CW01019906

Withdrawn

WB 8835164 5

Palgrave Macmillan Studies in Family and Intimate Life

Series Editors: **David Morgan**, University of Manchester, UK; **Lynn Jamieson**, University of Edinburgh, UK; and **Graham Allan**, Keele University, UK

Titles include:

Lynn Jamieson, Ruth Lewis and Roona Simpson (*editors*)
RESEARCHING FAMILIES AND RELATIONSHIPS
Reflections on Process

Carmen Lau Clayton
BRITISH CHINESE FAMILIES
Parenting, Relationships and Childhoods

David Morgan
RETHINKING FAMILY PRACTICES

Petra Nordqvist, Carol Smart
RELATIVE STRANGERS
Family Life, Genes and Donor Conception

Eriikka Oinonen
FAMILIES IN CONVERGING EUROPE
A Comparison of Forms, Structures and Ideals

Róisín Ryan-Flood
LESBIAN MOTHERHOOD
Gender, Families and Sexual Citizenship

Sally Sales
ADOPTION, FAMILY AND THE PARADOX OF ORIGINS
A Foucauldian History

Tam Sanger
TRANS PEOPLE'S PARTNERSHIPS
Towards an Ethics of Intimacy

Tam Sanger and Yvette Taylor (*editors*)
MAPPING INTIMACIES
Relations, Exchanges, Affects

Elizabeth B. Silva
TECHNOLOGY, CULTURE, FAMILY
Influences on Home Life

Lisa Smyth
THE DEMANDS OF MOTHERHOOD
Agents, Roles and Recognitions

Vilna Bashi Treitler (*editor*)
RACE IN TRANSNATIONAL AND TRANSRACIAL ADOPTION

Katherine Twamley
LOVE, MARRIAGE AND INTIMACY AMONG GUJARATI INDIANS
A Suitable Match

Palgrave Macmillan Studies in Family and Intimate Life
Series Standing Order ISBN 978–0–230–51748–6 hardback
978–0–230–24924–0 paperback
(*outside North America only*)

You can receive future titles in this series as they are published by placing a standing order. Please contact your bookseller or, in case of difficulty, write to us at the address below with your name and address, the title of the series and the ISBN quoted above.

Customer Services Department, Macmillan Distribution Ltd, Houndmills, Basingstoke, Hampshire RG21 6XS, England

---

CITY OF WOLVERHAMPTON COLLEGE

Understanding Families Over Time

Research and Policy

Edited by

Janet Holland
Professor Emerita, London South Bank University, UK

and

Rosalind Edwards
Professor of Sociology, University of Southampton, UK

Selection, introduction, conclusion and editorial matter © Janet Holland and
Rosalind Edwards 2014
Individual chapters © Respective authors 2014

All rights reserved. No reproduction, copy or transmission of this
publication may be made without written permission.

No portion of this publication may be reproduced, copied or transmitted
save with written permission or in accordance with the provisions of the
Copyright, Designs and Patents Act 1988, or under the terms of any licence
permitting limited copying issued by the Copyright Licensing Agency,
Saffron House, 6–10 Kirby Street, London EC1N 8TS.

Any person who does any unauthorized act in relation to this publication
may be liable to criminal prosecution and civil claims for damages.

The authors have asserted their rights to be identified as the authors of this
work in accordance with the Copyright, Designs and Patents Act 1988.

First published 2014 by
PALGRAVE MACMILLAN

Palgrave Macmillan in the UK is an imprint of Macmillan Publishers Limited,
registered in England, company number 785998, of Houndmills, Basingstoke,
Hampshire RG21 6XS.

Palgrave Macmillan in the US is a division of St Martin's Press LLC,
175 Fifth Avenue, New York, NY 10010.

Palgrave Macmillan is the global academic imprint of the above companies
and has companies and representatives throughout the world.

Palgrave® and Macmillan® are registered trademarks in the United States,
the United Kingdom, Europe and other countries.

ISBN 978–1–137–28507–2 CM

This book is printed on paper suitable for recycling and made from fully
managed and sustained forest sources. Logging, pulping and manufacturing
processes are expected to conform to the environmental regulations of the
country of origin.

A catalogue record for this book is available from the British Library.

A catalog record for this book is available from the Library of Congress.

CITY OF WOLVER ON COLLEGE
ST

306.874 HOL PR
-9 JUL 2014 8835164

£ 65.00 WOL

Contents

Tables

Series Editors' Preface

The remit of the *Palgrave Macmillan Studies in Family and Intimate Life* series is to publish major texts, monographs and edited collections focusing broadly on the sociological exploration of intimate relationships and family organization. As editors we think such a series is timely. Expectations, commitments and practices have changed significantly in intimate relationships and family life in recent decades. This is very apparent in patterns of family formation and dissolution, demonstrated by trends in cohabitation, marriage and divorce. Changes in household living patterns over the last 20 years have also been marked, with more people living alone, adult children living longer in the parental home and more 'non-family' households being formed. Furthermore, there have been important shifts in the ways people construct intimate relationships. There are few comfortable certainties about the best ways of being a family man or woman, with once-conventional gender roles no longer being widely accepted. The normative connection between sexual relationships and marriage or marriage-like relationships is also less powerful than it once was. Not only is greater sexual experimentation accepted, but it is now accepted at an earlier age. Moreover, heterosexuality is no longer the only mode of sexual relationship given legitimacy. In Britain as elsewhere, gay male and lesbian partnerships are now socially and legally endorsed to a degree hardly imaginable in the mid-twentieth century. Increases in lone-parent families, the rapid growth of different types of stepfamily, the de-stigmatization of births outside marriage and the rise in couples 'living-apart-together' all provide further examples of the ways that 'being a couple', 'being a parent' and 'being a family' have diversified in recent years.

The fact that change in family life and intimate relationships has been so pervasive has resulted in renewed research interest from sociologists and other scholars. Increasing amounts of public funding have been directed to family research in recent years, in terms of both individual projects and the creation of family research centres of different hues. This research activity has been accompanied by the publication of some very important and influential books exploring different aspects of shifting family experience, in Britain and elsewhere. The *Palgrave Macmillan Studies in Family and Intimate Life* series hopes to add to this list of influential research-based texts, thereby contributing to existing knowledge and informing current debates. Our main audience consists of academics and advanced students, though we intend that the books in the series will be accessible to a more general readership who wish to understand better the changing nature of contemporary family life and personal relationships.

We see the remit of the series as wide. The concept of 'family and intimate life' is interpreted in a broad fashion. While the focus of the series is clearly sociological, we take family and intimacy as being inclusive rather than exclusive. The series covers a range of topics concerned with family practices and experiences, including, for example, partnership; marriage; parenting; domestic arrangements; kinship; demographic change; intergenerational ties; life-course transitions; stepfamilies; gay and lesbian relationships; lone-parent households; and also non-familial intimate relationships such as friendships. We also wish to foster comparative research, as well as research on under-studied populations. The series includes different forms of book. Most are theoretical or empirical monographs on particular substantive topics, though some may also have a strong methodological focus. In addition, we see edited collections as also falling within the series' remit, as well as translations of significant publications in other languages. Finally we intend that the series has an international appeal, in terms of both topics covered and authorship. Our goal is for the series to provide a forum for family sociologists conducting research in various societies, and not solely in Britain.

Graham Allan, Lynn Jamieson and David Morgan

Contributors

Kathryn Backett-Milburn is Professor Emerita, Sociology of Families and Health, at the University of Edinburgh. She is a specialist in qualitative and longitudinal research, and her interests include lay perspectives on family and child health relevant issues, well-being, work–life balance, health promotion, and food and feeding. Recent publications include: J. Harden, K. Backett-Milburn, A. MacLean and S. Cunningham-Burley (2012) 'The Family–Work Project: Children's and Parents' Experiences of Working Parenthood', *Families, Relationships and Societies*, 1(2): 207–222 and D. Rankin, K. Backett-Milburn and S. Platt (2009) 'Practitioner Perspectives on Tackling Health Inequalities: Findings from an Evaluation of Healthy Living Centres in Scotland', *Social Science & Medicine*, 68: 925–932.

Sarah Baker is Programme Director of Culture + Context at the Victoria University of Wellington, New Zealand. Her research is focused on the consumption of design and the culture of everyday life. Recent research explores the consumption, production and representation of retro style for the home specifically in relation to class and gender identity. She is interested in exploring the processes with which the ordinary becomes spectacular as well as the ordinariness of practices that are viewed as exotic, alternative or elite. Sarah is the author of *Retro Style: Class, Gender and Design in the Home* (2013) and articles for the *European Journal of Cultural Studies*.

Joanna Bornat is Professor Emerita at the Open University, and her research interests are in secondary analysis, ageing and oral history. Recent publications include: 'Researching the Future with Older People: Experiences with the oldest generation', in J. Bornat and R. Jones (eds) *Imagining Futures*, (forthcoming) London; and J. Bornat, P. Raghuram and L. Henry (2012) 'Revisiting the Archives: A Case Study from the History of Geriatric Medicine', *Sociological Research Online*, 17(2). http://www.socresonline.org.uk/17/2/contents.html

Bill Bytheway recently retired from the Open University. Publications include: B. Bytheway and J. Bornat (2012) 'Family Images of the Oldest

Generation', in V. Ylänne (ed.) *Age, Image, Identity*, London: Palgrave Macmillan; and B. Bytheway (2012) 'Age Discrimination, Work and Retirement', *Public Policy and Aging Report*, 22(3): 14–16.

Carrie Coltart worked as a researcher on the Timescapes 'Men as fathers' project at Cardiff University in 2009–2011, contributing to various project strands, in particular work on the psychosocial dimensions of transitions to fatherhood and secondary analysis in qualitative longitudinal research. Prior to that she completed a PhD in women's studies at the University of York. She is currently on a career break to care for her two young children and is now based near Bath, Somerset.

Sarah Cunningham-Burley is Professor of Medical and Family Sociology at the University of Edinburgh and Head of the School of Molecular, Genetic and Population Health Sciences. She is based at the Centre for Population Health Sciences and is one of the founding co-directors of the Centre for Research on Families and Relationships. Her research interests include families, relationships and health; social issues in relation to new technologies and health; and public engagement in medical science. She is committed to promoting public engagement with research and knowledge exchange to influence policy and practice. She investigates the social and ethical context of developments in health and medicine, including new medical technologies and the development of record linkage for health research. Her current funded research includes: the Wellcome Trust Biomedical Ethics Strategic Award on 'The human body: Its scope, limits and future', in collaboration with the Institute of Science, Ethics and Innovation at the University of Manchester; the public engagement strand of the Farr Institute (e-Health Informatics Centre, Scotland); and most recently, with Martyn Pickersgill and Ian Deary, a project on 'Neuroscience and family life: The brain in policy and everyday practice' funded by the Leverhulme Trust. Recent publications include: S. Parry, W. Faulkner, S. Cunningham-Burley and N. Marks (2012) 'Heterogeneous Agendas around Public Engagement in Stem Cell Research: The Case for Maintaining Plasticity', *Science Studies*, 25(2): 59–78; and S. Wilson, A. Bancroft, S. Cunningham-Burley and K. Milburn (2012) 'The Consequences of Love: Young People and Family Practices in Difficult Circumstances', *Sociological Review*, 60(1): 1467–1954.

Rosalind Edwards is Professor of Sociology and Co-Director of the Economic and Social Research Council (ESRC) National Centre for

Research Methods at the University of Southampton. Her area of substantive interest falls broadly within the field of family studies, while her methodological interests encompass a range of qualitative, mixed and historical methods and methodologies. She is currently involved in research on brain science and early intervention; historical and comparative para-data; and accounts of voluntary action over time. Recent publications include *What Is Qualitative Interviewing?* (with J. Holland, 2013), *International Perspectives on Racial and Ethnic Mixedness and Mixing* (ed. with S. Ali, C. Caballero and M. Song, 2012) and *Key Concepts in Family Studies* (with J. McCarthy, 2011).

Nick Emmel has been doing research in the same low-income community since 1999. This qualitative longitudinal and mixed method research started with a health needs assessment for the local primary care group. In 2002 he was principal investigator of an ESRC research methods programme project, 'Developing methodologies', for accessing socially excluded individuals and groups, with Kahryn Hughes, Joanne Greenhalgh and Adam Sale. He continued this qualitative longitudinal research as part of the Timescapes programme, investigating intergenerational exchange with Kahryn Hughes and Lou Hemmerman. Between research projects, he has maintained close contact with residents and service providers in the community. Throughout the research, he has published on research methods, including Emmel et al. (2007) 'Accessing Socially Excluded People – Trust and the Gatekeeper in the Researcher–Participant Relationship', *Sociological Research Online* 12(2); and with Kahryn Hughes (2009) 'Small-N Access Cases to Refine Theories of Social Exclusion and Access to Socially Excluded Individuals and Groups', in D. Byrne and C. Ragin (eds) *The SAGE Handbook of Case-Centred Methods*. His substantive interests focus on interpreting and explaining vulnerability. Most recently this model was presented in Emmel and Hughes (2010) ' "Recession, It's All the Same to Us Son": The Longitudinal Experience (1999–2010) of Deprivation', *21st Century Society*, 5(2): 171–181. He teaches social research methods and the sociology and social policy of health inequalities and inequities at the University of Leeds. His most recent book is *Sampling and Choosing Cases in Qualitative Research: A Realist Approach* (2013).

Jeni Harden is Senior Lecturer in Social Science and Health at the Centre for Population Health Sciences and Co-Director of the Centre for Research on Families and Relationships at the University of Edinburgh. She has carried out research on children's and family health in a number of areas: parenting children with chronic illness; parent and child negotiation around everyday risks; the construction of young children's emotional well-being in schools; an exploration of how families reconcile work and family life over time; and low-income parents' food practices with young children. Current research includes an investigation of young people's experiences of information giving around epilepsy risks, and parental experiences of caring for a child with type 1 diabetes; and an evaluation of abortion provision within an integrated sexual health clinic, from the perspectives of women and staff. Recent publications include: J. Harden, K. Backett-Milburn, A. MacLean and L. Jamieson (2013) 'Home and Away: Constructing Family and Childhood in the Context of Working Parenthood', *Children's Geographies*, 11: 298–310; and L. Gibbs, C. McDougall and J. Harden (2013) 'Development of an Ethical Methodology for Post-bushfire Research with Children', *Health Sociology Review*, 22(2): 114–123.

Karen Henwood is Professor of Social Sciences in the School of Social Sciences at Cardiff University. Her research interests span the study of identities and subjectivities, families and personal lives, and living with risk from socio-technical hazards and environmental change. She has written extensively on qualitative methods in psychology and the social sciences. She leads the 'Energy biographies' project (2010–2015) that is part of the ESRC and Engineering and Physical Sciences Research Council's (EPSRC) Energy and Communities joint venture. The 'Energy biographies' project is utilizing creative, multimodal and longitudinal methodologies for understanding transitions in everyday consumption, sustainable practices and energy demand reduction.

Janet Holland is Professor Emerita in the Weeks Centre for Social and Policy Research, London South Bank University (LSBU). She was Co-Director of both the Timescapes study (2007–2012) and the Families and Social Capital ESRC Research Group (2002–2007) at LSBU. Her areas of research interest are wide and include youth, education, gender, sexualities and family life. She has a special interest in methodological development, in particular feminist and qualitative longitudinal methodology. Publications include *What Is Qualitative Interviewing?* (with Rosalind Edwards, 2013); 'Qualitative and Quantitative Longitudinal Research' (with Jane Elliott and Rachel Thomson, in *Handbook of Social Research Methods*, 2008); *Inventing Adulthoods: A Biographical Approach to Youth Transitions* (with Sheila Henderson, Sheena McGrellis, Sue Sharpe and Rachel Thomson, 2007); *The Male in the Head* (with Caroline Ramazanoglu, Sue Sharpe and Rachel Thomson, 2004); *Feminist Methodology: Challenges and*

Choices (with Caroline Ramazanoglu, 2002); and *Making Spaces: Citizenship and Difference in Schools* (with Tuula Gordon and Elina Lahelma, 2000).

Kahryn Hughes is Senior Research Fellow in Sociology at the University of Leeds. She has been funded by the ESRC for the past 11 years in research primarily aimed at methods innovation and development. Her current research interests are related to three overlapping areas: the sociology of health inequalities; sociological theory; and research methodology. More specifically, she is interested in addiction, poverty, time and identity. In research with Nick Emmel, funded under the ESRC Research Methods Programme and ESRC Timescapes, she has developed and sustained a number of effective networks with third sector organizations and has considerable experience and insight into enhancing impact through engaging a diverse audience. Most recently, she has won funding with Bren Neale under the ESRC Knowledge Exchange and Transformation scheme, for 'Changing landscapes for the third sector: Enhancing knowledge and informing practice'. This project brings together a national network of research projects and teams, to facilitate knowledge-sharing and secondary analysis, in addition to developing and refining the Timescapes archive at the University of Leeds.

Sarah Irwin is Reader in Sociology at the University of Leeds. As well as her work in qualitative secondary analysis undertaken as part of Timescapes, she has substantive interests in the areas of parenting, family, education and inequalities. Two examples of recent publications include S. Irwin and S. Elley (2013) 'Parents' Hopes and Expectations for Their Children's Future Occupations', *The Sociological Review*, 61(1): 111–130; and M. Winterton and S. Irwin (2012) 'Teenage Expectations of Going to University: The Ebb and Flow of Influences from 14 to 18', *Journal of Youth Studies*, 15(7): 858–874.

Lynn Jamieson is Professor of Sociology, Families and Relationships and is one of the founding co-directors of the Centre for Research on Families and Relationships. She has researched and published in the areas of intimacy; globalization and personal life; personal life, the environment and sustainable lifestyles; families, households and intergenerational relationships; and personal relationships across the life course. She is currently involved in the longitudinal study, 'Growing up in Scotland'. Recent publications include L. Jamieson and R. Simpson (2013) *Living Alone: Globalization, Identity and Belonging* and L. Jamieson and S. Milne

(2012) 'Children and Young People's Relationships, Relational Processes and Social Change: Reading across Worlds', *Children's Geographies*, 10(3): 265–278.

Carmen Lau Clayton is Director of the 'Following young fathers' study based at the University of Leeds (2012–2015), which is investigating the experiences and support needs of young fathers. Prior to this, she was the research fellow for the 'Young lives and time' project also at the University of Leeds. She is also a senior lecturer in family and child welfare studies at Leeds Trinity University. Other research interests include the Chinese diaspora and family dynamics for established and migrant households.

Alice MacLean is an investigator scientist within the gender and health programme at the Medical Research Council/Chief Scientific Office (MRC/CSO) Social and Public Health Sciences Unit, University of Glasgow. Alice's research interests include child and youth health, family practices in relation to health and the ways that help-seeking for illness, lay understandings of illness and experiences of illness vary and interact with gender over the life course. Current projects include an exploration of family food practices in relation to men's experiences of taking part in the 'Football fans in training' weight management and healthy living intervention and an analysis of UK newspaper representations of eating disorders in males. Recent publications include: A. MacLean, K. Hunt and H. Sweeting (2013) 'Symptoms of Mental Health Problems: Children's and Adolescents' Understanding and Implications for Gender Differences in Help-Seeking', *Children & Society*, 27: 161–173; and A. Maclean, H. Sweeting, M. Egan, G. Der, J. Adamson and K. Hunt (2013) 'How Robust Is the Evidence of an Emerging or Increasing Female Excess in Physical Morbidity between Childhood and Adolescence? Results of a Systematic Literature Review and Meta-analyses', *Social Science & Medicine*, 78: 96–112.

Sheena McGrellis is a visiting senior research officer in the Weeks Centre for Social and Policy Research at LSBU. She has been a member of the 'Inventing adulthoods' (IA) research team since 1996, for part of this time located in the University of Ulster. She directed 'Growing up in Northern Ireland', revisiting young people in the IA study in 2008–2010. Her interests are in youth research, youth transitions and identities, and health and well-being, with a particular concern for young people in Northern Ireland, and she has conducted a number of studies and published in these areas. Recent publications include: *Growing Up in Northern Ireland*, Report for Joseph Rowntree Foundation (2011); 'In Transition: Young People in Northern Ireland Growing Up in, and out of, Divided Communities', *Ethnic and Racial Studies*, (2010) 33(5): 761–778; 'Pushing the Boundaries in Northern Ireland: Young People, Violence and Sectarianism', *Contemporary Politics*, (2005) 11(1): 57–71; 'Pure and Bitter Spaces: Gender, Identity and Territory in Northern Irish Youth Transitions', *Gender and Education*, (2005) 17(5): 515–529, and many publications with the IA team.

Bren Neale is Professor of Life Course and Family Research in the School of Sociology and Social Policy at the University of Leeds. She specializes in policy-related research on the dynamics of family life, childhood and intergenerational relationships. As director of the ESRC Timescapes Initiative, Bren has contributed to advances in qualitative longitudinal research methods across the field of family, childhood and life- course studies. She has also supported the development of qualitative longitudinal projects across academia, government and the voluntary sector. Bren is currently tracking a group of young fathers to investigate the factors that influence their pathways through life; and scaling up and synthesizing evidence from a network of qualitative longitudinal projects that are investigating the dynamics of voluntary sector organizations ('Following young fathers' and 'Changing landscapes for the third sector': both ESRC funded). She is a founding editorial board member of the journal *Families, Relationships and Societies*. In 2010, she was elected as a member of the Academy of Social Sciences in recognition of her work in developing Timescapes.

Rachel Thomson is Professor of Childhood and Youth Studies at the University of Sussex, where she directs the Centre for Innovation and Research in Childhood and Youth. She has a long-standing interest in methods for researching the interplay of personal, social and historical change, as well as having conducted major empirical studies of transitions in the life course. Publications include (with Julie McLeod) *Researching Social Change: Qualitative Methods* (2009) and *Unfolding Lives: Youth, Gender and Change* (2009); (with Kehily, Hadfield and Sharpe) *Making Modern Mothers* (2011); and (with Henderson, Holland, McGrellis and Sharpe) *Inventing Adulthoods: A Biographical Approach to Youth Transitions* (2007).

Fiona Shirani is a research associate at the School of Social Sciences at Cardiff University. Her research interests include families and relationships, the experiences and implications of life-course events, and working with qualitative longitudinal methods. She currently works on the qualitative longitudinal (QL) 'Energy biographies' project.

Susie Weller is a senior research fellow in the Weeks Centre for Social and Policy Research at LSBU. Her research specializes in listening to and promoting the voices of children and teenagers. She is currently the principal investigator on an ESRC National Centre for Research Methods 'Methodological innovation project' that explores the potential of video telephony in qualitative longitudinal research with young people. Susie is author of *Teenagers' Citizenship: Experience and Education* (2007) and co-editor of *Critical Approaches to Care: Understanding Caring Relationships, Identities and Cultures* (with C. Rogers, 2012), along with over 30 peer-reviewed articles, chapters and papers exploring trajectories to adulthood during economic and political change; participation, citizenship and democracy in schools; friendship and social networks; caring relations, identities and practices; social capital and school choice; sibling relationships over time; and creative, participatory and longitudinal methods.

Mandy Winterton is Lecturer in Sociology at Edinburgh Napier University. Her interests cohere around social inclusion, and her research varies from qualitative studies of young people and inclusion (e.g. socio-economic dynamics and exercise, 'ethnicity' and youth organizations), non-traditional entrants to higher education, and military populations and relationships to welfare and/or education. She was a research fellow for ESRC Timescapes on the Secondary Analysis Project, and publications from that work include Winterton, M. and Irwin, S. (2012) 'Teenage Expectations of Going to University: The Ebb and Flow of Influences from 14 to 18', *Journal of Youth Studies*, 15(7): 858–874, and Irwin, S. and Winterton, M. (2012) 'Constructing Social Explanation: Lessons from Qualitative Secondary Analysis', *Sociological Research Online*, 17(2). Available at http://www.socresonline.org.uk/17/2/4.html.

1
Introduction to Timescapes: Changing Relationships and Identities Over the Life Course[1]

Janet Holland and Rosalind Edwards

What is qualitative longitudinal research?

At the heart of qualitative longitudinal research (QLR) is the desire to explore what social change through the passage of time means to those who experience it, and how people understand processes of change in their own lives in the context of broader social shifts. The method has recently undergone a resurgence of interest and adoption with some arguing that as a distinctive way of knowing and understanding the social world it is a methodology whose time has come (Thomson et al. 2003, Corden and Millar 2007). But there is nothing new about qualitative enquiry conducted through and in relation to time in the social sciences. It is part of a rich ethnographic tradition that spans fields as diverse as social anthropology, psychology, sociology and its multiple sub-disciplines, oral history and theatre studies (Walkerdine et al. 2001, Kemper and Peterson Royce 2002, Saldana 2003, Holland et al. 2006, Bornat and Diamond 2007, Henderson et al. 2007, Crow 2008). This disciplinary range is exemplified in the Timescapes projects that have contributed to this collection and enriched the work of the Timescapes study.

QLR is open-ended and intentional, involving a dynamic research process where research design and research process grow ever closer. The amount of time covered can vary with different disciplinary approaches and practical considerations, anthropological studies for example tend historically to have a commitment to spending a long time in the field using ethnography, itself a multi-method approach to data generation (Peterson Royce 2011). The Harvard Chiapas Project (Vogt 2002)[2] for

1

CITY OF WOLVERHAMPTON COLLEGE

example was driven by intellectual projects, which could change over the years as new researchers came into the team bringing new theoretical concerns and insights. In community studies, QLR can involve visits and revisits to key research sites by the initial and subsequent researchers. A famous in-depth sociological study of Middletown, US, seen by the researchers as an average or typical American small city (Lynd and Lynd 1929), 'became a sociological reference point' (Bell and Newby 1971: 82) that was revisited by the Lynds themselves during the Depression (1937) and many others subsequently (Caplow 1984, Smith 1984, Caccamo 2000).

Given the range of disciplines that employ QLR, specific definitions vary with disciplinary, theoretical and methodological focus. Amidst many insights, Johnny Saldana suggests that 'Longitudinal means a lonnnnnnnng time' (Saldana 2003: 1) emphasizing duration, time and change, as basic principles. He also extols the virtue of flexibility in the research process, a key aspect of QLR:

> I feel we should be flexible and allow a definition of change to emerge as a study proceeds and its data are analysed. Ironically yet fittingly, we should permit ourselves to change our meaning of change as a study progresses.
>
> (Saldana 2003: 12)

QLR is then an enduring tradition adopted in a range of social science and related disciplines, and has provided a wealth of theoretical, methodological and substantive contributions to social science. Qualitative longitudinal (QL) methods can offer fresh perspectives into established arenas of social enquiry, drawing attention to the psychological and biographical processes of lived experience through which social outcomes are generated and mediated. In this way it can illuminate important micro-social processes, for example how people subjectively negotiate changes occurring in their lives at times of personal life transition (to work or parenthood for example) and combine a concern for these micro as well as macro social processes and practices (Henwood and Lang 2005, Neale et al. 2012). The chapters in this book each describe the value and advantages afforded by QLR and provide excellent examples of these perspectives and insights.

In this chapter, we will describe the unique and innovative nature of the practice of QLR in Timescapes. We will outline the nine projects, seven empirical covering the life course and two that deal with secondary analysis/reuse and archiving, that together form the core of

Timescapes, all of which are represented in this volume. We will address the conceptualization of the study with its emphasis on biographical, historical and generational timescapes or flows of time, all laced through the chapters in the book, and we will explore the potential for the enhancement of policy in a range of areas that QLR and Timescapes offer. We will indicate the specific contributions of the chapters in this volume to family and related social policies, drawing out the policy implications, and illustrating the integrated and intersecting nature of the Timescapes study.

The Timescapes approach

The Timescapes' programme of research examines relationships and identities through the life course and has been carried out by a network of researchers from five universities in the UK (Leeds, London South Bank, The Open, Cardiff and Edinburgh) working in different disciplinary traditions that are sometimes combined in a multidisciplinary approach (sociology, social psychology, social policy, oral history, gerontology, health studies and cultural studies). The seven empirical projects in the study span the life course, from toddlers who were born in the course of a project on first motherhood and became participants, to grandparents over 75 years old. Together they investigate: siblings and friends, lateral relationships in childhood and youth; the unfolding lives of young people; the dynamics of motherhood; masculinities, identities, men as fathers; work–life balance in families with young children; grandparents and social exclusion; and the experiences of the oldest generation. Two further projects play a major part in the integration of the study: 'Making the long view' (Chapter 3) and the Timescapes secondary analysis project (Chapter 9; www.timescapes. leeds.ac.uk).

The projects
Here is a brief description of each of the projects:

'Siblings and friends: The changing nature of children's lateral relationships' Rosalind Edwards and Susie Weller at London South Bank University
The working title for this project was 'Your space: siblings and friends'. Building on three previous studies the project followed a nationwide (UK) sample of circa 50 children and young people (aged 6 and 13 in 2002–2005, 10–17 in 2007 and 12–19 in 2009) living in a variety of

family circumstances with three waves of interviews over eight years. The aim was to document the meanings, experiences and flows of their prescribed (sibling) and chosen (friendship) relationships, and explore how these were connected to their sense of self as their individual and family biographies unfolded over time.

'Young lives and times: The crafting of young people's relationships' Bren Neale, Anna Bagnoli/Sarah Finney/ Carmen Lau and Sarah Irwin at Leeds University

Building on an earlier study, the project followed a birth cohort of 30 young people with two further waves of interviews to chart the dynamics of their intimate, social and familial relationships. It explored their cumulative experiences and 'turning points' in their biographies and changing sources of morality as they constructed their identities. Further supplementary samples of young men and young fathers were also recruited in the second phase of the study. In this volume, Chapter 4 draws on three rounds of interviews with these young fathers.

'The dynamics of motherhood: An intergenerational project' Rachel Thomson, Mary Kehily, Lucy Hadfield and Sue Sharpe at The Open University

In 'The making of modern motherhood' (2005–2007), on which this project builds, a diverse sample of 62 pregnant women were interviewed before and after the birth of their first child to explore how women make sense of the meaning of first-time motherhood and the transition to a maternal subjectivity. Twelve intergenerational case studies (based on interviews with mother, grandmothers and a significant other, plus further methods) were constructed to examine the intergenerational processes involved. In the current project, the investigation of six of these case studies was extended to explore how mothers and families negotiate the arrival of a new generation.

'Masculinities, identities and risk: Long-term transitions in the lives of men and fathers' Karen Henwood, Mark Finn/Fiona Shirani at Cardiff University

'Men as fathers' (working title) draws on and extends a study of 30 fathers in East Anglia (1999–2000) interviewed up to three times before and after the birth of their first child. Nineteen of these men were interviewed again in 2008 and a further similar sample of 16 fathers was recruited in Cardiff (2008) to provide two geographically, socially and culturally diverse cohorts of first-time fathers. The studies examine how men narrate and account for their experiences of becoming a father, examining critical turning points in their life histories and how they make meaning of a significant biographical change. Through comparisons in and through time, the study examines the ruptures and uncertainties in people's relationships and lives flowing from the dynamics of socio-cultural change, and the making of paternal subjectivity.

'Work and family lives: The changing experiences of "young families" ' Kathryn Backett-Milburn, Alice MacLean, Sarah Cunningham-Burley, Lynn Jamieson, Jeni Harden and Sarah Morton at Edinburgh University

The study followed a sample of 14 families in differing socio-economic and labour-market conditions (22 parents and 15 children aged 9–12) with one group (family) and two individual interviews from October 2007 to 2010. The study aimed to explore how families reconcile work and family life over time in an effort to achieve a balance between competing responsibilities. The focus was on processes of negotiation and children's experiences, everyday family practices and the impact of changes in work and family circumstances including employment/unemployment.

'Intergenerational exchange: Grandparents, social exclusion and health' Kahryn Hughes, Nick Emmel and Lou Hemmerman at Leeds University

Intergenerational Exchange is nested in a ten-year programme of research that examines change and continuity in relationships across generations amongst hard to reach people in an estate in a northern city in the UK. The project deals with the experiences of grandparents aged 35–55 whose families are part of what has been called 'the precariat' – people whose lives are characterized by little in the way of stable income and social protection (Standing 2011) and described as vulnerable by service providers in the area, with whom the researchers also had ongoing relationships. The sample included 12 grandparents from eight families and retrospective life history accounts were drawn in the early interviews. Three further interviews both added to these accounts and generated prospective data on their ongoing lives and experiences. A visual family tree method tracked 319 immediate family members and significant others, with whom interviews were undertaken, and provided a prompt for highlighting relationships in the later interviews. The ethnographic approach also included formal and informal interviews with service providers associated with the estate who were also gatekeepers and facilitators of the research.

'The oldest generation: Marking time, relationships and identities in old age' Joanna Bornat and Bill Bytheway at The Open University

Like project 6, this study involved retrospective life history data from grandparents, with a focus on intergenerational relationships, and prospective tracking of their lives, this time for 18 months. Twelve families (UK nationwide, maximizing geographic and socio-economic diversity) were involved, with a Senior (aged over 75) interviewed twice and a Recorder – a family member who kept a diary of the Senior's day-to-day life, took photographs and made contact with the project on a monthly basis. The aim was to explore the dynamic nature of older people's relationships and identities in the context of changing structures of intergenerational support, and how families manage and account for time and change in the context of age and ageing.

'Making the long view: Sharing the "Inventing adulthoods" project' Sheila Henderson, Janet Holland, Sheena McGrellis and Sue Sharpe at South Bank University and Rachel Thomson at The Open University

The 'Inventing adulthoods' (IA) project had followed the lives of 100 young people in five socio-economically and geographically contrasting sites (urban/rural, inner city/leafy suburb) with up to six biographical interviews since 1996 (aged 11–18), and begun to archive the data. 'Making the long view' provided a model of archiving practice for Timescapes and continued archiving IA data, developed a method of (long) case history analysis, and here contributes an empirical chapter on young people in Northern Ireland revisited in 2008–2010.

The Timescapes secondary analysis project, Sarah Irwin and Mandy Winterton at Leeds University

The project involved cross-cutting work both across and within the Timescapes empirical projects to demonstrate and advance the potential for reuse of the data. Activities included conceptual and methodological work, analysis of responses to a small set of questions asked across all Timescapes projects and developing a methodological strategy to work across a subset of Timescapes data sets (described in Chapter 8), as well as in-depth analysis of single project data (from 'Young lives and times').

Close collaboration and considerable trust was required between this team of researchers and the researchers on other Timescapes projects who enabled them to access data while projects were still ongoing.

These descriptions indicate the commonalities and differences between the projects and suggest the core around which they coalesce, described shortly. Collectively the projects have followed the lives of over 300 individuals in varied families and diverse communities throughout the UK. The samples reflect the key social identifiers of gender, social class, race and ethnicity, cultural and geographical heritages, and locality. Each of these produces multiple intersections in the varied identities and life experiences of the participants. The projects use a range of methods, such as in-depth interviews, ethnographic techniques, visual methods, diaries, life histories and case studies, to capture the inner logic of people's lives as they unfold. QLR needs time for the full value of the method to be realized, so that the effects of changes and the existence of continuities can be seen in the accumulating data, and the complexity of the intersections and interrelationships can become more apparent. As you see from the descriptions above, in our research design six of the projects build on and incorporate data gathered from separately funded earlier phases of the specific research, which we have called heritage data. This extends their timescale to before the Timescapes five-year funded period. Further, some projects have successfully bid for additional funding to extend their work (projects 1, 2 and 3). These pre- and post-Timescapes extensions increase the longitudinal and historical reach of the work, and add time and value to Timescapes itself.

In QLR, as in any research, methods need to be tailored to specific research questions, samples and disciplinary concerns, and each of the Timescapes' projects stands alone with its own substantive and disciplinary focus, methodological approach and contribution to scholarship. But the common elements that they have all adopted and work within blend them together to produce a whole that is greater than the sum of its parts, the Timescapes study.

All of the projects pursue the major objective and theme of Timescapes: the dynamics of personal, intimate and family relationships, the identities that flow from these relationships and how they are worked out across the life course and within different generations. These processes are happening against a backdrop of widespread and significant changes in family and domestic life and intimacy. But as Timescapes itself demonstrates, such changes are accompanied by the continuing importance to people of relationality, and in particular relationships of intimacy, love and care over the life course and within and across familial and cohort generations. These changes in families themselves are taking place in the context of a changing economic situation following the near collapse of the world banking system and the subsequent economic austerity measures pursued by national governments that took place during the period of research (2008 and beyond). These economic and social upheavals have a negative effect on housing and welfare policies and conditions in general for already stretched families (Edwards and Irwin 2010).

All projects share the conceptual and methodological concerns that are the backbone of Timescapes, employing and elaborating three different timescapes: biographical, generational and historical. The inspiration for this approach comes from C. Wright Mills, who argued that we cannot hope to understand society unless we understand how biography and history are interwoven in real lives (1959). All of the empirical projects use prospective QL designs, tracking individuals through time to capture trajectories, transitions, changes and continuities as lives unfold, in some cases over quite long periods including heritage data. Chapter 2 for example relates experiences of children and young people followed for ten years in several related projects; Chapter 3 reports on a revisit to a group of young people in Northern Ireland in 2008–2010, interviewed six or seven times since 1996; in Chapter 5 first-time fathers visited in 1999/2000 are revisited in 2010; and in Chapter 9 the study of 'young' grandparents and intergenerational relations is embedded in an ongoing ten-year investigation. A wide variety of different and often innovatory techniques are used across the projects, as will be discovered in the following chapters. One example is from project 3 on motherhood. Researchers undertook 'day in a life' micro-ethnographies that involved spending an ordinary day shadowing mothers to document through visual data and detailed field notes the mundane everyday business of parenthood. This provides a new perspective on the unfolding family dynamic, capturing the agency of children and highlighting the very different lives of women mothering at the same historical moment. The different approaches and perspectives of each project can combine across the studies for particular shared purposes, for example using common or shared questions, sharing data and undertaking cross project/team analyses, and add richness and depth to interpretations. The secondary analysis project has led in these ways of working and provides examples of the analyses in Irwin, Bornat and Winterton (2012). In this article, they discuss inter-project analysis (project 4 on fathers and project 10 on the oldest generation) leading to a reframing of original data in project 10 to take into consideration the timing of fatherhood; and working across four project data sets to develop a conceptual framework to explore one of the common questions that was asked by all projects on experiences of critical moments/turning points in the participants' lives. In Chapter 8 of this volume they discuss using a gendered perspective to analyse data from project 5, 'Work and family lives', and to compare data from project 5 and project 4 on fathers.

The conceptual framework

QLR is distinguished by the deliberate way in which temporality is designed into the research process, making change and continuity over time a central focus of analytic attention and conceptual concern. As the title Timescapes suggests, time, its different meanings and the way that different temporalities intersect and interact, is at the heart of the investigation. Time here is seen as fluid, multidimensional and infinitely varied. As indicated earlier, there is a particular interest in three broad timescapes, or flows of time, and their intersection: biographical time, generational time and historical time, reflecting a concern to pursue individual and social processes at micro and macro levels.

In the case of biographical time, the flow of the individual life, the concern is with agency, causality and consequences. Frequent dipping into the biographical timescape with qualitative methods can give insight into causes and consequences of different events, experiences, critical moments and epiphanies through the understandings of the individual themselves (Thomson et al. 2002, Holland and Thomson 2009). The fluidity of time and the meanings ascribed to these events are captured in the present moment, but saturated with memory, knowledge and expectations of past, present and future; the past here being drawn on as a subjective resource in the present. Life is lived forwards yet understood backwards (Kierkegaard 1992[1846]). In Timescapes we can observe these processes in the reinterpretation, reworking and overwriting of memory and the past that can take place through time in the narratives offered by participants as we visit and revisit their (and indeed our own) moving present. All of the empirical projects are concerned in some way with biographical time, returning to their participants to track their trajectory through time. Most of the chapters use biographical interviews in one way or another. In Chapter 10 the approach is that of oral history, which creates a retrospective biographical account of the life as lived, while in this case also tracking participants for a short period.

Generational time refers to how individuals are located in what could be seen as a vertical generational convoy, where they simultaneously relate to their own generation, to older generations (parents and grandparents, and their contemporaries) and to younger generations (children and grandchildren, and their contemporaries), all travelling through the same segments of historical and social time together. Generational categories are fluid as people cross generational boundaries, move between different contexts or as key stages of life expand or contract. These issues are explicitly explored through the case of the 'small worlds' of young people's immediate and extended family relationships in Chapter 2. Indeed, in some instances generations are very compacted and close together in time, closely layered; a parent and their own child might be having a child at roughly the same time. On the disadvantaged site discussed in Chapter 9 this is a frequent occurrence, with complex sets of relationships and responsibilities emerging that raise issues around grandparents parenting, responsibility for children and dependence and interdependence. In Chapter 4, young fathers' narratives reveal similar complexities. The more general demographic context is that the age of onset of grandparenting is rising, although class inflected; and Chapter 10, about the oldest generation, reveals further aspects of intergenerational interaction with older grandparents. This area of the study throws light on the dynamics of intergenerational relationships and identities, and the shifting structures of family and kinship.

The interest in historical time refers to how individuals locate themselves in different historical epochs, and in relation to different external events, and wider social and structural conditions, both local and global. This calls attention to socio-economic and public policy norms and expectations, to technological and political landscapes. Here we are looking, for example, at the policy contexts that shape individual lives and through which people work out their relationships and identities. An example can be given from the IA project, which has been following young people through their transitions to adulthood since 1996. Part of the sample was located in Northern Ireland, so that individual transitions and identity construction took place in the complex historical context of 'the Troubles',[3] with paramilitary cease fires and their failures, the exigencies of the peace process and devolved government, and the economic boom; and as part of Timescapes the researcher returned to talk to them in a recession (2008–2010). There were dramatic historical, political, social and policy shifts and changes in the period, with significant effects on the lives and identities of the young people living through it. This material is drawn on in Chapter 3.

The conceptual questions about time that each of the projects has been concerned to pursue include:

- How are different timescapes (biographical, generational and historical) experienced? How do these timescapes intersect as lives unfold?
- What key events or 'critical moments' (biographical, intergenerational and historical) are significant for people and what impact do they have on life decisions and chances?
- How do people understand the causal links between their earlier and later selves, and their changing circumstances and experiences?

Each of the projects also pursues its own conceptual concerns, often advancing ideas of time and temporality facilitated by the QL approach. The ways that these questions have coloured the research and the range of answers produced can be seen throughout the publications produced by the projects, and in the chapters to follow.

Methodology

Part of Timescapes' work was methodological development, generating commitment and involvement in and enhancing the use of QL methods, and pursuing the ethical issues that arise in using these approaches. The issues are similar to the concerns of ethical qualitative research in general but exacerbated by the temporal dimension where data generation and analysis and interpretation are cumulative processes. In this case time can be a complicating factor, but also a resource for facilitating ethical practice. Considerations such as consent, the care of participants, confidentiality and the representation of lives, for example, need to be negotiated and revisited over time, and ethical dilemmas emerge and need to be engaged with as part of the ongoing research process. While broad ethical frameworks are available (Wiles 2012) and provide guidance for thinking about ethics and QLR, the Timescapes approach is based on situated and emergent ethics and 'careful judgement based on practical knowledge and attention to detail in context of time and place' (Edwards and Mauthner 2002: 27). The Timescapes team was constructed as a collaborative research network, and on key issues the entire team contributed through their experience and practice, as in the case of research ethics and in considering the potentialities and challenges for data sharing and archiving (Henderson et al. 2012, Neale and Hanna 2012). For example, Rosalind Edwards and Susie Weller have discussed how the sudden death of one of their young participants raised dilemmas about whether they had a moral obligation to keep his interview material confidential or to 'give back' something of their lost son to his parents (Edwards and Weller 2013).

In developing the methodology in this way, members of the Timescapes team have explored the use of QLR in different disciplinary contexts and so in relation to different methodological traditions. Projects 3 and 4 for example have taken a psychosocial approach in some analyses of their data (Finn and Henwood 2009, Thomson 2010a, Thomson et al. 2011); Bornat and Bytheway demonstrate the advantages of combining intensive diaries with extensive life history data in their oral history approach to investigating elders' family relationships (project 7/Chapter 10, Bornat 2013). The longitudinal approach enables elements of ethnographic participation and observation to run alongside other methods of data generation with repeat visits to participants' homes in many projects. Timescapes has also advanced multidimensional analysis and interpretation, particularly in the use of case history methodology (Thomson 2010b, Henderson et al. 2012) and framework matrices to capture the intersection of cases, themes and waves over time (Neale 2014). Edwards and Weller (2012) applied the analytical technique of I-poems alongside thematic analysis, discussing the differences and complementarity that emerged. Irwin and colleagues have developed methodological routes into secondary analysis/reuse of QL data (Chapter 8).

Archiving and secondary analysis

Archiving and secondary analysis or reuse of data is well established for quantitative longitudinal research in the UK, but extremely limited in the case of qualitative and even more limited for qualitative longitudinal research. As a major, funded longitudinal study, Timescapes was charged with producing an archive of the data generated by the research, and developing the potential for reuse of QL data through dissemination to and training for potential users of the data. Neither were easy tasks since what came to be a living multimodal archive, produced while the research was still in progress, is a complex, innovative and unique entity (Neale and Bishop 2012), and the issue of reuse of qualitative data has generated an extensive debate amongst qualitative researchers about even the possibility of this activity.

In this debate some see secondary analysis and reuse of qualitative research as a difficult endeavour for epistemological reasons, and stress the importance of the reflexive researcher as integral to data generation, part of the process of knowledge construction (Mauthner et al.

1998, Parry and Mauthner 2004, Mauthner and Parry 2010). A secondary analyst could not have access to the total research context and its understanding and mediation by the initial researcher. Crucially, for them, it is only a foundational epistemology that enables separation of data from the researchers who generated it. Others argue that this is a practical rather than an epistemological problem, since all data analysis requires reflexivity and processes of interpretation are core to qualitative analysis whether primary or secondary (Fielding 2004, James 2013). Necessary contextualizing data and metadata (data about the data) can be provided, in fact is essential in archiving (Bishop 2009). Yet other researchers try to bridge the divide, pursuing the possibility of archiving and data reuse from a range of philosophical and epistemological positions (Moore 2006, 2007, Mason 2007). Timescapes has contributed to this debate while producing its archive (e.g. Hadfield 2010, Irwin and Winterton 2011, 2012, Bornat et al. 2012, Irwin et al. 2012, Bornat 2013, 2014, Irwin 2013).

The projects have each deposited extensive data-sets in the Timescapes multimedia archive, and promulgated its use for data-sharing and reuse in a wide range of dissemination activities. The chapters in this book provide tasters of the type of data that is available for reuse in the archive, including in Chapter 8 an illustration of how to use it and the types of findings that can be generated. A series of methodological guidelines from each project as well as publications on theory, methods, ethics and substantive findings is accessible on and through the Timescapes website: http://www.timescapes.leeds.ac. uk/resources/publications.

Policy in the study

Studying families and individuals through time provides opportunities both to research the impact of social policies on their lives and to generate data that is of use in the development of policy. Policies and services that meet the needs of those at whom they are directed can be identified, as can failures of policy and needs that existing policies do not meet. Families and relationships were at the heart of the Timescapes study and so the data generated is of relevance to social policy, particularly in the areas of health and social care, well-being, social support for groups in different generations (children, young people, parents, older people) and the long-term resourcing of families. One of the aims of Timescapes was to provide a more holistic understanding of life-course processes and transitions and to this end a series of relevant research and policy questions have guided the team. We wanted to know how intergenerational dependencies and responsibilities worked out over time; how fluid patterns of intimacy and family life influence the long-term resourcing of families and the well-being of individuals in material and emotional terms; what the interplay between formal and informal care and support is over the life course, and how particular policy developments relate to individual biographical change; and how social policies intersect in the lives of individuals and families through time, what is their long-term impact and what are the lessons for policy development? By virtue of their particular substantive focus, the projects are each contributing to particular areas of policy, although findings relevant to gender and social class tended to emerge across the board.

The explanatory power of QLR derives from addressing 'how' and 'why' questions in their temporal context, paying attention to lived experiences over time, and subjective understandings of life-course dynamics and processes. Taking these temporal dimensions into account is crucial in order to generate more robust evidence about changing patterns of family life, parenting and intergenerational relationships and identities. Sensitivity to temporal processes is vital in policy processes and professional practice, where individuals who are the object of such processes and practices may be required to change their behaviour, to adapt to changing environments or transitions, or survive through difficult times.

An example of a question relevant to these issues that was taken across all of the projects is reported in a Timescapes special collection, exploring lived experiences of recession and drawing on contemporary and past accounts from varied households across the generations (Edwards and Irwin 2010). The contributions highlight the acute impact of recession on specific populations of families, and the important social, cultural and relational factors that affect resilience and well-being over time. The findings show how decisions surrounding education and employment, having children, moving house, taking early retirement or changing career are materially affected; how professional support becomes vital for survival for families with long-term experiences of low income and vulnerability; and how, despite all of this, families can and do pull together, offering support across the generations, showing the contrast between informal support and formal support in hard times. The research overall has pointed to the limitations of short-term and overly instrumental approaches to service provision and family and parenting intervention, approaches that fail to chime with the processes and rhythms of real lives (see, for example, Bornat and Bytheway 2010, Neale and Lau Clayton 2011 and chapters in this volume).

The chapters to come

A number of themes run through the chapters in this book, as would be expected given the common concerns that create Timescapes as an integrated QL study dealing with relationships and identities throughout the life course. In particular, as discussed earlier, the common conceptual underpinning of the study leads to a shared concern with biographical, generational and historical time and their intersection, refracted through the specific focus of individual projects and the lives of participants. Although each project has its major substantive focus on a particular segment of the life course, from that starting point they have all produced information on the linked, interrelated and entwined lives of other generations. Inter and intra-generational relationships in all their diversity as they develop and change through the life course, and in the course of the particular study, appear throughout the chapters.

A concern to demonstrate the value of QLR in general, as well as in the context of policy, follows from the aims of this volume. Many chapters refer to the particular policies pursued in the UK, where all studies took place, in the 2007–2012 timescale of Timescapes. This time frame encompassed a shift from a New Labour government to a Conservative/Liberal Democrat coalition government in 2010, and the introduction of austerity measures aimed largely at reducing expenditure on welfare services at all levels after the global economic meltdown and concomitant recession of 2008. An interesting slant was cast on the effects of austerity measures on the precariat by project 6. Participants were asked early in the recession what effect it would have on them, and the response was 'little', since they were still living with the experiences of an earlier recession that left large numbers of households persistently deprived and vulnerable, a situation unimproved in the intervening period of relative economic stability (Emmel and Hughes 2010). But in later visits the 2008 + recession had bitten into even this disadvantaged community, since local statutory and third sector services on which they were dependent were experiencing funding cuts (Chapter 9).

Other common themes emerging throughout the chapters are gender and gender divisions, social class and work and unemployment, all seen through a temporal lens. The sequence of chapters in this edited collection broadly follows the life course, first considering children and young people, then parenthood in various ways at different stages, and finally two ages of grandparenting. All of the chapters provide a more extensive description of the individual projects than given earlier in this introductory chapter, discuss their methodological and analytic approaches, and illustrate their arguments and discussion by drawing on their fascinating longitudinal data.

Chapter 2 plunges us into debates around generational conflict. Rosalind Edwards, Susie Weller and Sarah Baker reject the political rhetoric about intergenerational justice as fair reciprocity and obligation that pits generations against each other in generational conflict. In this narrative the post World War II baby boomers have 'systematically skewed the allocation of economic, social and cultural resources in their own favour at the expense of smaller, recent cohorts' and the policy solutions are reduced state expenditure and welfare state contraction, longer working lives and reduced pensions. The authors argue that this perspective obscures interdependencies by taking a cross-sectional rather than longitudinal view of the transfer of resources. The fact that the resources of the welfare state that the young enjoy are built on tax and work role contributions of the older generation and that younger generations have been financially dependent and receiving these resources for longer than previous generations are ignored. The narrative renders insignificant intra-generational cleavages, obscuring inequalities of class, gender and race/ethnicity and combining cohort and familial generations. Drawing on case studies from their project, which starts from the lateral relationships of children with siblings and friends and examines the small experiential worlds of generational relationships, the researchers show that there is fluidity and complexity in inter and intra-generational relationships over time, and that generations can weave unevenly across and within age cohorts in a family (as also seen in chapters 5, 6 and 9). Family generations are a relational practice rather than a series of categorical statuses. Turning the idea of parents' aspirations for their children on its head, the researchers sought the young peoples' aspirations and hopes for their parents, arguing that 'The desire for and morality of the transfer of cross-temporal resources is not only "downwards" from parents for the purpose of their children's future, but also upwards, with young people thinking of their parents' futures' and that intergenerational dialogue should be encouraged in political and media discussions and as a guide to policy. The next chapter also examines the lives of young people, this time in the broader context of dramatic social and historical change.

Chapter 3 is centrally concerned with the social, historical and policy context and its impact on the lives and experiences of young people growing up in Northern Ireland. The young people have been followed using up to six biographical interviews since 1996 in the IA project, the fieldwork shadowing the exigencies of the peace process,

and they were re-interviewed in 2008–2010. Using data from longitudinal case histories, the chapter indicates ways that the Troubles and
a history of generationally transmitted sectarian divisions and violence
have coloured how young people understand themselves and their relationships with families, communities, friends and politics, and have
affected their trajectories into adulthood. Sheena McGrellis and Janet
Holland found that the many policies for young people introduced in
the period were unevaluated so that it was not clear whether or not
they were effective. Major interventions had been transferred wholesale
from the UK setting into the quite different Northern Irish environment
with concomitant disjunctions and failures, and policies were compartmentalized into the different departments and agencies that provided
services for the young, resulting in many young people falling through
the cracks in provision. The authors review policies and experiences in
education and training, employment and housing. They highlight the
consequentiality of critical moments and life events that create shifts
and possibilities, or close off possibilities in the lived experience of this
group of young people. There is a brief description of the experiences
of young single fathers, providing a different view from that emerging in Chapter 4, although also indicating how crucial intergenerational
support is to their capacity to look after their children.

Chapter 4 forms a link between parts one and two of the book by
tracking 12 young men becoming fathers in varied circumstances over
an 18-month period, examining their perspective on how intergenerational support unfolds over time, and what this means for their ability
to establish and sustain a parenting role. Vertical care relationships are
highly significant when generations are closely layered, and may interfere with the development of lateral parenting relationships between
young parents. In this situation early parenthood has significance not
only for the young people involved but for their parents, who face
an unanticipated early entry into grandparenthood. Bren Neale and
Carmen Lau Clayton's material provides an interesting comparison with
the perspectives of young grandparents charged with caring for their
grandchildren in Chapter 9, often in similar types of disadvantaged families. A review of studies of parenting, intergenerational support and
social change reveals some mixed evidence on the nature and extent
of grandparental care in families with young parents, but suggests in
general that grandparents play an increasingly significant role in supporting both their children and grandchildren, which runs counter to
the idea of older people as a burden and a drain on their families and
the public purse. This chapter highlights movement from a 'leisure and

pleasure' model of grandparental care to a more active 'rescue and repair' model, appearing particularly in the case of family crisis. There is limited official recognition of grandparents' role in this type of care, and they are largely marginalized in legislation and social policy (Chapter 9). Notions of an intergenerational cycle of disadvantage where a culture of deprivation and parenting deficit are presumed to pass down the generations have become embedded in policy and practice thinking, despite evidence to the contrary, and might influence this marginalization of grandparents. The study reported here involved a longitudinal design and a participatory 'knowledge to action' approach, with the researchers working closely with a practitioner who was working with the young men. This collaboration helped to provide access to the sample, and to feed the findings into the development of appropriate support for the young men. In this chapter the authors draw on both current and retrospective accounts from the young fathers over three interviews to provide fascinating reports of how they disclosed the pregnancy to the older generation, what kinds of support (practical, financial, emotional) they received prior to and following the birth, how the support evolved over time, and the impact it had on the lives of the young fathers. Their parenting journeys revealed tensions that can arise across the generations around boundaries, where over-involvement of grandparents might marginalize the young men and the balance between support and interference (gift or curse) is difficult to manage, and the difficulties of sustaining intergenerational support over time, with in some cases both generations perceiving a lack of responsibility in the other. The authors suggest that 'A broader approach to policy and professional practice may be needed, that takes into account cross-generational relationships and support, as well as the dynamic relationship between the young parents themselves.' The next chapter examines fatherhood later in the life course.

Chapter 5 employs psychosocial concepts of intersubjectivity and relationality to examine the psychological investments that men make in ways of 'doing' and 'being' fathers, exploring how their lives are linked with others, and how intergenerational transmissions of classed masculinities and inherited paternal identities affect their experience of becoming fathers. The chapter draws on a number of publications by the current authors. Karen Henwood and her colleagues were in general concerned to explore the influence of the past on the present and ways that the present mediates the past, and to examine whether the current concern for fathers to be involved and intimate as opposed to the disciplinarian breadwinner of earlier generations travels from culture into practice. They review some of the growing literature on fatherhood and find little consensus about the extent to which men and their families support ideals of involved fatherhood in their everyday lives. There is discussion about the practical barriers to achieving involvement and a questioning of whether traditional models of fathering are still relevant. Building on heritage data Karen Henwood, Fiona Shirani and Carrie Coultart constructed a sample of 46 men who became fathers between the ages of 15 and 41, interviewed three times over this transition (in 2000 and 2008/2009). Revisiting the same participants over time in a QL project allowed the authors to see continuities and changes in their accounts in the immediate and longer term, building a detailed picture of fathering through time. The findings suggest that fathers' involvement during pregnancy and birth may be complicated, with the physical embodiment of pregnancy proving a practical barrier for some. During this period many men emphasized their input as an economic provider as a different form of caring for the family. The authors consider the intensive parenting debate, pointing out that, despite increased expectations of men's involvement, women have primary responsibility for childcare, and so the demands of this culture affect women and men differentially. The men in the study, for example, felt that their partners experienced more pressure in relation to the child's care, health and behaviour, while they felt the financial pressure to provide the best start for their child and to think about the child by planning for the future. But these fathers also wanted to be hands on with their children, not just a wallet. During the study changes occurred not only in men's personal biographies, but in wider society, with the global economic downturn having particular implications for some men's earning and caring in terms of awareness of greater financial uncertainty, constrained choice and a perceived need for financial risk-taking. In considering the implications of their findings for policy, the authors point out that QL insights have indicated that different issues continue, emerge or recede in men's fathering over time, which suggests they can be supported in different ways at different life stages. Policies that address practical barriers to fathers' involvement, for example government changes to parental leave, can play a part here. Educational practices aimed at eliminating gender stereotypes and encouraging the social and emotional development of boys and men to improve their capacity to care for themselves and others are also important. The following chapter is also concerned, amongst many other things, with the gendered division of labour, this time in the context of an examination of first motherhood and intergenerational relationships.

In Chapter 6 Rachel Thomson points out that the combination of the longitudinal and intergenerational aspects of the research design allows the researchers in this project to capture how historical change is mediated by families as well as how roles are constantly renegotiated over time, particularly in response to key moments of change such as the arrival of a new generation. They see motherhood as a historically located experience mediated within families by women who also see themselves as members of wider generations of women, so linking biographical and historical time. In this chapter the focus is on women encountering motherhood as workers, and interviews with mothers and grandmothers show how expectations about women's work and career have transformed over recent generations, indicating elements of progress, but also contradictions and intergenerational ruptures. The longitudinal perspective helps to understand how women experience the 'motherhood penalty', the impact of which takes time to emerge, and accommodate to its logic. The social changes in the gendered experiences of women in the workforce over time are outlined, with education and work now ubiquitous features of the individualized female biography and the acquisition of qualifications constituting new gender divisions *between* women. In this context attempts to guide policy on the basis of women's 'preferences' for home or work are criticized for ignoring the political, economic and cultural contexts in which 'choices' are made. It is also pointed out in the chapter that the brunt of the 2008 recession and austerity policies fall on women who occupy precarious positions in the labour market more often than men, and who by virtue of the domestic division of labour must absorb radical cuts to the welfare state.

Women in the study became mothers at different biographical points, and in different situations, and the chapter provides an overview of this range of experience from the perspective of work, family lives and practices, and intergenerational relations and changes. While working-class mothers were likely to see motherhood and paid work as complementary projects, middle-class mothers experienced the two as competing. Middle-class families in the group reflected intergenerational rupture in that mothers were better educated than their own mothers, established careers and relationships in their twenties, and came to motherhood later. The researchers argue that not only does motherhood have an impact on the kinds of workers women are, but that work influences the ways that women mother through the transposition of skills and values between work and home, and the need for them to absorb the effects of the 'stalled revolution' in which women's entry into the workforce has not been matched by a shift in the division of labour at home. A case study illustrates many of the points made in the chapter, and the authors consider motherhood – a singular and multiple experience that connects and divides women as daughters, mothers, non-mothers, grandmothers, employers and employees – as ripe for politicization. This chapter sets the experience of first motherhood in a broad social and historical context while examining closely intergenerational relationships between grandmothers and mothers and the experience of women as workers. In the next chapter the focus moves to a later part of the life course and the need for families with young children (aged 7–11 at the start) to balance the demands and needs of work and family life, with a focus on children and their roles in negotiating aspects of that balance.

The project described in Chapter 7 is concerned with the family life and practices of families with young children and is based on the concept of parental responsibility, currently seen as a key requirement by policy-makers, reinforced through public discourse and reflecting changes in family policy across Europe. Working parents are positioned at the intersection of family and employment policy, raising inherent tensions. Jeni Harden, Alice MacLean, Kathryn Backett-Milburn, Sarah Cunningham-Burley and Lynn Jamieson argue that the way this notion of responsibility features in parents' accounts of working parenthood has not been fully addressed and despite children being considered to be active family members, their views are absent in discussions of the issue. The study is designed to fill these absences by exploring the construction of responsibility through an investigation of the everyday lives and practices of working families. Responsibility is discussed through the notion of 'being there', the implications of competing responsibilities and the shifting nature of responsibilities in the context of change. Although other researchers (including in several chapters of this book – 5, 6 and 8) have observed that the burden of responsibility can be experienced differently by mothers and fathers in the domestic division of labour, the focus in this chapter is on comparing mothers' and fathers' views of their responsibilities with how their children understand them. In this study 'being there' was a moral narrative through which the concept of responsibility was expressed. Individual interviews were undertaken with parents and children (using child friendly methods) in the first and third waves of the study (over 18 months) with a family group interview at the second wave. The authors remark that a longitudinal approach is valuable for examining the dynamic experiences of working parenthood, responses to changes in work and family circumstances, and negotiations between parents and children, all illustrated in the findings presented in the chapter. The authors consider that parents are facing an impossible challenge in trying to give a 100% to both work and family life, but that is the aim they set themselves, while suggesting that any balance they did achieve was precarious and that they were often just getting by. One mother's 'plate spinning' failed when she forgot 'the tooth fairy'. Guilt around not 'being there' was strong in their responses and might have coloured the way they justified work as a necessity for the money, something that had to be dealt with rather than changed, as opposed to being fulfilling for themselves. Not surprisingly the children also seemed to feel powerless to change this situation. Increased responsibility for the children was often negotiated around transitions, for example from primary to secondary schooling, when new practical arrangements might also be required to keep the work/family balance afloat. The children did their bit to make life easier for their parents by modifying their behaviour, for example by doing what they were told in the mornings to facilitate the process of getting everyone where they needed to be. The 2008 recession also had an impact in that the uncertainty experienced about work could be a barrier to positive change. The next chapter discusses a secondary analysis of some of the Timescapes data, involving in particular chapters 5 and 7 above.

Chapter 8 is one example of work undertaken within the secondary analysis project. Here Sarah Irwin and Mandy Winterton explore and discuss strategies for the reuse and secondary analysis of data across two projects in Timescapes. In this instance, they were in a different position from most other secondary analysts in themselves being involved in the larger project and set of commitments. They were therefore already in a relationship with the primary researchers and able to liaise with them in accessing and selecting data for analysis. They were also provided with unique access to the data while essentially it was still 'live' and in use by the primary researchers, raising practical as well as ethical issues relating to data ownership. For the work reported in this chapter, after discussion with the Timescapes team, the researchers chose to work with data across projects 4 and 5. The projects had different disciplinary and conceptual bases, but the authors developed research questions relating to gendered experiences and manifestations of work–family conflict, exploring if and how they could work across very different data sets. For the presentation of their analysis here they provide a literature review of gender, paid work and family commitments, drawing on both quantitative and qualitative evidence from the UK and overseas, which also serves as support for statements made throughout this book on the gendered domestic division of labour. The authors describe in detail the processes they followed in analysing and then 'putting into conversation' the two primary projects, with judicious use of the data in presenting their findings. They conclude that this analysis 'complements wider evidence on the deep seated nature of economic and cultural drivers of gendered inequalities in experiences of time pressure in family life' and argue (as in Chapter 6) that policy must engage in an understanding of how 'choices' are framed in contexts that are taken as given.

Chapter 9 draws on a longitudinal study over ten years, in a site characterized by poverty and disadvantage, examining intergenerational relations and concerned with change and continuity in complex configurations of kinship in their relational networks. These networks crucially also included relations and interactions with service providers across health and social care in the public and third sectors, relationships that generate uncertainty and insecurity amongst the families concerned, particularly in crisis situations. For Timescapes, the study involved ethnography and interviews with young (35–55 years old) grandparents and their families, here focusing on the support grandparents channel to their grandchildren to improve their life chances. The researchers maintained close relationships with service providers in the area, some of whom facilitated access to participants, and observed up close experience of failures and problems with services. In this chapter, Nick Emmel and Kahryn Hughes draw on a theorization of time from Elias (1992), elaborating how the external compulsion from social institutions of time is converted into a temporal conscience, a pattern of self-constraint involving the whole life of the individual. This relates to the life course and generations so that people expect things, like fatherhood, motherhood, to arise at particular times in the life course. The authors' conceptualization of time is incorporated into a model of vulnerability, with four dimensions – an uncertain reliance on service providers, an assessment of material resources, resilience and time. This framework is used throughout the chapter, entwined with the presentation of case studies, to show how 'relations between socially institutionalized time as a means of orientation and experiences of generation have potential to explain the maintenance, amelioration, and exacerbation of vulnerabilities' (p. 23). For the authors, the temporal framing described in this research highlights a significant gap in social policy. Grandparents who are primary carers for their children and grandchildren are not considered in social policy literature in the UK, which can lead to particular institutional practices becoming embedded in health and social care provision to the detriment of the young grand-parents in this study. A teen child becomes a mother, catapulting her mother into grandmotherhood at the 'wrong' time; social services in the form of a teenage pregnancy and parenthood team hone in on the child with policies to facilitate her return to education, displacing the mother/grandmother and rendering invisible *her* needs in relation to supporting her child/grandchild. As the authors point out, confronting the assumptions supporting the conscience of generations could lead to strategies that could ameliorate significant vulnerabilities, in this case for young grandparents caring for their children and grandchildren. In the next chapter, the family and generational relationships of very old grandparents are examined.

In Chapter 10 Joanna Bornat and Bill Bytheway use life history inter-views and diaries combined in a retrospective/prospective investigation of the family relationships of the oldest generation, aged over 75. As in the last chapter, particular focus here is on the intergenerational relationship between grandparents and grandchildren. An overview of recent research into grandparenting provides a useful background for this and other chapters dealing with this generation, whether young or old. The review indicates a need for qualitative, temporal and multidi-mensional evidence, which the project reported here provides. A Senior (some of whose spouses actively participated) and a Recorder (who kept the Senior's diary, and took photographs) in each of 12 families UK-wide took part. Although the length of the study, 18 months, is short in longi-tudinal terms, it is long enough for both individual and familial change to emerge. Three case studies chosen to reflect the wide range of con-texts in which grandparenting was undertaken are discussed, exploring how events and changes in family life impinge on older people and their grandparenting. The case studies show how people make and are made by their grandparental status, and how various instabilities as they and their grandchildren change and grow older affect these relationships, which are an essential part of family life. Proximity aided contact and reciprocity, particularly when the grandparents were younger and more able to provide caring support. At this stage grandparents who were able to provide financial support did so, and often had done throughout, helping with the grandchildren's education. Free and accessible health care is important for older grandparents to avoid the need for practical support from younger family members. Should this change with future policy changes, and particularly in the case of social care, a looming problem for policy in the UK, then the situation would change, and more demands would be made on family members for care and support.

Funding cuts in social care budgets shift the balance between public- and family-based care. While an effective, free social care policy is available for the eligible in Scotland, in the rest of the UK this is not the situation, and the push will be from state to family provision, as pointed out in a number of the chapters in this book. And as ever, the burden on women is likely to increase and the parents in this study are liable to need to provide support to both younger and older family members, when they might often be grandparents themselves.

Conclusion

QLR enables researchers to explore social change over time as people experience and understand it. The contributions to this edited collection, individually and collectively as component projects of the Timescapes study stretching across the life course, demonstrate this major strength, focusing on micro-social processes of identities and relationships, and providing unique policy-relevant insights. We return to the lessons for social policies from these discussions in our overview conclusion to the volume. For now, having set the scene, we invite you to read the chapters themselves.

Notes

1. This chapter draws extensively on the work of the entire Timescapes team. Timescapes was funded by the Economic and Social Research Council in the UK, ESRC: RES 437 25 0003.
2. A long-term ethnographic study (from 1957) describing and analysing the Ezotzl-Maya cultures of the remote highlands of Chiapas, Mexico to understand how they are related to prehistoric Maya, and how their cultures change as they confront the modern world.
3. Briefly, 'the Troubles' describes the conflict over the constitutional status of Northern Ireland between the Protestant unionist community (wanting to remain in the UK) and the mainly Catholic nationalist community (wanting union with the Republic of Ireland). Over 30 years of violence in Northern Ireland (and mainland UK) involving republican and loyalist paramilitaries and the security forces of Northern Ireland and the Republic of Ireland began in the late 1960s.

References

Bell, C. and Newby, H. (1971) *Community Studies*, London: George Allen & Unwin.
Bishop, L. (2009) 'Ethical sharing and re-use of qualitative data', *Australian Journal of Social Issues*, 44(3): 255–272. Australian Council of Social Service. http://www.data-archive.ac.uk/media/249157/ajsi44bishop.pdf.

Bornat, J. (2013) 'Secondary analysis in reflection: Some experiences of re-use from an oral history perspective', in S. Irwin (ed.) 'Qualitative Secondary Analysis', *Families, Relationships and Societies*, special issue of FRS Open Space http://dx.doi.org/10.1332/204674313X667759.

Bornat, J. (2014) 'Epistemology and ethics in data sharing and analysis: A critical overview', in L. Camfield (ed.) *Research in International Development: A critical Review*, Basingstoke: Palgrave Macmillan (forthcoming).

Bornat, J. and Bytheway, B. (2010) 'Perceptions and presentations of living with everyday risk in later life', *British Journal of Social Work*, 40(4): 1118–1134.

Bornat, J. and Diamond, H. (2007). 'Women's history and oral history: Developments and debates', *Women's History Review*, 16(1): 19–39.

Bornat, J., Johnson, J. and Reynolds, J. (eds) (2012) *Secondary Analysis and Re-Using Archived Data in the Context of Ageing and Biography*, The Representation of Older People in Ageing Research, Series, no. 12. London: Centre for Ageing and Biographical Research and Centre for Policy on Ageing.

Caccamo, R. (2000) *Back to Middletown: Three Generations of Sociological Reflections*, Stanford, CA: Stanford University Press.

Caplow, T. (1984) 'Reply to Smith', *Qualitative Sociology*, 7(4): 337–339.

Corden, A. and Millar, J. (2007) 'Time and change: A review of the qualitative longitudinal research literature for social policy', *Social Policy and Society*, 6(4): 583–592.

Crow, G. (2008) 'Thinking about families and communities over time', in R. Edwards (ed.) *Researching Families and Communities*, London: Routledge, pp. 11–24.

Edwards, R. and Irwin, S. (eds) (2010) 'Lived experience through economic downturn in Britain', Special Issue of *21st Century Society: Journal of the Academy of Social Sciences*, 5(2): June. Contributions from six Timescapes projects.

Edwards, R. and Mauthner, M. (2002) 'Ethics and feminist research: Theory and practice', in M. Mauthner, M. Birch, J. Jessop, J. and T. Miller (eds) *Ethics in Qualitative Research*, London: Sage.

Edwards, R. and Weller, S. (2012) 'Shifting analytic ontology: Using I-Poems in qualitative longitudinal research', *Qualitative Research*, 12(2): 202–217.

Edwards, R. and Weller, S. (2013) 'The death of a participant: Moral obligation, consent and care in qualitative longitudinal research', in K. te Riele and R. Brooks (eds) *Negotiating Ethical Challenges in Youth Research*, Abingdon: Routledge.

Elias, N. (1992) *Time: An Essay*, Cambridge: Basil Blackwell.

Emmel, N. and Hughes, K. (2010) ' "Recession, it's all the same to us son": The longitudinal experience (1999–2010) of deprivation', *21st Century Society*, 5(2): 171–182.

Fielding, N. (2004) 'Getting the most from archived qualitative data: Epistemological, practical and professional obstacles', *International Journal of Social Research Methodology*, 7(1): 97–104.

Finn, M. and Henwood, K. (2009) 'Exploring masculinities within men's identificatory imaginings of first time fatherhood', *British Journal of Social Psychology*, 48(3): 547–562.

Hadfield, L. (2010) 'Balancing on the edge of the archive: The researcher's role in collecting and preparing data for deposit,' in F. Shirani and S. Weller (eds) *Conducting Qualitative Longitudinal Research: Fieldwork Experiences, Timescapes*

Working paper series no. 2: 60- ISSN 1758–3349. Available at www.timescapes. leeds.ac.uk/resources.

Henderson, S., Holland, J., McGrellis, S., Sharpe, S. and Thomson, R. (2007) *Inventing Adulthoods: A Biographical Approach to Youth Transitions*, London: Sage.

Henderson, S., Holland, J., McGrellis, S., Sharpe, S. and Thomson, R. (2012) 'Storying qualitative longitudinal research: Sequence, voice and motif', *Qualitative Research*, 12(1): 16–34.

Henwood, K. and Lang, I. (2005) 'Qualitative social science in the UK: A reflexive commentary on the "state of the art" ', *Forum Qualitative Sozialforschung/Forum: Qualitative Social Research*, 6(2): Art. 48. Available at: http://www.qualitative-research.net/index.php/fqs/article/view/16/35.

Holland, J. and Thomson, R. (2009) 'Gaining a perspective on choice and fate: Revisiting critical moments', *European Societies*, 11(3): 451–469. ISSN: 1461–6696; DOI: 10.1080/ 14616690902764799.

Holland, J., Thomson, R. and Henderson, S. (2006) *Qualitative Longitudinal Research: A Discussion Paper*, Working Paper No. 21, London: Families and Social Capital ESRC Research Group, available at http://www.timescapes.leeds.ac.uk/ events-dissemination/publications.php.

Irwin, S. (2013) 'Qualitative secondary data analysis: Ethics, epistemology and context', *Progress in Development Studies*, 13(4): 295–306.

Irwin, S., Bornat, J. and Winterton, M. (2012) 'Timescapes secondary analysis: Comparison, context and working across data sets', *Qualitative Research*, 12(1): 66–80. DOI: 10.1177/1468794111426234.

Irwin, S. and Winterton, M. (2011) *Debates in Qualitative Secondary Analysis: Critical Reflections*, Timescapes Working Paper 4, available at: http://www. timescapes.leeds.ac.uk/assets/files/WP4-March-2011.pdf.

Irwin, S. and Winterton, M. (2012) 'Qualitative secondary analysis and social explanation', *Sociological Research Online*, 17(2): 4, available at http://www. socresonline.org.uk/17/2/4.html.

James, A. (2013) 'Seeking the analytic imagination: Reflections on the process of interpreting qualitative data', *Qualitative Research*, 13(5): 562–577.

Kemper, R. and Peterson Royce, A. (eds) (2002) *Chronicling Cultures: Long-Term Field Research in Anthropology*, Walnut Creek, CA: AltaMira.

Kierkegaard, S. (1992[1846]) *Unscientific Postscript to Philosophical Fragments*, trans. and ed. H. V. Hong and E. H. Hong, Princeton, NJ: Princeton University Press.

Lynd, R. S. and Lynd, H. M. (1929) *Middletown: A Study in American Culture*, New York: Harcourt Brace.

Mason, J. (2007) 'Re-using qualitative data: On the merits of an investigative epistemology', *Sociological Research Online*, 12: 3. Available at http://www. socresonline.org.uk/12/3/3.html.

Mauthner, N., Parry, O. and Milburn, K. (1998) 'The data are out there, or are they? Implications for archiving qualitative data', *Sociology*, 32(4): 733–745.

Mauthner, N. S. and Parry, O. (2010) 'Ethical issues in digital data archiving and sharing', *E-Research Ethics*, available at http://eresearch-ethics.org/position/ ethical-issues-in-digital-data-archiving-and-sharing/.

Mills, C. W. (1959) *The Sociological Imagination*, New York: Oxford University Press.

Moore, N. (2006) 'The contexts of data: Broadening perspectives in the (re)use of qualitative data', *Methodological Innovations Online*, 1(2): 21–32.

Moore, N. (2007) '(Re)Using qualitative data?', *Sociological Research Online*, 12(3), available at http://www.socresonline.org.uk/12/3/1.html.

Neale, B. (2014) *What is Qualitative Longitudinal Research?* London: Bloomsbury (forthcoming).

Neale, B. and Bishop, L. (2012) 'The Timescapes Archive: A stakeholder approach to archiving qualitative longitudinal data', *Qualitative Research*, 12(1): 53–65.

Neale, B. and Hanna, E. (2012) *The Ethics of Researching Lives Qualitatively through Time*, Timescapes Methods Guides Series no. 9. Available at http://www.timescapes.leeds.ac.uk/resources-for-ql-research/publications.php.

Neale, B., Henwood, K. and Holland, J. (2012) 'Researching lives through time: An introduction to the Timescapes approach', *Qualitative Research*, 12(1): 4–15.

Neale, B. and Lau Clayton, C. (2011). *Following Fathers: The Lived Experience of Teenage Parenting Over Time*. Timescapes Policy Briefing Series. Available at: http://www.timescapes.leeds.ac.uk/assets/files/Policy-Conference-2011/paper-2.pdf

Parry, O. and Mauthner, N. (2004) 'Whose data are they anyway? Practical, legal and ethical issues in archiving qualitative data', *Sociology*, 38(1): 139–152.

Peterson Royce, A. (2011) *Becoming an Ancestor: The Isthmus Zapotec Way of Death*, New York: State University of New York Press.

Saldana, J. (2003) *Longitudinal Qualitative Research: Analyzing Change through Time*, Walnut Creek, Lanham, New York, Oxford: Altamira Press.

Smith, M. C. (1984) 'From Middletown to Middletown III: A critical review', *Qualitative Sociology*, 7(4): 327–336.

Standing, G. (2011) *The Precariat: The New Dangerous Class*, London: Bloomsbury Academic.

Thomson, R. (ed) (2010a) *Intensity and Insight: Qualitative Longitudinal Methods as a Route to the Psycho-Social*, Timescapes Working Paper No. 3: 4–6. Available at www.timescapes.leeds.ac.uk/resources.

Thomson, R. (2010b) 'Creating family case histories: Subjects, selves and family dynamics', in R. Thomson (ed.) *Intensity and Insight: Qualitative Longitudinal Methods as a Route to the Psycho-Social*, Timescapes Working Paper No. 3: 4–6. Available at http://www.timescapes.leeds.ac.uk/assets/files/WP3-final-Jan-2010.pdf.

Thomson, R., Bell, R., Holland, J., Henderson, S., McGrellis, S. and Sharpe, S. (2002) 'Critical moments: Choice, chance and opportunity in young people's narratives of transition to adulthood', *Sociology*, 6(2): 335–354.

Thomson, R., Kehily, M. J., Hadfield, L. and Sharpe, S. (2011) *Making Modern Mothers*, Bristol: Policy Press.

Thomson, R., Plumridge, L. and Holland, J. (2003) 'Editorial: Longitudinal qualitative research – A developing methodology', *International Journal of Social Research Methods*, Special issue on Longitudinal Qualitative Methods, 6(3): 185–187.

Vogt, E. (2002) 'The Harvard Chiapas project: 1957–2000', in R. V. Kemper and A. P. Royce (eds) *Chronicling Cultures: Long-Term Field Research in Anthropology*, Walnut Creek, CA: AltaMira.

Walkerdine, V., Lucey, H. and Melody, J. (2001) *Growing Up Girl: Psychosocial Explorations of Gender and Class*, Basingstoke: Palgrave.

Wiles, R. (2012) *What Are Qualitative Research Ethics?* London: Bloomsbury Academic.

Part I

Relationships and Life Chances of Children and Young People

2
Generations and Aspirations: Young People's Thinking About Relationships With Siblings and Hopes for Their Parents Over Time

Rosalind Edwards, Susie Weller and Sarah Baker

Introduction

Appeals to the social category of generation – particularly the differential opportunities available between generations – are found on both the political right and left as well as in the media in Britain.[1] In effect, generation is 'an emergent master-narrative on which actors of quite different persuasion converge as they seek to reshape prevalent conceptions of obligation, collective action and community' (White 2013: 217). Generation is posed as the central social division in society in an attempt to shape social policy in particular ways. It is questionable, however, whether or not such 'generationalism' has any purchase beyond its political practice, reflecting and creating wider social understandings.

In this chapter we use ideas about familial and cohort generations in the context of appeals to intergenerational justice to explore young people's thinking about their relationships with their siblings and other significant relatives, and their aspirations for their parents' future over time. We contrast what might be considered a rather simple portrayal of people's interests and thinking about generation and its political consequences, with the complex interplay between generation as age cohorts in larger society, as family lineage and solidarity, and as individual movement between childhood, youth and adulthood that are in play in young people's experiences as they grow older.[2] Our dual focus on young people's thinking about their relationships with their siblings and other significant relatives, and their aspirations for their parents' future reflects our concern about the neglect of the complexities and fluidity of inter and intra-generation in people's lives over time in political rhetoric. We will be exploring what Jaber Gubrium and Maude Rittman have referred to as the 'small worlds' of intergenerational relationships:

> A small world is an interpersonal domain of understanding. It is about what we happen to think, feel and do something about in particular situations. A small world has experiential boundaries.
>
> (1991: 94)

Gubrium and Rittman contrast these small, concrete worlds of everyday social relationships with the decontextualized 'global orientation' that animates public rhetoric about generational relations. They argue that people's perspectives on the nature of relations between the generations are rooted more in socially detailed circumstance than situation-free global abstracts.

We begin with a review of ideas around intergenerational justice that seek to influence policy, followed by an overview of the qualitative longitudinal study from which we draw our case studies. We then explore the subtleties and fluidity of young people's positioning of themselves and others in generational relationships, and move on to explore their hopes for their parents' future – an unusual but important and illuminating approach to understanding the 'small worlds' of intergenerational justice.

Generations and intergenerational justice

The concept of generation stretches across and holds together notions of society and family. On a societal level, generations can be understood in a purely demographic way; as birth cohorts of people born in a particular year or at approximately the same time and therefore all of a similar age. In this sense, society can be envisioned as layers of different age cohort generations. But cohort generation carries with it meaning beyond reference to chronological, demographic contemporaneity. As Karl Mannheim (1952) argued in proposing generation as a motor of social change, a complete understanding of generation as a basis for commonality and affiliation has to move beyond age. His emphasis on the formative and persistent historical, cultural and social events that young people live through and experience as significant has been subject to criticism as rooted in developmental thinking and overlooking children and older people (Pilcher 1995, Alanen 2001). Mannheim also acknowledged that while members of a cohort may experience the same historical and cultural events, these would not all touch their lives in the same way, thus constituting separate 'units' within a single generation.

Familially, the concept of generation is concerned with differential positioning within a family in the present – broadly, grandparental, parental and child generations; and also in terms of family lines of descent, stretching backward and forward in time. Within families, generation cross-cut with age is associated with asymmetries of dependency (youngest and oldest), power or authority (older), as well as associated flows of caring and providing obligations up and down generations. These flows involve a moral dimension of shoulds, oughts and the 'right thing to do', as studies of family life often reveal (Duncan and Edwards 1999, Ribbens McCarthy et al. 2003).

Political rhetoric about intergenerational justice as fair reciprocity and obligation draws on notions of both cohort and familial generations to drive social policy (White 2013), mimicking Mannheim's theoretical concern with generations as an explanation of social change. The topic of intergenerational justice has been the focus of a slew of recent popular and political publications that denominate current social policy issues in generational terms (access to higher education, employment, home-ownership, pensions, and so on): *How the Baby Boomers Stole Their Children's Future* (Willetts 2010), *Jilted Generation* (Howker and Malik 2010), *What Did the Baby Boomers Ever Do for Us?* (Beckett 2010). In such commentaries, generation usually becomes a central empirical social object in contentions that post-war 'boomer' generations, by virtue of belonging to larger cohorts, have systematically skewed the allocation of economic, social and cultural resources in their own favour at the expense of smaller, recent cohorts. In particular, older generations are said to have built and benefited from a generous welfare state but failed to steward it for sustainability. The younger generation suffers the consequent raw deal of strained public finances and pension systems; its members are immersed in debt and faced with a perilous future. As a result, commentators predict, the younger generation may renege on the social contract that binds generations together, abandoning any obligation to maintain the previous generation in old age.

Barbara Hirshorn (1991) has interrogated some of the means and consequences of this emphasis on generations as distinct, homogeneous masses whose interests are in conflict. On the one hand, interdependencies are obscured through a cross-sectional rather than longitudinal view of the transfer of resources. The flow of societal resources to the younger generation through the welfare state (education and health, etc.), built on tax and work role contributions from the older generation, is left aside. In addition, younger generations have been and are financially dependent and in receipt of such resources for longer periods than previous generations, with the extension of education and training (Furlong and Cartmel 2007). On the other hand, intra-generational social divisions are glossed over. Not all in the 'boomer' generations benefited from free higher education, bought their own home/s, had plentiful stable employment available to them, and have embarked on a life of cruising the Mediterranean on the back of a generous pension (the participants in Emmel and Hughes's study, Chapter 9, illustrate this well). The vertical ordering of such generational narratives cuts across, and renders insignificant, intra-generational cleavages (Kohli 2006, White 2013), obscuring inequalities of social class, gender, race/ethnicity and so on. In these two ways, generation is presented as a morally imbued category of injustice that requires rectification (White 2013).

The policy solutions put forward most often by generationalists are reduced state expenditure, welfare state contraction, longer working lives, reduced pensions and so on. The idea that cutting welfare provision for the older generation in fact places a burden on the younger generation who will need to care for them directly instead – a shift in responsibility from societal generation to family generation – is not addressed (White 2013, Bornat and Bytheway, Chapter 10, this volume).

Cohort generation and familial generation are woven together in ideas of intergenerational justice in other ways too. The generational idea

> brings with it a family metaphor: the idea of society as the kin group writ large [...] The family metaphor is prominent, conjuring links between the domestic world and the country at large. Our children are 'ours' both directly and figuratively [...] the country as a series of kin-like generations.
>
> (White 2013: 225/5)

Popular texts often connect the privileged and struggling generational cohorts together through reference to relations between parents and children, highlighting cross-temporal obligations where parents have a moral responsibility to rectify the consequences of their profligacy for the sake of their 'lost generation' of children, both individually and nationally. Ideas of intergenerational injustice leading to generational conflict also chime with images of generational tensions in relations between children and parents. Yet family researchers have long pointed out (such as Troll and Bengtson with McFarland 1979) that ideas about a 'generation gap' are simplistic; people's experiences of solidaristic and conflictual relations between the generations are more complex.

If the heady brew of cohort and familial generations invoked in ideas about intergenerational injustice has any purchase on social reality, and if youth experiences provide a contributing context for embedding attitudes, then it is important to explore how young people understand relationships within and between generations. We draw on qualitative longitudinal material from the 'Your space' study to do this.

The 'Your space' study

The strength of qualitative longitudinal research for studying the playing out of biographical lives, generational dynamics and wider social and historical processes is well demonstrated in this volume, as is the relevance of such in-depth temporal projects for providing insights into pressing social policy concerns, so we will be practising rather than rehearsing them here. The research from the Timescapes study that we draw on is the 'Your space: siblings and friends' project, which aimed to document the meanings, experiences and flows of children and young people's prescribed and chosen relationships, exploring how these connections related to their sense of self as their individual and family biographies unfolded over a period of up to eight years.

'Your space' brought together the notions of generation as cohort and familial discussed above. We followed over time a group of 50 children and young people who comprised a cohort of individuals sharing a similar location; they were born between 1989 and 1996. The participants were first interviewed when they were aged between 6 and 13 in 2002–2005 (wave 1); when they were 10–17 years old in 2007 (wave 2), and when they were 12–19 in 2009 (wave 3). Economically, these waves coincided with a period of apparent prosperous growth (wave 1), followed by the 'credit crunch' (wave 2) and then recession (wave 3) (Edwards and Weller 2010).[3]

From their cohort position, the 'Your space' participants shared a generational moment of economic recession as they moved towards and into young adulthood. But they did so from variable social and geographical locations, around a number of intra-generational cleavages. They came from a range of social circumstances, advantaged and disadvantaged, and housing conditions that included temporary accommodation, public housing estates, suburban semi-detached homes and gated communities. They lived in a variety of family formations, which meant that as an overall sample their sibling and parent relationships encompassed both biological and social ties. They were males and females from a diversity of majority and minority ethnic backgrounds. They were located across mainland Britain, from small villages in the Highlands of Scotland, to towns in the south of Wales, former industrial areas in the Midlands, suburban areas in the south and inner-city London. Further, social, familial and geographical situations shifted for some across the course of the study.

In addition to cohort generation as a feature of our sample, familial generation was built into the substantive concerns of the 'Your space' project. The key focus here was on the lateral generation of 'children' within family, on siblings. Topics that we asked about included: their relationships with their brothers and sisters; life at home, at school and in the neighbourhood; feelings of commonality and difference; times of help and support, and of argument and conflict; and so on. The children and young people also participated in activities that threw light on their sibling relationships, including circle maps, timelines and vignettes (Weller et al. 2011). Across the waves we also asked the children and young people about their relationships with their parents as these touched on their lives with their siblings and friends. In addition, in wave 2 we asked them about their hopes for their parents. A qualitative longitudinal approach means that we are able to understand these hopes in the context of the ebb and flow of relationships with their mothers and fathers over time.

Fluidity and complexity in intra- and intergenerational relationships over time

A number of social trends in family life do not sit well with cohort generational thinking. Diversity of family forms blurs the boundaries of 'the family' as a straightforward nuclear 'unit' and challenges notions of separate age groups (White 2013) because family generation lineage is not attached to chronological age. Young parenthood resulting in 'age-condensed' families, older parenthood in 'age-gapped' ones (George and Gold 1991, Emmel and Hughes, this volume), young children being aunts and uncles to older cousins, and large age gaps between siblings all mean that lineage inter and intra-generations can weave unevenly across and within age cohorts in a family. As one of our participants, Carl (aged 14), pointed out in his third interview: 'generation is a weird thing because everyone is having children at different times so you can't clearly cast a generation'. Although this was not Carl's direct experience in his immediate family, he had a large extended family in his parents'

Antipodean country of origin with cousins of all ages, who featured large in his sense of his connections.

Further, family generations are not merely a categorical status (sister, mother, grandfather) but importantly are a relational practice. It is the latter that is to the fore in people's 'small worlds' of generational relationships. We consider the implications of this for children and young people's understandings of generation in their lives in the context of relationships with their siblings and other significant relatives over time through two illustrative case examples: Daisy and Daniel.

Case study: Daisy

Daisy is a white British, lower-middle-class young woman. She lives in a village in Wales with her father, mother and brother, Mark (four years older), in an owner-occupied bungalow. Her father is a retired service-sector manager and her mother has part-time administration jobs. The basement of the bungalow is rented out to bring in additional income.

In her first interview in 2003 Daisy, then aged ten, alluded to the complexity of notions of generation in her life. She felt closely connected to her mother and Mark, but had a distant relationship with her father, who suffered health problems. In discussing her father's shortcomings as unapproachable and difficult, she presented a picture of intra-generational solidarity: Mark and Daisy sticking together at home, watching films to shut out conflict between their parents. She also gave examples of how Mark stepped in for her father: 'Dad used to show me [how to make things] but now he can't 'cos he has got arthritis in his arms, wrists, shoulders and feet'. In ten-year-old Daisy's 'small world' of generational relationships 14-year-old Mark had the potential to shift familial generation, remarking: 'if your brother or sister is older than you and your mum and dad die for no reason, like commit suicide, then your brother might be able to take good care of you'. Here the cross-cutting of generation with age, and indeed gender, is apparent, with Daisy believing her older brother could take responsibility for her. Daisy's narrative echoed others in the study, where power and caring relations in intra-generational relationships could be portrayed in terms of vertical intergenerational connections with some participants viewing (often older) siblings as 'second mums', 'strict parent types' or 'father-like'. This first encounter with Daisy revealed generation as a relational practice with the potential for relationships with siblings to be described, at times, as *intra*-generational bonds and at others as akin to *inter*-generational connections.

By the second interview, 13-year-old Daisy remained close to Mark
and they continued to share interests and enjoy spending time together.
She felt she was more able to talk to him than either of her parents, and
was concerned that when her brother left home she would have to confide in friends: 'because my brother is away at university and stuff I'd
have to talk to my friends more because I don't really feel comfortable
talking to an adult'. Thus Daisy positioned her relationship with Mark
as an intra-generational connection, united by a shared biographical
experience. Another dimension to her 'small world' of everyday social
relations emerged. Daisy spoke of her closeness to her maternal aunt,
who lived some distance away with her husband and young daughter.
Despite the age gap, the difference in life-course phase and her concerns
about confiding in an adult, she did not feel limits to what she could
divulge to her aunt:

> Me and [my aunt] get along quite well. It's very good because [my
> aunt] takes me out in the car with [my younger cousin and another
> cousin] sometimes and if the girls are asleep we can just like talk
> about stuff because nobody is around to listen. She's really nice to
> talk to as well and she understands better.

Other participants (male and female) similarly described aunts in particular as being 'like sisters', bridging conventional notions of intergenerational relationships.

Thus far Daisy's narratives had complicated notions of familial and
cohort generation. In her third interview, aged 15, the themes of closeness to her mother and brother, and distance from her father, continued.
Here the benefits of taking a longitudinal approach become evident.
Daisy had always looked up to her brother, albeit she slipped between
intra- and intergenerational relations in discussing this. In this interview, however, she introduced oscillating generational relations. For
instance, she felt Mark sometimes viewed her as an equal, or sometimes younger: 'Most of the time he just treats me like a friend kind
of, but, yeah, he sometimes treats me as a child'. Cleavages in intra-
generational relations become apparent during the 'betweenness' that is
the teenage years (Weller 2006). Generation as an individual movement
between childhood/youth/adulthood over time also points to challenges particularly of cohort-based notions of generation. Daisy's and
Mark's shared biographies are significant in their intra-generational connection, yet as Mark moved away from the contexts that shaped their
lives (such as school) to a different phase of the life course (employment,

independent living) so the 'gap' in their intra-generational relationship appeared to widen. Daisy's relationship with Mark is a good example of transcendence of conventional notions of intra- and intergenerational relationships, and also reveals how connections shift over time.

At 15 Daisy spoke less about the aunt with whom she previously felt so close, although maintaining contact with her by text. She discussed how women were more likely to understand than men, highlighting the ways in which gender cuts across generation. Now Daisy viewed their relationship as: 'In-between, not as a sister and not as an aunt but like a friend or something'. Talking about her three- and five-year-old cousins (conventionally occupying the same familial generation as Daisy), she said: 'I think they're in a younger generation. Life is going to be different for them when they're my age because it's going to be other stuff. At school life might have changed by then. Different, yeah'. School and technology formed important contexts for Daisy in terms of establishing an intra-generational relationship (technology can also be used for intergenerational connections, Tarrant 2012). Shared biographies and engagement with popular culture and technology were seen by several participants as significant in defining intra-generational connections, although common interests and spending time together helped shift seemingly vertical relationships into more lateral connections.

Case study: Daniel

Daniel is a British Filipino, lower-middle-class young man. He lives in east London with his mother, father and one of his sisters, Camille (eight years older), in an owner-occupied, small terraced house. His mother formerly worked as a secretary and is now a pastor, while his father is a bank clerk. His eldest sister Maria (16 years his senior) left home when he was five to start her own family. By six, Daniel was an uncle.

Daniel's 'small worlds' of generational relationships featured in his second and third interviews, at 15 and 16 years respectively. In the wave 2 interview in 2007, as with Daisy, notions of generation were neither fixed nor clear-cut for Daniel. He shared common interests and experiences with his sisters, enjoying spending time with them. For Daniel, the familial intra-generational connection meant that he could better confide in and relate to them than his parents: 'It's the generation thing. [My parents] compare how we are now with how they were before'. Yet because of his sisters' cohort age and life-course phase (employment, parenthood), Daniel also placed them in a similar generational position to his parents. Indeed, Daniel is closer in age to his nephew and niece than he is to Maria:

> Because [my sisters] are closer to [my parents'] age so can talk about the older things. But with me, I still come to them but sometimes it's limited and I have to talk about things that won't get them mad or something.

In his eyes, Daniel's sisters inhabited a fluid position, sometimes in the same familial generation as himself and sometimes more aligned with their parents. Dominant constructions of adult–child relations and life-course phases intersect with Daniel's understandings of intra- and intergenerational relations.

At 15, then, Daniel had regarded himself as treated at times as a child and at others like an adult. This 'betweenness' was still evident at 16, when Daniel commented: 'I'm able to look after the kids [nephew and niece] while [my Mum's] doing her own thing and I don't feel young. I only feel the youngest when I'm with my sisters'. Important, however, was Daniel's emphasis on shifts in his relationships with his sisters and his own growing maturity: 'The disadvantages [to having older sisters] would be having the age-gap, it kind of affects the way we get along. But as you get older you realize [and] they realize as well that things can change'. Nonetheless, Daniel reiterated his comments that his sisters shared a greater connection both with one another and with their parents because of their shared life-course experience: '[Maria] does things that my other sister can relate to and I can't. Like going out to certain places, she'll be able to get my sister involved but not me because it's not something that our generation would do'.

Daniel's case highlights the dynamic nature of generational boundaries. Shifts between life phases can morph lateral relationships into more vertical connections and vice versa. Over time Daniel's perception of his sisters' familial and cohort generational positioning fluctuated. Daniel illustrates the ways in which inter- and intra-generations can wend their way unevenly across and within age cohorts in a family where there are large age gaps between siblings, as well as where children become aunts or uncles at a young age, challenging notions of generations as distinct, homogeneous masses. Cohort and familial generational relationships cannot simply be equated with age or position in a family. Demarcating intra- and intergenerational relationships presents many challenges and the meanings ascribed to such connections vary by context. The examples of Daisy and Daniel challenge

conventional understandings of intra- and intergenerational connections, and suggest that the notion of a 'generation gap' is both simplistic
and naive.

Intergenerational justice: Hopes for parents over time

Much work on young people's aspirations focuses on their educational
and other outcomes, either through their own ideas for their possible future or their parents' hopes for them (for example, Perry and
Francis 2010, Carter-Wall and Whitefield 2012). This work resonates
with hopes that the next generation will do better than previous generations and fears about downward social mobility (Bourdieu 1993).
It seems a 'naturalism' that the future is associated with the younger
generation. Children and young people are understood in a future-
oriented time frame, in a process of becoming, transforming into adults.
The emphasis is on parental responsibility for this, with parents as primary in shaping the citizens and workers of the future (Prout 2000,
Harden et al. 2012). In turn, this focus on the younger generation as
the future and on the parental generation as responsible for their children's futures keys into preoccupations with intergenerational justice
where the younger generation's future is done down by an older generation who have had it all, and who have an obligation to rectify this
injustice.

We explore the purchase of these arguments through turning the
focus on parents' aspirations and plans for their children's future on
its head, to look at children and young people's hopes for their parents'
future over time. Exploring young people's aspirations for their parents
and how they might view their own role in this has something to tell
us about policy ideas that draw on notions of intergenerational justice,
where a younger generation is said to be set to rebel against any obligations towards the parental generation and a sense of solidarity is notable
for its silence.

Rather than focused on their own needs, the responses of participants
in the 'Your space' study were communicated with the 'good of the
family' or the wishes of their mother or father in mind. This was true
even of participants who had difficult relationships with their parents.
Across the interviews three types of response were common: hopes for a
'good' life, congenial family relationships and improvements in material
circumstances.

One of the ways that children and young people thought that the
'good' life could be obtained was by relocating in order to achieve a

more leisurely lifestyle. For example, in her second interview 13-year-old Daisy (see above) hoped that her parents would be able to retire to France or Spain once she and her older brother went to university. In the third interview, when Daisy was 15, her parents' plan to move to France looked more realistic and Daisy hoped that they would have a long and happy life there. For other children and young people a 'good' life also meant that their parents would be healthy, indicative of some of the problems that they think their parents face. They hoped that their parents would be able to work less and relax more, move to less stressful environments, and avoid the negative affects of ageing. These sentiments are a clear indication that children and young people, including those from middle-class backgrounds, do not view their parents as having easy lives.

Children and young peoples' hopes were also focused on family relationships. Where there were tensions between family members, they hoped that relationships would improve for the sake of their parents. In some cases, participants thought that if they were able to move out it would enhance their parents' lives. Children and young people also seemed more aware of 'getting on' with their families when new siblings arrived or new people moved into the home. A few also hoped that their parents would continue to have a good relationship with each other. For example, Daniel (see earlier) wished that the relationship between his parents, and his own with them, would improve in the future. But rather than for his benefit, he posed this as being good for the family. These findings indicate the complexities of intergenerational conflict and solidarity, as well as showing that difficult family relations do not necessarily lead to generation gaps, divisions or a lack of obligation.

Many of the participants also wanted their parents' material circumstances to improve in the future. Some hoped that their parents would have better houses, cars and incomes. Several looked forward to repaying their parents and felt a strong sense of responsibility towards them. This response often came from minority ethnic groups and those in close contact with their extended family. Over time it was common for their ideas about repayment to change from giving back material goods to returning care and the taking of responsibility. The issue of repayment is important to a discussion of intergenerational justice because it is illustrative of the ongoing reciprocity that binds generations together, rather than generational competition over a static pool of resources. To explore this issue, we present the case of Michael.

Case study: Michael

Michael is a black British, middle-class young man. He lives in south London with his mother, father, younger brother (three years junior) and older brother (four years senior), in a cramped owner-occupied terraced house. His father works in public transport and his mother as a nurse.

Michael talked about his hopes for his parents' future and repayment. He was 14 years old at the second interview in 2007, when he reflected on the freedoms he had gained since the previous interview. At the same time Michael was aware of the responsibilities that came with this freedom, saying 'as you get older, you get a bit more responsibilities and then it's more like a burden hanging over that you have to do certain things'. Indeed, Michael thought of himself as part of his parents' future. He wanted his parents not to have 'any problems with money or the house or anything', and said that eventually he 'will be able to help them out whenever'.

By 16 Michael's feelings of responsibility had intensified. At the time of the interview, he was waiting for his GCSE results as well as looking for a part-time job. The close relationship with his parents had continued. When asked about his feelings about his parents' future, he saw his mum's life getting easier because the children would 'grow up and get out of the house'. He was aware of how much work she did for him and his brothers:

> I guess as we all get older she wouldn't have to do so much for us so she can relax a bit more and then rather than her job being to look after us as we get older it sorts of switches around a bit and it will be our job to look after her and my dad.

Michael's response is typical of the gratitude that children and young people can feel towards their parents and the ethics of care and responsibility involved in generational relationships, especially as children get older. These sentiments challenge the idea of the competitive selfish individual (whether parent or child) on which models of intergenerational competition are based.

Michael was in regular contact with his extended family both in the UK and West Africa, and the strength of familial ties in his life may have contributed to his feelings of care and responsibility. Other children and young people in close contact with extended family, particularly those from working-class backgrounds, also saw themselves and their families as helping each other in the face of adversity. We look at this in relation to a young man, Rooney.

Case study: Rooney

Rooney is a white working-class young man. He lives in a city in the southeast of England with his father, mother, older sister and three older brothers, in a modern town house rented from a housing association. Both of Rooney's parents are long-term unemployed.

In his third interview, aged 16, Rooney talked about his family sticking with and up for each other: 'covering each other's backs'. When asked about the differences between his parents' generation and his own, he spoke of the difficulties in accessing social housing in comparison with his parents: 'Well, when my mum and dad were 16 they could get a flat easy, you know what I mean? They could just say, "Oh yeah, we need to move out because of our parents" and that, and they'd get a flat'. Rather than complaining about older generations or his parents taking all the resources, Rooney blamed politicians for mismanaging public provision and finances:

> Nowadays the government are funding crackheads with houses... they're funding them houses, and then you've got illegal immigrants who are coming over and they're funding them houses as well... If the future keeps going up and keeps going up in taxes, you know what I mean, people are going to end up giving up their jobs because they ain't going to be able to rent their houses and that, and they're going to be homeless.

Rooney experienced social inequalities alongside his family and friends, whatever their generation.

These cases, and the wider findings about young people's concerns for their parents' future, further illustrate the role that narratives of intergenerational justice have in obscuring distinctions and inequalities of social class, gender and race/ethnicity. Indeed, it gives weight to the argument that the concept of intergenerational justice is a white middle-class narrative that is only experienced by a minority who, due to economic conditions, are not able to 'have it as good' as their parents. Even then, as the 'Your space' qualitative longitudinal data has revealed, inter and intra-generational conflict and solidarity are far from the simplistic divisions that intergenerationalists would lead us to believe.

Conclusion

Throughout this chapter we have argued that generation is not the key societal division in young people's lives, as asserted in political and media rhetoric. Rather we have revealed the complex interplay between their cohort positioning in wider society and family lineage and solidarity, as the young people in our sample moved from childhood into youth and towards adulthood within their own, specific, everyday 'small worlds' of intra and intergenerational relationships.

With the benefit of qualitative longitudinal case studies we have been able to show that, in these small worlds, generation is not the simple cross-sectional affiliation of a cohort 'jilted' by 'baby boomers'. Rather it is a lived experience and relational practice, cross-cut by complex solidarities and challenges. Young people can experience a 'generation gap' with their sibling, and older siblings could be a 'second parent' and/or 'friend', switching generational positions at different moments in time and across the passage of time. The small worlds of who relates to whom and how challenge as well as confirm mainstream understandings of intra- and intergenerational connections and affiliations.

Simplistic ideas about intergenerational justice are equally thrown into question. The desire for and morality of the transfer of cross-temporal resources is not only 'downwards' from parents for the purpose of their children's future, but also upwards, with young people thinking of their parents' futures. Rather than feeling rebellious against any obligations, the young people in our study were concerned about the problems and stresses that their parents faced currently and might face in the future. They had hopes for their parents of a 'good' life, congenial family relationships and improved material circumstances. Many had feelings of family solidarity and wanted to repay their parents' efforts – even if the relationship was characterized by conflict or resentment.

Further, not all of the parental generation of the young people in our sample had the benefit of a higher education (whether free or not), stable and rewarding employment, and ownership of their home. Parents might face ill health or long-term unemployment, for example. The political rhetoric of intergenerational injustice as a rationale for social policy change is abstract and gains little purchase in diverse and intricate temporal small generational worlds. People's perspectives on the nature of relations between the generations are rooted more in socially detailed circumstance than situation-free global abstracts. They point towards the need to encourage intergenerational dialogue in political and media discussion, and as a guide to policy development, rather than ideas around intergenerational competition and injustice.

Notes

1. A topic with a history of being a 'contemporary' concern, especially in the US (Gubrium and Rittman 1991). Interestingly, the same 'baby boomer' generation now castigated in the UK was posed as the angry generation in the late 1980s in the face of greater resources and options having been available to older age cohorts than to them (Hirshorn 1991).
2. Other conceptualizations of young people and generation that we do not pursue here include childhood/adulthood as a two-generational order (Alanen 2001) and 'global generations' as a contemporary youth dynamic (Beck and Beck-Gernsheim 2009).
3. A further wave of data was collected in 2013.

References

Alanen, L. (2001) 'Explorations in generational analysis', in L. Alanen and B. Mayall (eds) *Conceptualising Adult–Child Relationships*, London: Routledge.

Beck, U. and Beck-Gernsheim, E. (2013) *Distant Love*, Cambridge: Polity.

Beckett, F. (2010) *What Did the Baby Boomers Ever Do for Us?* London: Biteback.

Bourdieu, P. (1993) *Sociology in Question*, London: Sage.

Carter-Wall, C. and Whitfield, G. (2012) *The Role of Aspirations, Attitudes and Behaviour in Closing the Educational Attainment Gap*, York: Joseph Rowntree Foundation: www.jrf.org.uk/site/files/jrf/education-achievement-poverty-summary.pdf [Accessed 1 September 12].

Duncan, S. and Edwards, R. (1999) *Lone Mothers, Paid Work and Gendered Moral Rationalities*, Basingstoke: Macmillan.

Edwards, R. and Weller, S. (2010) 'Trajectories from youth to adulthood: Choice and structure for young people before and during recession', Special Issue: Lived Experience Through Economic Downturn in Britain – Perspectives Across Time and Across the Lifecourse (eds. R. Edwards and S. Irwin), *21st Century Society*, 5(2): 125–136.

Furlong, A. and Cartmel, F. (2007) *Young People and Social Change: New Perspectives*. 2nd Edn, Maidenhead, Berks: Open University Press.

George, L. K. and Gold, D. T. (1991) 'Life course perspectives on intergenerational and generational connections', in S. K. Pfeifer and M. B. Sussman (eds) 'Families: Intergenerational and generational connections', Binghampton NY: Haworth Press. Also in Part 1/2, *Marriage and Family Review*, 16(1/2): 67–88.

Gubrium, J. F. and Rittman, M. R. (1991) 'Small worlds and intergenerational relationships', in S. K. Pfeifer and M. B. Sussman (eds) 'Families: Intergenerational and generational connections', Binghampton NY: Hawarth Press. Also appears in Part 1/2, *Marriage and Family Review*, 16(1/2): 89–102.

Harden, J., Backett-Milburn, K., MacLean, A. and Jamieson, L. (2012) 'Hopes for the future: Parents' and children's narratives of children's future employment orientations', *Sociological Research Online*, 17(2): http://www.socresonline.org.uk/17/2/13.html [Accessed 29 August 12].

Hirshorn, B. (1991) 'Sharing or competition: Multiple views of the intergenerational flow of society's resources', in S. K. Pfeifer and M. B. Sussman (eds) 'Families: Intergenerational and generational connections', Binghampton NY: Haworth Press. Also appears in Part 1, *Marriage and Family Review*, 16(1/2): 175–193.

Howker, E. and Malik, S. (2010) *Jilted Generation: How Britain Has Bankrupted Its Youth*, London: Icon.

Kohli, M. (2006) 'Generational changes and generational equity', in M. Johnson, V. L. Bengtson, P. Coleman and T. Kirkwood (eds) *The Cambridge Handbook of Age and Ageing*, Cambridge: Cambridge University Press, pp. 518–526.

Mannheim, K. (1952) *Essays on the Sociology of Knowledge*, London: Routledge and Kegan Paul.

Perry, E. and Francis, B. (2010) *The Social Class Gap for Educational Attainment: A Review of the Literature*, London: Royal Society of Arts: www.thersa.org/_data/assets/pdf_file/0019/367003/RSA-Social-Justice-paper.pdf [Accessed 1 September 12].

Pilcher, J. (1995) *Age and Generation in Modern Britain*, Oxford: Oxford University Press.

Prout, A. (2000) 'Children's participation: Control and self-realisation in British late modernity', *Children & Society*, 14(4): 304–315.

Ribbens McCarthy, J., Edwards, R. and Gillies, V. (2003) *Making Families: Moral of Parenting and Step-parenting*, Durham: Sociology Press.

Tarrant, A. (2012) 'Grandfathering: The construction of new identities and masculinities', in S. Arber and V. Timonen (eds) *Contemporary Grandparenting: Changing Family Relationships in Global Contexts*, Bristol: Policy Press.

Troll, L. and Bengtson, V. with McFarland, D. (1979) 'Generations in the family', in W. Burr, R. Hill, F. I. Nye and I. L. Reiss (eds) *Contemporary Theories About the Family: Research-Based Theories*, Vol. 1, New York: The Free Press.

Weller, S. (2006) 'Situating (young) teenagers in geographies of children and youth', *Children's Geographies*, 4(1): 97–108.

Weller, S. and Edwards, R. with Stephenson, R. (2011) *Researching Children's Lateral Relationships Over Time: Methodological and Ethical Lessons from a Qualitative Longitudinal Study*, Families & Social Capital Research Group Working Paper No. 30, London: London South Bank University.

White, J. (2013) 'Thinking generations', *British Journal of Sociology*, 64(2): 216–247.

Willetts, D. (2010) *The Pinch: How Baby Boomers Took Their Children's Future – And How They Can Give It Back*, London: Atlantic Books.

3
Growing Up in Northern Ireland

Sheena McGrellis and Janet Holland

Introduction

Young people in Northern Ireland (NI) have grown up during 'the Troubles'[1] and subsequent peace process, a period of significant political, economic and social transition. The 'Inventing adulthood' study has shadowed these changes since 1996. Politicians and those in positions of power and influence negotiated, renegotiated and thrashed out settlements and deals, while sectarianism and violence continued in the streets and communities where the young people lived. Ceasefires were agreed, and remained largely intact but the process of moving towards an inclusive and peaceful society was, and continues to be, delicate. The Troubles and the history of sectarian divisions and violence have had a strong impact on the lives of young people growing up in NI, colouring the ways they understand themselves, and their relationships with families, communities, friends and politics. This generation can be seen as falling between two eras (Mannheim 1952). They are children of the Troubles and at the same time the first generation to grow into adulthood in a post-ceasefire society – a society in its infancy in terms of governance, and very much at the early stages of building a shared future.

In this chapter we draw on data from the 'Inventing adulthoods' project to analyse, theorize and describe the lives of young people growing up in NI, bringing attention to the implications of findings from our study for policy and practice. The voices and stories of young people come from the analysis of longitudinal case histories that encapsulate their lives over the period of the study (Henderson et al. 2012).

Inventing adulthoods

The prospective qualitative longitudinal study, 'Inventing adulthoods' has been exploring young people's lives in their biographical,

48

social/historical and generational context since 1996.[2] The 100 young people who joined the study at the start were located in five socio-economically contrasting sites across the UK: a leafy suburb, an inner city location, an isolated rural area, a disadvantaged northern estate and a site in NI that varied in class and religion.

In up to six biographical interviews through time, we invited them to create a series of retrospective accounts of the past, and to project themselves into the future from the perspective of a changing present. A central concern has been to examine how biographies are shaped by structural factors such as location/place, social class, gender and family, and the concomitant personal, social, physical/material and economic resources available to the individual (Thomson et al. 2003, 2004, Henderson et al. 2007). The substantive and theoretical focuses for investigation have shifted across time with the sequential projects that were part of 'Inventing adulthoods', from values through the construction of identity and adulthood to social capital in an examination of the social and associational resources available to young people; and here focus on the impact on young lives of social and historical processes in NI. We have moved from the critique of postmodern theories of individualization and detraditionalization, while employing Giddens' concept of the reflexive project of self (1991), to developing conceptual and theoretical frameworks and tools from the data. Given the insights afforded by the methodological approach, we have been concerned throughout to develop aspects of qualitative longitudinal research and practice, including longitudinal case histories, in order to capture time and change (Henderson et al. 2012).

Inventing adulthoods in Northern Ireland

In 2004/2005, 27 of the young people in the NI group were interviewed; in 2009/2010 we returned to interview 18 of these for the seventh time (funded by the Joseph Rowntree Foundation (JRF) and part of Timescapes). We found a group of young adults who had moved between college, university, work and unemployment, and training; left from and returned to home and country; and accumulated shifting relationship statuses and caring responsibilities. The longitudinal approach allowed us (and the young people) to observe and reflect on 'critical moments' in their journeys and the consequences of these on different spheres in their lives over time (Thomson et al. 2002, McGrellis 2011). Young people identified a wide range of situations, events and experiences as critical or influential. These events could be family-related, such as moving home, illness and bereavement; education-related, such as leaving school, starting work; engaging in different leisure activities and moving into different social spaces; or significant moments in relationships. The ways that young people responded to these events, including those over which they had no control (illness, bereavement and family disruption for example), depended on the resources available to them, the timing, and if and how they changed their lives in the light of such events (Henderson et al. 2007). Critical moments feature heavily in the narratives on which this chapter draws.

Table 3.1 indicates the biographical life stages of the young people in the study alongside significant political/social/historical events, and the next section contextualizes their experiences by discussing the importance of community for them over this period.

Table 3.1   Biographical–political/social/historical timeline

Biographical	Age	Year	Political/social/ historical
	12	1994	Paramilitary ceasefires
GCSEs; education decisions; expanding social lives	14	1996	IRA bombs London, Manchester
Part-time jobs; more freedom and independence	15	1997	2nd IRA ceasefire
Leave (continue) school; college/FE	16	1998	Good Friday Agreement 71% support; Omagh bomb
Expanding social and leisure scene in NI; relationships; educational pressures	17	1999	Devolved government; Assembly set up
Leave home; relationships; social life; work/unemployment; training; FE/higher education; travel	19	2001	IRA decommission arms; power sharing
	20	2002	Assembly suspended
Completed university; work/unemployment; emotional health issues; global level opportunities; social networking; parenthood	23	2005	
	25	2007	Assembly reinstated
	26	2008	Recession UK
Work/unemployment; parenthood; relationships; emotional health; restricted opportunities; return to community/emigrate	27	2009	Increased dissident Republican activity

Communities: Together and apart

Context

In early interviews community relations loomed large and the young people gave accounts of how their lives were directly affected by sectarianism, conflict and segregation. They told of being 'put out', made to leave their houses/homes; of being part of or caught up in riots at interface sites; of fearing for their own, or their family's safety; of being expelled by paramilitaries, or merely feeling uncomfortable in communities where all around them were of a different religion. Over the years such accounts became less dominant but the legacy of conflict, segregation and sectarianism has extended into their adult worlds. Family, work, housing and their own children's education are priorities for these young people now, but these priorities continue to be shaped to a greater or lesser extent by the recent troubled history.

Young people's personal and family relations are worked out within the broader frame of the political and social environment, and woven within the fabric of their 'local' community, with its own distinct identity and values. Inter-community relations within NI (typically between Catholic and Protestant, but also between local communities and new-comers) remain an issue for both the government and the population as a whole. Building a 'shared future' of good community relations was one of the fundamental tenets of the Good Friday Agreement.[3]

Security and risk

Risk is part of life and is perhaps an expected part of growing up. In NI these concepts also take on meanings that are historically and locally specific, associated with conflict, policing, paramilitarism and territorialism. Although the ceasefire has remained in place, sectarianism and paramilitary activity continued to have a significant impact on the lives of young people, particularly those living in working-class areas. Their experience of space, place and mobility is often coloured by the fear or threat of violence or sectarianism, or the legacy of such experiences in their community. How they used and managed space was central to their coping and survival strategies growing up, and as data from this project suggest early experiences of conflict and sectarianism can influence future transitions. In Cynthia's case, recognition of these effects came later through personal experience.

Over the years, Cynthia professed and maintained a detached stance in relation to the community politics and sectarianism that surrounded her. It was not until she witnessed such activity more closely, and became more intimately familiar with it, that she appreciated the personal and community cost. In her latest interview in 2009, Cynthia expressed distaste for the growing number of punishment activities, saying 'they take their legs' to keep the members in line, and 'they think they are untouchable'. Bitterness still seeps through communities and young men are interested in joining paramilitary groups because, as she sees it, sectarianism is still rife. Parents are still 'teaching their children' to hate Catholics or Protestants: 'old men sit in pubs telling young boys stories about the good old days when they used to do this and do that. And their boys are just lapping it up, thinking "that's where I want to be in 30 years"'. Cynthia has personally witnessed how naïve and impressionable young men are 'built up' and 'railroaded', and 'before you know it you're all the way in'. She has also witnessed how the consequences and risk of this spill out to affect family and friends.

The young people's narratives illuminate many elements of risk and how these are mediated and managed over time. Their accounts highlight the sources of security they seek out to counterbalance and recover from exposure to challenging life events. When we first met, their concerns, and perhaps our interest, depicted the most difficult aspects of living in a divided community. They described and related to 'pure' and 'bitter' communities (McGrellis 2005), experiencing them as perpetuating hatred and instilling fear and suspicion. They relayed their experiences of delineating the boundaries of their own areas, of respecting or challenging and traversing these boundaries, and then more cautiously of linking with other communities. Young people also occupied many spaces within and beyond the confessional communities, defined rather by leisure, hobby and work interests for example, that took them beyond territorial boundaries and funnelled mindsets.

Close-knit communities and extended family networks fostered a strong sense of belonging and protection, and acted as sources and generators of social capital. Young people who encountered unexpected and challenging life events often retreated to the shelter of familiar spaces within communities and/or families. In the face of bereavement, unexpected pregnancies, paramilitary expulsion, education- or work-related stress, debt, job loss, relationship break-up or depression, young people journeyed back to families and familiar communities. The darker side of some close and tight-knit communities also emerged however, as young people who flouted community rules found that wanting to live outside the community boundaries both physically and normatively resulted in loss and rejection at a fundamental level.

Adele's trajectory reflects this process. First contacted in 1998, Adele was intent on leaving the restrictions of her home town for bigger cities and greater opportunities. She regards the place she lived as a 'wile rough area' full of 'gangs', 'drugs' and 'rackets'. Adele envisaged her passage out of what she saw as small spaces and small-mindedness through a career in hairdressing. Her defiance of territorial rules played a significant role in shaping her future. Despite the blatant reminders emblazoned on walls and the staunch unwelcoming stance of some members of her family, Adele walked her first Catholic boyfriend into her estate and her home, fully aware of the risk she was taking. Later Adele took a college training course as a means of fulfilling her dream to become a successful hairdresser working in a fashionable salon in a big city, a move that took her beyond her own tight-knit area and introduced her to people from different community and cultural backgrounds. Distracted and attracted by a social life previously unavailable to her, she gradually fell away from her studies. Alcohol and drugs played a part in her social scene, and arguments led to a decision to leave home. To qualify for social housing, Adele made herself homeless and left the hairdressing course.

She was housed in a different Protestant estate. At this time, she was in a steady relationship with a young Catholic man and within a few weeks she was intimidated out of her house by masked men. She saw no option but to move to a predominantly Catholic housing area, a move that further distanced her from her family, and gradually eroded this relationship. Her life became less structured, living on state benefit her social life increasingly revolved around house parties and drugs. But in 2009, aged 27, she had become 'fed up with a fried head,' and had given up drugs after eight years of use. At 27 Adele wanted a better future for herself, and any children she might have, but saw her choices as limited. With no qualifications, no formal work and dependent on housing benefit, Adele felt trapped and uncertain where to turn. With the country in recession and job opportunities limited, she felt even more disadvantaged and at risk. She wanted to 'stay away from drugs' but was aware that to do so might cost her her relationship and her social life. At a crossroads, Adele was unable to identify sources of help or guidance.

Policies for young people: Falling through the cracks

This chapter focuses on aspects of policy, and for the NI study we mapped policies for young people in NI in the last decade (McGrellis 2009). They were many and varied, but significantly there was little, indeed one could say no, evaluation of their effectiveness or follow-up on many of the initiatives started. In the face of the complexity of young people's lives and their intersecting identities and activities *across* policy areas, policies were compartmentalized into different departments and agencies, with young people generally falling through the cracks. These broad conclusions were supported by our JRF advisory group and a focus group, each consisting of policy-makers and practitioners in the youth area in NI, who commented on a 'silo mentality'. On the basis of our study, certain gaps in policy provision were identified and recommendations made (McGrellis 2011).

Key policy areas emerging in the interview data, particularly in the recent interviews in NI, are: mental health and well-being, including suicide rates; education; and drug and alcohol use (McGrellis 2011). Social disadvantage and the legacy of community conflict have been linked to the higher incidence of mental ill health in NI, where suicide rates are increasing compared with a drop across the rest of the UK. NI has one of the highest suicide rates in the UK and reports note a rise of more than a third in the number of young men taking their own lives since the end of the Troubles (Bennett 2007, O'Hara 2011). Statistics from the Public Health Agency (PHA) NI show that deaths from suicide remained relatively static over the second half of the twentieth century but rose by 64% between 1999 and 2008. Most recent figures available from the PHA (2008) suggest that suicides among the 15–34 age group accounted for the greater part of this rise (Hayes 2011). The NI government acknowledge that alcohol and drug misuse are compounding factors in the incidence of suicide and self-harm, and have developed strategy documents to address these issues. Mental health issues are considered in the section on critical moments below, but the following sections briefly trace the young people's experiences in the major policy areas of education, employment and training, and housing.

Education

The education pathways of young people in this group varied considerably. They became participants in the project initially, primarily, through schools; some from an integrated school, and others from either maintained (predominantly Catholic) or controlled (predominantly Protestant) schools. 'Traditional' educational transitions, moving from school to further or higher education and into professional careers, were the experience of just a few from this group – primarily from more middle-class backgrounds. A significant number of young people left school at 16 to follow a vocational course at a further education (FE) college, and some subsequently moved on to university from college. Amongst the young people in the study as a whole, those in NI were initially the most educationally aspirational. Reflecting on their educational experience in the latest interview, over half of the group expressed regrets at some level. These included regrets in relation to the choice of subjects, courses and career paths taken; regrets about leaving school for work; regrets about not pursuing a university degree; and indeed regrets about doing just that.

Noticeable within these regrets was the lack of education and career guidance, or a key mentor or teacher at decision-making times. Young people talked about being forced to choose between their best subjects in order to fit in with a curriculum timetable, of sliding from top of the class to 'basic' and subsequently failing when a good teacher was replaced by one 'who couldn't teach'. Others remained in school after 16 to follow the only vocational course offered but one in which they were not interested. Their decision was made less out of informed planning than fear (of leaving) and uncertainty about alternative choices.

The impact of critical moments in young people's lives on their education pathway was significant. Many experienced the loss of family and friends during their school and college years. While all employed different coping strategies and responded and recovered in different ways, sustained emotional support within the school environment was not readily accessible or used by these young people. Some reported on a 'grace' period when allowance was made for missed deadlines or lack of concentration, but the expectation to 'get back to normal' for them often came too soon in the bereavement process.

Pregnancy unexpectedly disrupted the educational pathway of a few; young mothers and fathers left education to care for their children and to find work to support them. Those who left for this reason reported an accelerated journey to adulthood. While they often retained unfulfilled educational and work ambitions, they did not envisage an easy return to such pathways. Shelagh's experience illustrates this critical moment in an educational pathway.

At 18 Shelagh became a mother. Before she was sexually active, she had mentioned that sexual health and protection was 'down to the girls, as fellas were not responsible in that department'. Her relationship ended 'because of sex'. The night they split he, much older than she, wanted sex and she did not, and so she left to go into the night, not knowing that she was already pregnant. On that occasion, she was on the pill but her prescription had run out and she took a chance. At that time NI had one of the highest rates of teenage pregnancy in Europe. For

Shelagh teenage parenthood made her grow up, feeding into her strong desire to take responsibility for herself and her child, to show that she could be an independent single mother. It made her feel 'tied down'; she never shirked her responsibility as a mother but needed to escape from it on a regular basis, to party with her friends, to forget and be young. It saw her give up her course at FE college and embark on a route to accelerated adulthood, with home and family at its core. She subsequently met another partner, with whom at the last interview she was buying a house, and had twins. She always worked, with her income often critical for the maintenance of her family.

Opting out of education was a choice that other young people made actively in order to secure a sense of competence and recognition – not readily available to them within the school system. Some achieved this through work, others within the domestic arena, and at least one in the leisure field. Attempts to return to education at a later point were thwarted by their age or by fees (course fees that were in excess of what was possible for them to pay on a low part-time wage as a part-time student), or by a developed dependency on state benefits.

Those who completed a university degree followed the more traditional and perhaps more socially valued route in education. In the current economic climate, some did not necessarily regard it as the best route. Accumulated debt, lack of work experience and increased competition have led to doubts about the 'piece of paper' they hold. The messages received from this group of young people reflecting on their educational journeys are for greater choice, more flexible learning conditions, easy return pathways to education and the need for individual guidance and mentoring throughout the school period, but particularly at key decision points. The seeming absence of this type or level of support is also reflected in the narratives of those who experienced significant trauma or disruptive life events while at school or college. The NI Department of Education's 'entitlement framework' implemented in 2013 addresses some of these areas, particularly the proposal to give students greater choice of academic and vocational courses.

Employment and training

While the NI economy has grown dramatically since the ceasefires, moving from a manufacturing based to a service-led, knowledge based economy, it has subsequently fallen into recession with the rest of the UK, Europe and the US (Group Economics, Ulster Bank 2008). Some analysts suggest that the factors sheltering NI from the 1990s recession (e.g. high dependence on public sector employment – 31% of the workforce in 2008 – underdeveloped private sector; significant government subvention in manufacturing) have made it particularly vulnerable to the recent downturn (Hutchinson and Byrne 2007). The collapse of the construction sector, for example, was dramatic, and followed by a sharp decline in the service sector and contraction of manufacturing industry (Group Economics, Ulster Bank 2008). Employment prospects for young people in the current economic situation are poor. The unemployment rate at the end of July 2012 was 8.2%, higher than the UK average; the unemployment rate for 18–24 year olds was 23.5% compared to the UK average of 19.3%. NI has a well-educated workforce but 65% of those who registered as unemployed in the past year have fewer than five GCSEs. Those with tertiary education are increasingly taking jobs for which they are overqualified, squeezing those with fewer qualifications out of the labour market.

Policy responses to youth unemployment in NI have largely followed Westminster government initiatives over time. The New Deal was introduced in 1998 as a training to work scheme for those in the 18–24 age group who had been unemployed for more than six months. In 2008 this scheme was replaced by the Steps to Work programme, aimed primarily at 18–24 year olds, and the Training Success programme for 16–18 year olds. A series of proposals to help address the current trend towards high economic inactivity in NI has been developed by the NI Adviser on Employment and Skills (NIAES 2010). These include a plan to strengthen state intervention, and to improve linkages across departments, government agencies, employers and local agencies responsible for welfare-to-work policies (Gray and Horgan 2010). If taken up, these could go some way to overcome the compartmentalization we have observed.

As time passed an increasing focus in interviews was the young people's transition from education to work, and how employment, or the lack of it, defined and influenced so many other aspects of their lives. Relationships and family support were a vital resource, helping young people to negotiate difficult phases, or providing social networks through which to access contacts and work. Social networks emerged as key as they endeavoured to find work. Some young people from more working-class backgrounds, for example young men in the construction industry, were adept at using such by-and-large local and family-based networks. For others these family-based networks extended to diasporic communities, in that way facilitating a specific working-class trajectory that was paradoxically rooted in the local but realized at a global level. As well as helping with finding employment, their networks were often useful for finding housing and providing leisure opportunities. But when these structures collapsed or evaporated in relation to work, a chasm was left in their wake. When last interviewed, about 50% of the young people in the NI study were in full-time employment and over a quarter unemployed.

A more middle-class trajectory can often seem smoother. For example, Maeve's career in the medical profession followed a well-planned path through the various necessary levels of education and work experience abroad, with considerable support from her parents, although since first starting university she had lived independently. At her latest interview, she and her partner of many years had returned to Ireland after a period extending their working experience and training in the Antipodes; coming back had been rather upsetting as the recession had really taken hold and they found the country depressed and depressing, and at first felt keen to turn round and go straight back.

> It's just the way things are at the moment isn't it, the reces-sion...when we left everything was fine, and when we came back this had all happened and we were like, what is going on, awful, all this bad news, bad news left, right and centre.

Later, however, she points out that

> When I came back...we were both like depressed, we weren't enjoy-ing being back at all and it took about a month I think, but I think it was just the transition and trying to settle. After a month or two we were grand again...now it's just kind of fading in to memory we don't feel we live there any more we live here now.

Long-term unemployment has been a feature of life for a small num-ber of study participants. For some cyclical training schemes, short-term work placements and casual work defined their 20s, and all such experi-ence had a significant impact on their sense of self-esteem and identity. Low self-confidence, previous poor experiences in education, training or social security, and uncertainty about options make their return to work or education significantly more difficult. We identified a gap in support and policy provision for those in their mid-to-late 20s with composite needs, who want to return to work, training or education (as does Adele above), and suggested that targeted support could be made available for this group. Investment is needed in youth and community provision, to provide a forum where support, training, career guidance and help with personal development could be easily accessed. This age group are normally seen as outside youth provision, and so ineligible for any provision that does exist for return to education, or specific youth programmes.

Housing

The social and political history of NI has left a segregated housing legacy, with almost 100% of public housing in Belfast segregated along religious lines. This pattern extends across the province to a lesser but significant degree. Reviews of policy and research in this area continue to illustrate the effects of such division in terms of the delivery and uptake of services, (health, leisure, education, employment), and in terms of attitudes and behaviour.

The 'shared future' (Community Relations Unit 2005) document is a significant initiative introduced in this area in recent years, and it has informed the new housing agenda, launched in 2008, which includes the development of mixed community housing. Research findings and reports suggest that an increasing number of young people and single parents rely on rented and social housing in NI, and are often restricted in housing options by the level of benefit entitlements. More than a quarter of all families with dependent children are headed by a lone parent, usually a mother, and findings from previous research show that single parent families have the lowest standard of living of any household type (Simmonds and Bivand 2008). The government's welfare reform programme aims to reduce the number of people on benefit and increase the numbers in paid employment, but since the NI Assembly did not adopt the Westminster national childcare strategy of 2004, it currently has no childcare strategy. Unusually and unexpectedly, amongst the five young people in the current study who are parents, three are young men. Luke (see later), Adrian and Patrick have four children between them and all have become single parents with complex parental trajectories and sometimes difficult legal battles in relation to their children (for young fathers' experiences see Lau Clayton and Neale, Chapter 4 in this volume). All have invested heavily in their role and identity as a father, a role that each has found both challenging and rewarding. Given the absence of other sources of support, family support has been essential in allowing them to act as key carers for their children. Immediate and extended family networks have facilitated their housing, their return to work and given them encouragement to plan a long-term future with their children.

Young people in the study have experience of various housing options over the years: living with parents; leaving the parental home for university and sharing with friends; returning home in the event of unemployment or for other reasons; living on their own; joining a reconstituted family; living in supported accommodation; sharing with a partner, a friend or with their child; and becoming homeless. As we saw earlier, Adele's need to live independently saw her forced, as she saw it, to make herself homeless and to give up her education in order to receive housing benefit. She then drifted into a long period of drug use.

Glen was homeless for large parts of the period that we were talking to him; that we were able to contact him each time for an interview is testament to the importance of the researcher/participant relationship in qualitative longitudinal research. The breakdown of his parents' marriage, and his mother's relationship with a Catholic man, had begun a spiral of events that undermined Glen's connection with place and community. Excluded from his Protestant home area, uncomfortable in his mother's new Catholic neighbourhood and unhappy in his father's new reconstructed family, he floundered. He periodically worked his way through a number of housing situations provided by social services, but failed to establish a home for any length of time, and largely relied on friends and girlfriends for a place to live. Pursuing his interest in music in a multi-denominational band provided a medium through which he could create a space beyond those communities from which he was excluded. Glen also used the internet and cyberspace as a way of crossing boundaries and making new contacts, and despite the insecurity that often beset his living arrangements, his narrative indicates how popular culture and globalization can have a positive impact upon young people's lives by providing space for a more expansive version of self than previously available to them.

The group in NI have been particularly mobile, more so than in the four other 'Inventing adulthood' study sites. Over the years, however, they have subscribed to the restrictions, and fallen into the pattern of living within segregated spaces. Those who left home, and country, for work or education and have since returned have almost all returned to their home area. Being close to childcare and family support was a significant factor for some, particularly those who became lone parents.

The availability and quality of housing in the private rental market meets a real need for young people who perhaps cannot wait for public housing, or cannot afford to live beyond the support of their own community. The volatility of young people's housing trajectories was particularly marked in this study and the impact of critical moments was stark. Life events such as unplanned pregnancy, bereavement, breakdown in family relations, parental separation and unemployment were all seen to have a significant, and often negative and long-term, impact on young people's housing pathways. The findings from this study suggest that young people are largely unprepared for such consequences and have little in the way of resources or knowledge with which to make sound choices. We have suggested that schools and colleges could help fill this knowledge and information gap by providing programmes promoting education and awareness around housing options and pathways. Those leaving care or prison could also be helped with possibilities and decisions concerning housing.

Segregation is still very much entrenched in working-class housing areas, but some young people from more middle-class backgrounds also had a desire to remain within the area they were raised, although there were the young people who valued the fact that their neighbourhood was 'mixed'. Despite this, shared housing projects seem quite unlikely for some areas at least. The practicalities of promoting and facilitating community integration and reconciliation through shared housing space are perhaps harder to achieve than to imagine. In 2010, the NI Life and Times survey suggested that 80% of people would be happy to live in a mixed housing area, but this is an aspirational challenge that needs very deliberate and interdepartmental policies to achieve. Creating a shared future, and building community relations within and across all communities can only be achieved by investment in a dedicated strategy driven by an independent body tasked with bringing the communities in NI closer to shared understanding and living.

Critical moments, life events and resilience

While not wanting to cast the stories of these 'ordinary' young people from the shadows, repeated accounts of stress, depression and despair made for a composite narrative that suggested increasing psychological pressure and vulnerability among young people. An equally notable and worrying observation was that many struggled through on their own without finding support, although the internet and social networking sites provided an outlet for some of them to 'talk' about their feelings.

As we have noted earlier, critical moments and life events can have an impact not only on young people's ability to cope but on their identities, their pathways and sense of self, as is evident from the following examples.

A series of significant life events including multiple bereavements, job loss as the construction industry collapsed, parenthood, relocation and a return to education overwhelmed Luke, who in the latest interview, aged 27, was carving out a new and demanding life as a single father. He set the scene by indicating that he was 'probably going through a bad patch at the minute.' He talked about his tendency to 'try and ignore things... try and put things over your shoulder, but things start to get heavy now and again'. When things got particularly 'heavy' Luke did not want to talk to his family, but went to his doctor who offered him anti-depressants. Luke refused these, reflecting that he just wanted 'a bit of advice or something like that'. But this brief opportunity to 'merely' express his feelings acted as a release valve for Luke, 'as soon as I walked out of there I felt a lot better, after talking, for some reason.'

Unemployment also featured in the narrative of Danny, who having successfully completed his degree enjoyed a lucrative job placement in the City of London. High earnings, a 'high life' and high expectations all came to an abrupt end when the company he worked for folded as markets collapsed. Danny had experienced depression at university, describing himself at that time as 'severely depressed' for about six months. He couldn't 'get out of bed, eat talk or socialize'. The recent experience of depression was linked to the end of a relationship and coincided with unemployment and loss of status, and Danny described himself as 'a wreck' and a 'disaster'. While Luke found 'talking' helpful, this is not one of Danny's coping responses:

> talking about emotional problems doesn't really help for me, because I talk too much and it just goes on and on and on. I get into loops and cycles and nothing gets resolved. I don't really resolve things by talking them through. I just have to stick it out then it goes away.

Although young women in the study, including Adele, also experienced and talked about stress, feeling down and depression, the number of young men who experienced emotional stress and feelings of depression was particularly striking. Also interesting were their coping strategies and the knowledge, or lack of knowledge, and access they had to support and resources.

Conclusion

We have examined the lives of a group of young people growing up in NI in the context of the challenging historical period through which the 'Inventing adulthoods' study followed their paths, putting them in comparative context with the rest of the young people in the study in other sites in the UK. The holistic qualitative longitudinal approach we adopt enables us to map these young lives in their social and historical perspective, and examine the impact of events at these levels in conjunction with their accounts of their biographical trajectory through time. It helps us to uncover the consequentiality of events and experiences, and identify critical moments that create shifts and possibilities, or close off possibilities in the lived experience. The focus of this part of the study was on policies for young people, and a detailed analysis of such policies over the period revealed gaps and deficiencies, and the impact of sectarianism on particularly, but not only, working-class young people and their families and communities. We discussed some of the routes they travelled through education, employment and training, and housing; key policy areas. We also drew on our analysis of critical moments in their lives to illustrate how their pathways, lives and identities might change after such experiences. We noted that depression and mental health issues arose amongst these young people, as in the rest of the UK, but seemingly to a greater extent, particularly, but not only, for young men. Our attention to politics and policies for young people has uncovered problems that emerge for them specifically at the stages of their lives that our qualitative longitudinal study followed, where gaps in policy provision, and a silo approach taken by the organizations and agencies tasked with support for young people, leave them falling through gaps and floundering. The current, ongoing economic crisis exacerbates the situation, particularly in relation to changes in welfare provision. In the face of often multiple vicissitudes, these young people have recounted considerable fortitude, resilience and imagination in the narratives of their lives that they have shared with us.

Notes

1. Briefly, the Troubles describes the conflict over the constitutional status of NI between the Protestant unionist community (wanting to remain in the

UK) and the mainly Catholic nationalist community (wanting union with the Republic of Ireland). Over 30 years of violence in NI (and mainland UK) involving republican and loyalist paramilitaries and the security forces of NI and the Republic of Ireland began in the late 1960s.
2. Research team: Sheila Henderson, Janet Holland, Sheena McGrellis, Sue Sharpe and Rachel Thomson. www.lsbu.ac.uk/inventingadulthoods.
3. The Good Friday Agreement, made between most political parties in NI, and between the British and Irish governments, was signed on 10 April 1998 and came into force on 2 December 1998. It established (i) the constitutional status of NI as part of the UK, (ii) institutions for devolved government in NI including the NI Assembly, and was the culmination of the peace process. Difficulties in implementation continued after it was signed.

References

Bennett, R. (2007) 'Young men face soaring suicide rates as Northern Ireland leaves the troubles behind', *The Sunday Times*, 20 June 2007. Available at: http://www.timesonline.co.uk/tol/life_and_style/health/article1957742.ece [Accessed 16 September 2011].

Community Relations Unit (2005) *A Shared Future: Policy and Strategic Framework for Good Relations*, Office of the First Minister and Deputy First Prime Minister, NI.

Giddens, A. (1991) *Modernity and Self-identity: Self and Society in the Late Modern Age*, Cambridge: Polity.

Gray, A. M. and Horgan, G. (2010) *Welfare to Work, Policy Brief* ARK Northern Ireland. Available at: http://www.ark.ac.uk/pdfs/policybriefs/policybrief1.pdf [Accessed 26 September 2011].

Group Economics, Ulster Bank (2008) *Northern Ireland Quarterly Review*, October 2008.

Hayes, C. (2011) 'Huge increase in NI suicides since the end of the Troubles'. Report in Irish Examiner 2 February 2011. Available at: http://www.irishcentral.com/news/Huge-increase-in-Northern-Ireland-suicides-since-the-end-of-The-Troubles-115093799.html.

Henderson, S., Holland, J., McGrellis, S., Sharpe, S. and Thomson, R. (2007) *Inventing Adulthoods: A Biographical Approach to Youth Transitions*, London: Sage.

Henderson, S., Holland, J., McGrellis, S., Sharpe, S. and Thomson, R. (2012) 'Storying qualitative longitudinal research: Sequence, voice and motif', *Qualitative Research*, 12(1): 16–34.

Hutchinson, G. and Byrne, T. (2007) *Northern Ireland Economic Overview*, Department of Enterprise Trade and Investment: Belfast NI. Available at: http://www.detini.gov.uk/edition_3_-_the_ni_economic_bulletin_-_2007__whole_document_.pdf.

Mannheim, K. (1952) 'The problem of generations', in P. Kecskemeti (ed.) *Essays on the Sociology of Knowledge*, London: Routledge & Kegan Paul, pp. 276–323.

McGrellis, S. (2005) 'Pure and bitter spaces: Gender, identity and territory in Northern Irish youth transition', *Gender and Education*, 17(5): 515–529.

McGrellis, S. (March 2009) *Growing up in Northern Ireland: Research and Policy Mapping Document*, Joseph Rowntree Foundation. Available at: http://www.lsbu.ac.uk/inventingadulthoods.

McGrellis, S. (2011) *Growing up in Northern Ireland*, The Joseph Rowntree Trust. Available at: http://www.jrf.org.uk/publications/growing-up-northern-ireland.

NIAES (2010) Northern Ireland Adviser on Employment and Skills. Available at: http://www.niacs.co.uk/News/Advice-on-Action-Needed-on-Youth-Unemployment-Tabl.aspx [Accessed 16 September 2011].

NI Life and Times Survey. Available at: www.ark.ac.uk/nilt/.

O'Hara, M. (2011) 'Sharp increase in suicide rates in Northern Ireland', *The Guardian*. Available at: http://www.guardian.co.uk/society/2011/mar/16/suicide-rates-northern-ireland [Accessed 28 September 2011].

Simmonds, D. and Bivand, P. (2008) *Can Work Eradicate Child Poverty?* Joseph Rowntree Foundation (November 2008, Ref: 2272). Available at: http://www.jrf.org.uk/sites/fi les/jrf/2272-employmentparenthood-poverty.pdf [Accessed 16 September 2011].

Thomson, R., Bell, R., Henderson, S., Holland, S., McGrellis, S. and Sharpe, S. (2002) 'Critical moments: Choice, chance and opportunity in young people's narratives of transition to adulthood', *Sociology*, 6(2): 335–354.

Thomson, R., Henderson, S. and Holland, J. (2003) 'Making the most of what you've got? Resources, values and inequalities in young women's transitions to adulthood', *Educational Review*, 55(1): 33–46.

Thomson, R., Holland, J., McGrellis, S., Bell, R., Henderson, S. and Sharpe, S. (2004) 'Inventing adulthoods: A biographical approach to understanding youth citizenship', *The Sociological Review*, 52(2): 218–239.

Part II
Parenting and Family Life

4
Young Parenthood and Cross-Generational Relationships: The Perspectives of Young Fathers

Bren Neale and Carmen Lau Clayton

Introduction

The entry of young people into parenthood has long been regarded as an issue for UK social policy and professional practice. The UK has one of the highest rates of teenage pregnancy in Europe, concentrated in the most socially disadvantaged areas of the country (DCSF/DoH 2010). Most of these pregnancies are unplanned and about half end in abortion, although whether this should be a cause for concern is a contested issue (Duncan et al. 2010). Most existing research and policy tends to focus on young mothers; we currently know little about the practices, values or support needs of young fathers, or what barriers and enablers exist to improve their life chances (Alexander et al. 2010). Research that takes a dynamic approach, exploring the varied pathways through which young men enter and attempt to sustain parenthood, is especially sparse. A small-scale baseline study, conducted under the Timescapes programme, is addressing these gaps in knowledge, utilizing qualitative longitudinal (QL) methods of enquiry. We have been prospectively tracking a sample of young men to explore how their journeys through varied public landscapes (education, health, housing, employment and financial security) intersect with their interpersonal journeys – the changing landscapes of family life, partnering and parenting.

An important theme emerging from this research concerns the nature of intergenerational relationships in families where there is an early entry into parenthood. The transition to early parenthood has significance not only for the young people but for their parents, who face an unanticipated entry into grandparenthood. Our baseline study revealed that young fathers may have a strong commitment to developing a fathering identity, and that unplanned children are not necessarily unwanted; the arrival of a new generation may give young fathers a new sense of purpose and responsibility. However, young fathers also face a raft of challenges in developing a parenting role, often requiring considerable support over time from their families and in some cases from health and social care professionals (Neale and Lau Clayton 2011). Family support that flows down the generations from grandparents to parents and their young children is often taken for granted in this context (Grandparents Plus 2010). But the nature of such grandparental support, and the extent to which it is sustainable and can therefore be relied upon over time, is much less clear cut – with implications for the provision of professional support for young parents. Currently our knowledge of this support comes largely from the accounts of grandparents; there is very little evidence on how it is perceived and experienced by young parents themselves, especially young fathers (Tan et al. 2010).

The QL design of this research enabled us to explore how intergenerational support is worked out in the aftermath of youthful entry into parenthood. By 'walking alongside' our participants as their lives unfolded (Neale and Flowerdew 2003), we were able to explore the micro-processes through which intergenerational support is worked out over time and to document how grandparental support – maternal and paternal – is perceived and experienced by young fathers in the context of a major and often unanticipated life-course transition. We explored the opportunities, tension and constraints that may arise across the generations in these circumstances; and the impact of grandparental involvement on the ability of young men to establish and sustain an identity and role as a parent. Before turning to the empirical study and our findings, we briefly set out the theoretical and policy contexts for this research.

Parenting, intergenerational support and social change

In the UK, there are approximately 14 million grandparents (Broad 2007). The average age of becoming a grandparent is cited as anything between 47 and 54, with significant age differences by socio-economic group; for example, working-class women are more likely to be young grandmothers (under 50) than middle-class women (22% compared with 5%; Grandparents Plus 2009). The proportion of the population who are grandparents has been increasing (to an estimated 28.4% in

2007) and approximately 25% of families with a child under 14 are now using grandparent care (Speight et al. 2009). Demographic changes, from a high-mortality/high-fertility to a low-mortality/low-fertility society, have impacted upon these processes, leading to a rise in 'longer' and 'thinner' 'beanpole' families with fewer family members per generation. Increased life expectancy and falling fertility rates mean that grandparents may live longer and healthier lives, with increased options to take on an active and sustained caring role. While this may be incongruous with other options that may open up in mid to later life, for example, through changing work patterns, retirement or relocation planning (Carter and McGoldrick 2005), there is widespread evidence that grandparents play an increasingly significant role in supporting their children and grandchildren. This runs counter to the idea of older people as a burden, a drain on their families and on the public purse (Phillipson 1998).

Research on intergenerational support suggests the need to rethink the nature of grandparenting. The rather sedate and voluntary 'leisure and pleasure' model of grandparental care now sits alongside a more active and engaged 'rescue and repair' model, particularly in the context of managing family crises or disruption, such as divorce, separation or unemployment; or where chronic disadvantage or vulnerability among the parent generation requires grandparents to act as facilitators of family life and hold families together (Griggs 2010, Hughes and Emmel 2011, and Chapter 9 this volume). Grandparent care has been described as part of the 'moral economy': a significant social resource and a form of social capital (Arthur et al. 2003). The provision of kin care by grandparents may be particularly important for young parents; those living in disadvantaged circumstances may have few resources to bring to parenthood and need ongoing care themselves (Swann et al. 2003). Such support tends to flow down the maternal line. Indeed, in some communities, women may provide kin care (as the main carers or substitute parents) to successive cohorts of young children for many decades (Townsend 2011). There is also evidence to suggest a vital role for paternal grandparents in providing practical help and housing for young fathers, and supporting and enabling ongoing contact between the young men and their children (Speak et al. 1997, Shepherd et al. 2011).

Research that evaluates such care and the value that it holds reveals a mixed picture. Grandmother care may have positive outcomes for young mothers and grandchildren, for example on mothers' mental health and educational attainment (Griggs 2010, Shepherd et al. 2011).

But studies also report negative effects and the undermining of care between parent and child (SmithBattle 1996, Culp et al. 2006, Glaser et al. 2010) – fuelling notions of a parenting deficit that is passed down the generations.

Whatever the effects on the parent generation and their children, there are likely to be mixed consequences for the grandparents themselves. Reliance on the older generation can result in a 'missing generation in the middle' with a double care burden for the grandparents, particularly where they step in to keep families together and avoid their grandchildren being fostered (Kropf and Burnette 2003, Chapter 9 this volume). This, in turn, can impact negatively on the grandparents' health, income and future lives. Concerns have been raised about the stress on younger grandparents who need to balance work and family commitments – this clearly becomes a multigenerational family matter rather than a challenge for younger parents alone (Hank and Buber 2008). It is clear that with the arrival of a new generation, the whole configuration of interpersonal relationships is disrupted and forced to change to accommodate the need for new roles and additional resources (Kehily and Thomson 2011). Ambivalence between the generations can occur, as family members experience and negotiate familial and social change on the one hand, and continuity on the other (Thomson 2008, Thomson et al. 2011). Overall, there appears to be no simple correlation between involvement of grandparents and positive outcomes for their children and grandchildren and for their own well-being – the picture is complex and requires a more nuanced understanding of the constellation of factors at play across the generations and over time.

The policy context: Grandparental care

The broad aim of policy since 1999 has been to ensure that young parents engage with education and employment opportunities and develop the skills needed to parent effectively, reflected, for example, in the ten-year Teenage Pregnancy Strategy, and early interventions such as Sure Start and the Nurse Family Partnership schemes. The place of grandparents in this process is rather nebulous. Despite some recognition of their role (DfES 2003), in the main, they are marginalized in legislation and social policy (Grandparents Plus 2010). For example, grandparents are ineligible for childcare tax credit or childcare vouchers (Grandparents Plus 2010) and their role is not defined or assumed in family law, although they can apply for leave to make an application for contact or residence for a grandchild (DfES 2006). Currently, it would seem that practitioners, service providers and policy-makers are often unaware of the contribution that grandparents make to families, or may lack professional mechanisms to translate this knowledge into practice (Hughes and Emmel 2011, and Chapter 9 this volume). Some of the ambivalence about grandparents in policy and practice circles may have been fuelled by notions of an intergenerational cycle of disadvantage, whereby cultures of deprivation and a parenting deficit are presumed to pass down the generations, requiring early interventions to break the cycle (Allen 2011). This idea has become embedded in policy and practice thinking, despite longstanding evidence that such cycles are not inevitable, and that parenting cultures are only one part of the complex web of factors – structural, economic, relational and environmental – that influence the fortunes of families (Shildrick et al. 2012).

Notions of an intergenerational cycle of disadvantage may have the unintended consequence of reinforcing a negative image of the legacy that grandparents hand down to their children and grandchildren. Moreover, the overriding policy focus on early intervention may detract from the value of sustained support over time, while the short-term targets and measures used to evaluate provision (such as those used for the Sure Start programme) may be out of step with longer-term needs and the tenor of real lives (Neale et al. 2013).

This brief overview reveals some mixed evidence on the nature and extent of grandparental care for young parents. In what follows we explore how intergenerational support unfolds over time from the perspective of young fathers, and we consider what this means for their ability to establish and sustain a parenting role.

The 'Following young fathers' study

The research for 'Following young fathers' was carried out as part of the 'Young lives and times' project (part of the Timescapes programme). In 2010, in consultation with a team of teenage pregnancy co-ordinators, we set up a small study on young fatherhood – designed to support practitioners who were struggling to identify, let alone meet the needs of, young fathers. The consultation led to a partnership with a local authority educational service, located in a northern metropolitan city, with high levels of youth unemployment (22.5%). We combined a QL design with a participatory 'knowledge to action' approach, working closely with the practitioner in the conduct of the research (Neale and Morton 2012). Through this route we recruited 11 young fathers, and could engage with a marginalized group that would be otherwise 'hard to reach' using indirect methods of recruitment or survey techniques. Our twelfth participant was recruited through snowballing and was without any professional support.

We tracked the young men over an 18-month period, using focus groups and three waves of qualitative interviews in which we gathered life history data about their past lives, and utilized timelines and relationship maps to reveal changes in life-course trajectories and relationships. The interviews took place at four to six month intervals between December 2010 and May 2012. The importance of grandparents emerged through the early waves of interviews, and became a particular focus of our third wave of interviews.

Sample characteristics and circumstances

At the time of the first interview, the 12 young men were aged between 16 and 22. One young man was expecting a child, seven had children under the age of one, two had children under the age of three, while the remaining two fathers had children under the age of seven. In ten cases, the fathers had been under the age of 16 when their child was conceived. Ten of the young men were of European descent and two of African Caribbean descent. While there was a great deal of variation in life circumstances across the sample, in ten cases the young men had experienced disadvantaged and often chaotic backgrounds. They commonly described their lives in terms of family 'troubles' during their upbringing, including incidents of parental drug addiction, prison sentences, mental health problems, physical abuse, frequent changes of abode, periods in social care and volatile relationships within and outside their families. The young men themselves were often 'troubled' during their childhoods, describing volatile behaviour, anger management problems, dangerous activities, involvement with the police and disengagement from school. In seven cases, they had been, or were the subject of intervention or support from statutory agencies such as social services and youth offending teams.

The young fathers had different levels of contact with their children and varied relationships with the child's mother and maternal grandparents. Five of the young men were in a relationship with the mother at the time of the birth. In one case, these relationships were described as positive and settled; in the remainder varied levels of difficulty and volatility were reported over time. The majority (ten young men) had more positive relationships with their own parents (the paternal grandparents), although these too could be volatile over time. The fluid living

arrangements of the young men reflected the nature of these relationships. All the young parents initially resided with their respective
parents, with the mothers and babies living with the maternal grandmother (although subsequently, three young couples managed to set up
home together in privately rented accommodation). Five young men
had changed abode since the arrival of their child; in three cases, they
changed residence during the course of the study.

According to the accounts of the young men, the paternal and maternal grandparents were under the average age of grandparenthood, in
their 30s or early 40s, as opposed to their 50s. There were marked similarities between the maternal and paternal grandparents in terms of
residence, employment status and relationships. Most sets of grandparents lived in the local area and were reported to be in receipt of social
welfare benefits. Those in full-time employment worked in manual to
semi-skilled professions. Most had separated and re-partnered with new
children. Where paternal grandparents had separated, the young men
often had limited contact with their fathers as a result (although in one
case, a young man had resided with his father after his parents' divorce).

The intensive tracking revealed fluid and sometimes volatile lives for
11 of the 12 young men, marked by frequent changes of residence and
the making and breaking of relationships over relatively short periods
of time. In ten of these families, the generations were closely layered
together, with entry into early parenthood a feature of the lives of the
grandparent as well as the parent generation and also evident among the
siblings of the young parents. Such close layering of the generations is a
relatively common feature of family life in disadvantaged communities.
It appears to generate distinctive patterns of parenting in circumstances
where young parents are grappling with a dual identity as both young
person and parent, while mid-life grandparents have both children and
grandchildren to support.

Tracing the journeys of the young men into parenthood, we draw
below on their current and retrospective accounts of how they disclosed
the pregnancy to the older generation, what kinds of support – practical,
financial and emotional – they received prior to and following the birth,
how intergenerational support evolved over time, and what impact this
had on the young men. These were strong and reoccurring themes
within our data set that enabled us to gain an insight into the nature
of intergenerational support from the young men's perspective over a
relatively short period of time. We are currently extending the longitudinal reach and value of this study over a further three-year period, with
follow-up funding from the Economic and Social Research Council; this

will enable us to extend and deepen the 'long view' of grandparental support as the study progresses.

Disclosing the pregnancy: Reactions and adjustments

Paternal grandparents in this study had mixed reactions to the news of the pregnancy. Only one grandmother was said to be happy with the news; the others expressed shock and concern for their child: 'My step dad was just like "yeah, you screwed your life up"' (Darren, aged 21, wave 3). This would seem to be a common reaction from grandparents (Shepherd et al. 2011). Such feelings were considered to be a natural reaction:

> Because of the age factor and the circumstances.... [It was a] shock for them. Cause at my age, at my point in life, circumstance wise, education wise, that wasn't the right time for, for me to come with the news that, like a baby was on the way. But I think that's a natural reaction if they care about someone...They were purely looking out for my best interest.
>
> (Dominic, aged 18, wave 3)

One grandmother in the sample offered to become the primary caregiver once the grandchild was born (cf. Maposa and SmithBattle 2008):

> Oh my mum...she was like 'if you can't look after him, I'll take him on as my own but he'll still be calling you mum and dad' and all this.
>
> (Darren, aged 21, wave 3)

The maternal grandparents can play a significant role in the continuation (or otherwise) of a pregnancy. Four of these young men (ranging in age from 16 to 20 at time of first interview) had originally planned with their partners for the pregnancy to be terminated. However, the maternal grandparents were highly influential in reversing this decision. Dominic (aged 18) and Callum (aged 19) were both partnered at the time of their child's birth, but subsequently separated. In these cases, the maternal grandparents' religious and personal beliefs were a factor in keeping the child:

> Her mum didn't want her to [have an abortion]. My ex girlfriend probably thought, 'my mum knows best'. You're going to listen to your mum, aren't you?
>
> (Callum, aged 19, wave 3)

Her mother is very religious and Catholic; she managed to persuade my ex-girlfriend to not have an abortion .... My ex hadn't spoken to me at all. It was down to her dad and mum saying 'we're having him'. And obviously I just felt 'this isn't your right, this isn't your right as a person to decide whether or not me and [my ex] should have this child'. And it's something that I've let it go now, you know, whatever's happened has happened But at the time I was like you know, 'what is your right to decide this?' It's down to me, me and [her].

(Dominic, aged 18, wave 3)

As Dominic shows, when decisions were made in this fashion without any further discussion, the young men expressed upset and anger that they had been excluded.

Once the decision to go ahead with the pregnancy had been made, Dominic, Tarrell and Callum adjusted to the idea and were supportive, despite perceiving difficulties ahead. However, Jimmy, one of the youngest fathers in the sample, felt differently. He described early parenthood as very difficult, with negative effects on his intimate relationship with his partner, his energy levels and his social networks. Over time he expressed growing unhappiness with the interference of the maternal grandmother and great-grandmother:

Her mum started saying 'oh you need to think about it because if you get rid of it, it's just like killing somebody'. So she just decided to keep it. And now her mum and her nana have a go, saying 'oh you shouldn't have had him if you can't look after him'. But they were the ones that said all that to her. And they seem to forget that.

(Jimmy, aged 16, wave 3)

Other fathers were also aware of the potential influence of the maternal grandparents, but their concern was that the young mothers-to-be (their partners) would be persuaded to have an abortion. To avoid this, the young couples did not reveal the news of the pregnancy to the maternal side of the family until after the first trimester (although, interestingly, paternal grandparents were informed much earlier in the process):

We managed to keep it a secret for five months. And obviously by then it were too late to get rid of it.

(Darren, aged 21, wave 1)

After the initial shock, grandparents in this study 'came around' once the grandchild was born. Our findings mirror those of Sadler and

Clemmens (2004) who found that grandparents often formed a deep attachment to the grandchild after resolving their initial shock and disappointment regarding the pregnancy and their ambivalence about becoming a young grandparent.

> I don't think my mum was that happy at first but she grew to be alright with it.
>
> (Jimmy, aged 16, wave 3)

> Yeah they absolutely love and adore (being a grandparent). And they really enjoy the time.
>
> (Dominic, aged 18, wave 3)

> Strong bond. Yeah like when my son grows up he's going to absolutely love his nana.
>
> (Adam, aged 16, wave 3)

The reactions to the pregnancy by the grandparents indicate the momentous change that entry into young parenthood entails for both generations. While the mother is seen as the primary decision-maker in relation to the pregnancy, by extension it is the maternal grandparents – particularly grandmothers – who exercise agency in these decisions, creating a marked contrast with the agency of the young men and their families. This reflects a broader pattern of decision-making and responsibility that resides in the 'vertical' cross-generational maternal household, rather than residing in the lateral relationship between the young people themselves. As we show below, this pattern is likely to continue into the early years of parenthood.

Grandparental support

In line with existing evidence, the grandparents in this study were the main providers of practical, emotional and financial support for their children and new grandchildren. The provision of a home (board and lodging) for the young parents was perhaps the most tangible dimension of the support provided; in each case mother and baby initially resided with the maternal grandparents while the fathers continued to live with their parents. Direct care of the baby was more usually provided by the maternal grandmothers than grandfathers, reflecting traditional gendered roles and responsibilities. Such support was valued by the fathers, who could not always be present at the maternal home in the early days of the child's life.

In the six cases where the young parents were in a relationship, the couple and child would visit and stay over at the paternal household, enabling the paternal grandparents to provide some support and forge a grandparental role. Where the young parents were not together, the fathers would negotiate times to visit the baby, or to take the baby to the paternal grandparents' house – although this process could generate some tensions.

Most fathers reported that their own parents also played a significant role as second or co-parents to their children, involved actively in feeding, bathing, changing nappies, playing, minding and taking grandchildren out on day trips and visits. This was particularly so for the youngest of the parents in the sample (cf. Griggs 2010):

She'll [paternal grandmother] just do everything we would really. Change her bum. She'll have cuddles with her, have a little play with her and she likes to bath her now and again as well.

(Callum, aged 19, wave 3)

She'll just do everything that a parent does basically, but she's grandma.... I don't think a grandma would do that much. She does the absolute maximum that she could do.

(Adam, aged 16, wave 3)

Dominic regularly brought his child to stay over at his parent's home and appreciated the support he received as a single parent:

I think I've lost a bit of support from not having a partner.... So yeah they'll help out.... If they see I just need a hand or if, you know, they could see I've got a lot to do.... I think they're spot on in terms of how they deal with my son, they're really good grandparents.

(Dominic, aged 18, wave 3)

In terms of financial support, this too tended to flow down the generations from grandmothers and grandfathers, rather than operating as an exchange between the young parents. Depending on the relationship between the young parents, young fathers could benefit indirectly from the support provided for the young mothers:

See my dad, he helps me out with money.

(Darren, aged 21, wave 3)

> She [ex-partner's mother] always took us places we needed to go and stuff like that. She did do quite a lot for us money-wise as well.
>
> (Callum, aged 19, wave 3)

Only one father (Dominic) was in full-time employment during the study. Of the remainder, four were at college and seven fell into the local authority category of NEETs (not in education, employment or training). Four young men were not eligible for social welfare benefits and were entirely dependent upon their parents for financial and material support. The young fathers in the study often spoke of the difficulties of being young, uneducated or unqualified in a context where they perceived a fathers' role to be that of a traditional 'provider' for their children, and for their partners if the relationship was still intact.

> I'm the one who's meant to support the baby. Obviously without my mother's financial support or anything, I don't know where I would have got the money from. I'd have really been stuck.
>
> (Senwe, aged 16, wave 2)

Even minimal help was greatly appreciated. However, some frustration was felt at having to rely on the grandparents, especially when their resources were also limited. This was the case for Karl, who, following a social services pre-birth assessment order, did not have funds to attend assessment meetings to see his child:

> It's £4.30 every time.... The social workers expect my dad to, like, give me the bus fare and all that. But he can't afford it.
>
> (Karl, aged 16, wave 1).

Emotional support was also of vital importance to the young men. While this could come from a number of sources, including the young mothers and their families, the most consistent support in terms of talking things through and being listened to was from the paternal grandparents, particularly the grandmothers (cf. Tan et al. 2010, and Shepherd et al. 2011, who report similar findings for the maternal household). Simon, for example, learned of the pregnancy shortly before his child was born and valued his mother's support:

> If she weren't always there then I reckon I could have got in a mess and trouble and stuff.
>
> (Simon, aged 16, wave 3)

Grandparents were perceived as better confidantes than friends, in a context where few of the young men's peers would understand the issues they were facing: for single parents like Dominic, grandparents were doubly important, providing both childcare and emotional support that may have otherwise been provided by the mother (Tan et al. 2010).

> I feel that I can go to them with – and vent and discuss how I feel about certain things regarding my son and ex-partner... I don't tend to have that same outlook with my friends.
>
> (Dominic, aged 18, wave 3)

Overall, the material, financial, childcare and emotional support provided by grandparents for the young parents and their babies was substantial, especially in the early days of parenthood. This reinforced a pattern of parenting that operates down the generational line within each household. In these early days, the young fathers in this sample did not assume a central role as part of a parental dyad; they were more likely to find themselves somewhat peripheral as front-line carers. The engagement of the grandparents was not simply a useful supplement to the care provided by the young parents; it was in many cases a crucial foundation for the care of the new generation. Grandparental support was generally welcomed by the young men in this study and could help in their assumption of a parental identity. However, as we show below, the nature and level of support provided was subject to change over time.

Gift or curse? Changing grandparental support over time

The parenting journeys of the young men revealed the tensions that can arise across the generations over the boundaries around parental and grandparental care, and the difficulties entailed in sustaining inter-generational support over time. As we noted earlier, SmithBattle (1996) suggests that grandparent involvement can be seen as a gift or a curse. Tensions may arise, firstly, over involvement of the grandparents in ways that may marginalize the young men. Getting the right balance between support and interference is a difficult matter that affected most of the young men, even where relationships were generally very good. Dominic, for example, brought his child to live in the paternal home for three days per week:

> I'm parenting my son as a father. They're spending time with my son as grandparents. If my son's being naughty, if he's being silly

or if he's doing something or if he's done something dangerous, me telling him off and saying, you know, 'it's quiet time for five minutes cause you've been bad', and my parents are pulling faces. Just kind of undermining me as a father.... They just want to enjoy him. Sometimes it does get heated and quite hard to live under one roof and to co-exist happily.

(Dominic, aged 18, wave 1)

By wave 3 (a year after the first interview), Dominic's ex-partner had reduced the amount of contact that he had with his son. Contact times were precious and he found it difficult to always share his son with his parents:

If I'm at home with my son, I know that my parents are gonna be there. And obviously there may be activities I want to [do] and spend [time] alone [with him], but just due to obviously living arrangements, it's not going to be like that.

Where mother and child resided with the maternal grandparents, similar concerns were raised. Often maternal grandparents appeared to 'know best' and would take over in a way that was described as 'annoying' and 'upsetting' for the young fathers. However, voicing their concerns might lead to conflicts and withdrawal of support:

I'd just like her to sit back and be a grandmother instead of a mother. Normally I would argue with people if they've tried to be so controlling and horrible, but it's not in my son's best interest, I just had to bite my tongue.

(Jason, aged 22, wave 1)

If over-involvement was a curse, so too was its opposite – a withdrawal of grandparental support. In both cases the source of the conflict was a blurring of the boundaries of parental and grandparental care, with both generations perceiving a lack of responsibility in the other. Tensions simmered but might then erupt into family arguments over household chores, infant care and the differing priorities of the generations (Sadler and Clemmens 2004), which could in turn trigger changes in arrangements. During the first two waves of interviews (three months apart), Jimmy reported that his mother had been very supportive, but by the third wave (three months after wave 2), she had withdrawn all her support due to a large family disagreement, leading to a change of abode for Jimmy, who moved to live with his friend.

> She used to do everything for [the baby]. Like watch him all the time whenever we needed her to and that. But now she's started this big argument. She's not a good mum or grandma.
>
> (Jimmy, aged 16)

The maternal grandmother had also withdrawn her support at wave 3 due to the development of a new romantic relationship with another man:

> Her mum could watch my son a bit more and pay a little bit more attention to him. Because then my girlfriend would get it easier. Like she'd be able to go to sleep on a night if her mum'd watch him, and [be able to] get up for school and go. But no, her mum's just awkward like that.
>
> (Jimmy, aged 16, wave 3)

In this context, grandparenting took the form of temporary 'helping out' while the parents adjusted to parenthood, rather than a longer-term commitment. Darren's mother, for example, had initially provided substantial grandparental care, but within a few months of the baby's birth she was seeking a new life without parenting responsibilities:

> She wanted to move ... and start afresh, which I can understand, but obviously still see your grandkids. But she doesn't want it like that. She wants to go up there, never come back.... She goes 'oh my life don't involve children now'. So I'm like, 'well that's nice'. So if it doesn't involve children it doesn't involve my son. And if it doesn't involve my son, it doesn't involve me .... You could ring her and she's like, 'well, I'm busy now, you'll have to ring back tomorrow'. I'm like, 'well I don't need you tomorrow, I need you now'.
>
> (Darren, aged 21, wave 2)

The relationship between Darren and his mother grew increasingly distant over the course of the study. As a result, he became closer to his partner's parents and relied more heavily upon the maternal grandparents' support by wave 3. Adam (aged 16) also experienced dramatic changes in his relationship with the maternal grandparents over the course of the study. Prior to his son's birth at wave 1, Adam had a tenuous relationship with the mother-to-be, and experienced hostility from her parents. However, the arrival of his son at wave 2 (three months later) mended relationships with the maternal household. At this point, Adam moved in with his partner and was receiving substantial help and support. By the third wave (nine months later), relationships had once more become fragile and grandparental support was withdrawn:

> It's hard just the two of us.
>
> (Adam, aged 16, wave 3)

Sometimes the problems between the generations were severe, with grandparental care perceived to be poor in quality, or tipping over into exploitation or policing of the young parents. Research more usually stresses grandparents' dissatisfaction with the younger generation, but these judgements may be reversed where young parents enter parenthood themselves. Five young fathers reported that grandparents were leading lifestyles that were non-conducive to 'good' grandparenthood or were misusing their role as custodians of their grandchildren's welfare benefits:

> When you're on drugs, you're not interested about anybody but yourself and the drugs.
>
> (Andrew, aged 16, wave 3)

> Like my son's child benefits and all that, she [maternal grandmother] claims them because my girlfriend's too young. And when my girlfriend asks...she won't give her it, she spends it on herself. So we can never...go buy him anything.
>
> (Jimmy, aged 16, wave 3)

As a final example, maternal grandparents could control, restrict or even block contact between a young father and their daughter and the new baby. This was the case for seven of the young men in this sample. Sometimes this was in the context of concerns over child protection issues, with social services involvement already in place, but nevertheless, the actions led to stressful situations, with the young men having to seek contact through the family law courts:

> Her mum won't let me go up to her house no more.... And, like, I want to see [my son].... It'd have to go through courts wouldn't

it? [But] I don't wanna do that cause then it'll just cause bigger arguments.

(Jimmy, aged 16, wave 1)

Overall, grandparenting could tip over into control of the pregnancy and child, policing of the young parents' behaviour or interference in their relationship. This reflects the potentially conflicting status of the young parents – responsible for their children, yet still the responsibility of the older generation. The young fathers' high expectations of and mixed levels of satisfaction with the older generation were important themes running through the young men's accounts, revealing a distinctive dynamic about relationships and practices of care across the generations.

Conclusion

The findings presented here reflect the complex constellation of family relationships at play when young people enter parenthood. Intergenerational or 'vertical' care relationships are highly significant where the generations are closely layered, and they may take precedence over and interfere with the development of 'lateral' parenting relationships between the young parents themselves. Grandparental involvement clearly has an impact on the ability of young men to manage the transition to parenthood and to establish a parenting role and identity. But the evidence here shows that such support can be highly variable, may have mixed effects on their parenting identities, and may be unsustainable over time, particularly in families with complex needs such as those who make up most of this sample.

If state support for families is to be effective, it is important that the realities of grandparental care, including in some cases its detrimental effect over the long term, are taken into account. Even where such care is of good quality and highly valued, finding the right balance between support, interference and neglect is notoriously difficult to achieve, and may result in blurred lines of responsibility that become a burden for both the young parents and the older generations. A broader approach to policy and professional practice may be needed, that takes into account cross-generational relationships and support, as well as the dynamic relationship between the young parents themselves. There would be scope, for example, to extend the partnership approach for working with parents (DfES 2006) to include grandparents too, and to offer bespoke support that would operate flexibly and in line with the shifting dynamics of kin care in families. Tailoring support for families where the generations are closely layered could lead to a better balance of care across the generations, and between the young parents themselves, enabling young men to play a more effective role in their children's lives.

References

Alexander, C., Duncan, S. and Edwards, R. (2010) ' "Just a Mum or Dad": Experiencing teenage parenting and work life balance', in S. Duncan, R. Edwards and C. Alexander (eds) *Teenage Parenthood; What's the Problem?* London: Tufnell Press, pp. 135–156.

Allen, G. (2011) *Early Intervention: The Next Steps*. An Independent Report to HM Government, London: Cabinet Office.

Arthur, S., Snape, D. and Dench, G. (2003) *The Moral Economy of Grandparenting*, London: National Centre for Social Research.

Broad, B. (2007) *Being a Grandparent: Research Evidence: Key Themes and Policy Recommendations*, Essex: Grandparents Association.

Carter, B. and McGoldrick, M. (2005) *The Expanded Family Life Cycle: Individual, Family and Social Perspectives* (3rd Ed.), Boston, MA: Pearson.

Culp, A. M., Culp, R. E., Noland, D. and Anderson, J. W. (2006) 'Stress, marital satisfaction, and child care provision by mothers of adolescent mothers: Considerations to make when providing services', *Children and Youth Services Review*, 28: 673–681.

DCSF/DoH (2010) *Teenage Pregnancy Strategy: Beyond 2010*, Nottingham: DCSF.

DfES (2003) *The Effective Provision of Pre-School Education Project*, London: Department for Education and Skills.

DfES (2006) *Childcare Act 2006: Chapter 21*, Norwich: The Stationery Office. [Online] Available at: http://www.opsi.gov.uk/acts/acts2006/pdf/ukpga_20060021_en.pdf. [Accessed 3 March 2011].

Duncan, S., Edwards, R. and Alexander, C. (eds) (2010) *Teenage Parenthood: What's the Problem?* London: Tufnell Press.

Glaser, K., Montserrat, E. R., Waginger, U., Price, D., Stuchbury, R. and Tinker, A. (2010) *Grandparenting in Europe*, London: King's College London and Grandparents Plus.

Grandparents Plus (2009) *Rethinking Family Life: Exploring the Role of Grandparents and the Wider Family*, London: Grandparents Plus.

Grandparents Plus (2010) *Grandparenting in Europe*, London: Grandparents Plus.

Griggs, J. (2010) *Examining the Role of Grandparents in Families at Risk of Poverty*, Oxford: University of Oxford.

Hank, K. and Buber, I. (2008) 'Grandparents caring for their grandchildren: Findings from the 2004 survey of health, ageing, and retirement in Europe', *Journal of Family Issues*, 30(1): 52–73.

Hughes, K. and Emmel, N. (2011) *Intergenerational Exchange: Grandparents, Their Grandchildren, and the Texture of Poverty*. Timescapes Policy Briefing Papers, Leeds: University of Leeds.

Kehily, M. J. and Thomson, R. (2011) 'Figuring families: Generation, situation and narrative in contemporary mothering', *Sociological Research Online*, 16(4): 16. Available at: http://www.socresonline.org.uk/16/4/16.html. [Accessed 18 August 2012].

Kropf, N. and Burnette, D. (2003) 'Grandparents as family caregivers: Lessons for intergenerational education', *Educational Gerontology*, 29: 361–372.

Maposa, S. and SmithBattle, L. (2008) 'Preliminary reliability and validity of the grandparent version of the grandparent support scale for teenage mothers (GSSTM-G)', *Journal of Family Nursing*, 14(2): 224–241.

Neale, B. and Flowerdew, J. (2003) 'Time texture and childhood: The contours of qualitative longitudinal research', *International Journal of Social Research Methodology: Theory and Practice*, 6(3): 189–199.

Neale, B. and Lau Clayton, C. (2011). *Following Fathers: The lived experience of teenage parenting over time.* Timescapes Policy Briefing Series. Available at: www.timescapes.leeds.ac.uk/assets/files/Policy-Conference-2011/paper-2.pdf.

Neale, B. and Morton, S. (2012) *Creating Impact through Qualitative Longitudinal Research*, Timescapes Methods Guides Series. Guide no. 20. Available at www.timescapes.leeds.ac.uk/resources.

Phillipson, C. (1998) *Reconstructing Old Age*, London: Sage.

Sadler, L. S. and Clemmens, D. A. (2004) 'Ambivalent grandmothers raising teen daughters and their babies', *Journal of Family Nursing*, 10: 211–231.

Shepherd, J., Ludvigsen, A. and Hamilton, W. (2011) *Parents of Teenage Parents: Research, Issues and Practice, Summary Report*, Brighton: Young People in Focus.

Shildrick, T., MacDonald, R., Furlong, A., Roden, J. and Crow, R. (2012) *Are Cultures of Worklessness Passed Down the Generations?* Report for the Joseph Rowntree Foundation. Available at: www.jrf.org.uk/sites/files/jrf/worklessness-families-employment-full.pdf.

SmithBattle, L. (1996) 'Intergenerational ethics of caring for teenage mothers and their children', *Family Relations*, 45: 56–64.

Speak, S., Cameron, S. and Gilroy, R. (1997) *Young Single Fathers' Participation in Fatherhood: Barriers and Bridges*, Oxford: Family Policy Studies Centre.

Speight, S., Smith, R., La Valle, I., Schneider, V., Perry, J., Coshall, C. and Tipping, S. (2009) *Childcare and Early Years Survey of Parents. Research Report DCSF-RR136*, London: DFE.

Swann, C., Bowe, K., McCormick, G. and Kosmin, M. (2003) *Teenage Pregnancy and Parenthood: A Review of Reviews*, Evidence briefing, London: Health Development Agency.

Tan, J. P., Buchanan, A., Flouri, E., Schwartz, S. A. and Griggs, J. (2010) 'Filling the parenting gap? Grandparent involvement with U.K. adolescents', *Journal of Family Issues*, 31(7): 992–1015.

Thomson, R. (2008) 'Thinking intergenerationally about motherhood', *Studies in the Maternal*, 1(1): Available at: www.mamsie.bbk.ac.uk.

Thomson, R., Kehily, M. J., Hadfield, L. and Sharpe, S. (2011) *Making Modern Mothers*, Bristol: Policy Press.

Townsend, P. (2011) 'The family life of old people: An investigation in East London', *The Sociological Review*, 3(2): 175–195.

5
Investing in Involvement: Men Moving Through Fatherhood

Karen Henwood, Fiona Shirani and Carrie Coltart

Introduction

Discussions of contemporary fatherhood often refer to how men today are expected to be more involved with their children than in previous generations. Major social and cultural shifts occurring in Western countries – including economic restructuring, changes to the labour market and the impact of feminism – are changing expectations and experiences of fatherhood today so that it is now more common to think of fathers as intimate and involved as opposed to the breadwinner and disciplinarian role often associated with fatherhood in previous generations. However, questions have arisen about the extent to which these changes can be observed in practice, with some research providing support for this contention (e.g. Pleck 1997) while others suggest that generational changes may be more noticeable in the culture rather than conduct of fatherhood (Walker and McGraw 2000).

Dermott (2003, 2008) argues that men's assertions that they have higher levels of commitment and involvement with their children than their own fathers is a recurrent theme in fatherhood research, and has invoked intimacy as a framework for resolving the apparent gulf between culture and conduct. In her own research with fathers, she found that the word 'involvement' was frequently used, suggesting this is seen as an essential part of modern fatherhood, albeit that the term itself is ambiguous, and may be used to refer to widely contrasting situations. Also, some commentators link the decline in traditional ideas about fatherhood to social problems while others see new ideas about intimate and involved fatherhood as positive.

Research by Miller indicates that there has been a shift towards positioning fathers as actively involved, intimate and emotionally engaged

(Miller 2010), offering new insights into the research literature remarked upon by Jamieson (1998) that men are less intimate and disclosive than women. As such, it starts to introduce some of the socio-cultural complexities involved when focusing on fatherhood in terms of its relationship to questions of gender relations, masculine identity and subjectivity (see e.g. Henwood and Procter 2003, Finn and Henwood 2009). Such 'disclosing intimacy' is not voluntary and equal in the context of the parent–child relationship (Jamieson 1998) but places importance on fathers 'being there' for and 'really knowing' their child (see also Harden et al., this volume, for a discussion of 'being there'). Snyder (2007) suggests that intimacy underlies notions of quality time rather than quantity time, thus is not about sharing equally in childcare with mothers (Featherstone 2010). Similarly, in their qualitative study of men's and women's accounts of parenthood, Clarke and Popay (1998) note a contradiction in men's accounts; while on the one hand men speak of a need for involvement, this is often tempered by a resistance conditional on cultural representations that motherhood is mandatory and fatherhood discretionary, thus fatherhood is seen as involving a greater degree of choice and interpretation (Miller 2010).

While fatherhood has become a topic of research and policy interest in recent years, there remains little consensus about the extent to which men and their families support ideals of involved fatherhood in their everyday lives, the practical barriers to achieving this, and to what extent 'traditional' models of fathering remain relevant. Research has indicated that men would like to be more involved with their children than they are able to be, the biggest barrier cited being lack of time due to paid work commitments (White 1994, Burgess 1997). Changes in aspects of fatherhood that are prioritized in different historical time periods have not displaced models such as the work-focused father; indeed, some argue that paid work is a manifestation of family commitment (Townsend 2002). Nonetheless, while still a central aspect of a fatherhood role (Premberg et al. 2008), breadwinning is no longer seen as a legitimate form of fatherhood where men are exempt from more active involvement. Although the overall proportion remains small, there are now increasing numbers of stay-at-home dads who are in a unique position to create new forms of masculinity, yet this experience can be potentially challenging (Doucet 2004, Shirani et al. 2013). Thus the picture of fathers' relationship to breadwinning remains complex and contradictory.

In this chapter we elucidate how the 'Men as fathers' (MaF) project has sought to explore some of these issues and the implications they raise regarding potential opportunities and barriers to strengthening fathers' involvement in family life (Coalition for Men and Boys 2008, Featherstone 2009). We approach paternal involvement as a currently predominant signifier of good fatherhood, interrogating men's ways of relating to it as a way of helping to inform socio-cultural understanding of the practices and meanings of fatherhood and masculinity and their possible future implications (Henwood and Procter 2003, Doucet 2004, Dermot 2008, Henwood and Shirani 2012). This involves making sense of the gap between some of the ideas about 'new' fathers and the lived reality of fathers' experiences and lives (Daniel and Taylor 1999), and offers productive ways for reflecting on further changes – particularly in relation to issues of gender equality – needed to strengthen father involvement. Approached in this way, paternal involvement is of interest to policy-makers and practitioners who are involved in supporting families as they respond to the challenges of living in times of rapid economic and social change, possible destabilizations of identity and relationships, and raised salience of future uncertainty.

We bring together a number of our project publications to consolidate our work on the theme of involvement, illustrate how a qualitative longitudinal (QL) research design has contributed to these insights and highlight the policy and practice implications arising from this work.

The study

The MaF project built on work from 2000 which involved interviewing a group of 30 expectant fathers from East Anglia once before and twice within the year after the birth of their first child (Henwood and Procter 2003). The study lay dormant for several years until becoming part of the Timescapes project when 19 of these original participants were interviewed again in 2008/2009. A further 16 men from South Wales were recruited in 2008 and interviewed three times over their transition to first-time fatherhood. In total, these groups provide a sample of 46 men who became fathers between the ages of 15 and 41. When recruited to the study, the majority of men were married (n = 30) or cohabiting (n = 13) with three men living separately from their partners. Of the men, 38 worked full-time, two part-time, three were unemployed and three were students. However, relationship and work status changed over the course of the study.

Many studies of fatherhood represent one-off 'snapshots' (Neale and Flowerdew 2003) from single interviews or survey questionnaires, giving little indication as to how men may think differently about fatherhood at other points in their life. In contrast, a QL study provides the opportunity to consider fluctuations and changes across the life course and their repercussions. Both quantitative and QL research consider issues of change over time, yet a qualitative approach towards transitions, such as Timescapes, recognizes that these changes are differentially experienced and interpreted. They thus seek to gain insight into 'the subjective experience of personal change' (Thomson et al. 2002: 337). Recognizing the need for more dynamic research on fatherhood over time (Lewis and Lamb 2007), the MaF project revisited men on several occasions over the transition to fatherhood and beyond. Using this strategy, we encountered the same fathers as they entered into and practised different approaches to fatherhood at different moments in their life. The study sought to explore the complexity of contemporary fatherhood, without losing sight of common themes, broader contexts and issues. Revisiting the same participants over time as part of a QL study enabled us to see the continuities and changes in their accounts in the immediate and longer term, thus building a detailed picture of fathering through time.

Exploring the data

Early experiences and expectations

The reaches of involvement now extend even further, as men are now not only expected to be involved with the child, but also engaged during the pregnancy and birth as an equal and active partner and parent. While at one time the proportion of fathers attending the birth was miniscule, today attendance figures are between 93% and 98% for those men who live with their partners (Kiernan and Smith 2003, NHS 2005) showing a dramatic shift towards emphasis on father involvement. All fathers in our study were present at the birth of their child and often attended antenatal appointments and classes beforehand, reflecting this trend towards men's early involvement. Most men were positive about their experience of antenatal services, although some felt ignored by health professionals and believed that they could have been provided with more information to enable them to support their partners. However, this was something they found difficult to express, as, while wanting to be involved, they were reluctant to detract any attention or care from their partners.

One issue many men discussed during the pregnancy was access to good quality information. There appeared to be no shortage of information provided to expectant parents, so much that several men described feeling 'bombarded'. The difficulty arose in discerning what information was reliable or good quality. One way in which this was achieved was for partners to 'filter' information and provide the men with 'just the bits you need to know'. Most men were keen to find out more about what to do when the baby arrived (rather than pregnancy and birth) in order to play a useful role:

> I think that there is a lot about the pregnancy and what women can expect. But it's after it and thinking how am I going to know what to do with this; am I going to feed it, how many times am I going to feed it?...I don't want to be a complete you know um duffer and not know anything about it. To be forewarned is forearmed I think, a little bit of an inkling of what's going on, and that I don't feel like a complete spare part.
>
> (Ashley, 29, pre-birth)

Although keen to be involved during the pregnancy, there was some concern and scepticism about attending antenatal classes. For example, some felt it would be 'breathing and things. I've been doing that for the last 34 years so I know how to do it', while others had preconceptions based on TV programmes which gave them a negative impression. For some, antenatal classes represented a public sharing of what was otherwise seen as a private experience:

> I think having a child is personal, it's private isn't it really? Although eventually it won't be, because the nature of having to give birth anyway, but it's quite a private issue and I found, I found it quite embarrassing.
>
> (Malcolm, 32, pre-birth)

An additional challenge of antenatal classes was the assumption that all men would attend the birth, which made things difficult for the small number who felt unsure or did not want to attend. This assumption of involvement was also accompanied by some assumption of knowledge, which several men felt made it difficult to raise questions or concerns. A small number of those who attended National Childbirth Trust classes had access to men-only sessions, where they could ask 'silly' questions and share their existing knowledge with other expectant fathers, which they appreciated (Shirani et al. 2009). The greater availability of such sessions may help men to feel more involved and knowledgeable about their impending parenthood and ability to support their partner and child during this time.

These findings suggest a complicated relationship exists with father involvement during pregnancy and birth. The expectation is that men will be involved from the earliest stages, however not experiencing the physical embodiment of pregnancy proved too much of a practical barrier to this for some. For example, Draper describes the way in which men may find it difficult to engage with the reality of the pregnancy, despite their desire to be involved, resulting in a sense of redundancy and distance. She notes how:

> In a culture which espouses a model of involved fatherhood, this sense of detachment can challenge men's early experience of pregnancy. They can experience therefore a tension between the ideal image of involved fatherhood, shored up by contemporary representations, and the reality which is grounded in their experience.
>
> (2002: 568)

This tension reflects the experiences of several men in our own study, who, during this period, described involvement as a future experience, focusing on when the baby was born and how they would contribute to its care. During this period, many men emphasized their input as an economic provider, highlighting this as a different form of caring for their family (Shirani et al. 2013).

Caring for and about

It has been suggested that contemporary parenting is becoming particularly demanding as parents experience increasing pressure to ensure their child's positive future development. Theorists of intensive parenting culture have argued that parents are required to invest in their child emotionally and practically (in ways that require both time and money) while relying on 'expert' guidance to do this in the most appropriate way; for example, using parenting 'manuals' such as Gina Ford's book *The Contented Little Baby* (Ford 2006). Subsequently, intensive parenting can be seen as a process of 'making' the child through 'concerted cultivation' (Vincent and Ball 2007). The assumption is that parents are able to shape the lives of their children (Wall 2010), ensuring they become responsible citizens (Lister 2006), thus any risks can be managed out through attentive parenting. In addition, the social standing of parents can be seen as contingent on child accomplishments and intelligence, as well as the parental effort put into achieving this, placing parents into competition with one another in achieving desirable child outcomes (Wall 2010).

The term 'intensive parenting' stems from work on intensive mothering (Hays 1996). However, while the term parenting is used, implying gender neutrality, research points to the way in which, despite increased expectations of men's involvement, women continue to have primary responsibility for childcare. Therefore the demands of 'intensive parenting culture' are subsequently seen to fall predominantly on women. Our own analytical work on intensive parenting culture (Shirani et al. 2012) explores this gender division, suggesting the pressures of intensive parenting culture may be differently weighted. For example, men felt their partners experienced more pressure in relation to the child's care, health and behaviour, while the men themselves talked extensively about financial pressure to provide the 'best start' for their child. In this way, responsibilities were differently negotiated between parents (see Harden et al., and Irwin and Winterton, this volume).

> I think it's just the way men think; you think that you're the one who needs to make sure the finances are in place that you can afford to look after them ... My wife and I earn similar levels of money and both work just as hard, you just feel in yourself that it's your responsibility to make sure that's in place and so you take on a bit more of that, more of the planning and the organizing, and make sure you've got the funds. But something my wife's taken on or just naturally seems to worry about more is the childcare side of things, so with Poppy starting nursery she worries a lot more than I do whether it's the right nursery and if she should be going there or not ... So she takes on that worry and I take on the financial worry.
>
> (William, 30, post-birth)

Another aspect of men's involvement was described in 'thinking about' the child by planning for the future, for example saving for the child to go to university. While these varying forms of care may be differently valued, a recognition of men's anxieties in relation to providing suggests the need to account for men's paid work as a manifestation of family commitment or 'care through work' (Townsend 2002: 137) rather than an attempt to avoid the demanding work of hands-on care. For example, men in our study did not feel providing alone constituted good fatherhood but demonstrated a commitment to greater involvement in childcare and knowledge about children's everyday worlds:

the father's got to get really hands-on involved here, they cannot just be a wallet in the sense of passing the money over to the mother and the mother goes and buys the stuff for the child, that's not parenting. You've really got to get engaged completely with them, you've got to know everything about your child; you've got to know everything that's going on.

(Barry, 36, post-birth)

While paid work continues to remain relevant for fatherhood identity (even for those who are not in employment), men who choose to take on primary childcare may uphold alternative standards of masculinity (Shirani et al. 2013). The QL design of the project, involving men being interviewed on multiple occasions, enabled us to explore how these negotiations around earning and caring were worked out over time (see also Irwin and Winterton, Chapter 8, for another interpretation of our data set on this topic). Changes occurred not only in the men's personal biographies but in wider society, with the global economic downturn having particular implications for some men's earning and caring.

Involvement and the economic downturn

Our work on fathering during the economic downturn further highlights some of these tensions between providing cash and care (Henwood et al. 2010). Although one might reasonably expect that those with the most limited financial means would feel the biggest strain, we wanted to explore the accounts of men who on the surface may appear relatively insulated against the recession. For example, the recession led to difficulties for some participants in buying suitable family homes, while others experienced constrained incomes at a time when finances may already be strained due to periods of maternity leave. For some there were longer-term implications as they revised down the number of children they felt able to have. While in response to direct questions these men often said they had been relatively unaffected, several findings emerged by posing questions about changes to these men's anticipated futures brought about by the economic downturn: awareness of greater financial uncertainty, constrained choices and a perceived need for financial risk-taking.

One example of these changes in circumstances can be seen in Jeffrey's account. In the second interview with Jeffrey when his son was a few months old, soon after the recession had hit, he did not relate any financial concerns, instead highlighting the benefits of delaying the transition to fatherhood until his 40s as he had had a longer period of earning. He had also reached a career stage where he was able to stipulate his working conditions to an extent, particularly around working away from home:

> I've not had any problems... we're doing [project name] and there's been a call for volunteers to go out there and I've said no I'm not interested, it's too far, I've got a small baby, I'm not bothered. The company have accepted that, that's fine.

Nine months later when we revisited Jeffrey, the family had moved to a larger house, which required a 'stupidly large mortgage' and subsequently increased pressure for Jeffrey to be earning. However the company he worked for had been affected by the recession so Jeffrey felt less secure in his ability to refuse particular working conditions. For example, in the period between interviews he had spent several months living away from the family home, working on the project he had described refusing in the previous interview:

> So it's all a bit up in the air at the moment about are there gonna be more redundancies, I think there will be. And there is a lot of talk at work about you having to go where the work is... It's not ideal but it's a job and it pays the mortgage so... all you can do is try and grin and bear it and work your way through.

Although Jeffrey was relatively accepting of the situation, recognizing the necessity for the company to make changes, this resulted in a significant departure from the lifestyle he had envisaged before the birth of his son. This also led to feelings of guilt when he was absent during the week; from both the care burden placed on his wife and the lack of time to invest in his son. It is interesting that despite a precarious financial situation the family had taken the risk of moving to a large house in a more family-friendly area in order for their son to have the benefit of growing up with more space and in a preferred location. Threats to the men's ability to provide the best start for their child challenge contemporary ideals of good fatherhood; providing this was often seen as non-negotiable and meant compromises had to be made in other areas, such as time spent with the child. These findings from our work on men's experiences of the economic downturn therefore corroborate aforementioned points about men seeing their role as financial providers as a form of care for the family, which was also often a source of pride. However, this role can also raise anxieties (Coalition for Men and Boys 2009), particularly in the context of the contemporary intensive parenting culture and changes to state support, about providing the best start for the child. A possible scenario is that new social risks, not simply benefits, will arise in relation to fathering in response to shifting moral evaluations of everyday parenting practices (Henwood and Pidgeon 2012). Ways of acknowledging these (involving insight as well as foresight) may need to be part of building resilience to the significant changes currently underway in ideologies of welfare state provision.

Changing relationships to involvement

In addition to exploring the unfolding repercussions of the economic downturn, the QL design of our study also allowed us to explore how men's relationships to involvement changed over time in relation to their life experiences (Shirani and Henwood 2011). As noted earlier, during the pregnancy men could feel excluded and often looked forward to their baby arriving so they could be involved. However, post-birth some men were surprised that involvement was more limited than they had imagined. One barrier cited by several men was breastfeeding. Although men were often supportive of breastfeeding and the associated health benefits, after the birth many of the men were surprised at the strong reactions they had to breastfeeding, which frequently made them feel excluded from having a close relationship with the baby in the way their partner did. For example, Premberg et al. (2008) discuss how some men experience breastfeeding as an impediment in the relationship between father and child in the light of the way it limits opportunity for contact. Inability to feed the child was also a source of frustration for the men as they were unable to be involved in all aspects of care:

> I don't enjoy at all having to look after him when he's crying when I know full well that I'm powerless to do anything about it because actually what he wants to do is feed ... he has to go to his mum and there's nothing else I can do about it ... when that does happen I find it remarkably frustrating, much more frustrating than I'd imagined.
>
> (Simon, 35, post-birth)

Although they participated in most other aspects of childcare, breastfeeding was viewed as a special activity for bonding with the child and therefore preferable to other activities such as nappy changing or bathing. However, some men found ways to feel included in this activity, for example reading to the child while it was being breast-fed. Other barriers to involvement described by the men included the demands of paid work, or the child's immaturity and lack of responsiveness. For example, pre-birth many imagined father–child relationships focused on a young child rather than a baby, with some men finding caring for a baby less rewarding than anticipated due to a lack of 'feedback'. To help to guard against feelings of exclusion amongst fathers and to promote their involvement in family life in the longer term, more could potentially be done to highlight the positive contributions fathers can make in the early stages (such as changing nappies, bathing, reading or playing music to baby). For example, images of involved fathers in the 'Birth to Five' booklet (National Health Service) could be reinforced by supporting text.

Feelings of exclusion often came as a surprise to men who were aware of and aspired to discourses of father involvement, prompting some to look towards the future to a time when they could be more involved:

> I want some feedback, I want response, and it's horrible to wish away his time but I'd like him to get older and bigger. That's what I'm looking forward to, the interaction and sort of teaching him things and telling him things.
>
> (Keith, 31, post-birth)

Revisiting some men eight years later, several of these practical barriers to involvement were no longer relevant and the majority of men felt that they were more involved with their children, the exception being those men who had separated from their partners and no longer co-resided with children. However, having a high level of involvement in both paid work (as discussed above) and family life meant many fathers experienced their time as pressured. This prompted some men to look forward to a time in the future when they would have fewer family responsibilities and more time to themselves:

> You want them to become more and more mature as people so you can relate to them in a more adult to adult level and lose the kind of parenthood thing a bit. [...] Some people have this thing of being quite devastated when their children leave home and that they've lost their life purpose, I don't think so, I think I'll be quite looking forward to it (amusement) to doing something else you know.
>
> (Rick, 43, 8-year-old child)

In contrast, other men described the increased level of involvement as a more enjoyable experience and intimated that a sense of value was achieved from being busy at home and work. In some cases, the prospect of being less involved with their children in the future was a more daunting one:

> I can sort of project forward to a time when they don't need us in the sense that they need us now, perhaps our role becoming a bit redundant then. I don't look forward to that bit...I don't know how redundant I'll be (amusement) you know I don't know how much they'll still feel that they want to come and talk to me and take my advice, do you know what I mean? You know that is the unknown...they might not feel that I'm necessarily the person that they want to talk to.
>
> (Kenny, 49, 8-year-old child)

By drawing on a QL data set, we are able to consider how men's relationships to discourses of involvement change over time and in relation to life circumstances. While involvement remained a central concept for fathers across all stages of the research, the extent to which it was realized and enjoyed showed considerable variation. This longer-term perspective served to illustrate some commonalities in the data set; men predominantly described becoming increasingly involved with their children over time. This suggests that men may need to be varyingly supported in their fathering at different life stages, particularly to overcome early feelings of exclusion in some cases, as previously discussed.

Fathering across generations

The QL design of the study also enabled us to develop and extend our efforts to elucidate psychosocial aspects of men's experiences and practices of fathering. Psychosocial research is concerned with aspects of identity formation that are not easily spoken about, or are otherwise obscured from view (e.g. because they are incoherent, or do not follow normative cultural logics). Typically it draws attention to the constitutive and regulatory role of cultural discourses (which are conceptualized as multiple, contradictory, coexisting), while also asking questions about issues such as affective intergenerational transmissions (i.e. ones energized by feelings that lie outside representation) to deepen understanding of intangible, dynamic forms of (in our case – paternal) subjectivity.

One of our published studies (Coltart and Henwood 2012) reports a psychosocial, narrative analysis of the ways in which intergenerational transmissions of classed masculinities affect men's experience of becoming a father. Use of the term 'psychosocial temporalities' (Henwood and Finn 2010) foregrounds a developing interest in the dynamic and multimodal constitution of masculine identity and paternal subjectivity (Henwood et al. 2008). The study also highlights two particular psychosocial concepts: intersubjectivity (processes of mutual regard and recognition between people) and relationality (assemblages of meaning and affect that hold together self and other, rather than posit them in the form of binary opposites, which are explored in relation to multiple conditions and flows of time). The article explores the influence of the past on the present – classed masculine transmissions and inherited paternal identities – and ways in which the present mediates the past. Novel experiences – such as caring for a new baby – and 'new' socio-cultural and relational contexts are brought into particular focus in terms of how they prompt a recasting of inherited paternal identities as a means of seizing opportunities or to accommodate change. The longitudinal lens afforded by the study allowed fathers' attempts to reconcile 'old' and 'new' discourses and identities to be tracked as they responded to the opportunities, demands and concerns arising out of particular circumstances. This longer-term perspective also shed light on the dynamics of continuity and change in fathers' experiences and subjectivities, including the ways fathers arrive at particular 'settlements' between past, present and future over time.

An example of these dynamic and unfolding psychosocial temporalities (discussed extensively in the published paper) is given in Richard's account. Richard (aged 37) described himself as coming from an 'upper-middle-class' background and worked full-time in a senior position as a professional theologian. In his pre-birth interview, tensions around involvement seemed to be affectively freighted for Richard in connection with his negative childhood memories of his own father's 'workaholic-type pattern', which was at odds with the current cultural emphasis on active paternal involvement. In response, Richard sought to reconcile his competing investments in work and involvement through appeals to discourses of 'quality time' and intimacy. Subsequently, in his first post-birth interview, unexpected events seemed to herald a more fundamental transformation in his paternal horizons. Richard's wife's traumatic birth and post-partum health complications thrust him unexpectedly into the position of primary carer in the very early stages of his daughter's infancy. The 'joyous' and 'very special' bond he established with her in the first months prompted a dramatic reimagining of his anticipated home/work life trajectory:

> It has caused a fundamental change in where I see myself going ... the whole idea about staying at home I'd have been horrified about 10 months ago, but now I think that may have become a real possibility at some point.

This potentially fundamental change did not prompt a severing of links with his paternal legacy. There is a notable difference here between Richard and some of the self-described 'working-class' fathers in the sample, who strongly distanced themselves from their fathers' 'macho' identities. In contrast, Richard was able to emphasize positive continuities with his own father's fathering, highlighting their shared socio-economic position and creating the 'type of environment' and 'range of experiences' capable of promoting children's development.

Psychosocial analysis of intergenerational transmissions of such a valued and persuasive middle-class identity may go some way to explaining Richard's original 'horror' at the thought of being a main carer to his child and why, by the second and third interviews, he speaks of a tension between a 'push' towards highly involved fatherhood and the 'pull' of established priorities around work-based opportunities and achievements: 'the reality ... is I suspect I will drift back into doing the amount of work I was doing before Beca was born', 'I'm too driven by the work I do'.

Richard's experience of hands-on parenting ignited his interest in being a highly involved father, but the radically new course opened up by his novel experience as primary carer could not be easily integrated into his established senses of self and stable middle-class masculinity as a positive paternal inheritance and resource for identity construction. Accordingly, Richard is pushed away from a more 'stay-at-home' trajectory despite this being economically and relationally viable with Richard's wife – also career minded – supportive of his choices either way. Richard appears to resettle instead upon his earlier resolution of being an affectionate father who makes a regular effort to have 'quality time' with family.

The findings suggest that psychosocial investments in masculinity (and associated ideas of class and culture) pull men back towards inherited or more traditional fathering models. This is apparent even in those cases when the opportunity or conscious desire for change is pushing men towards more involved and less gender-differentiated parenting, as in Richard's case. This perspective is in tune with other gender and fatherhood researchers (e.g. Featherstone 2009) who suggest that theory and policy need to take account of complex gendered and generational issues. It would be beneficial if men's chances of coming to a settlement with their family legacies could be improved in ways that promote self-esteem and positive, mutual recognition among family members.

Conclusion

The chapter brings together insights related to father involvement from our analytical projects in order to consider and consolidate the implications of these findings for policy-makers and practitioners. Our findings lend support to existing work that stresses the importance of the concept of involvement in understandings of contemporary fatherhood. However, the MaF project has expanded on these existing studies by foregrounding QL insights showing how relationships to involvement alter over time and in relation to life experiences. This approach has enabled an exploration of how different issues continue, emerge or recede in men's fathering over time, which has implications for how they can be supported at different life stages. For example, while the ideal of involvement was central to men's experiences at all stages of fatherhood, many of the men in our study increased their level of practical involvement over time as their children got older. Further work to consider the extent to which this continues into teenage years, and the subsequent implications of this, would therefore be beneficial.

Ideals of father involvement and commitments to an egalitarian model of parenting appear to be widely upheld amongst fathers; however, practical barriers can prevent ideas of involvement from becoming a reality. Policies which attempt to address these barriers may have significant effects on family life and research will be needed to establish the impact of government changes to parental leave on patterns of working and caring in different families. However, a view which considers paid work as necessarily restricting father involvement may overshadow the way in which paid work represents a manifestation of family commitment for many men (Townsend 2002). Fathers in our study saw themselves as making important contributions to family well-being and resilience, but the resources fathers offer are shaped by practical restrictions, and many other forces including popular cultural understandings of masculine and paternal 'roles' and identities. Practitioners and policy-makers still need to promote and remove barriers to non-traditional contributions by men as fathers. For example,

promoting educational practices aimed at eliminating gender stereotypes and encouraging the social and emotional development of boys
and men in ways that improve their capacity and potential to care for
themselves and others; while highlighting the positive contributions
fathers can make to family life during the early stages may help to guard
against feelings of exclusion.

While this chapter may be seen to highlight gender differences in
focusing solely on fathers, it is important to consider similarities with
women's experiences. For example, how to balance paid work, other
interests and relationships with the responsibilities, anxieties and pleasures of childrearing are concerns for both men and women (Lupton
and Barclay 1997) and remain important for understandings of contemporary family life (see also Harden et al. and Irwin and Winterton, this
volume). In drawing out insights we have adopted a relational approach,
acknowledging that the experiences of one parent hold implications for
the other, and supporting recommendations to foreground the mother–
father relationship in more joined-up approaches. As well as addressing
the practical barriers to father involvement, this perspective could create
new opportunities for mothers in the work of earning and caring.

References

Burgess, A. (1997) *Fatherhood Reclaimed: The Making of the Modern Father*, London:
Vermilion.

Clarke, S. and Popay, J. (1998) ' "I'm just a bloke who's had kids": Men and
women on parenthood', in J. Popay, J. Hearn and J. Edwards (eds) *Men, Gender
Divisions and Welfare*, London: Routledge.

Coalition for Men and Boys Report (Author: Sandy Ruxton) (2009) *Man Made:
Men, Masculinities and Equality in Public Policy*: http://www.comab.org.uk/.

Coltart, C. and Henwood, K. (2012) 'On paternal subjectivity: Qualitative longitudinal and psychosocial case analysis of men's classed positions and transitions
to first-time fatherhood', *Qualitative Research*, 12(1): 35–52.

Daniel, B. and Taylor, J. (1999) 'The rhetoric versus the reality: A critical perspective on practice with fathers in child care and protection work', *Child and
Family Social Work*, 4: 209–220.

Dermott, E. (2003) 'The "Intimate father": Defining paternal involvement', *Sociological Research Online*, 8(4). Available at http://www.socresonline.org.uk/8/4/
dermott.html.

Dermott, E. (2008) *Intimate Fatherhood: A Sociological Analysis*, London: Routledge.

Doucet, A. (2004) ' "It's almost like I have a job but I don't get paid": Fathers at
home reconfiguring work, care and masculinity', *Fathering*, 2(3): 277–303.

Draper, J. (2002) ' "It's the first scientific evidence": Men's experience of pregnancy confirmation', *Journal of Advanced Nursing*, 39(6): 563–570.

Featherstone, B. (2009) *Contemporary Fathering: Theory, Policy and Practice*, Bristol:
Policy Press.

Featherstone, B. (2010) 'Writing fathers in but mothers out!!!', *Critical Social Policy*, 30(2): 208–224.

Finn, M. and Henwood, K. (2009) 'Exploring masculinities within men's identificatory imaginings of first time fatherhood', *British Journal of Social Psychology*, 48(3): 547–562.

Ford, G. (2006) *The New Contented Little Baby Book: The Secret to Calm and Confident Parenting*, London: Vermilion.

Hays, S. (1996) *The Cultural Contradictions of Motherhood*, New Haven, CT: Yale University Press.

Henwood, K. and Finn, M. (2010) 'Researching masculine and paternal subjects in times of change: Insights from a QLL and psychosocial case study', in R. Thomson (ed.) *Intensity and Insight: Qualitative Longitudinal Methods as a Route to the Psycho-social*, Timescapes Working Paper Series 3. Available at http://www.timescapes.leeds.ac.uk/assets/files/WP3-final-Jan-2010.pdf.

Henwood. K. and Pidgeon, N. (2012) Risk and identity futures (DR18) *Foresight: The Future of Identity*, London: UK Government Office for Science.

Henwood, K. and Procter, J. (2003) 'The "good father": Reading men's accounts of paternal involvement during the transition to first-time fatherhood', *British Journal of Social Psychology*, 42(3): 337–355.

Henwood, K. and Shirani, F. (2012). 'Researching the temporal', in H. Cooper (ed.) *Handbook of Research Methods in Psychology*, Vol 2, Chapter 13. ISBN 978–1–4338–1003–9, Washington, DC: APA Publications.

Henwood, K., Shirani, F. and Coltart, C. (2010) 'Fathers and financial risk-taking during the economic downturn: Insights from a QLL study of men's identities-in-the-making', *21st Century Society (now Contemporary Social Science)*, 5(2): 137–147.

Henwood, K. L., Finn, M. and Shirani, F. (2008). 'Use of visual methods to explore paternal identities in historical time and social change: Reflections from the "men-as-fathers" project', *Qualitative Researcher*, (9), September: 2–5. Available at: http://www.cardiff.ac.uk/socsi/qualiti/QualitativeResearcher/QR_Issue9_Sep08.pdf.

Jamieson, L. (1998) *Intimacy: Personal Relationships in Modern Societies*, Cambridge: Polity Press.

Kiernan, K. and Smith, K. (2003) 'Unmarried parenthood: New insights from the millennium cohort study', *Population Trends*, (Winter 2003): 23–33.

Lewis, C. and Lamb, M. E. (2007) *Understanding Fatherhood: A Review of Recent Research*, York: Joseph Rowntree Foundation.

Lister, R. (2006) 'Children (but not women) first: New Labour, child welfare and gender', *Critical Social Policy*, 26(2): 315–335.

Lupton, D. and Barclay, L. (1997) *Constructing Fatherhood: Discourses and Experiences*, London: Sage.

Miller, T. (2010) *Making Sense of Fatherhood: Gender, Caring and Work*, Cambridge: Cambridge University Press.

Neale, B. and Flowerdew, J. (2003) 'Time, texture and childhood: The contours of longitudinal qualitative research', *International Journal of Social Research Methodology*, 6(3): 189–199.

National Health Service (2005) *NHS Maternity Services Quantitative Research* (October). Prepared by TNS System Three for Kate Hawkins, London: Department of Health.

Pleck, J. (1997) 'Paternal involvement: Levels, sources and consequences', in M. Lamb (ed.) *The Role of the Father in Child Development* (3rd Ed.), New York: Wiley and Sons.

Premberg, A., Hellstrom, A. and Berg, M. (2008) 'Experiences of the first year as father', *Scandinavian Journal of Caring Sciences*, 22(1): 56–63.

Shirani, F. and Henwood, K. (2011) 'Continuity and change in a qualitative longitudinal study of fatherhood: Relevance without responsibility', *International Journal of Social Research Methodology*, 14(1): 17–29.

Shirani, F., Henwood, K. and Coltart, C. (2009) *Men's Experience of Antenatal Services: Findings from the 'Men as Fathers' Study*. Research Report. Available at: http://www.cardiff.ac.uk/socsi/research/researchprojects/menasfathers/publications/antenatalreport.pdf.

Shirani, F., Henwood, K. and Coltart, C. (2012) 'Meeting the challenges of intensive parenting culture: Gender, risk management and the moral parent', *Sociology*, 46(1): 25–40.

Shirani, F., Henwood, K. and Coltart, C. (2013) ' "Why aren't you at work?": Negotiating economic models of fathering identity', *Fathering*, 10(3): 274–290.

Snyder, K. A. (2007) 'A vocabulary of motives: Understanding how parents define quality time', *Journal of Marriage and Family*, 69: 320–340.

Thomson, R., Bell, R., Holland, J., Henderson, S., McGrellis, S. and Sharpe, S. (2002) 'Critical moments: Choice, chance and opportunity in young people's narratives of transition', *Sociology*, 6(2): 335–354.

Townsend, N. (2002) *The Package Deal: Marriage, Work and Fatherhood in Men's Lives*, Philadelphia: Temple University Press.

Vincent, C. and Ball, S. (2007) ' "Making up" the middle-class child: Families, activities and class dispositions', *Sociology*, 41(6): 1061–1077.

Walker, A. and McGraw, L. (2000) 'Who is responsible for responsible fathering?', *Journal of Marriage and Family*, 62(2): 563–569.

Wall, G. (2010) 'Mothers' experiences with intensive parenting and brain development discourse', *Women's Studies International Forum*, 33: 253–263.

White, N. R. (1994) 'About fathers: Masculinity and the social construction of fatherhood', *Australian and New Zealand Journal of Sociology*, 30(2): 119–131.

6
Expectations and Realities: Motherhood and the Female 'Choice' Biography[1]

Rachel Thomson

Introduction

> Many, probably most, women feel that their range of choices is greater than that of their mothers with regard to work, marriage and reproduction. Yet [...] in the post-war world an increasing gap has opened up between women in terms of opportunity and autonomy. One of the most significant differences of income and expectation in late twentieth-century society must be that between the teenage unmarried mother, unable to escape from dependence on state benefits, and the professional woman in her late thirties, married to another professional, having her first child and able to pay for a nanny.
>
> (Lewis 1992: 10)

Becoming a mother can be seen as a profound moment of personal change that ties women to the past, the future and each other. Yet what it means to be a mother is shape-shifting in line with women's increased participation in work and education. The general trend is towards later motherhood, delaying the birth of a first child until education is completed and a career is well established. Emotional stability, financial security and the 'right' relationship are expected to fall in line with this life trajectory, making birth the apex of achievement for grown-up girls living the success story narrative of contemporary times. Yet for some young women first pregnancy comes early. Marked by disaffection from education, lack of opportunity and poor socio-economic circumstances, young motherhood may be the first act of adulthood rather than the highly prized goal of deferred gratification. Could it be that motherhood is becoming the site of a new social division between women?

The increasing participation of women in further and higher education and the labour force since World War II has transformed the shape and meaning of women's biographies (Lewis 1992), reflected in a trend towards later motherhood. Yet this change has been uneven, with stagnation in social mobility and widening inequality heightening differences *between* women, reflected in differential patterns of family formation depending on educational and employment status (Crompton 2006). The social polarization of motherhood is one of the most distinctive demographic trends of the post-war period, reflected in a movement towards later motherhood for the majority, and early motherhood for a minority. In 2010 the average age for a woman giving birth in England and Wales was 29.5 – an increase of 2.7 years over a 20-year period. The most obvious manifestation of this polarization has been the intensive public focus on teenage pregnancy as a social problem, where a concern with age replaces earlier concerns around illegitimacy and marriage as markers of autonomy and respectability (Arai 2009). Although later motherhood tends not to raise political concerns about economic dependence, it does become visible through popular concern over the availability and ethics of infertility treatment, the supposed 'intensification of parenting' and the commodification and delegation of domestic care.

The 'Making of modern motherhood' study set out to capture and relate two dimensions of social division – division that exists *between* generations (as captured in relationships between grandmothers, mothers and daughters) and division *within* generations (as captured by women simultaneously becoming mothers for the first time). Recognizing the complexity of this task, we maintained a substantive but relatively narrow focus on the experience of first-time motherhood and the transition into a maternal subjectivity. Located in the unique space of late pregnancy, our research encounters women as they approach birth, then follows a small number of case studies through into the first year of motherhood and subsequently as babies became toddlers. A central objective of our approach has been to capture the paradoxical way that motherhood is both one thing and many and for this reason we generated an initial sample of 62 pregnant women that was diverse in terms of age, social class, ethnicity, nationality, fertility history, disability and sexuality. Two research sites, an inner-city borough and a new town, generated a diverse sample of women linked by the common experience of becoming a mother. The initial interviews were conducted in 2005 in the midst of the New Labour project of widespread change in social welfare, health and education. Subsequently, women and their families were revisited during the first year of the child's life. Five of these families continued to be involved in the research until the end of 2009, taking us through the credit crisis and the appointment of a coalition government with a very different perspective on family support. The combination of a longitudinal and intergenerational research design allows us to capture the ways in which historical change is mediated by families as well as the ways in which roles are renegotiated constantly over time and in particular in response to key moments of change such as the arrival of a new generation.

In designing this study, we were keen to capture and address two forces that hold the category of motherhood in tension (Thomson 2011). On the one hand we wanted to engage with the question of diversity within the contemporary moment and the way that motherhood both provides the potential for identifications between women as well as the ground for women to experience differences in a heightened way. On the other, we wanted to add to this brew a temporal perspective on mothering as experienced by chains of women within families and between generations more collectively as expressed through control over resources, institutions and representations. For us this involves exploring motherhood as a historically located experience that is nevertheless mediated within families between grandmothers, mothers and daughters, who in turn locate themselves as members of wider generations of women. In terms of our research design, we have translated this into a desire to research motherhood in two directions: horizontally, as relations between women who share a historical moment; and vertically, as relations between intergenerational chains of women within families. It is an approach that seeks to move between an understanding of biographical time as experienced by individuals and within families, and a more collective sense of historical time as experienced by generations and the relationships between generations.

This chapter explores women's experiences of encountering motherhood as workers. By drawing on interviews with mothers and grandmothers, we show how expectations in relation to work and career have transformed over generations – pointing both to elements of progress in women's social position but also to contradictions and intergenerational ruptures. Planning around maternity leave and returns to work were characterized by much anxiety, and the longitudinal perspective enabled by the study allows us to understand both how women experienced the 'motherhood penalty' and how they accommodated to its logic.

Women and working

An ever-increasing level of female employment, including mothers with dependent children, has been a distinctive feature of post-war British society, paralleled by an overall improvement in living standards yet a rise in inequality. The 'family wage' that was consolidated during the second half of the nineteenth century began to unravel in the later decades of the twentieth, giving way to dual-earner households and a slow and incomplete convergence in male and female pay (Ferri and Smith 2003). Much of the continuing disparity between the earnings of men and women can be explained by the 'motherhood penalty' that has been estimated to diminish women's average earning capacity by one fifth (Davies et al. 2000). In comparison to other developed economies, the UK has high levels of female employment but low levels of subsidized childcare and a survey of seven industrialized countries found the UK had the highest motherhood pay penalty (Harkness and Waldfogel 1999). Mothers are far more likely than fathers to take time out from paid work, or to work part-time, in order to care for their children, with higher skilled women much more likely to return to work after the birth of a child and lower skilled women being more likely to stay at home (Crompton 2006: 46). The campaign organization the Fawcett Society sums this up as follows: 'becoming a parent marks the start of the great divide between women's and men's pay. Motherhood has a direct and dramatic influence on women's pay and employment prospects, and typically this penalty lasts a lifetime' (Woodroffe 2009).

The cultural significance of these social changes has been characterized in terms of labour having become feminized (increasingly precarious and communication-based) and women having become labourized (considered as workers first and as mothers second) (Power 2009). Education and work are now ubiquitous features of the individualized female biography, with the acquisition of qualifications constituting new gender divisions between women. Young women are outperforming young men at school and university and taking up many of the new places created by the expansion of higher education. Consequently, the social divisions that matter for the young are increasingly those constituted around poverty and qualifications rather than around gender, sexuality or race. Angela McRobbie captures this change through the idea of a post-feminist sexual contract, which celebrates educationally successful young women as the active and aspirational subjects of social change. Extended periods of education and work on an apparently level playing field delay motherhood for the majority. By the time these women encounter the motherhood penalty, they may find themselves without the political and cultural resources of feminism. McRobbie argues that 'How successful the individual heterosexual woman might be in achieving equality in relation to domestic labour and childcare then becomes a private affair, or rather evidence that she has chosen well from the range of possible partners, her life-plan in this regard has worked to her advantage.' (McRobbie 2007: 18).

It is little surprise then that the contemporary politics of motherhood are fragmented and privatized, played out through a splitting of destinies on the grounds of consumption, age and choice. Academic debates over working parenthood are also caught up in this maelstrom, with attempts to guide policy according to women's 'preferences' for home or work (Hakim 2000) criticized for failing to capture the political, economic and cultural contexts in which 'choices' are made (Gattrell 2005, Crompton 2006, Armstrong 2010). For those such as Adkins (2009), mass female employment and the socialization and commodification of childcare are a sign of the end of the patriarchal order as we knew it associated with a gendered division of labour within a private sphere. The divisions that should most matter now for feminists are between women.

Work in biographical perspective

The women in our research approached motherhood at very different stages in their biographies. The youngest were still in secondary education and experienced pregnancy either as a disruption to that education and associated career plans or as a different pathway to maturity and responsibility than that promised by the extended forms of youth associated with further and higher education. For some, the experience of being pregnant gave them insight into new possibilities, encouraging an interest in midwifery and childcare as potential areas of training and work. Others, like Kim, significantly downscaled their ambitions in the face of new motherhood, drawing on the support provided by a young mothers project to rework a dream of being a lawyer into a pragmatic plan to train as a florist. The oldest of our new mothers tended to be well established in their careers and in a position to privilege motherhood over work, or at least to control their work in such a way that they could exercise a high level of choice in regard to how they managed the relationship between parenting and career. For 40-year-old Pauline, it meant having the confidence to ignore the disapproval of her sister and leave a job as a nursery manager, embarking on motherhood without work and supported by benefits. Older mothers were more able than most to make their work fit around their mothering rather than vice versa. In the middle age group, women's attitudes towards combining work and motherhood were shaped in large part by the nature of their work, including how well they were paid, whether or not they understood themselves as being in a career and the extent to which it was possible to disrupt this career path.

Of the 62 women that we interviewed in late pregnancy 47 were in work, eight were students and seven unemployed. Overall we classified 36 women as falling within a lower-middle-class category, 21 as working class and just five as upper middle class. The kinds of work that women were involved in were diverse, spanning public and private sectors as well as salaried and self-employment. Occupation did not map neatly onto our judgement of social class positions, being complicated by factors including migration and the occupation and resources of partners and families. However it is our contention that the kind of paid work that women were involved in shaped their experience of motherhood significantly.

A sense of choice?

> I was talking to somebody at work and I said, 'Oh I have got to decide about what I want to do about going back to work and all this that and the other', and she said, 'Can I say something and I hope you will take this in the way it is intended, at least you have a choice. I didn't have a choice when I was your age, when I had my kids I had to resign and that was it, I stayed at home'. And I thought, Oh is it better to have choice or no choice? No if somebody said right you have got to resign now and go and have a baby, would I be like, 'This isn't fair!', or would I be, 'Oh okay then.'? (laughs) You know it is funny.
>
> (Deborah: 33)

At the time of our initial fieldwork the statutory entitlement for maternity leave was still only six months, although the policy change of extending this to a year was in discussion. Most women were eligible for maternity leave, although a couple had recently changed jobs and so lost out on their full entitlements. Many of the women that we interviewed were uncertain about their return to work, and several felt pressurized by the need to let their employers know how much time they would be taking off. How much maternity leave women were able to take was generally dictated by their financial situation and the generosity of their maternity package. Several were clear that their return to work after the six months was motivated purely by 'financial reasons'. Sofia for example, who was the main breadwinner in her family, felt that she had no choice but to go back to her work as a beauty therapist after just four months of maternity leave. Others explained their choice as involving a desire to work, associating employment with independence and good mothering. For example, 23-year-old supermarket worker Farah looked to work as a source of independence. She could not countenance giving up her job and remaining at home with her unemployed husband and mother, asserting that 'no-one can stop me working' and that she would 'work for myself and for my child'. A similar account came from 21-year-old chef Lorraine, whose son lived for a period with his father in the Caribbean enabling her to work long hours, a pattern of parenting that had shaped her early life also (Reynolds 2006, Phoenix 2008). Some of the youngest mothers in our study, who had often been disaffected by school in advance of the pregnancy, drew on their experiences to imagine a working future in areas such as midwifery, childcare or floristry (a course often provided in young mother support projects). For these young women, a commitment to work is an integral element of a narrative of self-improvement and economic independence that is promoted by service providers working with teenage mothers (Ponsford 2011, Rudoe 2011).

Others welcomed the prospect of escaping work for a period of time. Again this might be for a range of reasons – because they were unsatisfied with their work, wanted to change their priorities, or felt that they were sufficiently secure in their working lives to be able to 'afford to take some time out'. A significant group of women had decided to take an extended period out of work, choosing to be stay-at-home mothers. In general these women were in couples where it was financially viable to survive on a single wage, and where the calculation had been made that the financial and personal costs of childcare were greater than the loss of a salary. For 29-year-old administrator Sharon

> it all depends on money really, child minding fees don't appear to be cheap and I think if I look into it, it's got to be a case of well it's worth it, because I would hate to pay to go to work just to pay child

minding fees and just walk out with a couple of hundred pounds in my pocket.

For others, the choice to stay at home was presented as part of a moral project of self and a self-conscious embrace of a child-centred model of parenting. Women's deliberations depended largely on the overall economy of the household. For some the demand to pool resources was very challenging. Journalist Vickie, 33, talks about her panic on stopping work; having been financially independent since her teens, it was hard to re-conceptualize herself and her money as part of a 'family' or a 'team'. However, others, such as Anastasia, considered themselves to be unemployed rather than stay-at-home mothers, finding it impossible to afford the childcare that would allow her to return to work and having no alternative but to stay at home, where she sells second-hand clothes on eBay to make some money.

Women's accounts of being pregnant at work and planning around maternity leave do not simply reflect their different biographical situations. They also communicate something important about variability between and within workplaces in terms of how pregnant workers are treated. The most difficult experiences appear to be associated with small-scale organizations and businesses and those dominated by gender-neutral discourses of the good worker. In these contexts, the pregnant body may be unwelcome and disruptive and the pregnant worker may be constructed as demanding and disloyal. Women working in these kinds of organizations may see it as easier to withdraw rather than fight for their rights. Larger organizations with established traditions of human resource management, health and safety standards and negotiations with unions appear to provide a more promising environment for the negotiation of flexible working and quality part-time work (Lyonette et al. 2010). Whether women see motherhood and paid work as compatible or not depends in part on their circumstances, the extent to which they are invested in work and the kind of workplace, if any, that they would return to.

Making motherhood work

The combination of work and motherhood is nothing new for many groups of working-class, migrant and minority women, who, far from perceiving tensions between motherhood and work, may see work as an arena through which competence as a mother and a provider is demonstrated (Duncan et al. 2003, Gillies 2006, Reynolds 2006, Armstrong

2010). Yet for much of the white middle class, working motherhood constitutes an intergenerational rupture, especially where daughters are better educated than their mothers and becoming parents much later (Sharpe 1984). These patterns were reflected in our study, with middle-class mothers and grandmothers having much more to say about work and how work and education complicate their relationships. Where their own mothers had tended to marry early (compressing childbearing and rearing into their 20s, and returning to employment in their 30s), this generation of young women spent their 20s establishing themselves in careers and relationships (Crompton 2006). The way in which these grandmothers responded to this generational change varied. Most were delighted that their daughters had access to educational and professional opportunities that they had perhaps missed. Yet they also expressed concern about the double burden of working and mothering that their daughters faced, feeling that the tempo of mothering had become much more intensive. Sixty-five-year-old Jean Woolfe acknowledged that she was relatively unusual to be 'born in the generation that enabled me to be a stay-at-home mother when my children were young, and at the same time to have the experience of being a professional person. That's ideal'. It is not something that is available to the young mothers that she works with in a university context for whom 'there's almost intolerable pressures on them to do both, it's impossible'.

Grandmothers in our study tended to be very careful about how they described their daughters' situations and choices, distinguishing between the imperative to fulfil one's own potential and the imperative to prioritize the needs and well-being of children. Avril, who had a long and successful career in teaching, explains that

> years ago teachers were not allowed to work when they were married. It had to stop. I suppose we've come a long way in that respect. But I think it's good if you can work and still feel that you can give your child what they deserve, then that's fine. I wouldn't have liked to have had a job that I couldn't do that.

Tension between self-actualization and the realization of children's potential forms a vital dynamic in intergenerational relationships, amplified when children face the prospect of becoming mothers themselves.

Each new mother faces the challenge of negotiating work and care from the position of having been mothered herself, which means that she must engage in an intergenerational conversation about the shape of the female biography (Lawler 2000). Women respond differently: some daughters of working mothers are keen to reproduce something like the model provided by their mother, while others embrace the possibility of being at home full-time. Those whose mothers felt frustrated by their own lack of opportunities may find themselves involved in a kind of recuperation of thwarted ambition, while others are distressed by a sense that they are not providing their children with the 'hands on' parenting that they had enjoyed themselves.

The practical, moral and interpersonal complexities involved in this terrain are inadequately served by concepts such as work/life balance that dominate policy discussions and much of the academic literature (Everingham et al. 2007). A more promising approach is offered by those promoting a 'new sociology of work', who call for attention to be paid to the 'matrix' through which household labour and the market economy interact, including the interplay of processes of consumption and production, paid and unpaid 'work' (Pettinger et al. 2005). Yet what still seems to be missing most from this debate is a sense of the kinds of emotional, psychic and creative work involved in being good enough as a parent and a worker. Rosemary Crompton suggests that it is worth looking closely at the divisions of labour that are struck within families, and the kinds of gender relations that these make possible and available (Crompton 2006). In her view certain responses to the challenge of parenthood (such as dividing work and care, or simply delegating care to the market) can create or confirm traditional gender roles, while other strategies (such as fully sharing the tasks of breadwinning and care) may unpick them. It is in the small but growing body of qualitative research on mothering that we find evidence of how individuals and families work through the limits and opportunities of their situations, demonstrating the local and contingent factors that shape ideas of good mothering (Duncan et al. 2003) and the everyday practices through which mothers combine, breach and separate the worlds of home and work (Cunningham-Burley et al. 2005).

The final section of this chapter involves a single case study of a working mother, whose account captures something of the intergenerational change that characterizes the socially mobile new middle class. Middle-class women with careers had a great deal to say about combining work and motherhood, experiencing the two as competing projects. As illustrated earlier, working-class working mothers were more likely to understand motherhood and paid work as complementary projects and consequently had less elaborate accounts. Informed by the spirit of the new sociology of work, the case study brings together an analysis of paid and unpaid work, tracing the consequences of private deliberation over childcare and the division of labour for the kinds of gender relations that arise. The case study benefits from a longitudinal perspective, including two interviews with the mother, before and a year after the birth, and interviews with the grandmother.

Case study: Deborah Rickard

We met Deborah Rickard at the beginning of her maternity leave from a full-time post as information specialist in public sector organization. At this time Deborah was moving between 'plan A' (returning to work full-time after six months maternity leave and placing her child in nursery) and 'plans B–F' that involved longer maternity leave and part-time return. This was a fraught time for her relationship as she and her partner communicated previously unspoken feelings about their perceptions of each other and their attitudes to work and parenting. Deborah is upset when her partner expresses his view that she should return to work full-time after 18 weeks, using his own work colleagues as an example of the 'norm'. They argue over whether there is a financial need for her to return so quickly to work, with Deborah asserting that they are relatively well off and could afford to cut down on their expenses. She also reported his concern that women in his workplace 'go back part-time and they seemed very frustrated because they were stuck at the level they left at and are not able to progress in their careers'. She reported his words as follows: 'You have worked so hard and you have got to where you want to be and I don't want to see you throw it away'. While she appreciates his sentiment she is exasperated that he cannot understand that she might want to take a break from work.

Deborah's initial strategy is to suspend decisions about work until the baby is born, predicting that her partner

> WILL want me to stay home when the baby arrives, I don't think he will like the idea of me going back to work. He is quite a sensitive soul. It will upset him putting the baby in the nursery.

She has also had to fight with him over paternity leave, recalling a recent episode when he announced that he would only take a weeks' paternity leave while at a meal with friends. In Deborah's words, she 'went ballistic', upset that he had not first discussed it with her. At this stage she is deeply uncertain as to her priorities. In an ideal world she would like 'to work part-time, still get promoted and still have a fantastic salary', but feels that this is unrealistic. Yet, working full-time feels like an overwhelming prospect:

> forty hours a week and have someone else look after your child and then come home and you spend 10 minutes with it before it goes to bed so you miss it crawling you miss it talking all those kind of things.

As she faces the birth of her first child Deborah has no clear sense of how she will deal with this challenge, explaining that she 'will cross that bridge when I get over it. I may want to go back to work full-time in January or I may want to stay home bake cakes and keep chickens'.

We interviewed Deborah's mother, Judy, eight months after baby Ruby was born. Judy explained that when Deborah shared the news of her pregnancy she had burst into tears having 'made up my mind that she wasn't going to have any, when she reached that age, I thought oh she's decided not to bother you know, she's going to go for the career'. Education and work loom large in the relationship between mother and daughter. Judy expressed regrets that she had given up paid employment when she had had children. Not only does she worry that she does not have a pension (unlike many of her friends) but she also asserts that she may have been a more 'interesting person' if she had a career. Nevertheless she is confident that she did a good job bringing up her children and illustrates her priorities by telling a vivid story of going for a job interview as a school secretary but realizing that she had miscalculated the hours and deciding that she could not leave her daughter for that long.

There is a sense throughout the interview that Deborah's university education and career success created a gulf between mother and daughter. The arrival of a granddaughter has made this a little easier. Judy feels that Deborah is 'different' now she is a mother: they have more to talk about and she doesn't feel 'bozeyed' like she did when Deborah talked to her about her job. Her sense of connection with her granddaughter is also strong. Yet Judy struggles to align her own experience of motherhood with Deborah's situation. She asserts that her daughter has shown her an alternative way of doing motherhood which allows women to have more 'independence', while also recounting conversations where Deborah has questioned whether it is possible to 'have it all'. Judy's assertion of hope that Deborah will 'make the most of her education' by returning to work after her maternity leave is followed by the admission that she herself would have liked to go to university but feels she is 'not clever enough' and her concerns that her second daughter who did not go to university will miss out on the 'modern experience'.

When we meet Deborah again over a year after the birth of her daughter she is much less ambivalent about work, explaining that she found she was 'really glad to go back, and I didn't have any qualms about leaving her either'. Deborah started off working three days a week, which she claims was long enough to feel 'organized at home but disorganized at work', and then started working four days a week, which she claims 'makes me feel disorganized everywhere'. When she is at work she reverts to being 'pre-pregnancy Debbie' but as soon as the nursery calls her she becomes 'mummy Debbie': 'I'll just be, not torn, but I'll be completely mummy Debbie there is no middle way'. She attributes her ease at returning to work partly to her daughter's 'confidence' and her ability to 'settle' into nursery, although she acknowledges that a second child could disrupt this delicate balance.

Deborah describes her work environment as having been supportive and attributes this to the fact that it is dominated by women and many of her colleagues have children. She has found that her four-day week is actually a full-time job but feels that any less days would not make her feel the same sense of 'value' that she gets from working four days a week, attending important meetings and so on. She reports experiencing a form of prejudice from a colleague who expressed the view that part-time staff with children only work their hours and want to return home to their children. She felt offended that this suggested that she had less 'commitment' than non-mothers. Outside of work she has noted differences with her peers from the antenatal groups, some of whom have commented on her 'fancy job title'. She also feels different from her peers who just see work as 'something they do', unlike Deborah. She also reports feeling a 'bit out of it' when mothers arrange to meet, not being part of either 'the stay-at-home set or the full-time set'.

Deborah is in a relatively privileged situation compared to other women in the study: she and her partner could afford for her to stay at home and her wages are sufficiently high to pay for childcare. She had achieved a position of some status at work before she became pregnant and was able to maintain that on her return from maternity leave. Having some 'choice' over how they would manage the division of labour within the family gave rise to intensive negotiations within the couple's relationship involving ideas about appropriate masculinity and femininity as well as what constitutes good parenting. However it is Debbie who appears to be shouldering the burden of the identity work involved, attempting to square the circle of 'having it all'.

Rethinking the 'choice' biography: Conclusion

In our research we found a proliferation of local work-based cultures, but find that within the same organization women workers may experience very different working conditions and norms. The evidence in this chapter suggests that not only does motherhood have an impact on the kinds of workers that women are, but that work influences the ways in which women mother, not simply in terms of their presence or absence, but through the transposition of skills and values between fields of work and home. The extent to which motherhood influences the workplace itself is much more limited. For most middle-class women at least, work and mothering continue to be constituted as conflicting projects that must be 'balanced' – most often with work being fitted around children or less often with children fitted around work (Everingham et al. 2007). Moving beyond this involves a radicalizing of the couple relationship and inspecting the centrality of work to ideas of success and well-being (Stacey 1998). The relationship that a woman strikes in relation to work appears to be highly consequential in the kind of mothering project that she subsequently embarks on, including how she orients to expert advice, consumption and childcare. A longitudinal approach enables the complexity of this project to be captured and the ways in which the full impact of the 'motherhood penalty' takes time to emerge.

One of the shocks associated with pregnancy is being made to feel female at work. The dominance of a gender neutral discourse within workplaces creates a bifurcated world where questions of embodiment, care and reproduction are constituted as private matters that do not belong in the workplace yet are implicitly assumed through a reliance on an increasingly female workforce. This is the post-feminist contract conceptualized by McRobbie, where the right to assert sexual difference is traded for the right to be treated as the genderless worker. Yet sexual difference continues to exist in workplaces and our case studies illustrate the kind of work that can go into making this invisible, or at least untroubling for colleagues and employers. Despite appearances, working and mothering are entangled and entwined, creating insights that are both exciting and intolerable. One reason for this may be the divisions that motherhood asserts between women and between genderless workers. In forging private solutions to public problems women provide solutions for each other as childminders, and formal and informal carers. Again women are drawn into holding tensions between exploitation and solidarity and between instrumental and intrinsic forms of care (Maher et al. 2010). There is no inevitable correlation between female employment and the evaporation of traditional gender relations. The micro-politics through which domestic labour and childcare are shared, delegated and entrusted to others is important moral terrain in the contemporary politics of motherhood. Thinking about mothers as workers forces us to recognize the politics of class and qualifications, and chains of care that may connect families (Ehrenreich and Hochschild 2003, Chavkin and Maher 2010). By capturing women at the same biographical moment (maternity), we also capture the fragmentation of women's biographies along class lines, and the difficulties for forging solidaristic relations between women.

During the five years that we have been involved in this research, we closely followed media coverage of motherhood observing the way in which mainstream discourses of motherhood are more or less split into either/or debates (Hadfield et al. 2007). So, for example, the core issue in discussions about working mothers is whether the place of mothers is in work or at home. If they try to do both, they are not fully appreciated in either place. Present in these debates, however, is also the desire to 'rethink' or move beyond, or incorporate both sides of the argument. Social change influences new ways, perhaps more pragmatic ways, of thinking about motherhood. Women who stay at home argue that this is an independent 'choice', that being with children is not oppressive but interesting and challenging. This is not a surprising choice, when we read that even professional women suffer discrimination at work and feel undervalued and demeaned.

This research has spanned an important political transition. After 13 years of New Labour government that brought with it a commitment to support vulnerable children (realized through family tax credits, Sure Start, extension of maternity leave to one year, right to request flexible work, basic paternity leave, child trust bonds), we now have a coalition government intent on remaking the welfare state. We are seeing divisions between women on the basis of social class hardening as families seek to defend their children against downward social mobility, monopolizing the best in state provision or opting into private provision if necessary and possible. The spaces in which mothers mix diminish as state provision is reduced and targeted on the most disadvantaged. As in previous generations women are bearing the brunt of the recession both in terms of occupying the most precarious positions in the labour market, and in terms of absorbing the radical cuts to the welfare state (Thomson et al. 2010). A longitudinal research design that incorporates an intergenerational approach enables us to bring together a longer history of how previous recessions have been experienced by families with a nuanced account of the ways in which families adapt to a changing economic landscape.

By researching families in real time, we gain insights into the relationship between historical change and the making of history in the present. The relationship between feminism and motherhood has been generative yet complicated, providing a focus for activism yet also raising divisive issues concerning the centrality of biology to women's oppression, whether motherhood is part of women's self-actualization, and enduring tensions between female, maternal and child subjectivity and well-being. In 1997 Arlie Hochschild wrote about a 'stalled revolution' suggesting that the historical shift constituted through women's entry into the workforce had not been matched by a shift in the division of labour at home. She subsequently characterized feminism as 'escaping the cage' of its radical origins, increasingly put to the service of an expanding form of neoliberal global capitalism that seeks to enter and make business out of domestic spaces that women had escaped (Hochschild 2003). Over time the commercial substitutes for family activities 'often turn out better than the real thing [...] in a sense, capitalism isn't competing with itself [...] but with the family, and particularly the wife and mother' (2003: 37). Thus 'a cycle is set in motion': 'As the family becomes more minimal, it turns to the market to add what it needs and, by doing so, becomes yet more minimal' (2003: 37). In commodifying care the market incites forms of excellence and achievement that go far beyond the standards of 'good enough mothering', but which increasingly set benchmarks for new forms of distinction in a wider context of downward social mobility.

This 'slicing and dicing' of the mother's role is not entirely new, the delegation of care has a long history in upper-class households. The contemporary market for commercialized care is created by middle-class working women, and serviced by poor women, often involved in global chains of care, where mothering is displaced and reconstructed down the line (Chavkin and Maher 2010). Writing about Silicon Valley at the turn of the century, Hochschild captures something of the state of things to come for many developed Western economies. Motherhood is ripe for another round of politicization, constituting both a singular and multiple experience, connecting and dividing women, as daughters, mothers, non-mothers and grandmothers, as well as employers and employees.

Note

1. This chapter draws on Chapter 6 of *Making Modern Mothers* by R. Thomson, M. J. Kehily, L. Hadfield and S. Sharpe © (2011) reproduced by permission of

The Policy Press. The chapter uses 'we' in keeping with the original text of the book, however it is the work of the author.

References

Adkins, L. (2009) 'Feminism after measure', *Feminist Theory*, 10(3): 323–339.

Arai, L. (2009) *Teenage Pregnancy: The Making and Unmaking of a Problem*, Bristol: The Policy Press.

Armstrong, J. (2010) 'Class and gender at the intersection: Working class women's disposition towards employment and motherhood', in Y. Taylor (ed.) *Classed Intersections: Spaces, Selves, Knowledges*, Aldershot: Ashgate.

Chavkin, W. and Maher, J. (2010) *The Globalization of Motherhood: Deconstructions and Reconstructions of Biology and Care*, London: Routledge.

Crompton, R. (2006) *Employment and the Family: The Reconfiguration of Work and Family Life in Contemporary Societies*, Cambridge: Cambridge University Press.

Cunningham-Burley, S., Backett-Milburn, K. and Kemmer, D. (2005) 'Balancing work and family life: Mothers' views', in L. McKie and S. Cunningham-Burley (eds) *Families in Society: Boundaries and Relationships*, Bristol: Policy Press.

Davies, H., Joshi, H., Rake, K. and Alami, R. (2000) *Women's Incomes over the Lifetime: A Report to the Women's Unit*, London: Cabinet Office.

Duncan, S., Edwards, R., Reynolds, T. and Alldred, P. (2003) 'Motherhood, paid work and partnering: Values and theories', *Work, Employment and Society*, 17(2): 309–330.

Ehrenreich, B. and Hochschild, A. (2003) *Global Woman: Nannies, Maids and Sex Workers in the New Economy*, London: Granta Books.

Everingham, C., Stevenson, D. and Warner-Smith, P. (2007) 'Things are getting better all the time? Challenging the narrative of women's progress from a generational perspective', *Sociology*, 41(3): 419–437.

Ferri, E. and Smith, K. (2003) 'Partnership and parenthood', in E. Ferri, J. Bynner and M. Wadsworth (eds) *Changing Britain, Changing Lives: Three Generations at the Turn of the Century*, Bedford Way papers, London: University of London Institute of Education, pp. 105–132.

Gattrell, C. (2005) *Hard Labour: The Sociology of Parenthood*, Maidenhead: Open University Press.

Gillies, V. (2006) *Marginalised Mothers: Exploring Working-Class Experiences of Parenting*, London: Routledge.

Hadfield, L., Rudoe, N. and Sanderson-Mann, J. (2007) 'Motherhood, choice and the British media: A time to reflect', *Gender and Education*, 19(2): 255–263.

Hakim, C. (2000) *Work-Lifestyle Choices in the 21st Century: Preference Theory*, Oxford: Oxford University Press.

Harkness, S. and Waldfogel, J. (1999) *The Family Gap in Pay: Evidence from Seven Industrialised Countries*, CASE paper 29.

Hochschild, A. (2003) *The Commercialization of Intimate Life: Notes from Home and Work*, San Francisco, Los Angeles and London: University of California Press.

Lawler, S. (2000) *Mothering the Self: Mothers, Daughters, Subjects*, London: Routledge.

Lewis, J. (1992) *Women in Britain since 1945*, Oxford: Blackwell.

Lyonette, C., Baldauf, B. and Behle, H. (2010) ' "Quality" part-time work: A review of the evidence,' University of Warwick, Institute for Employment Research/Government Equalities Office. Available at: http://sta.geo.useconnect.co.uk/pdf/Review%20of%20Evidence.pdf.

Maher, J., Lindsay, J. and Bardoel, A. (2010) 'Freeing time: The family time economies of nurses', *Sociology*, 44(2): 269–287.

McRobbie, A. (2007) 'Top girls?: Young women and the post-feminist sexual contract', *Cultural Studies*, 21(4–5): 718–737.

Pettinger, L., Parry, J., Taylor, R. and Glucksmann, M. (2005) *A New Sociology of Work?* Oxford: Blackwell.

Phoenix, A. (2008) 'Claiming liveable lives: Adult subjectification and narratives of "non-normative" childhood experiences', in D. Stauneas and J. Kofoed (eds) *Play in Power*, Copenhagen: Danmarks Paedagogiske Universitesforlag.

Ponsford, R. (2011) 'Consumption, resilience and respectability amongst young mothers in Bristol', *Journal of Youth Studies*, 14(5): 541–560.

Power, N. (2009) *One Dimensional Women*, Winchester/ Washington: Zero Books.

Reynolds, T. (2006) *Caribbean Mothers: Identity and Experience in the UK*, London: Tufnell Press.

Rudoe, N. (2011) *Young Mothers, Education and Exclusion*, unpublished PhD, the Open University.

Sharpe, S. (1984) *Double Identity: The Lives of Working Mothers*, London: Pelican.

Stacey, J. (1998) *Brave New Families: Stories of Domestic Upheaval in the Late Twentieth Century America*, Los Angeles: UCLA Press.

Thomson, R. (2010) 'Using biographical and longitudinal methods: Researching motherhood', in J. Mason and A. Dale (eds) *Understanding Social Research: Thinking Creatively about Method*, London: Sage.

Thomson, R., Hadfield, L., Kehily, M. J. and Sharpe, S. (2011) *Making Modern Mothers*, Bristol: The Policy Press.

Thomson, R., Hadfield, L., Kehily, M. J. and Sharpe, S. (2010) 'Family fortunes: An intergenerational perspective on recession', *Twenty-First Century Society Journal of the Academy of Social Sciences*, 5(2): 149.

Woodroffe, J. (2009) *Not Having It All: How Motherhood Reduces Women's Pay and Employment Prospects*, London: Fawcett Society.

7

Responsibility, Work and Family Life: Children's and Parents' Experiences of Working Parenthood

Jeni Harden, Alice MacLean, Kathryn Backett-Milburn, Sarah Cunningham-Burley and Lynn Jamieson

Introduction

In the UK, more children than ever before are being brought up by parents who are engaged in some form of paid employment outside the home (Philo et al. 2008). This change has been met with interest by academics, policy-makers and indeed employers, with particular concern about how the demands of work and family are managed by parents and the impact this has on children's lives. The challenges of reconciling the competing demands of paid work and family life on parents' time have been acknowledged at a political level (OECD 2007) and research has offered insights into how the competing frameworks of work and family are constructed and managed by parents (Daly 2001, Cunningham-Burley et al. 2006, Backett-Milburn et al. 2008, Ba 2010). In particular it has been noted that working parents express a feeling of being 'harried' (Southerton and Tomlinson 2005), of being constantly busy (Brannen 2005) and of their time being 'squeezed' (Southerton 2003).

Implicit in these discussions of working parenthood is the notion of parental responsibility. Emphasis is placed on the challenges that working parents experience in 'juggling' their work and parental responsibilities, specifically addressing the potential negative impact that working parenthood can have on children's lives by limiting the amount of time and the nature of time spent with children. The concept of responsibility lies at the heart of the government's vision for how the UK should change. In an article in *The Guardian* in 2010, Prime Minister David Cameron said 'At the heart of the breakdown of trust in society is a breakdown of personal responsibility. Personal responsibility is the foundation of an ethical society. Without it we cannot hope for people to ask the right questions of themselves' (Cameron 2010). What is most pertinent here is that while this is presented as an inclusive concept involving everyone taking responsibility for their communities, parents are singled out for attention. In 2008 David Cameron said that parental responsibility was the 'task for a generation' (Ryan 2008).

However, the way in which this notion of responsibility features in parents' accounts of working parenthood has not been fully addressed. Moreover, despite children being considered to be 'active family members' playing a key role in how families reconcile work and family life (Ridge 2007), their views are often absent from the discussion. In this chapter, through an investigation of the everyday lives of working families (children and parents), we explore the construction of responsibility; how this is reflected in family practices, that is, the everyday routines that families engage in (Morgan 2011), and how it may change over time. This chapter draws on data from a qualitative longitudinal study with working families and considers the ways in which children and parents[1] construct and negotiate responsibility in relation to their everyday experiences of working parenthood. We discuss responsibility through the notion of 'being there'; the implications of competing responsibilities; and the shifting nature of responsibilities in the context of change. As various researchers have observed, the burden of this responsibility may be experienced rather differently by mothers and fathers (see Irwin and Winterton, and Henwood et al. in this volume) but the focus of this paper is on comparing parents' views, mothers and fathers, of their responsibilities, with how their children understand them. Experiences of working parenthood are dynamic, changing in response to changes in work and family circumstances, including those in the lives of children, and negotiated, between parents and children. A qualitative longitudinal study offers the opportunity to explore these dynamics and negotiations over time. Before going on to discuss the findings, we will outline the project from which the data are drawn.

The study

In this chapter, we present data from a three-year qualitative longitudinal study entitled 'Work and family lives: The changing experiences of 'young' families' (WFL). The aim of the study was to investigate processes of negotiation between parents and their primary-school-aged children in addressing issues raised by working parenthood; how such issues impacted on family practices; and how these changed over time. The sample comprised 14 families recruited from a variety of employment, community and education sites. Fourteen mothers, eight fathers and 16 children participated, of whom five were lone-mother households and nine heterosexual couple families.[2] Children were aged between 7 and 11 years at the inception of the research. This age group was chosen because the children still required childcare but were also entering a period of transition, particularly as they moved on to secondary school (Borland et al. 1998). All parents were in paid employment apart from two fathers who were retired due to ill health. We aimed to recruit a range of working families in terms of job type and income. Of the 20 employed parents, 11 worked full-time and nine part-time. Eleven parents worked in the public, six in the private and three in the third sector. Recruitment was based on a form of quota sampling with the intention of recruiting ten lower income (i.e. below the UK average £33,956) and ten higher income families. However despite many different recruitment strategies, it was only possible to recruit four lower income families.[3]

The study entailed three waves of data collection: individual interviews conducted with parents and children separately in waves 1 and 3, and a group interview conducted with all family members in wave 2. The waves were carried out approximately nine months apart, from 2007 to 2009, with the time between the wave 1 and the wave 3 interviews averaging 18 months. While this is a fairly short period of time in families' lives, it was possible to explore the ways in which they experienced change in the context of working parenthood. Each fieldwork wave had a specific thematic focus (e.g. experiences of time during a working day; experiences of leisure time and holidays; values in relation to employment). Changes over time in relation to work and family and the spaces between them (e.g. childcare, leisure) were also explored longitudinally. The concept of responsibility was addressed directly in the interviews but was also embedded in much of the parents' and children's discussion of their experiences and concerns. In order to build a rich and complex picture of everyday family life and practices, we took a multiple perspectives approach (Harden et al. 2010) by eliciting parents' and children's viewpoints. Individual interviews were semi-structured and lasted one to two hours for parents and 30 minutes to an hour for children. Children's interviews included some activities (e.g. drawing, vignettes, choosing from stickers of faces showing a range of emotions) as a springboard for discussion (Harden et al. 2000); parents also responded to some of the vignettes. All interviews were audio recorded, transcribed verbatim and potential identifiers were anonymized.

As an advantage of our longitudinal design we were able to include family group interviews, a method rarely used in family sociology due to concerns about silencing children in the context of generational power dynamics (Harden et al. 2010). It has been claimed that family interviews, through the interaction they stimulate, can reveal the 'tone and personality of a family [...] in a way that interviewing individual family members cannot' (Eggenberger and Nelms 2007: 290). While we do not view the family group interviews data as wholly 'naturally occurring' (Smithson 2000) or representing a straightforward reflection of family dynamics and power relationships present on a daily basis, we used this method as a means of shedding some light on the group dynamics and interplay of personalities within each family. We conducted the family group interviews in-between rounds of individual interviews, in order that the research relationships built during the first wave would facilitate discussions and, particularly, creating the possibility that children would feel empowered by having been listened to in their first interview and, consequently, better able to voice their opinions in the presence of parents and siblings. In order to engage both children and parents in the group discussion, careful consideration was given to the methods used and topics raised. Family interviews were also semi-structured and lasted one to two hours. They featured activities designed to encourage interaction and discussion between family members. There were very few examples of parents talking for, or instead of, children. Nevertheless, parents influenced children's contributions in a number of ways, including facilitating them by asking additional questions, modifying them by disagreeing or presenting an alternative point of view, and controlling them by quieting dominant children in order to give others a say. There was also evidence of parents modifying and policing one another's accounts as well as of children questioning and contradicting parents' and siblings' accounts, suggesting that it is by no means clear how power relations will play out within the research process (MacLean and Harden 2012).

Analyses were conducted iteratively between interviews and waves to inform analytical reflections and enhance subsequent data collection. Analysis initially focused on family groups in team analytic discussion meetings. This provided an in-depth exploration of the roles and identities constructed by family members across the different research contexts and over time. While this focus on the multiple perspectives within families has proven to be a rich source of data, we also identified a need for an across families overview; this enabled us to compare and contrast children's and parents' accounts from their generational stand-points as well as the experiences of families in similar socio-economic circumstances, and with similar family structures.

As part of our multiple perspectives approach, one of our analytic tasks was to ensure equal consideration was given to children's and adults' accounts, despite the former often being less voluminous and in a different form due to the use of 'child friendly' methods. The analytical process was further complicated by the fact it involved analysing and comparing individual and group interview data that were very different in nature. The individual interview data reflected the more focused and detailed one-to-one interaction between the researcher and the participant, whereas the family group interview data were characterized predominantly by interaction between participants themselves, and there was potential for this to affect the direction and depth of the discussion. Analysis of the individual interview data involved interpreting participants' responses and considering ways in which the researcher had contributed to their construction. Analysis of the family interview data paid attention to the ways in which the group context and interaction between family members influenced the data which were generated and the way in which children's and parents' accounts may have been controlled, inhibited or facilitated by one another's presence and utterances, as well as those of the researcher. We have reflected in more detail on aspects of analysing multiple perspectives over time, particularly issues of power and truth (Harden et al. 2010). Analysis was facilitated by NVivo wherein transcripts were systematically coded according to a range of broad emergent themes. As a longitudinal study, the identification of change over time was a strand of analysis which cross-cut all themes.

Responsibility as 'being there': When worlds collide

Morgan (2011) refers to the 'ethical turn' in family studies, noting the significance of both public moralities, (re)enforced through public discourse such as the discourse of parental responsibility, but also the embeddedness of moral narratives in everyday decision-making and in the routines he describes as family practices. Parents' accounts are also often moral tales, containing value statements about their own or others' actions (Ribbens McCarthy et al. 2000), often conveyed through shorthand concepts that mask the complexities of what lies beneath them (see the chapters by Irwin and Winterton, and Henwood et al. in this volume for discussion of the gendered nature of these accounts). In our study, 'being there' was a moral narrative through which the concept of responsibility was expressed.

'Being there' was present in the parents' and children's accounts of the challenges that the articulation of work and family created. In much of the work/family literature, there is a discussion of the challenges of synchronization of individual family member's schedules leading to an actual or perceived increased tempo at which life is experienced (Southerton and Tomlinson 2005). In our study, the need to 'be' in several places at specific times was described by many of the parents and children as problematic. For example Jack said,

> Well we all have to rush and stuff, it's a bit tiring and stuff, my mum gets a bit grumpy because she needs to get to work and today she was in a mega rush because she had to have meetings just before school started.
>
> (Jack Erskine, aged 8, mother working part-time)

Most of the children were also involved in a range of activities, often on weekdays, and parents made considerable efforts to try and ensure that their work did not limit the children's opportunities to participate. This reflects the notion of parents' perceived responsibilities to 'be there' as a facilitator for children's extracurricular activities, as Fiona Christie described:

> I think where I find it hard is work is, you know, fairly demanding. And, you know, you go and you put your work hat ... But surrounding all of that is trying to keep everyone else doing what they do to make their lives enjoyable and to let them to progress in any way that they want.
>
> (Fiona Christie, couple, working part-time)

Family practices reflected structured, time-oriented routines through which the, often competing, demands of school, work and family were attended to. Many of the parents knew, to the minute, how long it would take them to get from their child's school to their workplace. These routines were an important part of the day, ensuring that the basic tasks of getting everyone where they needed to be on time were met, particularly during the hot spots of the day, most notably weekday mornings (Harden et al. 2012):

> So you've got a kind of routine that we're all conforming to on most days. Which is about getting up, getting out the door, getting the packed lunches made and then for me it's like stage two of the day which is then the commute to work. Stage three of the day is being at work.
>
> (Nicci Rankin, lone parent, working part-time)

However, the routines and organization did not dispel the emotions expressed by parents about 'being there'. There were feelings of guilt described by parents of not being around at key times such as school shows, but more generally of not giving enough of their time for their children:

> I suppose that's where the guilt comes in sometimes though because I don't feel like I give him enough... I don't feel I listen to him enough. Or my life, I put my life in front of his sometimes.
>
> (Debra Grieve, couple, working full-time)

There were times when the conflict between parents' work and parenting responsibilities was clearly the topic of discussion between parents and children as in the case of Gail, who works with children in her social work role:

> They get annoyed about it if I'm not there and she says quite openly that, you don't care about me, you only care about the children that you work with.
>
> (Gail Adams, lone parent, working full-time)

Parental absence in their lives has been described by young people as a key factor in their lack of well-being (Margo et al. 2006). Many of the children in our study expressed concerns about parents not 'being there'. For example Abbey said,

> It would be okay if she like worked maybe less hours but... the same amount of time only spread out a bit more so that we could see her more during the day.
>
> (Abbey Christie, aged 11, mother working full-time, father retired)

Concerns over the timing of parents' work were also expressed through the children's attitudes towards after-school care. In addition, for some, the sense of wanting to be with their parents was hard to disentangle from a desire to be at home because they would then have more opportunities to play with their friends or to play with their own things (Harden et al. 2013).

The difficulties parents described related not only to the impact of work on 'being there' at home or in transporting children to activities, but also the impact that parental responsibilities had on work. Jan Ritchie spoke of feeling guilty about her family commitments impinging on her work:

And then you get to work and then you pray to goodness that the phone is not going to go, that it's not going to be the school saying the kids are sick or the nursery saying the baby's sick or whatever... You feel like you're looking at the clock all the time and taking more time off probably than people who don't have children. So it's a real juggling act and sometimes you feel quite guilty.

(Jan Ritchie, couple, working full-time)

Many parents expressed similar concerns to Jan and there was a sense that responsibility for work meant 'being there', that is being visible in the workplace, and that arriving later than others or having to leave earlier to collect children, or to be off at times when the children were ill, was frowned upon as Rachel Erskine described:

I feel at the moment that my boss is not happy, that I've not done enough of this, or enough of that... although I do a lot of hours at home, they're invisible hours to her.

(Rachel Erskine, lone parent, working part-time)

This clearly has implications for whether flexible working arrangements, which are intended to address some of the issues working parents face, are dealing with the kind of challenges discussed above.

The significance of availability was also discussed in terms of the parents 'being there' at home. While children value parents 'being there', it has been argued that children also value control over their time (Solberg 1997, Lewis et al. 2008) and to spend 'ordinary' time as a family rather than dedicated 'quality' time (Christensen 2002). Many of the parents in our study indicated that they were aware that their children wanted them to be around more at home, that is to be available though not necessarily always to spend time with them. As Julia noted,

> I think the reality is he does like me being in the house. Although he's never in. He just likes to know that I'm there.
>
> (Julia Fisher, couple, working part-time)

Yet being there and being available is not always straightforward. Two fathers in the study worked considerable amounts of time, or entirely, from home and in these cases there was a flexibility about being able to be in the house when children came home from school but there still remained an expectation that children would fit around their work schedules. Graham Reid works from home and described some of the difficulties of distinguishing between when he was there and available and there but not available:

> He [his son] says you're always on your computer and I do have to say, look not now I'm working ... Like this morning I was working, twenty past seven he woke up and came through and ... I was chatting away to him for a bit and I said, look Lewis you need to go away now because I'm trying to do some work.
>
> (Graham Reid, couple, working full-time)

Despite the fact that for most of the parents in our study there was a physical separation between work and home, there were many ways in which the boundary between the two and so the sense of 'being there' was blurred. For some parents this meant taking work home in order to 'catch up' on work left unfinished as a result of having to leave to be home for the children. Even when not bringing work home, many parents described a sense of not being able to be fully switched off about work when at home, or vice versa, and described it as a shifting focus between 'work mode' and 'mum mode' (Gillian Nicholson, lone parent, working full-time). Some of the children discussed the implications of this. Here Hannah gave an example of when her mum was working at home:

> Once Mum was doing her work and I said, 'Can you help me with my knitting?' ... It's like she says, 'I'll do it once I've finished my work' ... So when she did it I asked her, 'Can we do it now?' and she said, 'No it's too late' .... I felt a bit upset and a bit disappointed

and I also felt, err, well let's just say I felt really dreary and I started to sob a wee bit...It's like you've lost a bit of trust. She said she'll do something with you, like then she just doesn't do it.

(Hannah Phillips, aged 10, mother working full-time)

The implications of competing responsibilities

It is clear from the data discussed above that parents often struggle to find a balance between their competing responsibilities, as Maggie Clarke described:

The whole responsibility is all bein' put onto the parents' shoulders to deal with everythin' all at the one time.

(Maggie Clarke, couple, working full-time)

Many of the parents, mostly the mothers, described being tired, exhausted, frazzled or grumpy. It was not simply the amount of work, but the sense of not being able to do any of it well that was the source of stress as Marie Wilson described:

Sometimes you feel like you're not doing 100% as a parent, some-times you feel you are not giving 100% to your work and it is just, it can be quite a stressful situation sometimes.

(Marie Wilson, couple, working full-time)

This attempt to give 100% to work and family life is perhaps an impossible challenge yet it was the bar that parents seemed to set them-selves. Nevertheless they described the ways in which any balance they achieved was precarious and that often they were just 'getting through'. For the parents in this study there had been points in their lives during which this had proved an impossible task, as a result of marriage break-down or depression following the birth of a child, but there were also everyday occasions when the attempts to do this 'plate spinning' failed. Rachel Erskine described one such incident:

I forgot the tooth fairy money one night...and he came through in tears the next morning. The fairy didn't come! And that was a huge guilt mummy moment.

(Rachel Erskine, lone parent, working part-time)

The children were very aware of their parents' moods, and often described them as tired or grumpy, relating this directly to work:

[after] she's home from work she's a bit crabbit.[4]

(Ashley Clarke, aged 9, parents working full-time)

Moreover, we have described elsewhere the ways in which the children contributed or shared the responsibilities arising from working parenthood by modifying their own behaviour, for example by doing what they were told in the mornings, in order to make life a bit easier for their parents; by contributing to domestic chores; and by engaging in acts of self-care or care for others (Harden et al. 2012).

Shifting responsibilities: The negotiation of change

As a longitudinal study we had the opportunity to explore the families' lives over time, discussing changes in children's and parents' circumstances and the impact of these on work and family life. Some of the children made the transition from primary to secondary school during the study and spoke of changes of practice in the lead up to and following the start of secondary school. For example, Simon Nicholson wanted to be given a key in his final year of primary school so that he could come straight home from school, but was told by his mother that this could not happen until he was in secondary school. By the final interview he had started secondary school and his mother described the transition that had occurred in the final months of primary school, during which time a key was left with the neighbour; Simon would come home from school, collect the key and go into the house to get changed and then go back over to the neighbour's house. Like Simon's mother, many of the parents described responsibility as something the children would grow into and, as this example indicates, the transition to secondary school was usually a key marker of change. This can be understood in part as an indication of the significance of this change in children's lives, and responsibility was linked in this context to the belief that children should become more independent as they made this transition. However negotiation of responsibility at this point should also be understood as a response by parents to the challenges presented by the lack of after-school care for children beyond primary school age.

The move from primary to secondary school was referred to as incurring changes for all family members. For example, children who had moved to secondary school outlined changes, such as having to get up and leave the house earlier, and travelling further and by public transport (instead of walking or being driven by parents). Even for the younger children in these families, it was no longer simply their parents' work but also their older siblings' school timetables which now shaped their morning routine, as was the case for Charlotte Phillips (aged 10) who had to go to a breakfast club before school because of her older sister needing to be at secondary school earlier. By their nature, such transitions provided children and parents with new temporal and spatial challenges to negotiate.

Change also occurred for a small number of families as parents moved jobs or returned to work after a period of childcare. For example, when Sheila Watson began working full-time she was no longer at home when her son Lewis came back from school, although his father, who worked at home, was there:

> Well he [dad] still works at home and on Tuesdays, Thursdays and Fridays my mum's at work all day. So my dad looks after me after school on those days. She gets home about half five... But yeah, that's fine, 'cause it's not long after school when she gets home, 'cause'... But my dad's on the computer, so I just go in the garden or play with the Lego or something.
>
> (Lewis Watson, aged 9)

Change within families can also arise from wider social changes. The timing of the study coincided with the onset of the recession in 2008 and we have discussed elsewhere the families' responses to this (MacLean et al. 2010). At that time, the families did not experience significant change in the form of job losses, but for some the uncertainty engendered by the recession was a barrier to positive change. Archie Ritchie spoke in the first interview of wanting to change jobs to be closer to home, making him more available for the family. By the third interview, he hoped for 'no change' to his job and planned to keep his 'head down' in his current position. He described his concerns about not being as much a part of his children's life as he would like, yet feeling that there was no choice in this:

> And also the kids, you miss them during the day and it's just... like I said it's the best part of your life, it is, it hurts when you have to go away and not spend time with them but it's just the practicalities of living isn't it?
>
> (Archie Ritchie, couple, working full-time)

This powerlessness to bring about change was also, perhaps more predictably, expressed by the children. For example, Ryan Clarke (aged 9) spoke about not liking the after-school club because there was a boy that he did not like there, but when asked whether that put him off going he said 'It doesn't matter, I dinnae get to choose if I want to go or not'. The children also seemed restricted in their sense of being able to discuss this topic or to negotiate any change. However we have to understand this through the significance of work in the parents' accounts of their families.

In both the children's and the parents' accounts work was presented as a taken for granted assumption in their lives, 'it's just what they do' (Calum Ritchie, aged 10), and so limited the nature of any negotiation of change that could be made. Many of the families described themselves through work, for example Jane Heath spoke of her family as a working family, that is, work was 'in their nature'. In addition, both parents and children referred to the financial need to work. Our findings suggest that parents drew on monetary incentives as a shorthand way to explain their need to work to children, rather than conveying their views of work as bringing enjoyment, fulfilment and opportunities for social interaction. The latter sentiments were often tempered by feelings of guilt, as Nicci Rankin described:

> I do have an element of guilt but I have to bring myself back from that because you can't live your life like that. Because if I didn't have fulfilment at work I probably wouldn't be a very good parent.
>
> (Nicci Rankin, lone parent, working part-time)

Given the feelings of guilt that parents expressed around 'being there', it may be more difficult for parents to justify their work to their children as something that they *want* to rather than *have* to do. When parents, particularly mothers, can read media reports of their 'selfishness' and the damage that working causes their children, this response is perhaps not surprising (Easton 2009). As a result, the juggling of work and family life, despite presenting difficulties that have an impact both on parents' and children's lives, was often normalized and presented as something to be dealt with rather than changed.

Conclusion

Recent years have seen an increasing focus in policy on parenting as the foundation of society and 'good' parenting as the key to addressing many of society's present ills (Lupton 2004, Gillies 2008). Parental responsibility is presented as a moral obligation and failure to perform that obligation adequately may be considered as a moral failure with implications for society's future (Wyness 2000). As Lister notes, 'it is as citizen-workers of the future that children figure as the prime assets of the "social investment state" ' (Lister 2006: 322). This emphasis on parental responsibility reflects current changes to family policy across Europe (Churchill 2011). Working parents are often positioned at the intersection of policies that raise inherent tensions (Driver and Martell 2002). The power of parenting as a social panacea is reflected not just in family policy, but also in employment policy. However much the value of parenting in general is stressed, there is, in tandem with this, a clear expectation that it is *working* parents who are particularly valued and who are best meeting the ideal of the responsible, active citizen.

We have shown how longitudinal research with families over time enabled us to explore the ways in which responsibility is experienced and negotiated between parents and children in the context of working parenthood. Consistently across time and circumstances, parents described responsibility to others, both parental and in employment or education, as involving 'being there'. For parents, this understanding of responsibility was the idiom for expressing feelings of being torn between and of juggling different parts of their lives, although the practical dilemmas faced changed over time, with new demands and insecurities in employment for parents and with children's transitions from primary to secondary school. However, it also represents a reality in which the competing demands on parents' and children's time are experienced. Both children's and parents' lives are structured by the need to synchronize their times and both expressed a sense of living life at speed. Family practices in part then become focused on routines and organization with which everyone is expected to comply.

'Being there' reflects the way responsibilities are experienced in different spheres of life, and by parents and children. For parents 'being there' means fulfilling their perceived parental responsibilities, which can involve spending time with their children, as well as a more general sense of being able to be around when they are needed. Equally, it refers to being visible in the workplace, that is, being *seen* to be fulfilling their work responsibilities. For children, 'being there' reflected a desire to spend more time at home with parents but also, as Christensen (2002) found, it meant having parents around even if they were not engaged in family activities. Being there is therefore connected to place, to being in a particular place whether it be home or work, but also relates to availability. This is most apparent when parents work from home or bring work home with them. While physically present in the home, they are not always available for children – there but not there. This also reflects the blurring of the boundaries of work and home as parents juggle their dual responsibilities often feeling that they are never fully 'being' in either role. Change was restricted by the financial circumstances of their lives, and the experience of juggling the competing demands on their time, though causing anxiety and stress, was often considered unavoidable and was to a large extent normalized. This normalization, emphasizing the responsibility to work as a necessity for sustaining family life while remaining relatively silent on any personal pleasures or benefits from it, helped adults manage their guilt and rebuff objections to not 'being there'.

Particular notions of child–adult relations are embedded in the concept of parental responsibility, reflected in policies. Children are the object of parental responsibility, reflecting particular constructions of childhood as a stage in life that should be characterized, in part, by the absence of responsibility (Wyness 2000). Within the context of working parenthood, Miller and Ridge (2008) present a more reciprocal notion of responsibility, with both parents and children as active in the everyday processes that construct the 'family–work project'. Indeed, research with children indicates that responsibility is a key part of their identity construction, and their relations with peers and parents (Such and Walker 2004). Within our study there was evidence of responsibility as contested between parents and children.

The children, to a large extent, accepted working parenthood and the implications this had for their lives. They complied with the everyday routines, and contributed through various forms of caring. Yet at times they also disrupted routines, asked for more time from parents, questioned parents' commitment to them or their need to work. Responsibility was defined primarily by both parents and children as an adult concept, as something that adults possess and that children will grow into, earn or be given by adults. Moreover, children's capacity for bringing about any change in their circumstances was limited by the extent to which the change fitted with adult perceptions of children's responsibility and the demands of working parenthood. There were particular age expectations around when children should, and could, be given more responsibility, for example in domestic chores and in coming home alone after school. This was most evident in the negotiation of change associated with the period of transition to secondary school, which both parents and children used as a bargaining tool. For children in our study, having responsibility was often described in terms of having control over their own time. The issue of whether or not they were regarded as responsible was brought to the fore by being allowed to be at home without co-present parental supervision.

Responsibility was therefore central in understanding families' experiences of working parenthood and reflects and shapes the way in which these experiences are constructed and negotiated over time. Qualitative longitudinal research with parents and children allows us to present a more complex picture of working parenthood, the challenges families face and how these challenges are perceived and addressed over time.

Notes

1. We refer here to parents and do not discuss the differing experiences of mothers and fathers. A secondary analysis of the data from this project, focusing on gender relations has been conducted and is included in this book (Chapter 8).
2. In one of the heterosexual couple families, a father declined to participate resulting in this portion of the sample being made up of nine mothers and eight fathers.
3. The income for lone parents was above the UK average of £16,744 for lone parents working 16 hours or more, while the sample included couple families whose incomes ranged from significantly below to well above the UK average of £33,956 for coupled parents both working 16 hours or more (Philo et al. 2008).
4. Scottish word for grumpy.

References

Ba, S. (2010) 'Meaning and structure in the work and family interface', *Sociological Research Online*, 15(3). Available at http://www.socresonline.org.uk/15/3/10. html#.

Backett-Milburn, K., Airey, L., McKie, L. and Hogg, G. (2008) 'Family comes first or open all hours? How low paid women working in food retailing manage webs of obligation at home and at work', *Sociological Review*, 56(3): 474–496.

Borland, M., Laybourn, A., Hill, M. and Brown, J. (1998) *Middle Childhood: The Perspectives of Children and Parents*, London: Jessica-Kingsley Publishers Ltd.

Brannen, J. (2005) 'Time and the negotiation of work-family boundaries: Autonomy or illusion?', *Time and Society*, 14(1): 113–131.

Cameron, D. (2010) 'Return to responsibility', *The Guardian*, 27 February 2010. Available at http://www.guardian.co.uk/commentisfree/2010/feb/27/david-cameron-personal-responsibility.

Christensen, P. (2002) 'Why more "quality time" is not on the top of children's lists: The "qualities of time" for children', *Children and Society*, 16: 77–88.

Churchill, H. (2011) *Parental Rights and Responsibilities: Analysing Social Policy and Lived Experiences*, Bristol: Policy Press.

Cunningham-Burley, S., Backett-Milburn, K. and Kemmer, D. (2006) 'Construct-ing health and sickness in the context of motherhood and paid work', *Sociology of Health and Illness*, 28(4): 385–409.

Daly, K. J. (2001), 'Deconstructing family time: From ideology to lived experi-ence', *Journal of Marriage and Family*, 63: 283–294.

Driver, S. and Martell, L. (2002) 'New labour, work and the family', *Social Policy and Administration*, 36(1): 46–61.

Easton, M. (2009) 'Selfish adults damage childhood', *BBC News Online*. Available at http://news.bbc.co.uk/1/hi/7861762.stm.

Eggenberger, S. and Nelms, T. (2007) 'Family interviews as a method for family research', *Journal of Advanced Nursing*, 58(3): 282–292.

Gillies, V. (2008) 'Perspectives on parenting responsibility: Contextualizing values and practice', *Journal of Law and Society*, 35(1): 95–112.

Harden, J., Backett-Milburn, K., Hill, M. and MacLean, A. (2010) 'Oh, what a tangled web we weave: Experiences of doing "multiple perspectives" research in families', *International Journal of Social Research Methodology*, 13(5): 441–452.

Harden, J., Backett-Milburn, K., MacLean, A., Cunningham-Burley, S. and Jamieson, L. (2013) 'Home and away: Constructing childhood in the context of working parenthood', *Children's Geographies*, 11(3): 298–310.

Harden, J., MacLean, A., Backett-Milburn, K. and Cunningham-Burley, S. (2012) 'The "family-work project": Children's and parents' experiences of working parenthood', *Families, Relationships and Societies*, 1(2): 207–222.

Harden, J., Scott, S., Backett-Milburn, K. and Jackson, S. (2000) 'Can't talk, Won't Talk?: Methodological issues in researching Children', *Sociological Research Online*, 5(2). Available at://www.socresonline.org.uk/5/2/harden.html.

Lewis, J., Noden, P. and Sarre, S. (2008) 'Parents' working hours: Adolescent children's views and experiences', *Children and Society*, 22(6): 429–439.

Lister, R. (2006) 'Children (but not women) first: New Labour, child welfare and gender', *Critical Social Policy*, 26(2): 315–335.

Lupton, D. (2004) ' "A grim health future": Food risks in the Sydney press', *Health, Risk & Society*, 6(2): 187–200.

MacLean, A. and Harden, J. (2012), 'Generating group accounts with par-ents & children in qualitative longitudinal research: A practical & eth-ical guide', *Timescapes Methods Guide Series*, Guide No. 8. Available at http://www.timescapes.leeds.ac.uk/assets/files/methods-guides/timescapes-harden-generating-group-accounts.pdf.

MacLean, A., Harden, J. and Backett-Milburn, K. (2010) 'Financial trajectories: How parents and children discussed the impact of the recession', *21st Century Society*, 5(2): 159–170.

Margo, J., Dixon, M., Pearce, N. and Reed, H. (2006) *Freedoms Orphans: Raising Youth in a Changing World*, London: Institute for Public Policy Research.

Millar, J. and Ridge, T. (2008) 'Relationships of care: Working lone mothers, their children and employment sustainability', *Journal of Social Policy*, 38(1): 103–121.

Morgan, D. (2011) *Rethinking Family Practices*, Basingstoke: Palgrave Macmillan.

OECD (2007) 'Babies and bosses: Reconciling work and family life: A syn-thesis of findings for OECD countries', *OECD Social Issues/Migration/Health*, 20: 1–217.

Philo, D., Maplethorpe, N., Connoly, A. and Toomse, M. (2008) *Families with Children in Britain: Findings from the 2007 Families and Children Study* (FACS), Department for Work and Pensions: Research Report 578, London: Department for Work and Pensions.

Ribbens McCarthy, J., Edwards, R. and Gillies, V. (2000) 'Moral tales of the child and the adult: Narratives of contemporary family lives under changing circumstances', *Sociology*, 34(4): 785–803.

Ridge, T. (2007) 'It's a family affair: Low income children's perspectives on maternal work', *Journal of Social Policy*, 36(3): 399–416.

Ryan, R. (2008) 'Cameron: Parental responsibility is "task for a generation" ', *The Guardian*, 10 April 2008. Available at http://www.guardian.co.uk/politics/2008/apr/10/conservatives.davidcameron.

Smithson, J. (2000), 'Using and analysing focus groups: Limitations and possibilities', *International Journal of Social Research Methodology*, 3(2): 103–119.

Solberg, A. (1997) 'Negotiating childhood: Changing constructions of age for Norwegian children', in A. James and A. Prout (eds) *Constructing and Reconstructing Childhood: Contemporary Issues in the Sociological Study of Childhood*, London: Falmer Press.

Southerton, D. (2003) ' "Squeezing time", allocating practices, coordinating networks and scheduling society', *Time and Society*, 12(1): 5–25.

Southerton, D. and Tomlinson, M. (2005) 'Pressed for time: The differential impacts of a "time squeeze" ', *The Sociological Review*, 53(2): 215–239.

Such, E. and Walker, R. (2004) 'Being responsible and responsible beings: Children's understanding of responsibility', *Children and Society*, 18: 231–242.

Wyness, M. (2000) *Contesting Childhoods*, London: Falmer Press.

8
Gender and Work–Family Conflict: A Secondary Analysis of Timescapes Data

Sarah Irwin and Mandy Winterton

Introduction

Recent decades have seen a growing interest in the reuse of extant qualitative data and a remarkable expansion in the possibilities for doing so with the exponential growth in electronic data storage and archiving capacity. Research funders have sought to encourage reuse and data sharing through investing in archiving infrastructure and requiring research bids to include proposals for depositing and sharing data (Van den Eynden et al. 2011, Neale and Bishop 2012). The secondary analysis of large data sets is a standard practice in quantitative research, but the secondary analysis of qualitative data entails unique challenges. There has been some controversy over the logic of undertaking secondary analysis of qualitative data. The orientation of qualitative research to context, specificity and meaning, and the embeddedness of data in the purposes of the primary researchers, in their disciplinary and theoretical concerns, and in the specific contexts through which they generate data makes their secondary analysis a potentially fraught undertaking. Alongside epistemological issues and methodological questions are a range of ethical challenges. These issues are widely discussed and addressed in detail elsewhere (e.g. Bishop 2006, 2009, Mason 2007, Hammersley 2010, Irwin and Winterton 2012, Mauthner and Parry 2012). Most concur that secondary analysis has a role to play both in enhancing sociological understanding, as well as a potentially valuable role in informing policy.

Qualitative secondary analysis was an integral part of the Timescapes programme. As well as a range of secondary analytic activities within and across the project teams, Timescapes included a dedicated secondary analysis project. The latter was undertaken by the current authors and ran within the final two years of the overall five-year Timescapes project duration. In this period we sought to develop insights into, and resources for, undertaking secondary analysis of qualitative data through substantive worked examples. One of these revolved around exploring the scope for working across different primary project data sets. The research questions we evolved in advancing this work related to gendered experiences and manifestations of work–family conflict, working with data from two of the Timescapes projects (see Irwin and Winterton 2011b for an account of how we arrived at research questions). Before exploring the methodological issues we confronted, we offer a brief account of literature and evidence relating to gender and work–family conflict.

Gender, paid work and family commitments: Experiences of 'work–family conflict'

The latter decades of the twentieth century saw a very significant increase in the employment participation rate of mothers of young children, a pattern underpinned by a complex set of intersecting social and economic processes (Walby 1997, Irwin 2005, Perrons et al. 2005). In a longer-term historical context, the developments amounted to a partial undoing of the breadwinner/component wage earner pattern of family resourcing (Creighton 1999). The prior (highly gender unequal) twentieth century 'accommodation' between paid employment and childrearing commitments occurred through a marked division of labour by gender. This model gave way to a dual-earner model, in which women's earnings became more important to reproduction, and women's work more the norm in the period of family building (Crompton 2002, Irwin 2005). A significant increase in mothers' paid employment rates since the 1970s reflects some improvements in opportunities in education and employment, albeit with uneven outcomes for women. It has been accompanied by ongoing asymmetry in the domestic sphere, in which women remain positioned as primary carers (e.g. Perrons et al. 2005). In the UK, the increase in mothers' paid employment participation occurred despite limited state support for childcare. This means that people find pragmatic solutions as best they can, and see work–life tensions as a private problem to be resolved or accommodated within families (Perrons et al. 2005, Crompton and Lyonette 2006, Edlund 2011, also Harden et al., this volume). Commonly women seek a part-time work solution, often at the expense of pay and prospects. Where both parents work, they may work shifts, manage childcare 'around' their work, draw on their own parents for care provision or pay for formal workplace or private childcare. Frequently families absorb the tensions of managing discrepant childrearing and employment time schedules into the fabric of day-to-day family and personal life.

A range of analyses of large-scale quantitative data allow international comparisons of the extent of work–life conflict, which appears notably high amongst full-time employees in the UK context, particularly as hours are high and state supports for dual-earner families minimal (e.g. Crompton and Lyonette 2006). Although the proportion of men's time contributing to domestic work has increased over recent decades, domestic tasks remain highly gendered (Kan et al. 2011; and reviewing US and international evidence, Bianchi and Milkie 2010). Overall the evidence reveals a growing problem of work–family conflict, and experience of time stress amongst fathers as well as mothers, but the weight of this falls disproportionately on working mothers (e.g. Crompton and Lyonette 2006, Edlund 2011). Extensive qualitative research documents household level experiences and perceptions of conflict in managing paid work and childrearing commitments. Analyses across different country contexts document the highly gendered divisions of labour within childrearing, and in managing work–life balance itself (e.g. Vincent et al. 2004 in the UK, Forsberg 2009 in Sweden, Morehead 2001 in Australia). Ongoing gender differences are a complex outcome of economic and social structural arrangements and cultural norms (e.g. Latshaw 2011). The gendered asymmetry in experiences of work–family conflict is not only an outcome of how women are situated 'between' formal paid work and childcare and childrearing commitments. For Vincent, people make choices but they

> work within a 'dominant cultural script' [...] that posits men's involvement [in childcare] as laudatory but still voluntary.
> (Vincent et al. 2004: 383)

Cultural processes exert an overlapping but independent influence in positioning women as the primary carer (Vincent et al. 2004, cf. Doucet 2009). Even where women take on extensive employment responsibilities this does not absolve them from societal, and deeply engrained personal, assumptions.

Across diverse country contexts researchers have documented the still highly gendered 'resolutions' made to reconcile competing demands, with women bearing a disproportionate weight (e.g. Morehead 2001, Forsberg 2009). Evidence also points to ways in which women take on themselves the task of synchronizing conflicting timetables and the work of 'managing' work–life balance; that is, making arrangements around childcare, managing who will do what and carrying the mental and emotional work of ensuring that everyone's needs are met (Morehead 2001, Forsberg 2009). Further evidence suggests that where women experience or perceive difficulties, they see these in terms of their own inadequacies or failures and rarely as a systemic failing (Rose 2011, Thomson et al. 2011). Some have argued for further research into the specific contexts in which particular gendered experiences and practices are manifested (e.g. Latshaw 2011) to enhance understanding of how these are underpinned. Researching gendered experiences of work–family conflict, and if and how this varied across contexts, became an objective of our own secondary analysis.

Methods

We have elsewhere discussed various epistemological, conceptual and methodological issues confronting secondary analysts of qualitative data (e.g. Irwin and Winterton 2012). We provide a brief indication of some of the challenges we needed to address. The secondary analysis project was included within the overall Timescapes grant and time-frame, and run within a two-year period across the final stages of the overall project. This meant that it ran concurrently with primary projects. The Timescapes archive was in its design stages. The timing meant that some projects were still undertaking fieldwork, and new waves of data generation, and most were still preparing data for the archive, as well as undertaking their analysis and writing. We therefore sought access to data directly from teams where they were ready to make it available for reuse purposes. The process raised challenging practical issues for primary and secondary teams, along with ethical issues relating to data ownership and access (see Neale and Bishop 2012).

In our secondary analysis work as a whole, we undertook a range of different activities. This included conceptual and methodological work (e.g. Irwin and Winterton 2011a, b); exploring the scope for working across qualitative and quantitative data (e.g. Irwin 2011); undertaking analysis of responses to a small set of questions asked in common across the Timescapes projects (Irwin et al. 2012); and undertaking a qualitative longitudinal case-based analysis of social class and teenagers' evolving biographies and expectations about accessing higher education drawing on data from the Timescapes 'Young lives and times' project (Winterton and Irwin 2012). In this chapter we discuss an analysis of data which was part of our efforts to follow another secondary analysis strategy, specifically working *across* a subset of Timescapes data sets, centring on themes they held in common and asking whether we could engender a meaningful analytic conversation across them.

We needed to decide on new research questions we might meaningfully ask within and across projects. The starting point was of necessity an unusual one: designing research questions to suit the available data. We came to projects with broad conceptual questions that we then sought to refine on reading available data on specific substantive themes. We had familiarized ourselves with the projects' aims, research designs and fieldwork instruments. We had gained an early understanding of projects too through our work on the small set of common questions asked across all projects. We further explored the data supplied to us directly by the project teams, and generated a list of themes and potential questions for further exploration. We documented these (Irwin and Winterton 2011b) in a discussion document shared with the project teams. Having invited their reflections upon it, and on our evolving research questions, we then met with the teams to explore with them our understanding of the data sets, and concerns they held relating to undertaking secondary analysis of 'live' project data. We settled on a set of questions relating to gender in contexts of parenting young families, a theme within three of the Timescapes projects and an area of interest to us as analysts. We focused on the longitudinal data to which we had access across two of the projects: 'Work and family lives' (WFL) and 'Men as fathers', both the subject of other chapters in this volume.[1]

Recognizing the nature of data as contextually produced is important to effective qualitative research. For us, working across projects as well as with longitudinal data highlighted the contextual situatedness of data. The significance of the research designs, their samples, methods and interviewers' interests were particularly visible. In respect of data relevant to analysing experiences of work–life conflict, the two projects we drew on had very different disciplinary and conceptual underpinnings, different sets of research questions and different kinds of sample. It was therefore important to consider if, and how, we could work in a way which would allow a meaningful analytic 'conversation' across the differently constituted data sets.

In the analysis below, we consider gender and time stress in the family lives of parents with young (primary school age) children.[2] In our initial readings of the available data we were struck by the extremely gendered, at times seemingly almost stereotypical assignation of gendered roles and manifestation of different experiences amongst mothers and fathers in families with young children. There were working mothers who sounded almost at breaking point; managing childcare, feeling always on call, anxious about the phone ringing at work in case it was school requiring them to leave work to collect a poorly child, even managing social relationships with an eye to help with childcare, and feeling guilt about compromising, not achieving their best for their children and not performing as they would like to at work. There were some fathers who seemed to experience time stress yet even when they did they were typically at a remove from the hurly burly of practical arrangements and took a secondary role in childcare. Where fathers had an unusually close involvement with practical issues, they still referred to shutting themselves away in the loo for half an hour or retreating to a garden shed. Elsewhere so-called 'work–life balance' issues amongst men appeared to be struck much more on terms of their own choosing, finding space for independent leisure activities for example, or asserting autonomy and authority over time.

Through a reading of data across data sets, we chose to focus in on two themes:

- that women managed family time and the scheduling of work and care differently to men, and perceived greater tension in managing demands which they experience as competing;
- that men were more likely to maintain greater control and autonomy over their time scheduling, and less likely to experience work and family commitments as competing.

We formulated these questions in this gendered way since gendered differences appeared to be very strong on our initial reading of data, both within WFL, where we could compare mothers' and fathers' accounts, and in 'Men as fathers', where a male gender coding was very evident amongst many fathers' accounts. However, we needed to confront the risks of working with a 'gender model' of analysis (cf. Feldberg and Glenn 1979, see also Henwood et al. 2008). Concerned we were reading the evidence through a 'gender lens' we were keen to explore contexts in which these sorts of expressions were made, but also ensure that we would 'hear' working mothers who were not stressed, or working fathers who were.

Issues of gender and work–family conflict in the WFL data set

We first explored in-depth data from WFL. This project is described in detail in Chapter 7, to which we refer the reader for an account of the research design, method and sample. We note here that all parents were in paid work, excepting two fathers who had retired early for health-related reasons, and that the sample comprised 14 families. We first read across all transcripts of adult participants in households where they were co-residing with their partner or spouse. On this basis we sought to 'map' individual cases with reference to the specific dimensions of experience in which we were interested. On our readings, the data related well to extant evidence on experiences of gender and time pressure. For example, women across diverse circumstances appeared more likely to *manage* the work of work–life balance than did men, and where they had extensive paid work (full-time or approaching full-time hours) they were likely to experience pressure, and they expressed a substantial degree of guilt and anxiety about sufficiently meeting their commitments. Due to the nature of the sample there was not the numerical breadth that would allow us to isolate differing contextual influences on parents' experiences of work–life conflict. The longitudinal structure of the data set perhaps best lends itself to detailed case studies, wherein particular cases can be adduced to illuminate wider social processes. An example might be the important question of how parents' experiences evolve as children grow older (as discussed by Harden et al. this volume). For our secondary analysis we read and explored data across the one-to-one interviews with mothers and fathers, and across successive waves of data generation, but most of the data cited below is drawn from wave 1 interviews where participants were asked about parenting and work in some depth.

The analysis was based not on answers to a specific question but on an assessment of experiences of time pressure, and the linked management of day-to-day scheduling of work and care commitments, as manifested in participants' accounts. In line with extant evidence our analysis suggested that those who were mothers *and* had extensive paid work (or, in one case, study) commitments were the ones most likely to talk about managing their work and family commitments in terms of compromise, conflict and spreading themselves thinly. Such anxieties were not absent from some male accounts but it was a more common and marked motif amongst working women. For example, Jan worked full-time and described her experience as follows:

> it's the constant time pressures that I find really difficult...you feel like you've already done a day's work in the house, before you've left the house in the morning. And then you get to work and then you pray to goodness that the phone is not going to go, that it's not going to be the school saying the kids are sick.

Emma, a professional single mother of two daughters who was working four days a week, appeared extremely stressed with managing arrangements. She was asked what it was like being a working mum, and described how she had been called the previous week to get her daughter who was ill and her need to be at the management team meeting at work:

> So you're sort of torn between the two...Most days you think ooh I'll get her straight away, but some days you think, I'm paid to be here, so I should really be here, but there is no Plan B.

Jan's husband Archie described guilt and an experience of being stretched by conflicting time commitments:

> you want to be a major influence on [the kid's] life...you don't really want to see them for [only] half an hour at night and then you're away the next morning. So that's where you feel torn with that. I've got an extremely busy job. I come back and I usually work at night as well...and it's just trying to juggle all that. But I suppose I'd feel guilty if I couldn't provide for them either.

Archie however was unusual amongst male participants. While expressions of time pressure were present in fathers' accounts, they did not tend to describe themselves as being pulled in different directions or as feeling compromised. Further comparisons within couples are of some interest here. For example, Debra was studying full-time at university while also doing some part-time work. Her husband managed a restaurant and they had an eight-year-old child. She appeared stressed about how she managed her time and anxious that her son was suffering from this. She and her husband worked in a shift pattern so they could look after their son and the family spent little time all together. She said that:

> the reason I am [at university] is so that we can have … a better life. I can have a job and we can have more security. And that's not just for me that's for Logan but I feel sometimes that my focus on that detracts from the amount of time that I spend with him

She went on to talk about the difference between her previously imagined ideal of being a mother and her current reality: 'I do have a lot of guilt about being a bit crap'. This was in marked contrast to her husband Kenny who said:

> if there's things to be done with Logan then I'll take him out and I'll do it all … I suppose being a dad is just how you slot into … your routines as well, what you have to do … it's interesting

It might be observed this is simply a gender coded or male way of expressing the same concerns, that 'interesting' is a catch all for more difficult emotions which women express more easily. It may be also that in doing a degree and being supported by her husband, Debra's guilt reflects a rather particular anxiety about whether she is being selfish. However, the asymmetry of gendered experiences is much broader. In mapping parents' experiences of challenge and conflict in managing the daily scheduling and experience of care and work commitments, the difficulties were experienced and recounted much more vividly by mothers who had extensive paid work commitments. Women working less extensively in part-time employment, and men in general, were less likely to foreground such challenges within their accounts.

We wanted, within a numerically small sample, to find some basis on which to explore gendered manifestations of work–life conflict and the contexts giving rise to them. Might atypical household resourcing arrangements offer further insights? We chose then to focus on the experience of two families in which the mothers worked full-time or near full-time and their husbands had retired through ill health. In both cases, the men were able to take on quite extensive childcare responsibilities. It might be supposed that accounts of work–life stress and conflict amongst mothers in these contexts would attenuate given the availability of practical domestic support. However this was not the case, and the mothers in question described aspects of their lives still in terms of stress. There may be particular reasons for this, not least the men's background of ill health, but the examples remain consistent with wider evidence on the cultural positioning of women as primary carers, which overshadows their immediate economic circumstances (e.g. Vincent et al. 2004, Doucet 2009).

Fiona and her husband John had three children, she worked four days a week as a project manager in the public sector and he, having retired early through ill health, took on significant domestic and childcare responsibilities. John's intermittent recurrence of illness placed Fiona under more stress than if this were a straightforward role reversal situation. Nevertheless, interestingly when she was reflecting on her role as a worker and mother, her account echoed those of other working women with working partners. So while she talked about the fact that she was not in a traditional mum's role and her husband does a 'lot of the houseworky things', she said being a mum was 'kind of competing demands all the time' and that 'wherever I am, I'm always thinking that I should be doing something else'. She went on: 'I think, for me, it's always feeling like you're not devoting quite what you should to whatever task that it should be. And so… it is that, just you feel you're spreading yourself thinly'.

Sally worked full-time as a police officer, her husband had retired from the police force through ill health. She described some flexibility around childcare and had support locally, for example, and they had just the one child. Nevertheless, even with her husband describing his active involvement with their son, doing school runs, cooking and helping with his homework, Sally still felt she was compromised:

> there was still the guilt (when her son was cared for by her own parents) but certainly not to the extent that I feel it now that I've gone back full-time. And I know that it's silly, I shouldn't, because he's got his dad there all the time. But it's still not the same as me being there.

The WFL data was consistent with wider evidence of a pattern where working mothers retain extensive responsibility for managing care and the domestic domain, and experience conflict and compromise more extensively than men do. Women across diverse circumstances appeared more likely to manage the work of work–life balance than men did, scheduling time and care arrangements, being more 'on call' for their children when they were at work, anticipating and reacting to contingencies, and thereby carrying much of the hidden work of managing work–life balance along with their more extensive practical care giving.

They generally appeared more prone than fathers to experience pressure, and often guilt, when they held extensive paid work commitments. This evidence echoes that of other qualitative research on women's experiences of time pressure and of 'feeling guilty'. Alongside the greater importance of women's paid work for the resourcing of family life and the next generation, mothers remain positioned as their children's primary care giver, absorbing the structural dilemmas into personal, and often stressful, solutions (cf. Thomson et al. 2011).[3]

Working across data sets: Seeking to engender analytic conversation across diversely constituted project data

In our secondary analysis, we wanted to bring the WFL data into conversation with data from the project 'Masculinities, identities and risk: transitions in the lives of men as fathers (abbreviated to 'Men as fathers', or MaF). In this project, men were interviewed about their own identities and experiences as these evolved from before the birth of their first child to when this child was eight years old. Primary research from the MaF project is explained and further references indicated in Chapter 5. The original waves of data collection, in East Anglia, were conducted between 1999 and 2001. A fourth wave of interviews was undertaken in 2008 as part of Timescapes. The team provided us with access to this data set. In bringing it into comparison with WFL data we needed to exercise caution, as the data reflect their project contexts, designs and methods. In MaF, only men were interviewed. The design of MaF meant that the way the male participants were oriented – by the study design, by the lines of questioning and by the fact that within their families it was only they who were interviewed – all press towards rather different kinds of account than in the contexts of the WFL interviews. The project was shaped by a different theoretical and social psychological disciplinary grounding to that of WFL. Interviews explored men's own personal, masculine identities as these evolved through their experiences of being a father. Questions were very different to those asked in the WFL project. We read full transcripts to gain a feel for the men as individuals, and then focused on areas of the interview where men discussed issues relating to the intersection of work and care commitments, for themselves and their partners.

We began with a deductive way of entering into the project data set, exploring cases which looked potentially 'productive' with respect to our questions, based on project metadata (supplied to us by the team) about household divisions of labour, for example where there was a high density of paid work within households. We then read 'outwards' across the sample. We chose for in-depth analysis men who seemed at ease within a conventional division of labour and others who both worked extensively *and* desired extensive practical hands-on care of their young children, and examples where managing both work and family commitments seemed more of an issue. Echoing the strategy for WFL data, we then sought to compare experiences as they related to more conventional, and less conventional, divisions of labour. In the following, we consider men who manifested different degrees of ease with their work–family 'balance'. We draw below on data from the men's fourth wave interview, when they had at least one young (primary school aged) child.

Kenny was situated within a conventional division of labour in which he was the main breadwinner as a self-employed chiropodist building his own practice. At his final interview, he and his wife had two children aged eight and six. In an early interview when his first child was a baby, and he was unemployed, he had envisaged a more progressive division of labour in the future than in fact came to pass. Consistent with his primary earner situation, he offered a male coded account. To illustrate, in answer to a question about being an involved caring father, looking back over eight years, he said,

> I mean I don't know what percentage out of the hundred that I'd hoped for, Michelle'd probably say its less than she'd hoped for. I would probably say it's about as good as I can manage.

Kenny conveyed no evidence of unease with their work–family balance, and saw it as an outcome of decisions made about work commitments and a suitable division of labour between him and his wife. We can then compare this quite unproblematic rendering of work–family balance with the perspectives of two working fathers who appeared committed, unusually, to an ongoing and extensive, hands-on, practical caring commitment to their children.[4]

Bruce was a school teacher and head of a department within school, and his partner worked full-time as director of her own company. He desired extensive practical caring involvement and commented on how for him and his partner 'I am more of a mum and she is more of a dad ... there is almost a role reversal in the traditional roles'. Bruce spoke about work–life balance in a relaxed manner, yet combining roles was very much on his own terms, facilitated by extra, bought-in support, since the family had a nanny. Interestingly, also, in respect of changing work practices, and unlike in women's accounts in WFL and elsewhere, he saw the compromise as his to make, an aspect of his authority. A potential time pressure 'tension' was perceived and experienced very differently than was the case amongst mothers, in part due to the bought-in support, and in part facilitated by his work identity. Another example of a man who desired an extensive practical caring commitment with his children was Malcolm, who had three children. Unlike Bruce, Malcolm, who worked as a manager within a prison, felt he had limited control over his own time. He therefore was situated in a circumstance more similar to the working women discussed earlier. He talked of chores and domestic planning and described a level of practical involvement in childcare that was relatively unusual for men in the MaF data set. Additionally he recounted his experience of compromise and unease about whether he was effective in managing his time across work and family life:

> So yeah it's um, if you'd interviewed me a couple of months ago you'd see a different me sitting here 'cause I was stressed, I was under a lot more pressure but you don't always realize it . . . I've never particularly been that stressed in the prison service before, it was impacting at home, I just felt stressed about everything and it was all about time time time, not enough of it.

Malcolm, who desired extensive practical care involvement and experienced limited control over his work time, comes closest to echoing some of the stress and conflict routinely described by mothers with extensive work commitments. Overall, then, we could speculate that fathers become more like mothers in experiencing stress when, and this is unusual, they desire extensive practical hands-on care of children *and* they are relatively inflexible in their work commitments. Even in such instances, it should be emphasized, there was no evidence of equivalence in caring responsibilities and there was allusion to a still taken for granted division of gendered roles.

Conclusion

In this chapter, we have sought to illustrate some of the challenges but also the possibilities that arise from the secondary analysis of qualitative data. In our Timescapes secondary analysis work, we were guided by methodological as well as substantive questions. There is an array of possibilities for qualitative secondary analysis which have expanded significantly due to the currently available electronic and data sharing infrastructure. Existing data sets have the potential to offer insights beyond the original analyses of primary research. Researchers must not underestimate the time needed to develop an adequate understanding of relevant data sets, and the challenges of doing so. Data analysis requires, amongst other things, a detailed and nuanced understanding of context, and this is a particular challenge for secondary analysts who were not involved in the proximate contexts of data generation. In addressing our research questions, we made some use of data from across successive time waves but did not undertake a systematic longitudinal analysis of gender and work–family conflict. Our questions were not ones which shaped the original research design, and we did not gain sufficient purchase on longitudinal dimensions to our questions to pursue a fully longitudinal analysis. Nevertheless qualitative longitudinal data promises particular insights when it comes to both tracking and also conceptualizing parents' evolving experiences and behaviours.

We have described some of our strategies, and discussed our approach to working with data across Timescapes projects. Amongst the challenges we faced, the Timescapes programme design required that we needed to access, and work with, data which was still 'live' for primary project teams, raising ethical as well as practical challenges. We evolved research questions on the basis of available data across two data sets. It is of course possible to bring together data from different projects in a quite direct way where it is clearly comparable, but we exercised caution due to the very different project contexts in which the data was generated. We endeavoured to translate our research questions across the project data, so these questions had integrity within the project contexts but were also commensurate, allowing us to bring project data into a meaningful analytic conversation.

Having 'mapped' diversity within WFL data, with reference to our research questions, we chose then to further explore diverse contexts in which gendered work–family settlements and experiences were shaped. We then followed a parallel strategy with the MaF data. We found a marked gendering in accounts of childrearing commitments and experiences of work–family conflict, even in contexts where working women were 'more like men' in having their spouse undertake extensive childcare at home, and in contexts where men were 'more like working women' in their commitment to work and to provide extensive practical hands-on childcare. This gendering is no surprise and entirely consistent with an array of wider evidence. However, it offers further and poignant illustration of extensive experiences of conflict and compromise for many working mothers. Our secondary analysis complements wider evidence of the deep-seated nature of economic and cultural drivers of gendered inequalities in experiences of time pressure in family life. Parents, but most markedly mothers, of children of primary school age and under cope with time stress, frequently feel themselves to be making compromises and manage the associated pressures as an effectively personal or private (if common) challenge. Policy needs to engage with an adequate understanding of the ways in which 'choices' are framed within contexts which are effectively taken as given. Currently such contexts commonly leave parents, and mothers in particular, with relatively constrained choices between work and care, or feeling stressed and compromised in effectively meeting their commitments.

Notes

1. 'Work and family lives: the changing experiences of young families' was directed by Professor Kathryn Backett-Milburn at the University of Edinburgh. We are grateful to Kathryn and her team for providing us with access to the WFL data and for having a dedicated project meeting with us in winter 2010–2011. 'Masculinities, identities and risk: transition in the lives of men as fathers' was directed by Professor Karen Henwood at the University of Cardiff. We are grateful to Karen and her team for providing us with access to the MaF heritage data from interviews conducted in Norfolk from 2000–2008 and for having a dedicated project meeting with us in winter 2010–2011.
2. We are grateful to the WFL and MaF project teams and, in particular, Jeni Harden and Karen Henwood, for their comments on an earlier draft of our analyses relating to their project data. The analysis we report on is our own and does not necessarily correspond with the primary analysts' views.
3. Some commentators distinguish 'work to family' conflict, and 'family to work' conflict, where domestic commitments shape experiences within paid work (e.g. Bianchi and Milkie 2010). Evidence suggests that mothers may be more prone to experience constraints on work-based entitlements, for example due to how they are positioned informally by supervisors and colleagues (Perrons et al. 2005, Thomson et al. 2011). This was echoed in the WFL data but we have no space to explore it here.
4. As a prelude to our secondary analysis, we read several publications by the project team, but came to read Finn and Henwood (2009) only after our own analysis. Interestingly both Bruce and Malcolm were important in their psychosocial analysis as men with quite particular commitments to involved fatherhood (from the interviews just before and after the births of their first children).

References

Bianchi, S. M. and Milkie, M. A. (2010) 'Work and family research in the first decade of the 21st century', *Journal of Marriage and the Family*, 72: 705–725.
Bishop, L. (2006) 'A proposal for archiving context for secondary analysis', *Methodological Innovations Online*, 1(2). Available at: www.methodological innovations.org.uk/wp-content/uploads/2013/07/2.-Bishop-pp10-20.pdf.

Bishop, L. (2009) 'Ethical sharing and reuse of qualitative data', *Australian Journal of Social Issues*, 44(3): 255–272.

Creighton, C. (1999) 'The rise and decline of the "male breadwinner family" in Britain', *Cambridge Journal of Economics*, 23(5): 519–541.

Crompton, R. (2002) 'Employment, flexible working and the family', *British Journal of Sociology*, 53(4): 537–558.

Crompton, R. and Lyonette, C. (2006) 'Work–life balance in Europe', *Acta Sociologica*, 49(4): 379–393.

Doucet, A. (2009) 'Gender equality and gender differences: Parenting, habitus and embodiment' (The 2008 Porter Lecture), *Canadian Review of Sociology*, 46(2): 1103–1121.

Edlund, J. (2011) 'The work–family time squeeze. Conflicting demands of paid and unpaid work among working couples in 29 countries', *International Journal of Comparative Sociology*, 48(6): 451–480.

Feldberg, R. L. and Glenn, E. N. (1979) 'Male and female: Job versus gender models in the sociology of work', *Social Problems*, 26(5): 524–538.

Finn, M. and Henwood, K. (2009) 'Exploring masculinities within men's identificatory imaginings of first-time fatherhood', *British Journal of Social Psychology*, 48: 547–562.

Forsberg, L. (2009) 'Managing time and childcare in dual earner families. Unforeseen consequences of household strategies', *Acta Sociologica*, 52(2): 162–175.

Hammersley, M (2010) 'Can we re-use qualitative data via secondary analysis? Notes on some terminological and substantive issues', *Sociological Research Online*, 15(1). Available at http://www.socresonline.org.uk/15/1/5.html.

Henwood, K., Parkhill, K. and Pidgeon, N. (2008) 'Science, technology and risk perception: From gender difference to effects made by gender', *Journal of Equal Opportunities International*, 28(8): 662–676.

Irwin, S. (2005) *Reshaping Social Life*, London: Routledge.

Irwin, S. (2011) 'Working across qualitative and quantitative data: Childhood, youth and social inequalities', *Forum 21. European Journal on Child and Youth Research*, 6: 58–63.

Irwin, S., Bornat, J. and Winterton, M. (2012) 'Timescapes secondary analysis: Comparison, context and working across data sets', *Qualitative Research*, 12(1): 66–80.

Irwin, S. and Winterton, M. (2011a) *Debates in Qualitative Secondary Analysis: Critical Reflections*, Timescapes Working Paper no. 4. Available at http://www.timescapes.leeds.ac.uk/assets/files/WP4-March-2011.pdf.

Irwin, S. and Winterton, M. (2011b) *Timescapes Data and Secondary Analysis: Working across the Projects*, Timescapes Working Paper no. 5. Available at http://www.timescapes.leeds.ac.uk/assets/files/WP5-March-2011.pdf.

Irwin, S. and Winterton, M. (2012) 'Qualitative secondary analysis and social explanation', *Sociological Research Online*, 17(2). Available at http://www.socresonline.org.uk/17/2/4.html.

Kan, M. Y., Sullivan, O. and Gershuny, J. (2011) 'Gender convergence in domestic work: Discerning the effects of interactional and institutional barriers from large scale data', *Sociology*, 45(2): 234–251.

Latshaw, B. A. (2011) 'The more things change, the more they remain the same? Paradoxes of men's unpaid labour since "The Second Shift" ', *Sociology Compass*, 5(7): 653–665.

Mason, J. (2007) ' "Re-using" qualitative data: On the merits of an investigative epistemology', *Sociological Research Online*, 12(3). Available at www.socresonline.org.uk/12/3/3.html.

Mauthner, N. and Parry, O. (2012) 'Open access digital data sharing: Principles, policies and practices', *Social Epistemology: A Journal of Knowledge, Culture and Policy*, 27(1): 47–67.

Morehead, A. (2001) 'Synchronizing time for work and family: Preliminary insights from qualitative research with mothers', *Journal of Sociology*, 37(4): 355–369.

Neale, B. and Bishop, L. (2012) 'The Timescapes archive: A stakeholder approach to archiving qualitative longitudinal data', *Qualitative Research*, 12(1): 53–65.

Perrons, D., Fagan, C., McDowell, L., Ray, K. and Ward, K. (2005) 'Work, life and time in the new economy. An introduction', *Time and Society*, 14(1): 51–64.

Rose, J. (2011) 'Finding time to balance: Perceptions of time pressure and work-life balance', paper presented to *Community, Work and Family 4th International conference*, University of Tampere, Finland, 19–21 May 2011.

Thomson, R., Kehily, M. J., Hadfield, L. and Sharpe, S. (2011) *Making Modern Mothers*, Bristol: Polity Press.

Van den Eynden, V., Corti, L., Woollard, M., Bishop, L. and Horton, L. (2011) 'Managing and sharing data: Best practice for researchers', UK Data Archive.

Vincent, C., Ball, S. J. and Pietikainen, S. (2004) 'Metropolitan mothers: Mothers, mothering and paid work', *Women's Studies International Forum*, 27: 571–587.

Walby, S. (1997) *Gender Transformations*, London: Routledge.

Winterton, M. and Irwin, S. (2012) 'Teenage expectations of going to university: The ebb and flow of influences from 14 to 18', *Journal of Youth Studies*, 15(7): 858–874.

Part III
Older Lives and Times

9
Vulnerability, Intergenerational Exchange and the Conscience of Generations

Nick Emmel and Kahryn Hughes

Introduction

In this chapter, we are concerned with grandparents between 35 and 55 years old. The grandparents' experiences reported here are all firmly positioned in a group recently labelled the precariat (Standing 2011); a group churning between low-paid low-skilled employment, underemployment and unemployment (Shildrick et al. 2012) and characterized by high levels of insecurity on all measures of economic, social and cultural capital (Savage et al. 2013). This is a relatively large social class and our focus in this chapter is an important minority of excluded low-income grandparents and their families. Grandparents in the UK are getting older, reflecting increasing life expectancies. There are, however, approximately 1.5 million grandparents under the age of 50 years. Furthermore, investigation by Grandparents Plus (2009) of the difference in age of grandparents reveals important divergence between socio-economic groups. Women from a working-class background are four times more likely to become a grandmother before their 50th birthday when compared with middle-class groups.

This chapter considers the cases of low-income marginalized grandparents with whom we undertook qualitative longitudinal research over three years. This research, a part of Timescapes, is nested in a ten-year longitudinal programme of research through which we have insight into how relations across generations between grandparents, children and grandchildren change and stay the same. Our concern is far wider than the household with the focus of our studies on the ways in which change and continuity within complex configurations of kinship are understood as embedded in the relational networks of which they are part.

A significant part of these networks are the relations and interactions with service providers across health and social care in the public and third sectors. Despite the frequency of contact observed and recorded, we have described the insecurity felt by participants due to their reliance on the response of service providers in a crisis as an important feature of these relationships (Emmel and Hughes 2010). Participants are uncertain in their relationships with service providers across health and social care, and this insecurity is most keenly felt in response to crisis. Service providers listen and do not listen and act or do not act to address need.

An uncertain reliance on service providers to respond to crisis is one axis of a model of vulnerability we have developed (Watts and Bhole 1993, Emmel and Hughes 2010, Emmel et al. 2011). This model includes two further dimensions: an assessment of material resources to address everyday basic needs; and resilience characterized across a range, from a perceived ability to address need in the present and plan for the future through to a stubborn lack of capacity to respond to any crisis. We describe this model of vulnerability as the 'Toblerone model', referring to the shape of the Swiss chocolate confectionary, a triangle in cross section exhibiting the three dimensions described here, and a fourth dimension, time, through which these co-ordinates of vulnerability change, to explain the dynamic experiences of vulnerability described in this model.

In this model of vulnerability time has been conceptualized as cross sectional, linear and determined (Emmel and Hughes 2010). Events, such as the death of a family member for example, have been interpreted as propelling already precarious families into vulnerability. In this chapter we consider the impact of cross-sectional events and their effect on experiences of vulnerability, but we add to this analysis with new conceptualizations of time. In particular, through engaging with the temporality of relationships between grandparents and grandchildren mediated through particular institutional practices embedded in health and social care provision, we reveal a more finely textured and nuanced account of the processes of vulnerability. These relations between socially institutionalized time as a means of orientation (Elias 1992) and experiences of generation have the potential to explain, in part, the maintenance, amelioration and exacerbation of vulnerabilities.

It is notable, for example, that the group of grandparents that are the focus of this chapter (those between 35 and 55 years old) have been described as '*very* young' (Grandparents Plus 2009: 11 – emphasis added). This choice of term, we suggest, reflects particular social institutions of time (in this case age and generation). Like the examples that will be elaborated in the two cases presented in this chapter, it articulates external compulsions, which in turn are expressed in social policy and practice and have the potential to exacerbate precarious experiences of grandparenting leading to vulnerability.

Before presenting two cases of grandparenting from which we refine a model of vulnerability, we detail the method used in the study 'Intergenerational exchange', and its relationship to our programme of qualitative longitudinal research.

Method, ethics and time

The evidence we report here is drawn from a qualitative longitudinal programme of three separately funded studies conducted on a low-income estate in a northern English city between 1999 and the present. We have described the objectives and methods from these three studies in detail elsewhere (Emmel and Malby 2000, Emmel et al. 2007, Emmel and Hughes 2010), so here key issues are identified to contextualize the substantive and methodological issues considered in this chapter.

'Intergenerational exchange', as part of the qualitative longitudinal initiative Timescapes, is a study of the ways that young vulnerable grandparents in a low-income urban community support their grandchildren. It was conducted from 2007 to 2010. Our objective was to investigate how low-income grandparents describe what they do for their grandchildren in order to improve their life chances. Our sample comprised 12 grandparents from eight families. We recruited two of these grandparents (a couple, and an estranged and now widowed grandmother) and their families in an earlier study that investigated methodologies for accessing socially excluded individuals and groups (Emmel et al. 2007). The remaining six grandparents were recruited to this study through service providers in the public and third sectors who deliver services in the geographical estate and with whom we have longstanding relationships. The criteria for selection included being grandparents between the age of 35 and 55, and either they or their families were considered by service providers to be vulnerable, as understood within current policy and practice discourse (see for instance DWP 2011).

In addition to recruiting the 12 grandparents in eight families, we tracked 319 immediate family members using a visual family tree method (Tsey et al. 2004). This participatory exercise was conducted in the first of four rounds of in-depth life history interviews carried out at six-monthly intervals throughout the study. The family tree was a prompt used in later interviews in which relations with many of the family members identified through this method were discussed. The first interview also focused attention on life's ups and downs, what participants felt their lives were like and by what routes they became the person they are today. We enquired about everyday routines, how life is now and how it might change or stay the same. In the second interview, a key focus was on the people and agencies who help and the experiences of being a grandparent. In the third interview our focus was on place, for example where grandparenting happens and cannot happen. The fourth and final interview paid particular attention to pressures within and beyond the family, crisis and the life-course of their grandchildren. We asked participants to imagine their grandchildren's futures. Each of the interviews also included a catch-up on changes since we last met.

Catching up has always been an important part of our qualitative longitudinal method. Describing the interview schedule as we have done here gives the impression of cross-sectional interviewing across time. We sought to bridge the six-month gaps between interviews through asking participants to reflect back on events since we last met, always aware of course that the past is 'recreated, reselected, preserved, and evoked afresh in the light of new knowledge', as Barbara Adam (1990: 143) observes. We have tried to overcome this reconstitution of the past, at least to some degree, through meeting with our participants between formal interviews. We have maintained contact with participants in the research, with service providers through two third-sector organizations that have their offices on the low-income estate and with the health visitors and community workers based on the estate. Most often these meetings are informal, popping in for a cup of tea, meeting for a drink in the social club or accepting an invitation to a party.

If we are to incorporate what we hear informally into the ongoing research, then the ethical implications of the inclusion of these data must be considered. We have found it important to regularly remind participants that we are researchers and what they tell us cannot be dissociated from our larger research programme. This means frequently negotiating ongoing verbal informed consent in all informal and formal interactions.

However informal, participants in the research and service providers have always been aware that we are researchers and our observations and conversations will be recorded in field diaries and discussed among the research team. This ongoing contact with participants in sustaining relationships provides important data for the research, as do the socio-economic, political and policy changes that happen through time and are seen by participants, service providers and us as important and mediating in the relationships we are investigating. Together with the interviews, these data form the small *n* cases in our research (Emmel and Hughes 2009, Emmel 2013), which are both organizational structures for the data and methodological strategies for interpretation and explanation.

In qualitative longitudinal research, ethical and methodological practices like the constitution of cases that include participants' accounts and wider contextual description are always proposed and enacted with reference to time. Similarly, the research questions that inform these ethical practices and methods are framed temporally. In addition, longitudinal research foregrounds time, obliging us to explain what we mean by time in the research. This opens up new lines of enquiry. As Elias (1992: 1) asserts at the beginning of his investigation of time, through 'exploring problems of time one can find out a good deal about human beings [...] that were not properly understood before'. A temporal framing of sociological problems, like the ways in which grandparents in low-income households support their children and grandchildren and how service provision intervenes in that support, makes accessible mechanisms that hitherto could not be seen and explained. These temporally framed insights can inform social policy, as we show through the presentation and interpretation of two cases from the research.

Ruth and Bridget

The (northern) city council-based teenage pregnancy and parenthood team works with schools and other agencies to ensure that school-age parents get the help they need to continue with their education. This team liaises with specialist midwives and health visitors in locally based children's centres in the city. Together they develop and disseminate maternity and care pathways intended to ensure referral to appropriate services for young women who become pregnant while in statutory full-time education.

A focus of this pathway construction and service delivery is Bridget, a 13-year-old mother and the subject of her mother Ruth's observations below. Ruth presents a paradox. She strongly approves of service interventions put in place to support Bridget, while at the same time recognizing that the focus on Bridget as a mother undermines her relationship with her daughter in significant ways, which have practical implications and the potential to exacerbate vulnerabilities within the household.

> I had visions of, like I say, old fashioned times with children get-ting married, grow, go, leaving home, then coming back, Yeah, we're having a baby, and me, you know, spoiling the baby because all my children had grown up. It didn't turn out the way I wanted it. It was, er, a bit of a shock. Yeah, a pretty big shock. Bridget's attitude was: Yeah. Aren't I clever? I've had a baby, even though she didn't know what to do with it, erm, relied on me too much, it's like, Mum, do this. Mum, can you do that? Erm, it's just she wouldn't get up and do anything for herself, as in find out about that, er, child benefit, that sort of thing, that were all left up to me as well.

The teenage pregnancy and parenthood team's focus is on Bridget as a mother rather than as Ruth's child. The team's efforts are to facilitate Bridget's return to education and support access to welfare ben-efits. A designated health visitor provides extended support, including frequent visits.

This approach to services delivery has quite specific impacts on the relationship between Ruth and her daughter, as Ruth explains. She observes that despite the baby being Bridget's she is mother to both child and grandchild. And as she goes on to say, of her grandchild, 'I've got another baby to look after', while describing her daughter as 'very, very young…she is a baby herself'. Bridget is too young, inexpe-rienced and, in her opinion, immature to be mother to her child. After all, she notes, Bridget is not even capable of collecting child benefit from the post office. Ruth's support of Bridget is ignored in service delivery. She is rendered invisible to service provision. Pre-existing generational relations between Ruth and her daughter are undermined and vertical generational structures reinforced with their focus on the mother to the neglect of the grandmother.

Ruth's role as grandmother is also undermined at an affective level. She is finding it difficult to come to terms with and understand her role as grandmother. In observing that 'it [grandparenting] didn't turn out the way I wanted it', Ruth is expressing a collapsing of expected generational relations, where, as she notes later in the interview, her role should be one of knitting baby bootees and hats, not dealing with the everyday nursing needs of her newborn grandchild.

Ruth finds the role of being a grandmother difficult, even confusing. Repeatedly she observes that she is simply the wrong age. And those whom she meets feel she is the wrong age to become a grandparent as well. Her uncertainty in a generational role that does not fit with her age is intensified through the ways in which she perceives others thinking of her:

> And I used to get really strange looks. You know, cos people think as, grandmas as being, you know, old, walking stick, and stuff like that. But I was, I don't know if I was sad because I'd been made a grandparent, or if I was happy. I was in sort of two minds.

Ruth's identity as a young grandparent is ambiguous. Her identity as a grandmother is undermined through her everyday interaction with friends and acquaintances. Her experiences of caring for daughter and grandchild reinforce a mothering, not grand-mothering role. Yet, vertical relations of generation are reinforced. There is a tension between the socially institutionalized time of grandparenting ascribed in policy and societal norms of grandparenting on the one hand, and the experiences of grandparenting (and parenting) for Ruth on the other hand.

As well as unsettling relations between Ruth and her daughter, there are practical implications in the delivery of services that are underwritten by particular ways of seeing generation at odds with the experiences of generation in the family. Service interventions direct money and other resources towards Bridget. As Ruth contends, making ends meet is harder as these resources would have helped her in household budgeting.

Geoff and Margaret, and Warren

Until recently Warren, his mother Hannah and his three cousins lived with their grandparents, Geoff and Margaret. The three cousins, all girls and aged between four and 12, the daughters of Geoff and Margaret's middle daughter, were placed with their grandparents by social services. They had been removed from their mother, a chaotic heroin user (Hughes 2007), late one evening and left with Geoff and Margaret who were assured that social workers would visit the following morning. Geoff and Margaret called this informal type of placement the 'midnight drop'. It is an event regularly reported by many of the grandparents and the local voluntary organization working with grandparents that we spoke to in the research. Concerned to remove children from risky settings, social workers leave them with close relatives, often late at night and invariably with a promise that they will return in the morning to address practical and financial issues. Rarely does the follow-up visit happen. In this case, too, social services did not resume the expected contact and so started an ongoing and intensive process of interaction between Geoff and Margaret, social services and the family courts to formalize arrangements for the granddaughters' care and access to financial resources.

This household is precarious and vulnerable along a dimension of material vulnerability. Both Geoff and Margaret are in receipt of welfare benefits and at the time of the study they were both deemed unfit to work, as Geoff explains:

> We've always had to fight for things in life, er, me wife being disabled. Erm, you've really gotta fight and sometimes you don't know which way to turn, you don't know who to go to, who to see, er, and to me it's frustrating, a lot of people get frustrated over it and you can understand why because she's entitled to it. It's not as though you're asking for summat for nothing. I've worked all me life. You know I mean unfortunately I've had to pack me job in.

The way that this low-income household manages their household economy, which includes the care of their grandchildren, is, as Geoff points out, mediated to a significant extent by advice workers. In their case, these advice workers are from third-sector organizations. They are important in understanding the relation Geoff and Margaret have with service providers and the ways in which they can provide leverage in pursuit of the entitlements Geoff mentions.

Geoff and Margaret discuss their understanding of entitlement in terms of another relationship. They are not just grandparents; they also became great-grandparents during the study (while still meeting our age criteria for inclusion). Their grandson, Warren, who is 15 years old, has a child with a 14-year-old girl, Michelle. As the following quote suggests, Michelle's mother is restricting Warren's access to his newborn son. What is also evident is the confidence with which Margaret asserts that Michelle's mother does not have the right to restrict access:

> See it's a funny situation at the moment with them. The mother of the girl, won't, she doesn't trust Warren to be on his own at her house . . . . So I were talking to somebody, and they says, 'She can't call the shots'. Her mother can't. For the simple reason, it's because with them being under-aged they're under social services. And if they say that Warren can have him on his own, that's all right.

During the interview, it emerges that Warren is also supported by an advice worker. She counsels Geoff and Margaret who in turn support

Warren in his communications with social services that are essential in asserting his rights and maintaining contact with his young son.

In a similar way to Bridget, discussed in the first case, Warren's parenting is supported through the intervention of service providers. And also, like Ruth, who it will be recalled found coming to terms with her identity as a young grandmother difficult, so too Warren has found the affective identity of young fatherhood difficult. As Margaret observes, the process of becoming a dad has not been straightforward. In her opinion it is made more difficult by those around him, in particular Warren's father, Dennis:

> And Warren's come to terms with it now [being a father]. And he's, you know, he's always talking about [his son], you know, what he's done with him, and, in that, you know. And they've all come to terms with it now, I think. The only one that I think is holding our Warren back on most of this is his dad [Dennis]. His dad still can't come to terms with it.

As Bren Neale and Carmen Lau Clayton discuss in Chapter 4 of this volume, parents and grandparents express shock and dismay at the announcement of prospective fatherhood for young men. Similarly, for Warren as a young father, Ruth as a young grandmother and Bridget as a young mother, we have shown how their experiences of taking on new generational identities have been difficult to manage and frequently considered to be wrong by themselves, their families, neighbours and acquaintances. Furthermore, as these two cases reveal, service providers with whom they interact reinforce particular generational identities. Ruth and Bridget's case, in particular, has shown how maternal and grandparental identities are 'situated, entangled, and dynamic', as Rachel Thomson (2009: 21; and Chapter 6 of this volume) observes in her discussion of the generational succession, rhythm and flow of the historically located experiences of motherhood. In the next section, we consider a particular sociological theory of time to explain these changes; our focus is on the powers, liabilities and dispositions institutionalized in temporal processes, drawing on the work of Norbert Elias. We note in particular how interpretations of time underwrite particular social policy formulations and practices.

Time and the conscience of generations

For Elias (1992) the question of time centres on the way two or more events are placed in relation to each other to produce a series. Time becomes a social institution represented and segmented through clocks only when it can be compared and juxtaposed with a second sequence of events that occurs regularly. These 'recurrent patterns in the second sequence then serve as standardized reference points by means of which, since they represent the return not of the same thing but of the same interval, can be compared indirectly' (Elias 1992: 10).

We are compelled to make these comparisons, as Ruth does when she notes that grandmothers should be much older than she is, evoking the symbols of the process of ageing, 'old, walking stick, and stuff like that', to mark out a particular generation who should be grandparents. Ruth has recourse to a standard reference point, which Elias (1992: 12) relates as the 'positions of physical or natural becoming, of social becoming and of course an individual life'. As Cipriani (2013) emphasizes, these symbols reach a high level of conformity with reality, in which it becomes difficult to distinguish the symbols – the generations and the cadence of life course – from reality.

Ruth neither conforms to the symbols, nor to the reality. Her experiences of grandmothering, her feeling that she is the wrong age – expressed through her accounts of the way she feels some of her neighbours judge her and people in the street think about her – is, we suggest, an expression of the lack of harmony between societal symbol and her reality.

Time as a symbol raises conscience about the external compulsion and relations of social institutions. We learn from an early age to regulate 'our behaviours and feelings in keeping with the social institutions of time' (Elias 1992: 11). As Ruth's experience suggests, if we do not conform to these social institutions then life can become difficult in some way or another. Indeed Elias argues that conforming to time is part of the civilizing process:

> The conversion of the external compulsion coming from the social institutions of time into a pattern of self-constraint embracing the whole life of an individual, is a graphic example of how a civilizing process contributes to forming the social habitus.
>
> (Elias 1992: 11)

The external compulsion by social institutions into a temporal conscience marks this civilizing process. Life course and generation are no different in this regard. As Ruth's experience suggests, key times are marked out in particular ways. Similarly, events like fatherhood are expected to happen at particular, even right, times in the process of people's lives. Warren's family's must 'come to terms with' his impending fatherhood. This most of his family do, but as Margaret points out, Warren's father still cannot come to terms with his son's early fatherhood. We might be tempted to interpret this as a problem of values and a moral disposition. But Warren's father was of a similar age to Warren when he fathered his son. These considerations of the right and wrong time are better explained though a theoretical lens where the mothers', fathers' and grandparents' experiences are compared and found to be at odds with the symbols of social institutions, processes of social habitus and a temporal conscience of generations.

Like Warren's father, the teenage pregnancy and parenthood team would far prefer that teenagers did not become parents, although their reasoning is quite different; they use a different series in arriving at the disposition of a right time to have a child. Wide-ranging health education campaigns are implemented to promote contraception in areas of high teenage pregnancy prevalence, including the low-income estate where this research was conducted. The justifications for these campaigns are provided through another kind of social symbol, epidemiological data. As a policy document written by this teenage pregnancy and parenthood team notes, 'the infant mortality rate for babies born to teenage mothers is 60% higher than for babies born to older mothers.' (NHS 2009: 2). Although the risks are more nuanced than this assertion suggests (see Phipps et al. 2002), the emphasis on this headline measure in policy documents points to the ways in which risk, in this case risk to a child, is constructed as a series and juxtaposed against age, which in turn allows for a 'civilisatory conversion of external compulsion by the social institutions of time into a kind of temporal conscience' (Elias 1992: 11).

This temporal conscience is not immutable, however, as becomes evident once Bridget becomes a mother at 13 years old and Warren a father at 15. The teenage pregnancy and parenthood team focus on Bridget as a mother, and social services on defending Warren's rights of access as a father. The external compulsion changes as well, social policy is directed by evidence that teenage mothers who successfully complete education and training are more likely to be employed, and young dads who are engaged in parenthood contribute to the child's well-being. The events in the series are rewritten and the civilizing conversion changes. Teenage parenthood is valorized in this process. The conscience of generations is reconfigured making the grandparents invisible to service provision. These temporal changes have implications in explaining vulnerability. These we consider in the next section.

Time and vulnerability

Time is the fourth dimension in the model of vulnerability described earlier. Most often in discussions of vulnerability time is conceptualized as cross-sectional, linear and determined (Watts and Bhole 1993, Blaikie et al. 2004). Key events tip precarious groups and individuals into vulnerability. Similarly, as we have shown in the case of Geoff and Margaret, the 'midnight drop' of their three granddaughters by social workers propelled a precarious household into vulnerability. Geoff uses the evocative metaphor of a black hole in recounting the experiences of trying to support the three young girls during that time:

> It's just ... I don't know I can't explain it. It's like, like I keep saying to [the support worker] sometime at [the third-sector grandparents organization], all the time before we like, we're going through putting in for [child support benefits] it's like you're in a black hole and you can't see the light, you try to crawl up it but now I can because when they informed us we got [the benefits], it were just, it were like a miracle, you just couldn't believe it but now I can see the light at the end of the tunnel, I'm going up there you know what I mean. I mean sometimes before I were going up there and coming down and, er ....

There is, however, a further significant theme in this quote to explain the process of vulnerability. Geoff extends his metaphor to include light, which he and his family are able to crawl towards (almost literally we feel as we read the transcript in full) with the support of advice workers from third-sector organizations. That the 'midnight drop' compromises two dimensions of the model of vulnerability is obvious; material resources to address everyday basic needs are significantly eroded and resilience as capacity to respond to the crisis reduced. In part this is because there are three more girls' basic needs to meet in a low-income household, but this does not determine their vulnerability. According to Geoff it is the failure of service provision to respond to their condition that impacts on them most significantly. Furthermore, the intervention of the advice worker to ensure that Geoff and Margaret receive the benefits and support to which they are entitled is identified as the mechanism that staves off vulnerability in that moment.

In this chapter we have considered time as more than cross-sectional, linear and determined. As shown, the temporal conscience of generations is processual, relational and mutable. More than this, its relation to social institutions has significant implications for the vulnerability of individuals and households. In Ruth and Bridget's case the writing of care pathways for Bridget means Ruth, who considers herself mother to both Bridget and her child, is not considered by service providers. She observes that this focus has material effects on the planning of household income and expenditure and the potential to exacerbate vulnerability. For Warren, a focus on him as the child's father, despite the resistance of Michelle's mother, can be seen to decrease vulnerabilities for Warren and his child as his rights of access are enforced through an external agency.

This qualitative longitudinal research brings into view cross-sectional events and the mutable conscience of generations. These temporal processes contribute to the interpretation and explanation of vulnerability. In the final section, we consider the implications of these insights for social policy.

Vulnerability, intergenerational exchange and the conscience of generations: Conclusion

We would argue that through the temporal framing in the research we gain insights that have real and practical implications for social policy and practice. In this research, for example, we have charted the significant ways in which advice workers have supported grandparents, their children and grandchildren. At the time of writing, this third-sector organization, whose value is reflected in Geoff and Margaret's case, has closed. The advice workers no longer provide clinics and support services in the city. There is no known replacement. We have little reason to doubt that there are other families like Geoff and Margaret's who will be thrown into the 'black hole' of vulnerability in the process of caring for their grandchildren. The significant difference now is that there are no advice services to ameliorate that vulnerability.

We have also made a case for a temporal conscience of generations, showing how the framing of events of becoming a grandparent and teenage parent make valid certain generational relations at the expense of others. This analysis shows how vulnerabilities are exacerbated through making the grandparent generation invisible. Evidence across social policy suggests this is a common issue. Strategies for early intervention with vulnerable children, for example, provide examples of the absence of grandparents in social policy. Two recent reports prepared for the UK coalition government (Field 2010, Allen 2011) make a strident case for early interventions with young children (aged zero to three years) to give them:

the social and emotional bedrock they need to reach their full potential; and to those [interventions] which help older children become the good parents of tomorrow.

(Allen 2011: xiii)

Graham Allen's (2011) report makes only one reference to grandparents. This is a discussion of the much-discredited notion of a generational transmission of a culture of poverty. Frank Field (2010: 64) offers a more nuanced view of parenting, observing that 'services need to welcome all parents and carers, including fathers, and grandparents', but that service planning and service provision often assume that the mother is the main or only carer.

We have shown how a temporal conscience of generations underwrites policy and practices and how generational practices at odds with these symbols of social institutions exacerbate vulnerabilities. The temporal framing in this research highlights a significant gap in social policy. Grandparents acting as primary carers for their children and grandchildren do not seem to be considered in social policy literature in the UK. This leads to particular institutional practices becoming embedded in health and social care provision, such as we have shown in care pathways written by the teenage pregnancy and parenthood team. Confronting assumptions that underlie the conscience of generations in policy and practice may lead to strategies to ameliorate significant vulnerabilities for very young grandparents caring for their children and grandchildren.

References

Adam, B. (1990) *Time and Social Theory*, Cambridge: Polity Press.
Allen, G. (2011) *Early Intervention: The Next Steps*, London: The Stationary Office.
Blaikie, P., Cannon, T., Davis, I. and Wisner, B. (2004) *At Risk: Natural Hazards, People's Vulnerability and Disasters*, Abingdon: Routledge.
Cipriani, R. (2013) 'The many faces of social time: A sociological approach', *Time & Society*, 22(1): 5–30.
DWP (2011) *A New Approach to Child Poverty: Tackling the Causes of Disadvantage and Transforming Families' Lives*, Department for Works and Pensions, London: HM Government Stationary Office.
Elias, N. (1992) *Time: An Essay*, Oxford: Basil Blackwell.
Emmel, N. (2013) *Sampling and Choosing Cases in Qualitative Research: A Realist Approach*, London: Sage.

Emmel, N., Davis, L. and Hughes, K. (2011) *The Aspirations of Vulnerable Grand-parents and the Life Chances of Their Grandchildren*, Leeds: University of Leeds.

Emmel, N. D. and Hughes, K. (2009) 'Small N access cases to refine theories of social exclusion and access to socially excluded individuals and groups', in D. Byrne and C. Ragin (eds) *The Sage Handbook of Case-Based Methods*, London: Sage.

Emmel, N. D. and Hughes, K. (2010) ' "Recession, it's all the same to us son": The longitudinal experience (1999–2010) of deprivation', *21st Century Society*, 5(2): 171–182.

Emmel, N. D., Hughes, K., Greenhalgh, J. and Sales, A. (2007) 'Accessing socially excluded people-trust and the gatekeeper in the researcher-participant relation-ship', *Sociological Research Online*, 12(2). Available at: www.socresonline.org.uk/12/2/emmel.html.

Emmel, N. D. and Malby, B. (2000) *Meeting Health Needs in Gipton – Regeneration and Health*, Leeds: East Leeds Primary Care Group.

Field, F. (2010) *The Foundation Years: Preventing Poor Children Becoming Poor Adults*, The report of the Independent Review on Poverty and Life Chances, London: HM Government Stationary Office.

Grandparents Plus (2009) *The Poor Relation? Grandparental Care: Where Older Peo-ple's Poverty and Child Poverty Meet*, London: Grandparents Plus and the Equality and Human Rights Commission.

Hughes, K. (2007) 'Migrating identities: The relational constitution of drug use and addiction', *Sociology of Health & Illness*, 29(5): 673–691.

NHS (2009) 'Update on current interventions to reduce teenage pregnancy'. Available at http://www.leeds.nhs.uk/Downloads/Corporate/Board%20Papers/2009/March%202009/February%202009/Teenage%20Pregnancy.pdf. Accessed May 2013.

Phipps, M. G., Sowers, M. and DeMonner, S. M. (2002) 'The risk for infant mortal-ity among adolescent childbearing groups', *Journal of Women's Health*, 11(10): 889–897.

Savage, M., Devine, F., Cunningham, N., Taylor, M., Li, Y., Hjellbrekke, J., Le Roux, B., Friedman, S. and Miles, A. (2013) 'A new model of social class? Findings from the BBC's great British class survey experiment', *Sociology*, 47(2): 219–250.

Shildrick, T., MacDonald, R., Webster, C. S. and Garthwaite, K. (2012) *Poverty and Insecurity: Life in 'Low-pay, No-Pay' Britain*, Bristol: Policy Press.

Standing, G. (2011) *The Precariat: The New Dangerous Class*, London: Bloomsbury Academic.

Thomson, R. (2009) 'Thinking intergenerationally about motherhood', *Studies in the Maternal* 1(1): Open Research Online The Open University's repository of research publications and other research outputs. Available at www.mamsie.bbk.ac.uk/back_issues/issue_one/journal.html.

Tsey, K., Wenitong, M., McCalman, J., Whiteside, M., Baird, L., Patterson, D., Baird, B., Fagan, R., Cadet-James, Y. and Wilson A. (2004) 'A participatory action research process with a rural Indigenous men's group: Monitoring and reinforcing change', *Australian Journal of Primary Health*, 10(3): 130–136.

Watts, M. J. and Bohle, H. G. (1993) 'The space of vulnerability: The causal structure of hunger and famine', *Progress in Human Geography*, 17(1): 43–67.

10
Grandparenting Across the Life Course

Joanna Bornat and Bill Bytheway

> Oh I was delighted, as a matter of fact I was getting ready to adopt grandchildren. I says What is the matter with my sons, are they are not having any family?... And Fred I said, Oh god I am not going to get any grandchildren. I was desperate. I love children really, but er mind you sometimes when they were young we used to mind them, but I was always glad to see them away (laughs) sometimes you know. Some brah memories.
>
> (Man interviewed in 2007, aged 78, who became a grandfather at 58)

> Well I was 80. Absolutely, well the only trouble is where I could go and take care of them and help out you know with the children, I can sit with her on my knee and I can talk to her and she's as happy as anything. But I can't carry her about, I can hold her but I can't carry her about. She's a very big baby.
>
> (Woman interviewed in 2009, aged 81, becoming a grandmother for the sixth time)

Introduction

Mass grandparenting is a twentieth-century phenomenon. The likelihood of being a grandparent or great-grandparent has become more the norm as greater numbers of people have survived into later life (Herlofsen and Hagestad 2012: 30). For the oldest generation and their children, grandchildren and great-grandchildren, this has brought new experiences and relationships (Antonucci et al. 2011). Recent research and policy papers have tended to focus on what is referred to as 'active grandparenting' or 'active ageing' (see for example Harris-Johnson 2010, Van Bavel and De Winter 2011, Sahlen et al. 2012, Walker and Maltby 2012), contributing to campaigns that encourage participative and healthy lifestyles in later life with the aim of reducing health and social care costs. At the same time, an increasing number of grandparents are contributing care and support to their families during times of austerity (Arber and Timonen 2012: 253–256, Grace 2012). Grandparents' support to family members conflicts with policies that aim to reduce the cost of pensions by delaying the age of retirement (Gray 2005). Moreover such policies tend to elide an ambivalence which more accurately describes relationships in late life, particularly where an older generation is seeking or expected to pursue independently fulfilling lifestyles (Luescher and Pillimer 1998, May et al. 2012). Policy debates such as these provide helpful structural frameworks for understanding the interactions and complexities which determine intergenerational relations and contribute to the shaping of how people understand and give their own meanings to being a grandparent. What is missing is a recognition that to effectively engage with grandparenting social policies need to allow for changes during the later life course which inevitably affect perceptions and levels of activity as well as relationships of reciprocity.

Overall, there is little hard evidence about how, in the UK, demographic changes and the economic downturn have affected intergenerational relationships within families; nor about the effect of proposed policies which threaten solidarities and ties with accusations of blame and selfishness directed at older generations (Willetts 2010). Much of the available research is based on cross-sectional studies which neglect how 'intergenerational exchanges change over time, especially in the face of exogenous changes as in the availability of state support' (Grundy and Henretta 2006: 720). The aim of this paper is to provide relevant evidence of such changes. How does grandparenting fit in with the everyday life of people over 75 years of age? What part does it play in their lives and how do they feel about changes in grandparenting roles over time?

We begin with an overview of recent research into grandparenting, before going on to outline our own research. We then introduce three case studies that we draw on in a concluding discussion of the policy implications of a perspective on grandparenting that focuses on change during late life.

Grandparenting in time

It is claimed that there are 14 million grandparents in the UK (The Grandparents Association 2012a). Large-scale surveys show how important grandparents are to families, with 90% of grandparents providing financial support and 25% of the grandchildren being looked after by a grandparent (Hawkes and Joshi 2007). Detailed accurate information is hard to come by, though this may be changing (Chambers et al. 2009, Arber and Timonen 2012). A review of available research demonstrates that a number of factors are leading to an increasing differentiation between grandparents and the roles they play (Chambers et al. 2009, Ch. 6). Thus the type of help which grandparents report providing is associated with age, with people over 75 being more likely to give financial than practical help (Grandparents Plus 2011). Similarly the gender of the grandparents, and of the intervening generation, affects the nature and strength of attachments and relationships (Chan and Elder 2000, Dench and Ogg 2002, Tanskanen and Danielsbacka 2012). Grandparenting roles are also affected by distance. Geographical mobility generally has had the effect of separating the generations, with this tendency becoming greater. Nevertheless, over one in three grandchildren has a grandparent living within 15 minutes' travel (Gray 2005). The likelihood of grandparents providing care was found to be dependent on the health of the grandparents and on their employment status. The fact that over 60% of grandparents are not the oldest members of their family (Grandparents Plus 2011) points to another source of differentiation within the category 'grandparent': the increased likelihood that some will also be providing care and support to their own parents or to another older relative or friend (Gray 2005). But research suggests that this varies according to the size of the family and, in particular, the number of adult children (Grundy and Henretta 2006: 717). Class also leads to distinctions, with the affordability of formal childcare playing a part in whether or not grandparents are called on to provide care, sometimes to the detriment of their own health (Thomas et al. 2000). There is evidence that lower-income generations tend to live nearer to one another and to have more grandchildren than non-manual groups (Gray 2005).

   The notion that grandparenting is a universally applicable state is further undermined by evidence that, as family types become increasingly varied, the contexts within which grandparenting develops are becoming increasingly diverse. The result is 'uncertainty in intergenerational relations and expectations (which) has specific effects on life course role transitions' (Lowenstein et al. 2011: 1078). As more women and men survive into grandparenthood, sharing grandchildren becomes a factor and differences between grandmothers and grandfathers in their relations with grandchildren also have significance (Mueller and Elder 2003, Mann et al. 2009).

The two people who are quoted at the start of this chapter express some of the desires and dilemmas of grandparenting. As an aspired status and an enjoyable relationship, it brings rewards. Yet, as they acknowledge, it also has limits, self-determined and imposed, and its timing is outside their control (See Emmel and Hughes, Chapter 9 in this volume, for a discussion of midlife grandparenting in low-income families). Grandparents may play an active part in supporting their grandchildren at any time from birth into adulthood. A time comes when the grandchildren no longer need routine care and, conversely, a time may come when the grandparent is no longer able or willing to provide such care. When this happens the implicit reciprocities in relationships inevitably shift the focus towards grandparent care and away from grandparent caring (Merz et al. 2008).

Currently there is evidence of increasing numbers of grandparents, especially grandmothers, helping younger people to remain in employment, by caring for grandchildren, sometimes 'retiring' from paid work themselves in order to do so (Thane 2011, Herlofsen and Hagestad 2012). At a time of economic recession, grandparents may feel that there are new responsibilities to be addressed, particularly if family breakdown leads to unexpected housing or childcare needs (see Emmel and Hughes, Chapter 9). One in three working mothers say they rely on grandparents for childcare, and this is true of one in four working families (Grandparents Plus 2011). Allowing for all the many ways in which grandparenting may be experienced and played out, how are shifts in relationships marked and achieved in the day-to-day and week-to-week negotiations over who does what, when and for whom? What can be learned from these experiences to helpfully inform today's policymaking? How does the meaning of grandparenting change, as both younger and older generations grow older?

Methods: The oldest generation

This review of contemporary research indicates a need for evidence that is qualitative, temporal and multidimensional. This is available in our research into the changing position of older people in family life (Bornat and Bytheway 2012). We recruited a sample of 12 diverse families by calling for volunteers through the extensive UK-wide Open University network. In each family, one member over the age of 75 years, 'the Senior', was to be interviewed in 2007 and again 18 months later, and another person, 'the Recorder', was to keep a diary and take photographs.

Forty families responded to our call and we selected a sample of 12. We do not claim that it is in any sense statistically representative but we did use selection criteria that maximized diversity (see Bytheway and Bornat 2010, for details). Inevitably those who responded tended to be from middle-income families who, at the time, felt that their families were able and willing to participate. Several perceived real benefits for the Senior and the family in the proposed activities. Nevertheless, we suspect that most would not have responded one year later: for them, the call to participate had come at a propitious moment that soon passed. Only one family dropped out, shortly after the first interview, and was replaced by another. Over the course of the 18 months, two Seniors died and in each case a proxy, a son and two daughters respectively, took their place at the time of the second interview. So we would claim that, over the course of the 18 months, some of our sample came to represent family situations that are rarely accessible through cross-sectional research methods.

The interviews explored the life history of the Seniors, including their experiences of being grandparented in the first half of the twentieth century as well as their current involvement and attitudes to family life. In addition, however, the strategy of recruiting a Recorder who was in contact with the project office on a monthly basis meant that, potentially, we were in constant touch as events unfolded in the lives of the participants. The Seniors were the focus of the project and we are heavily reliant upon their participation and that of the 12 Recorders, but the research casts light on the wider, unfolding histories of intergenerational relationships within the 12 families. In respect to grandparenting, it is important to note that, with the Seniors being 75 or more, the focus is on expectations and experiences in this stage of life. Although just one person in each family was selected to be the Senior, some of their spouses actively participated, as will be evident from the case studies below. Much research on later life generates a seemingly static image of everyday life; one made up of routine activities and normative ways of maintaining relationships. While comparatively few major life transitions are fully completed in 18 months, it is long enough to uncover change, both individual and familial. In what follows we provide three case studies, using data from the interviews and diaries, to explore how events and changes in family life impinge upon older people and their grandparenting roles. All names have been anonymized, and all diary entries are dated.

Three case studies

A large family

This first case study illustrates how a grandparent describes changes in family life, and the experience of observing her grandchildren growing up. Marie Rees, born in 1931, and her husband, Ally, live on one of the Scottish islands. They have four daughters (all living close by) and a son who lives in Edinburgh. Marie and Ally had by far the largest number of grandchildren within our sample. In her first interview in August 2007, Marie was asked if she saw her family often. She replied:

> So, probably once a week, they're all very busy of course, as women nowadays, they all work and have families. So we've got 18 grandchildren and two great-grandchildren with another two on the way. But of course the grandchildren scattered about a bit now [...] one's out in Dubai and one's in England, and the family that live in Edinburgh, of course they're down there.

Early in the interview she illustrated how they still had large family gatherings, just as they had had when she was a child, describing a visit three months previously by her brother and family. There were nearly 40 at the get-together. Later in the interview, she was asked how intergenerational relations more generally had changed:

> I don't know. I think they're all fairly close to their parents as they always were. Of course they're moving away sooner than we did. I mean we just all stayed at home until we married and now well they're moving away either for university or whatever, [...] the trend seems to be to marry later but they all seem to be, well, three are married and one grandson who's living in Edinburgh with his fiancé. They're getting married next year. Another grandson's going to move in with his girlfriend shortly and, you know, it's just different, you know. It's not a case of staying at home until you get married. There's more moving out. [...] So I think it's different in that way.

This is a clear account of how Marie viewed changes both within her family and within the wider culture. The diary (written by the Recorder, one of her daughters, but in Marie's voice) echoes much of this, recording many visits and celebratory meals. She still enjoyed the company of her teenage grandchildren and their friends: when the four granddaughters from Edinburgh visited (27 March 2008) for example, she was pleased to see how they got on with their island cousins. They arrived late in the evening because 'they were just having a "cruise" around the town as young folk do'. At times she was actively involved in their transition into adulthood. For example, she went to view a house that a grandson had put an offer on, and noted in the diary how difficult it was 'for youngsters to get on the property ladder' (16 March 2008). And, when she travelled to Edinburgh for his wedding, she 'went up town' with her granddaughters and had 'a lot of fun' purchasing a dress for the wedding (8 August 2008). As her grandchildren joined up with partners and moved into their own homes, she was aware of how the family was extending: she met some future 'in-laws' for example, when another grandson became engaged (25 December 2007). In 2007, she still had school-age grandchildren to stay when their parents left for a holiday, or when the children were off school and their parents had to go to work. She was well aware, however, of how the generations age. One Sunday only one of their grandsons was with them for lunch, and she commented on the change from when there were 'four small boys' sat round the table (9 December 2007). Following another 18th birthday, she noted that exactly half their grandchildren were now aged 18 or more (28 September 2008).

Regarding the great-grandchildren, their fourth was born in England soon after the first interview in August 2007, and Marie met him for the first time six months later. This was an opportunity for her to reflect in the diary on changes in parenting practices:

> Parents nowadays are more involved in the 'psychology' of raising children whilst I feel 'we' just got on with it & didn't worry about what was right or wrong! They seem to go to a lot of parenting classes and learn more about it. However it makes me wonder what I did wrong! However if I had my time to live over again I'd probably do exactly the same things.
>
> (14 April 2008)

Contact with another granddaughter reminded her of her own youth:

> Julia reminded me of what it felt like to be 16 and worried about what she would say to impress others! I thought how easy it was to remember back to my own teenage years & the worries one has at that age.
>
> (29 March 2008)

So, through frequent contact with her grandchildren, Marie had ample opportunity to reflect and act upon changes within her family. She was also active in visiting old friends in hospital and more significantly, between the two interviews, Ally, her husband, became progressively more ill and disabled. In May 2008, he was admitted to hospital and re-admitted a number of times over the subsequent 12 months. She noted how he was pleased when their fifth great-grandson was named after him. When she was visiting Ally in hospital in Aberdeen, she was also able to have meals with a granddaughter, a student there. They went shopping in 'shops I'd never have gone into' (28 November 2008). This is typical of the positive attitudes she expressed when writing about her grandchildren. There is no indication that Ally's illness may have prevented her from enjoying family life more fully.

In the follow-up interview in April 2009, Marie was asked if, 18 months later, she was seeing as much of her grandchildren:

> Not as much as I was, 'cause they're sort of branching – they're at the age when their mum and dad hardly sees them, I suppose.

She saw them 'once or twice a month' whereas she used to see them two times a week: 'But that's the way it goes, isn't it?' So, she was well aware of how relationships were changing. Ally's illness had become the dominant demand upon her time and energy. As he was becoming more dependent on her, their grandchildren were conversely becoming more independent. Marie herself was still in good health and able to enjoy opportunities to sustain her relationships with their grandchildren, but she was of the generation that was increasingly needing the support of the wider family. It was their children's generation that was becoming engaged in active grandparenting.

A dispersed family

This case study is of a smaller family in which grandparenting was a more diffuse and intermittent activity but no less meaningful. In 2007, Marion Arthur and her husband, Adam, lived in a village in the north of England where they had moved after retiring from their business. Their middle child, a daughter, had died in early adulthood and had had no children. Their other two daughters were married, each with two children, one living in Edinburgh and the other in the south of England.

Adam was the Recorder and his wife, Marion, the Senior. Both were born in 1920. Their grandparenting was done largely through email and telephone, and biannual visits at Christmas and in the summer. From the interviews it seemed that Marion's contacts with the grandchildren were limited, with much news coming to her via Adam's email correspondence. Moreover, her memory and mobility problems (which were more evident by the time of her second interview) were limiting her further in communicating with the grandchildren. The following exchange in the first interview illustrates how they were disappointed not to see more of their grandchildren, and how they had closer and more regular contact with Alec, the oldest grandchild and the only grandson:

Interviewer: And do you see much of your grandchildren?
M: Not really, no, I, Adam, we see Alec because he comes and stays with us for a few days but, er, not the others.
A: Well Joan brings Kath.
M: Yes.
A: Sometimes when she…
M: Well she was here…
A: But she whistles up and down the world and whenever she's sort of passing she grabs…
M: She comes…
A: (Laughing) And brings her here for a day or two…
M: Yes, that's right.

Later in the interview, Adam returned to Alec:

A: Very thoughtful as a grandson, he takes a lot of effort to keep in touch with us, sends us emails from wherever he is and he's sent lots of pictures and he visits us whenever he's around which I think is very good he's a very relaxed lad, I mean you wouldn't think he'd get anywhere but he's extremely bright (laughs) and so, so long as he finds someone really nice to marry, and I hope it'll be marry, I think that people who don't are (pause) it's very hard.

He then turned to their granddaughters:

A: Kath is very harder type, she's determined to be a doctor, er, and has been for years now, although she's fifteen coming up sixteen. The other two girls are very much softer, and have a lovely home surrounding because Ellen and Peter have a good range of friends and they always have wonderful parties for children and they do a lot together which is, I think great, because things that stick in my mind are our family holidays.

M: Yes, that's right.

A: And so if they can, yes we've tried to contribute to make sure they are alright, to get any education they want, and if you can give them education then you can't do much more.

This is the clearest indication in the interviews that Adam and Marion had helped with the cost of the education of their grandchildren, and how it was this rather than more practical help that had characterized their experience of grandparenting.

In the diary, there are some references to Kath and her school successes and teenage adventures, and to the two youngest grandchildren but limited largely to Christmas and birthday presents. In contrast, there are many references to Alec. In 2007, he was an undergraduate student studying in Taiwan: 'they are working him quite hard' (8 December 2007). He regularly attached photographs to his emails and the 'exciting package' of gifts that Alec posted for Christmas had 'something for everyone, with suitable translations ... some were edible – amazing tastes' (25 December 2007). Adam appeared to gain some vicarious pleasure from Alec's emails; a week in Hokkaido was 'very cold but beautiful, and with active volcanoes, and hot pools and a trip in an icebreaker to see the ice floes in the Sea of Okhotsk' (11 February 2008).

In July 2008, Alec, in Japan, kept Adam informed of a visit by his mother and sister, Kath. Upon their return, Adam noted that they would have been 'quite lost' without Alec as there were no signs or menus in English (6 July 2008).

In September 2008, Alec was back in Britain with his girlfriend, Holly, and he phoned to arrange for them to visit Adam and Marion. They were delighted and Adam's description of Alec is full of grandparental pride and affection:

> He is still tall, and almost hidden by a huge rucksack (25kg) and a large guitar in its case [...]. Luckily China still has left luggage offices, so he left it for 2/3 weeks while touring round China. Alec's soft voice & huge smile are still unchanged. We fed him on vegetable lasagne and new potatoes & veg. Appetite still huge.
>
> (8 September 2008)

That autumn, Alec started his final year at university and he was planning to obtain a certificate of competence in Chinese: 'We think he is extraordinary' (9 September 2008). In the evening Alec and Adam went to a local pub: 'he much enjoyed the pub atmosphere which he had not seen for 18 months' (9 September 2008). During this stay, Alec and Adam played chess; both were 'rusty' as their last game had been 15 months previously. 'We have enjoyed his visit – a really lovely lad' (10 September 2008).

In the follow-up interview, Adam and Marion reported that, given Marion's mobility problems, Adam would attend Alec's graduation ceremony on his own. They were then asked about Alec's plans when he returned to Taiwan:

Interviewer: ...does he want to stay out there, do you think?
M: I don't know.
A: Difficult to say, it looks to me as if he'd be very happy as a permanent student. Very easy going and er...not one of these go-getters or anything, but he's very bright.
Interviewer: And he's the one of your grandchildren that you see most of I think, that's what you said last time? But maybe the others have got a bit...
A: Yes they have, well Joan occasionally brings Kath along. At Christmas time they all turn up which is very nice of them. They spend two days then they're off. That's what you have to accept. But er...they're very good these grandchildren. They all seem to enjoy being here. They've got busy lives to...
Interviewer: Yes, how do you keep in touch with them?
A: Well, not very much really (laughing). Occasionally you'll get a very nice little letter from one of them which is usually in response to something we've done but er...we don't write letters I'm afraid. Well my writing is so awful (laughing).

Again this is evidence of a certain regret that they were not able to see more of the grandchildren. Overall, Adam and Marion recognized that the children were growing up and that Alec, their oldest, was already making his own independent relationship with his grandparents. Living at a distance and now well into their 80s, they grandparented through gifts, money and hospitality. They relied heavily upon communication at a distance and in this respect it was Adam rather than Marion who had the necessary capabilities and resources.

A close-knit family under pressure

The Senior in this family was Geoff Roberts, born in 1926. He and his wife, Lettie, have three daughters, a son and two granddaughters:

Georgina, aged 27, and Amy, aged eight. They all live in the same part of a city in the north of England. When Geoff was interviewed in September 2007, Lettie was being treated for dementia and the family as a whole were providing Geoff with virtually daily support. Judy, their youngest daughter, was the Recorder and she kept a diary from August 2007 through to a few weeks before Geoff died in October 2008.

Georgina visited Geoff and Lettie fairly frequently. In August 2007, when she was moving into a new flat, Geoff and Lettie's house was being renovated by the council and Geoff joked about staying in her flat while this was underway. In December, the flat was ready and Georgina invited them to see it, to enjoy a games night and to meet her new boyfriend, Jack. The whole family was there. Two weeks later, Christmas Day was a busy day, in which Georgina played a major part. Judy wrote in her diary:

> Called at Mam & Dads early, along with Ann, John & Amy to exchange presents. Dad loved all of his and they were all surprises. Things were chaotic as we all opened and watched people open. Dad loves us all to be together and can think of nothing more enjoyable. We left to visit Sally's – Dad sitting with tinsel around his neck. Mam & Dad were being taken to Georgina's for lunch with Peter & Len. Gerry and I went there for tea where we all played cards, family fortunes and Pictionary. Mam & Dad left at 1am so they had a good day. Uncle Ray rang Dad in the morning to wish him Merry Xmas.
>
> (25 December 2007)

Geoff and Lettie had several encounters with Georgina over the following week and, occasionally, over the subsequent months. In contrast, Amy was a grandchild of school age. In the diary, there are frequent mentions of Geoff picking her up from school and he and Lettie providing meals. Amy would help with the washing, shopping and housework. In August 2007, Geoff and Lettie went to her school assembly 'as they were doing a drama'. Amy's mother, Ann, told Geoff off for being loud during the recital: 'they all said Amy was the best' (17 October 2007).

In November, Geoff saw a lot of Amy over the course of one week and it is clear from the diary entries that he was particularly attached to her. On the Monday:

> Dad picked Amy up from school. Once at home Dad remarked to something Amy said with the statement 'When you get home' and Amy replied that 'this is home'. Dad was really touched by this.
>
> (12 November 2007)

And then, on the Friday and the Saturday:

> Amy slept over at Mam & Dads while Ann and John had a night out –
> they had been to the horse racing in the afternoon. Dad let Amy stay
> up late watching *Children in Need*. When she did go up to bed Dad sat
> with her and made up a story (he used to do this would sit for ages but
> now finds it makes him sleepy). After one story Amy said she would
> tell Granddad one. Amy's story was about a little boy who wanted
> to be a girl who had a sister who wanted to be a dog! Dad thought
> how different stories are these days to his old fashioned subjects like
> pirates.
>
> (16 November 2007)

> Before John picked Amy up she gave Dad a big cuddle and sat very
> contented watching TV like when she was younger (now 8). Dad liked
> this and was disappointed that they could not sit for longer.
>
> (17 November 2007)

In May 2008, Geoff gave Amy a fish aquarium for her birthday and, a
few days later, they all went to a garden centre to get her some goldfish.
In August, Amy and her mother 'spent quite a bit of the day' at Geoff
and Lettie's, and played a few board games but by this time Geoff was
not well and he slept a few times while they were there. He died two
months later. In 2009, Judy and Ann, Amy's mother, were interviewed.
This is how they commented on the impact on Amy of the loss of her
grandfather:

> A: I miss him in that way so does Amy cos my daughter, she's ten
>   now, and I mean me mam hasn't been able to or willing really to
>   look after her for a few years since she's been, the way she's been
>   but me dad was always, he would have done anything for Amy,
>   wouldn't he?
> J: uh uh
> A: He would pick her up from school if I needed him to or whatever
>   and I mean that's a practical thing but obviously that's a big miss
>   and I mean she misses him, because they were close. [...] she used
>   to love that when he picked her up and she said they would never
>   stop talking all the way from school all the way home.

This was a family that was under pressure: there was the long-
running refurbishment of Geoff and Lettie's house; problems with

unemployment and housing costs; and Lettie's health, a constant and growing source of concern. His daughters acknowledged that much had depended upon Geoff, and his death was a great loss and added further pressure on the family. At the time of the second interview, they were exploring the possibility of Lettie being admitted into residential care.

Two of the 12 Seniors had no grandchildren. Of the other ten, three were widowed. Their experiences of grandparenting were distinctive in that one was living with a daughter, son-in-law and granddaughter, and a second spent much time visiting her two daughters who lived some distance away. She stayed put in order to be near her oldest daughter who had a severe learning disability. The third widow resembled Marie Rees in that she enjoyed close contact with all her grandchildren, while at the same time having lifelong responsibilities for a seriously disabled brother.

Ten of the 12 Seniors were grandparents and the three case studies were selected to represent the wide range of contexts in which grandparenting was undertaken. Apart from Marie Rees, none had more than five grandchildren and so she was exceptional. Arguably the Arthurs were similar to two others who had grandchildren living in distant places. In one case, serious efforts were made during the course of the 18 months to enable the grandparents to move to live nearer their daughter and her family. The Roberts family represents two others characterized by working-class histories and retaining a degree of residential proximity. Finally, in reviewing the 12 Seniors, it is important to note that five, including the two without grandchildren, had quasi-grandparent relationships as a result of adoption or reconstituted families.

Conclusion

Through interviews and diaries, constructed at different points in time, and through time, we have been able to see how older people experience the 'taken-for-grantedness and great symbolism' of grandparenthood (Cunningham-Burley 1986: 469). The three case studies demonstrate how people both make and are made by their grandparental status, and how relationships are affected by various instabilities as they and their grandchildren change and grow older. It is clear that distance plays a part in the closeness and frequency of grandparent–grandchild contacts. Living far apart can limit relationships, but those grandchildren who are older and more independent can make their own relationships through email and visiting. Living close facilitates varied types of reciprocity, as the balance of care needs changes and with it the nature of support.

The commitment and attachment of grandparents to grandchildren, through the intervening generation, is strongly in evidence, yet for these three Seniors, their contribution to the day-to-day care of young children is limited, except in the case of the Roberts, a closely knit family with only one young grandchild. What is evident, in all three, is that grandparents are 'an essential part of family life' (Chambers et al. 2009: 19) even when living at considerable distances from their grandchildren. Moreover, in our data there is no evidence that grandchildren and grandparents compete with each other for family resources. However, this could alter as the bases for the independence of the oldest generation change within families. A balance is in part secured by the availability of free and accessible health care: those grandparents with deteriorating conditions appear to be receiving appropriate NHS treatment without the intervention of other family members. When it comes to social care, the situation could be very different. Of the 12 families in our sample, seven are at risk of being among the two million older people in the UK with care-related needs who get no support from public or private sector agencies. This proportion is likely to increase as eligibility for public funds for social care is further restricted (Age UK 2012) and publically funded services, including networks and advice services, are cut back or eliminated. Finding their own social care, through private networks, can mean an individualization of decision-making and responsibilities that is risky and sometimes costly for older people and their families. Funding cuts in social care budgets have the effect of shifting the balance between public and family-based care in ways that may test the abilities of the generations to manage and sustain relationships which are valued by all family members. In Scotland, where a popular and effective policy of free social care is available to those assessed as eligible, the rising cost and unevenness of provision is being debated (Audit Scotland 2008, Barnes 2012). Throughout the UK, the response to further cuts and rising costs could result in a push towards provision which might be described as more southern European in nature (Lowenstein and Katz 2010: 192–194), one that places expectations on the family rather than the state as care providers.

The balance between state and family, in relation to care and support in late life, is also threatened by the availability of transport alternatives as circumstances change. In families living in areas well served by a network of public transport, such as the Roberts, the oldest generation were able to remain mobile and within easy reach of younger family members. However in the case of the Arthurs, where distances between the generations were great and local public transport virtually non-existent, preferred options for independent living, and opportunities for grandchildren to visit in the future, are greatly reduced when car driving becomes no longer possible for the grandparents. We would argue that the availability and accessibility of public transport networks deserves to be given a much higher profile in policies for care and support in late life if family support networks are to avoid being stretched to their limits.

We have highlighted social care and transport as both are policy issues that are basic to the sustainability of family ties and relations between the generations. Maintaining a balance between the state and families which supports grandparenting and intergenerational family relationships is essential if active and independent roles are not to be threatened and if families are not to be forced to choose between more and less deserving care recipients within and between the generations.

Regarding future research on grandparenting we would advocate a temporal perspective, allowing for changing needs and expectations in how families live out the daily experience of intergenerational relations. Through interviews and diaries it has been possible to hear how people account for and sustain family life, how they initiate or respond to changes in circumstances and relationships. We have gained insights into the preferences, potential tensions, choices and likely decisions of members of the oldest generation.

References

Age UK (2012) *Care in Crisis 2012*, London: Age UK. Available at http://www.ageuk.org.uk/documents/en-gb/campaigns/care_in_crisis_report_2012_report.pro.pdf?dtrk=true.

Antonucci, T. C., Birditt, K. S., Sherman, C. W. and Trinh, S. (2011) 'Stability and change in the intergenerational family: A convoy approach', *Ageing & Society*, 31: 1084–1106.

Arber, S. and Timonen, V. (2012) 'Grandparenting in the 21st century: New directions', in S. Arber and V. Timonen (eds) *Contemporary Grandparenting: Changing Family Relationships in Global Contexts*, Bristol: Policy Press, pp. 247–264.

Audit Scotland (2008) *A Review of Free Personal and Nursing Care*, Edinburgh, Audit Scotland. http://www.audit-scotland.gov.uk/docs/health/2007/nr_080201_free_personal_care.pdf. Accessed 04 October 2012.

Barnes, E. (2012) 'Call for reform as cost of personal care for elderly rises by 150% in 7 years', *The Scotsman*, 29 August. Available at http://www.scotsman.com/news/health/calls-for-reform-as-cost-of-free-personal-care-for-elderly-rises-by-150-in-7-years-1-2493159. Accessed 11 October 2012.

Bornat, J. and Bytheway, B. (2012) 'Working with different temporalities: Archived life history interviews and diaries', *International Journal of Research Methodology*, 15(4): 291–292.

Bytheway, B. and Bornat, J. (2010) 'Recruitment for "the oldest generation project" ', in F. Shirani and S. Weller (eds) *Conducting Qualitative Longitudinal Research: Fieldwork Experiences*, Timescapes Working Paper Series No. 2. Available at http://www.timescapes.leeds.ac.uk/assets/files/WP2-final-Jan-2010.pdf.

Chambers, P., Allan, G., Phillipson, C. and Ray, M. (2009) *Family Practices in Late Life*, Bristol: Policy Press.

Chan, C. and Elder Jr., G. (2000) 'Matrilineal advantage in grandchild-grandparent relations', *The Gerontologist*, 40(2): 179–190.

Cunningham-Burley, S. (1986) 'Becoming a grandparent', *Ageing and Society*, 6: 453–470.

Dench, G. and Ogg, J. (2002) *Grandparenting in Britain: A Baseline Study*, London: Institute for Community Studies.

Grace, E. (2012) 'How to be a healthy and active grandparent', http://www.proudgrandparents.co.uk/how-be-healthy-active-grandparent.html. Accessed 18 September 2012.

Grandparents Plus (2011) Policy Briefing Paper 01, available at www.grandparentsplus.org.uk. Accessed 18 September 2012.

Gray, A. (2005) 'The changing availability of grandparents as carers and its implications for childcare policy in the UK', *Journal of Social Policy*, 35: 557–577.

Grundy, E. and Henretta, J. C. (2006) 'Between elderly parents and adult children: A new look at the intergenerational care provided by the "sandwich generation" ', *Ageing and Society*, 26: 707–722.

Harris-Johnson, D. (2010) *The Parent Part of Grandparenting: A Guide for Today's Active Grandparents*, Bloomington: Xlibris.

Hawkes, D. and Joshi, H. (2007) 'Millennium cohort study: Grandparents', *Briefing 4*, available at www.cls.ioe.ac.uk/shared/get-file.ashx?id=1404&itemtype=document. Accessed 18 September 12.

Herlofsen, K. and Hagestad, G. (2012) 'Transformations in the role of grandparents across welfare states', in S. Arber and V. Timonen (eds) *Contemporary Grandparenting: Changing Family Relationships in Global Contexts*, Bristol: Policy Press, pp. 27–49.

Lowenstein, A. and Katz, R. (2010) 'Family and age in a global perspective', in D. Dannefer and C. Phillipson (eds) *The Sage Handbook of Social Gerontology*, London: Sage, pp 190–214.

Lowenstein, A., Katz, R. and Biggs, S. (2011) 'Rethinking theoretical and methodological issues in intergenerational family relations research', *Ageing & Society*, 31: 1077–1083.

Luescher, K. and Pillimer, K. (1998) 'Intergenerational ambivalence: A new approach to the study of parent-child relations in later life', *Journal of Marriage and the Family*, 60: 413–425.

Mann, R., Khan, H. and Leeson, G. (2009) 'Age and gender differences in grandchildren's relations with their maternal grandfathers and grandmothers', *Oxford Institute of Ageing Working Papers*, Oxford, Working Paper 209.

May, V., Mason, J. and Clarke, L. (2012) 'Being there yet not interfering: The paradoxes of grandparenting', in S. Arber and V. Timonen (eds) *Contemporary Grandparenting: Changing Family Relationships in Global Contexts*, Bristol: Policy Press, pp. 139–156.

Merz, E.-M., Schuengel, C. and Schulze, H.-J. (2008) 'Inter-generational relationships at different ages: An attachment perspective', *Ageing and Society*, 28: 717–736.

Mueller, M. and Elder Jr., G. (2003) 'Family contingencies across the generations: Grandparent-grandchild relationships in holistic perspective', *Journal of Marriage and Family*, 65: 404–417.

Sahlen, K.-G., Löfgren, C., Brodin, H., Dahlgren, L. and Lindholm, L. (2012) 'Measuring the value of older people's production: A diary study', *BMC Health Services Research*, 3: 12–14.

Tanskanen, A. and Danielsbacka, M. (2012) 'Beneficial effects of grandparental involvement vary by lineage in the UK', *Personality and Individual Differences*, 53: 985–988.

Thane, P. (2011) 'There has always been a "Big Society"', available at http://www.historyworkshop.org.uk/there-has-always-been-a-big-society/. Accessed 18 September 2012.

The Grandparents Association (2012a) 'General leaflet', available at http://www.grandparents-association.org.uk/images/general_leaflet2010.pdf. Accessed 18 September 2012.

Thomas, J., Sperry, L. and Yarbrough, M. (2000) 'Grandparents as parents: Research findings and policy recommendations', *Child Psychiatry and Human Development*, 31(1): 3–22.

Van Bavel, J. and De Winter, T. (2011) *Becoming a Grandparent and Early Retirement in Europe*, Bamberg: European Science Foundation. Available at http://www.vub.ac.be/SOCO/demo/papersonline/Van%20Bavel%20and%20De%20Winter%202011.pdf. Accessed 2 October 2012.

Walker, A. and Maltby, T. (2012) 'Active ageing: A strategic policy solution to demographic ageing in the European Union', *International Journal of Social Welfare*, 21: S117–S130.

Willetts, D. (2010) *The Pinch: How the Baby Boomers took their Children's Future – and Why They Should Give it Back*, London: Atlantic Books.

11
Conclusions

Janet Holland and Rosalind Edwards

An overall picture

In the chapters of this book the relatively dry descriptions of the Timescapes study in the introduction come to life through the experiences of the participants as they are described, analysed, explained and compared by the researchers who have followed their lives for a space of time. The intersection of biographical, historical and generational timescapes, a major interest of the research, leapt from the pages carried on the words of children, sisters and brothers, friends, mothers and fathers, and grandparents and grandchildren, demonstrating through their narratives the use and value of qualitative longitudinal research for understanding these temporal processes.

In the introduction to this book we generated a series of questions in an attempt to gain a more holistic understanding of life-course processes and transitions, and we have seen the answers to these questions spilling through the chapters in the book. The chapters have shown us how intergenerational dependencies and responsibilities can work out over time; how fluid patterns of intimacy and family life can influence the long-term resourcing of families and the well-being of individuals in material and emotional terms; what the interplay between formal and informal care and support can be over the life course; and how particular policy developments relate to individual biographical change. They have also revealed how social policies intersect in the lives of individuals and families through time, their long-term impact and potential lessons for policy development. The effects of policy and policy changes can be clearly seen in these lives, from, for example, the constraints that policies of austerity place on the life and plans of a well-established, middle-class father as his work became less secure, to the damage that they can wreak on those caring grandparents who thought they could tumble no further down society's ladder until their local support services were no longer funded and the cost of caring took them even further into poverty. Only qualitative longitudinal research can provide such depth of understanding of these effects and their impact on individuals, families and generations through time.

Emerging themes

We live as ever in interesting times, and the research conducted as part of the Timescapes study has straddled changes in social, family and welfare policies across a change in government in the UK from New Labour to a Conservative–Liberal Democrat coalition. Many chapters drew attention to the contingent changes and some of the effects they have had on the groups the researchers have been studying. In this conclusion, we will draw together the major themes emerging in the book and the policy implications associated with these themes.

Timescapes was grounded in investigating the intersection of biographical, generational and historical time in the lives of participants located along the life course. This starting point led all projects into the linked, interrelated and entwined lives of those in other generations and the diversity of inter and intra-generational relationships as they developed and changed over time, through the life course and in the course of each qualitative longitudinal study. Not surprisingly a major theme emerging in all chapters is that of generational relationships. The major social divisions of gender and class came into view also throughout the chapters and were threaded through analyses of the specific timescapes under study. Given the family focus of the Timescapes study, these latter themes were also explored through consideration of the relationship between work and family life, with an interesting methodological and analytical contribution from Sarah Irwin and Mandy Winterton's secondary analysis project (Chapter 8) that provided a different interpretation of primary data from the two projects in which the data was generated (see chapters 5 and 7).

Generational relations

The changes in UK social, family and welfare policies based on the predicated need for austerity (because of the 2008 financial crash) mesh onto the political concerns and ideologies of the departing New Labour government and the incoming Conservative–Liberal Democrat coalition government (in 2010). These concerns form the backdrop of the

Timescapes study, and the effects run through all of the chapters, including their impact on generational relationships.

Starting at a general level, in Chapter 2 Rosalind Edwards, Susie Weller and Sarah Baker took issue with political rhetoric that proposes that intergenerational justice is fair reciprocity and obligation; a rhetoric that pits generations against each other in proposing that the baby boomer generation 'had it all', have skewed the allocation of resources in their own favour, and that the imbalance should be reversed. The policy solutions proposed by proponents of this scenario are reduced state expenditure and welfare state contraction, longer working lives and reduced pensions. It is here that a longitudinal and historical perspective on generation draws attention to the fact that the baby boomers themselves have worked to generate and support the expanded social provision that later generations have enjoyed, and that a generational conflict approach obscures the operation of other intra-generational cleavages such as the social divisions of class, gender and ethnicity.

The political rhetoric also ignores the intricacy, fluidity and complexity of intra and intergenerational relations, particularly given that generations can weave unevenly across and within age cohorts in closely layered generations, as we also saw in chapters 4 and 9. Any reduction of social and welfare provision of the older generation is liable to throw a burden of care onto the younger, a point that Joanna Bornat and Bill Bytheway also made in Chapter 10, where they suggested that this type of policy pressure is likely to produce a situation in the UK more similar to that in southern Europe, where care for the older generation rests with the family not the state. But the main intent of Edwards and colleagues was to show that these broad global generational injustice arguments in support of particular social policies have little purchase in the 'diverse and intricate temporal small generation worlds' that their research explored, and they advocated intergenerational dialogue in political and media discussion and as a guide to policy development.

In Chapter 2, children were asked for their aspirations for their parents, demonstrating caring and concern for the parents' future happiness and material well-being, sometimes recognizing an obligation to repay the care they had themselves received. These concerns and the direction of care from younger to older were also seen in the responses of children and younger people in chapters 7 and 10. In chapters 9 and 10 we learned about caring in the more usual direction, here about grandparents and their relationships with younger family members. In Chapter 9, Nick Emmel and Kahryn Hughes show how young grandparents in the precariat, often part of closely layered generations and so carrying responsibility for both their children and grandchildren, were thrust into grandparenthood before they felt ready. Here policy weighed heavily on these poor families, and even when there was provision of welfare and a policy focus (for example on pregnant young people, addressing their education and potential work future) the grandparents and their caring and material contributions to the younger generation remained unrecognized and social service providers could be unaware of the extent and significance of that support. Emmel and Hughes pointed to a tension between the socially institutionalized time of grandparenting seen in policy and societal norms on the one hand, and the experiences of grandparenting and parenting in the lives of the participants in their study on the other. Austerity cuts to statutory and third sector services that provided advice and support for these families created further difficulties for them.

Chapter 4 gave us insight into intergenerational relationships and grandparental care from the perspective of young fathers in relatively similar families to those discussed by Emmel and Hughes in Chapter 9. In Chapter 4, Bren Neale and Carmen Lau Clayton rejected the 'cycle of disadvantage' argument (where cultures of deprivation and parenting deficit are assumed to pass down generations) that they identified as embedded in policy and practice thinking; assumptions made despite considerable contrary evidence. For them and other opponents of this position in this edited collection, parenting cultures are only one part of the complex set of structural, economic, relational and environmental factors that affected the lives of families they studied. Grandparental care as gift and/or curse is discussed in this context, and Neale and Lau Clayton's policy suggestion is to tailor support for families where generations are closely layered to produce a better balance of care across generations, and between the young parents, enabling young fathers and mothers to play an effective role in their children's lives.

Chapter 10 turned to older grandparents; here Bornat and Bytheway gathered retrospective and prospective accounts of the oldest generation's relationships with grandchildren. They revealed the emotional, practical and material support that flowed from older to younger generations, varying in type and amount over time in these long lives. By this age grandchildren may not need direct, practical grandparenting, and the direction of care and support may have reversed in some respects, but hands-on grandparents did remain in this group of over-75s. Policy concerns here are that reduction in welfare, health and particularly care support from the state to these older people might throw responsibility back onto their children/families, already squeezed in providing for themselves and their own children. Bornat and Bytheway high-lighted social care and transport as policy issues that are basic to the sustainability of family ties and relations between the generations.

Families and intergenerational relationships were also of crucial importance for the participants discussed in Chapter 3, in which Sheena McGrellis and Janet Holland were centrally concerned with the social, historical and policy context of the changing situation in Northern Ireland over the last 15 years, and its impact on young people in their study. They found that in the face of the complexity of young people's lives and their intersecting identities and activities across pol-icy areas, policies and services were compartmentalized into different departments and agencies, with young people generally falling through the cracks. 'The Troubles' and a history of generationally transmitted sectarian divisions and violence coloured how young people under-stood themselves and their relationships with families, communities, friends and politics, and affected their trajectories into adulthood. These effects could be seen in the major policy areas considered in the chapter. In education few schools were integrated, the majority experience was segregation; and in housing segregation was the rule, often because people wanted to live close to their families, but enforced by sec-tarian communities in many instances when they did not. In work and employment the recession led to job loss and unemployment or underemployment for many, austerity measures exacerbating economic contraction. McGrellis and Holland identified a gap in support and pol-icy provision for those in their mid- to late 20s with composite needs who wanted to return to work, training or education, and suggested that targeted support could be made available for this group, usually seen as outside youth provision and so ineligible for specific youth pro-grammes. They give a brief description of the experience of a group of young single fathers with complex parenting histories, differing from that of the young men in chapters 4 and 9, but highlighting the impor-tance of the physical, emotional and material intergenerational support from parents, which enabled them to look after their own children.

Fathers were the focus in Chapter 5 and a consideration of gen-erational relationships led us into issues of classed transmission and inherited paternal identities. The starting point for Karen Henwood, Fiona Shirani and Carrie Coltart was increasing policy concern around fatherhood and the idea of involved fatherhood as an ideal in contrast to the more traditional breadwinner father. Ideals of father involve-ment and commitment to an egalitarian model of parenting were widely upheld by the fathers in their study, but practical barriers often prevented them from becoming a reality. Policy attempts to address this, for example introducing parental leave, can have an impact on patterns of working and caring in different families. Moving back along the life course, Henwood and colleagues suggested that practitioners and policy-makers need to promote educational practices to eliminate gender stereotypes and encourage the social and emotional development of boys and men to improve their capacity and potential to care for themselves and others.

One way that some fathers dealt with barriers to their involvement, and with a feeling of exclusion they experienced when their wives were pregnant and particularly breastfeeding, was to translate their role in caring for the family to be that of providing for them materially, part of the traditional male role. The longitudinal approach in this study, as in the other studies, enabled an exploration of how different issues continue, emerge or recede over time, in this instance in men's fathering. This helps to identify how fathers can be supported by different policies at different life stages. Henwood and colleagues point out that the experiences of fathers have implications for mothers, and the mother–father relationship should be recognized in policy-making, since addressing practical barriers to father involvement could create new opportunities for mothers in earning and caring. Such an approach could also help provide potential solutions for the basic problem discussed in the following section: gender inequality in the domestic division of labour.

Gender, class, work and family life

The themes of gender, class, work and family life ran through most of the chapters providing complementary information from their analysis and interpretation, with the most sustained contribution coming in Chapter 6 where Rachel Thomson examined women as (first time) mothers and workers. The negative effect on women of the change of government and policies was specified here. New Labour was committed to supporting vulnerable children with family-oriented policies, whereas the coalition government has sought to roll back the welfare state, cutting down or dropping these provisions in the name of austerity. In addition, women have borne the brunt of the recession in occupying the most precarious positions in the labour market, and in absorbing the radical cuts to the welfare state. This has occurred in terms of their work (many worked in the public sector and have lost their jobs in cuts) and increased demand for their caring services in their family when welfare provision disappeared, by virtue of the domestic division of labour.

Compounding the recent pressures on women are the effects of the fundamentally differentiating experience of motherhood itself on the situation of women in employment and the labour market. Here women experience the 'motherhood penalty' of lower levels of occupational achievement/success and lower pay than men. As the Fawcett Society (Woodroffe 2009) points out, motherhood has a direct and dramatic influence on women's pay and employment prospects and typically lasts a lifetime. Motherhood marks the return of the iron grip of the domestic division of labour, as Irwin and Winterton indicated in Chapter 8 through an extensive analysis of gender difference and inequality in the division of labour in the home. Institutionalization of the double burden of paid work and domestic labour for mothers was a major contributor to this situation and exemplified by austerity-led policy changes that pay no heed to their effects on women.

Chapters 6 and 8 take on the issue of choice for women in this regard. In the former Thomson argued that attempts to guide policy on the basis of mothers' preferences for home or work ignore the political, economic and cultural contexts in which such 'choices' are made. Chapter 8 spelt out this hollow choice in detail, drawing on wide national and international research literature and a secondary analysis of data from two other Timescapes projects by Henwood and colleagues and Harden and colleagues, respectively (chapters 5 and 7). From their analysis of the latter source, Irwin and Winterton concluded that even when mothers have extensive employment responsibilities this did not absolve them from societal and deeply engrained personal assumptions about their domestic, childcare and childrearing responsibilities, and pointed to the deep-seated nature of economic and cultural drivers of gendered inequalities in experiences of time pressure in family life. They suggest that policy should engage with an adequate understanding of how 'choices' are framed in contexts that are effectively taken as given.

This is not to deny of course that there have been changes in women's working lives and experiences of education in recent decades. Thomson used interviews and family case studies in Chapter 6 to reflect how expectations about women's work and careers have transformed in recent generations; there has been progress but also contradictions and generational ruptures. By identifying women at the same biographical moment (maternity), the fragmentation of women's biographies along class lines and the difficulty of forging relations of solidarity between women was also captured. The middle-class families reflected intergenerational rupture in that mothers were better educated than their own mothers, expected work and career, and were likely to see motherhood and paid work as competing. The working-class mothers saw these as complementary projects. Divisions between women on the basis of social class were seen to be hardening as middle-class families sought to defend their children against downward social mobility.

Many of the issues discussed here emerge in Chapter 7, where Jeni Harden, Alice MacLean, Kathryn Backett-Milburn, Sarah Cunningham-Burley and Lynn Jamieson focused on 'working families', families with working parents and young children, and how they managed the pressures on family lives that this entails. Their research compared mothers' and fathers' views of their parental responsibilities with how their children understood them. Harden and colleagues suggested that parental responsibility is currently seen as a key requirement by policy-makers, with 'good' parenting regarded as a potential solution to many of society's ills. This 'responsibilization' is reinforced through public discourse and reflects changes in family policy across Europe. Working parents are positioned at the intersection of family and employment policies, raising inherent tensions; with competing demands on individuals played out in family practices.

In the study, parental responsibility is discussed through the notion of 'being there', competing responsibilities and shifting responsibilities in the context of change, where the longitudinal method is particularly useful. Harden and colleagues discerned that 'being there' was a moral narrative through which the concept of responsibility was expressed. Parents in their study accepted the parenting responsibility, but also felt the pressure for meeting the requirements and responsibilities of work, often feeling that they were falling short of the demands they made on themselves in both, never fully 'being there' in either, resulting in feelings of guilt and anxiety. Both parents and children seemed to regard work as taken for granted, something that was normalized and could not be changed; the whole family required to adjust to its demands.

In conclusion

Qualitative longitudinal data and analysis brings to life the conditions and circumstances in which people live out their lives. Following people over time gives insight into how they create and respond to different events, experiences and consequences; a concern with biographical timescapes. It illuminates the way that they are simultaneously embedded in familial and cohort generations, yet shifting their own generational position from, perhaps parent to grandparent, and from younger to older generation; layering a concern with generational timescapes onto biographical. And it reveals the way that biographies and generations are located in different epochs, characterized by particular local and global social, economic and cultural conditions and events, and underlying historical timescapes. These are the lived timescapes that policy seeks to address, and which shape and are shaped by policy initiatives, expectations and values.

In this concluding chapter we have drawn out the way that education, social services, housing, health and care policy-relevant themes run through the various analyses of the qualitative longitudinal data from the Timescapes study reported in the book. Rather than treating these policy related areas separately, qualitative longitudinal research can reveal how they interrelate and weave together in people's lives over time. These inter-relationships can be followed across the life course, from childhood and youth, through parenthood and parenting, to grandparenting and later life. Indeed it is because qualitative longitudinal data and analysis shows how individual and generational lives shift through historical moments that it can provide depth and nuance of understanding of how policy develops, not only in the past and present but also indicate how policy initiatives of the future will touch on, shape and be shaped by the timescapes of the future.

Reference

Woodroffe, J. (2009) *Not Having It All: How Motherhood Reduces Women's Pay and Employment Prospects*, London: Fawcett Society.

CITY OF WOLVERHAMPTON COLLEGE

Index

Printed and bound by CPI Group (UK) Ltd, Croydon, CR0 4YY

CW01019905

*Opposite: Lord Shiva delighting in
the cosmic dance with his musicians*

TOUCHED BY
TRUTH

A CONTEMPORARY HINDU
ANTHOLOGY

COMPILED BY
SANDY & JAEL BHARAT

William Sessions Limited, York, England

TOUCHED BY TRUTH: A CONTEMPORARY HINDU ANTHOLOGY
COMPILED BY SANDY & JAEL BHARAT

First published by Sandy and Jael Bharat 2006

Text copyright Sandy and Jael Bharat 2006, Oxford, England.

Design: Sandy and Jael Bharat. The Om on the front cover is from the Himalayan
Academy collection, available on CD. www.himalayanacademy.com/art

ISBN 1-85072-355-9

All rights reserved. Except for brief quotations in critical articles or reviews, no part of
this book may be reproduced in any manner without prior written permission from the
publishers.

The rights of Sandy and Jael Bharat as author have been asserted in accordance with
the Copyright, Designs and Patents Act 1988.

A CIP catalogue record for this book is available from the British Library.

Printed on environmentally friendly paper by Sessions of York, the Ebor Press,
                              Huntington Road, York YO31 9HS,
                              England
                              Tel +44(0)1904 659224
                              www.sessionsofyork.co.uk

Information on other books by Sandy and Jael Bharat
                              www.spiritualityfordailylife.com

ROYALTIES

Royalties from this book will go to relevant charities associated with
the contributors including
THE LOOMBA TRUST
that aims to educate the children of poor widows throughout India.
The inspiration for the Trust deed came from Raj Loomba's late mother,
Shrimati Pushpa Wati Loomba, who became a widow at the age of 37
and succeeded in educating her seven children single-handed.
Find out more, sponsor a child and donate online at
www.theloombatrust.org

Help educate a needy child in India and also help that child's family escape
from abject poverty.

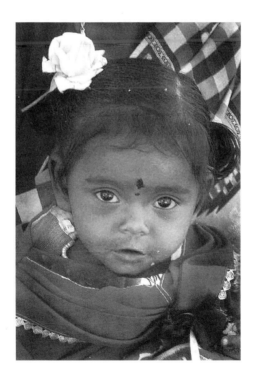

NAMASTE

AND WELCOME TO THIS BOOK.
This traditional Hindu greeting means
'I bow to the God in you and in me.'

ॐ ॐ ॐ ॐ ॐ ॐ ॐ ॐ ॐ ॐ ॐ ॐ ॐ ॐ

Touched by Truth

I salute the supreme teacher, the truth, whose nature is bliss;
Who is the giver of the highest happiness;
Who is pure wisdom;
Who is beyond all qualities and infinite like the sky;
Who is beyond words;
Who is one and eternal, pure and still;
Who is beyond all change and phenomena and who is
the silent witness to all our thoughts and emotions.
I salute truth, the supreme teacher.

- Ancient Vedic Hymn -

CONTENTS

ॐ ॐ ॐ ॐ ॐ ॐ ॐ ॐ ॐ ॐ ॐ ॐ ॐ ॐ ॐ ॐ ॐ ॐ

PREFACE

The contributors to this book are all Hindus from various spiritual paths and walks of life. They have reflected on some special Hindu influence or inspiration in their lives and the impact this person or text or event has had on them. What they have learnt or felt may speak to you also and give you some hope, encouragement, insight into your own spiritual journey. Certainly we have been touched by their openness and experiences. We thank each one of them for sharing their stories. It has been a delightful project.

Behind all of the included stories are special people and texts. Some of them are internationally famous. Some are spiritually illustrious. Others are known best to their families, those who have benefited most from their love and wisdom. Gratitude to them all for the influences and inspiration they have been and continue to be.

Added to each story is some wisdom related to the story itself. This includes poems, verses, and thoughts from great spiritual personalities and scriptures. May their Light and Love illuminate and transform all our lives. Om.

Our thanks to all the kind people and organisations who gave permission to use their texts and photos. Thanks also to Gwyneth Little for proof reading and for sharing some helpful suggestions.

After careful consideration we decided to leave the reflections with their mix of English and American English spellings so that every reader has some contentment with the way things are!

In this book, whenever you read 'Gita' it is short form for the Bhagavad Gita (Song of God), one of Hinduism's most sacred scriptures. As Hindu words are transliterated, there may be several versions of words eg. Bhagavad-Gita, Bhagavad Gita, Bhagavadgita. In this case, we have introduced some uniformity, using Bhagavad Gita as the norm. Quite often words are used with and then without an 'a' at the end, eg. Mahabharata, Mahabharat, referring to one of Hinduism's great epics. Sanskrit scholars could elucidate on all the reasons for this! Check out the Glossary for information about unfamiliar words used.

Om shanti, shanti, shanti
(Hindu invocation of peace)

Sandy and Jael Bharat
Oxford August 2006

www.spiritualityfordailylife.com

FOREWORD

This collection of texts gives a personal glimpse
into the lives of many of its contributors. Some
of them I have known personally and there are
others about whom I have heard so much. They
reflect the value Hinduism has placed in them
and reveal how Hindu values and spiritual
insights can resonate with and have meaning for
others as well as for Hindus.

All religions have similar basic values at their core – truth, respect, empathy,
compassion, tolerance and love amongst others. The values we often subscribe
to our own beliefs are also reflected in other religions. The vast Hindu
community in Britain has observed at first hand life in a predominantly
Christian country. Isn't it remarkable that there has been no conflict in the way
we have developed our economic and social life here? No longer are we seen
as a misunderstood religion worshipping deities. What people talk about are
the values we represent.

Immigration to this country since the early fifties has stood the test of time. It
has also proved that the affinity between different religions is based on values
we attach to our own beliefs and the values others attach to those ideals. It is
by recognising and understanding this commonality that people of all religions
can live together in harmony. There are many examples of how a lack of understanding and acceptance has led to disquiet and, often, violent conflict in
locations around the world. They mark a move away from these core values
and an emphasis on differences rather than similarities.

I welcome the thoughtful contributions to this book with their reflections on
some inspiring people and values within Hinduism and the contribution they
have made to integration, peace and individual enrichment.

The Lord Dholakia of Waltham Brooks OBE DL
London, January 2006

INTRODUCTION

Jill Gant, a good friend, not a Hindu, suggested that it might be helpful to introduce some of the characters and texts that contributors write about in the pages that follow. It seemed a good idea so included in the Glossary, amongst common Hindu words, are brief reviews of some of the special people that have influenced and inspired some of our contributors and who have also played important roles on the broader Hindu stage. You might like to look there before engaging with the reflections.

WHAT IS HINDUISM?

Two eminent Hindu scholars can help us with this. The first is a contributor to this book. The second wrote the description especially for our interfaith book and some extracts are included here.

Prof Seshagiri Rao:

Hinduism is not a founded religion. There is no single person, whose life and ministry started Hinduism; there are many seers and sages who have contributed to the tradition, but none of them is regarded as its founder. It has no beginning in history; no single historical event marks its birth. Actually, Hindus hold that Truth has no beginning and no end; that is why it is called *sanatana dharma*, eternal religion. Hinduism is not a 'creedal' religion. There is no creed that regulates Hindu beliefs….Hinduism is not a missionary religion; proselytization has no place in Hinduism….Nor is it a dogmatic religion. It is a religion based on experience and realization.

Hinduism is not an ecclesiastical religion. Hindus have never been an organized church body. Although there is a place in the tradition for congregational worship practices, the Hindu community, as a whole, does not belong to any church nor does it accept any ecclesiastical head as the sole spokesperson for the whole community…. The aim of Hindu sages has been to illumine faith in its various forms and consolidate values, and not to condemn or destroy any particular form of faith or worship. Hinduism has practiced an approach of harmony *(samanvaya)* and reconciliation *(samadhana)* towards different sects within and outside the tradition. Truth is one, paths are many.[1]

---

[1] K L Seshagiri Rao, 'Hindus in America and the Emerging World Culture,' paper presented to Symposium 'Hindus in America and the Emerging World Culture,' organized by the Sri Venkatesvara Temple, Pittsburgh. Also in Sandy Bharat, *Christ Across the Ganges: Hindu Responses to Jesus*, O Books, May 2007.

Prof Anantanand Rambachan:

Many of the common features of the Hindu tradition are derived from the scriptures known as the Vedas. Orthodox Hindus consider the four Vedas as revelation. Particular Hindu groups regard many other texts as revelation, but the Vedas enjoy an almost unanimous recognition as revealed knowledge….

Wealth (*artha*) and pleasure (*kama*) are among the four legitimate goals of life. Wealth and pleasure must be sought by being responsive to the demands of the third goal, referred to as *dharma. Dharma* is violated when we obsessively pursue private desires that destroy the harmony of the community on which our lives depend. Non-injury (*ahimsa*) is the best expression of *dharma.*

Hinduism's highest goal is liberation (*moksha*). It is a common view in the Hindu tradition that ignorance of the true nature of the human self (*atman*) and God (*brahman*) is the fundamental human problem and the underlying cause of suffering. Liberation cannot be obtained without right knowledge of reality….In its essential nature, the self is eternal. Consciousness and bliss constitute its essence. Ignorant of the true nature of the self, one wrongly identifies it with the body and mind and becomes subject to greed and want. Desire-prompted actions generate results (*karma*) that lead to subsequent rebirths (*samsara*). *Moksha* is consequent upon the right understanding of the nature of the self. It implies the recognition of the self to be different from the psychophysical apparatus and to be immortal. Such an understanding of the self's essential nature, brings an end to the cycle of death, birth and rebirth. For all traditions of Hinduism, *moksha* implies the cultivation of compassion for all beings and freedom from hate and greed.

Hindu sacred texts and tradition remind us constantly that, in relation to God, our language is always limited and inadequate….A God whose nature and essence could be entirely captured in our words or who could be contained within the boundaries of the human mind would not be the absolute proclaimed in Hinduism. No representation of the divine in image or words can ever be final or complete. As it is impossible to capture the limitless within the boundaries of our religion or to define it comprehensively through the limited language of our theology, Hinduism teaches that we must be open to meaningful insights from others that may open our understanding to the inexhaustible nature of the divine….Religious arrogance is the consequence of thinking that one has a privileged relationship with and understanding of God….Hinduism is not challenged by the fact of other traditions claiming revelation from, encounters with and knowledge of God.[2]

[2] Sandy and Jael Bharat, *A Global Guide to Interfaith: Reflections from around the world*, O-Books, May 2007.

REFLECTIONS

TRUTH NEVER LIES
ARUN GANDHI

As a grandson of Mohandas Karamchand Gandhi it should come as no surprise that I would regard him as my mentor. I learnt so much from him. He was such a great influence on my life. For example, sixty years ago, as a ten-year-old, I was growing up on a hundred-acre farm amid a sea of sugar cane fields in South Africa. Apartheid, the government policy of racial discrimination, had already burned its ugly brand across this fertile land. We lived on Phoenix, established by my grandfather. It was the only island of sanity in a colour-crazed South Africa. All prejudices, hate, anger, and discrimination were left outside its borders. Fifteen miles away in Durban, all these feelings were unleashed in gale force.

My grandfather

One Saturday afternoon in Durban, while others enjoyed a siesta, I walked to a little store to spend the sixpence Dad had given me for candy. Up ahead three white men loitered on the curbside. As I drew even with them, they decided to have some fun and excitement. They blocked my way and one grabbed my collar. All three pounced on me. Blows came from all sides. When I fell they kicked me in the ribs. This was my first encounter with the physical violence of apartheid. It filled me with tremendous rage. A few months later, in another part of the city, several Zulus stopped me at a street corner. As I tried to pass, one of them tripped me. When I stumbled and fell, he kicked me in the ribs. Everyone was laughing.

The wounds of humiliation from both blacks and whites would not heal. I joined a health club and worked to become big and strong. My anger manifested itself in other ways. I became an introvert and collected stones and a brass 'knuckle-buster' to protect myself. By then Grandfather was out of prison in India. It had been a long time since we visited the family there, and my parents decided it was time to go. One of the first things he did was to ask me to describe the circumstances of the beatings I had suffered. He listened intently as he put his arms around me in a gesture of love and comfort. 'I can understand your anger,' he said. 'But do you know they acted out of ignorance? They do not know what they are doing.'

'Do you know,' he went on, 'that anger is like electricity?' When I asked what he meant, he told me, 'Anger can be as powerful and destructive as electricity. Do you know what happens if a bolt of lightning falls somewhere or if you touch a live wire?' 'Yes,' I said. 'It destroys or kills.' 'Well, anger is the same. If you don't harness your anger as we harness electricity then anger, too, will destroy and kill. Anger should be used the same way we use electricity.'

He encouraged me to write an anger diary. He said every time you feel the surge of anger, write your feeling in a diary. Writing will give you an outlet for your anger and will also be a record of your feelings. When you are calm, you can read the diary and decide how you should have used the anger positively rather than negatively. At the end of my eighteen months visit with Grand-father, I understood much of the concept of peace that he taught and lived.

Although I believe categorically that grandfather was the greatest Hindu, some diehard believers would refute this claim since they did not agree with his interpretation of Hinduism. He regarded himself as a Sanatani Hindu but he was not dogmatic in his beliefs and detested the pomp and pageantry and the meaningless rituals introduced in the traditional worship. Above all, he could not reconcile to a religion that condemns one fourth of its believers as less than human. So the question that arises is: Was Gandhi great because he was a Hindu? Or, was he great because he was a humanitarian?

As a small child,
with my grandfather.

I believe he was great because he was a humanitarian who respected all people and all religions as 'though they are my own.' Through his life's work he attempted to remove the canker of competition from religion and introduce respect for all beliefs. He believed: 'A friendly study of all scriptures is the sacred duty of every individual.' He made the friendly study and discovered that none of the religions could claim to 'possess' the whole Truth. Our practice of religion must be to 'pursue' the Truth with all honesty and diligence. All religions, in reality, are based on the foundation of Love, Truth, Understanding, Compassion and Respect for all. That all the religions have buried the foundational principles and built a garish and, one might even say, 'Godless' edifice of exploitation is a shame. We must now reclaim the essence of goodness that exists in every religion and display to the world the wisdom that exists in each by living it, not proclaiming it.

The good that Gandhi found in Hinduism is its openness and acceptance, which does not exist in any other religion. It is the most accommodating and accepting. This makes Hinduism more than a religion in the widely accepted sense. Hinduism, in a sense, is about *Dharma* – Duty – which enjoins upon those born into this fold to perform their duties diligently, not to a temple or a priest but to humanity at large. In the 1870s Mohandas Gandhi's parents attempted to live Dharma. They not only respectfully learned about all the different religions but they incorporated into their daily life the wisdom from other Faiths in order to enhance their own. This is why people from different Faiths lay claim to their allegiance. Some believe the Gandhis were Jains while others believe they were Christians. In fact Louis Fischer, a devout Catholic, has written a book on which the Attenborough film *Gandhi* is based in which Fischer proclaims, 'The most Christ-like person on earth was not even a Christian.'

I think what Gandhi practiced is the true spirit of Faith and religion - that one's beliefs and one's practice should make one so lovable and respected that everyone would want to claim you. Visiting temples, Churches and Mosques or any other House of Worship ten times a day and performing all the rituals and pujas diligently does not make a true believer. Building monumental edifices at the cost of billions of dollars and encouraging worships like pouring milk over stones and feeding those who don't need to be fed when millions starve to death is not the kind of worship I believe in. Very early in his life Gandhi boycotted temples because of the practice of caste discrimination and much senseless exploitation. As a Sanatani Hindu he held public worship in which thousands from different Faiths participated every day and we all sang each other's hymns.

The Hindu concept of *sarvodaya* means the good of all people and in our attempt to establish a society based on this concept of sarvodaya we must work for the good of all residents of a nation, not for a select few.

Gandhi's earthly possessions: dinner bowls, wooden fork and spoon, famous porcelain monkeys, his diary, prayer book, watch, spittoon, letter opener and two pairs of sandals.

Believers will condemn me as a heretic for saying this but the priests in all religions are responsible for misleading and distorting religion so that they can manipulate and mould the thinking of the people. And we, the people, have allowed ourselves to be meekly exploited. We, the believers, in our ignorance, have elevated the priests to the position of mediators between God and the common man.

This raises another, a more important, question: Who is God? What is God? The common assumption in all religions is that there is a supernatural being somewhere in heaven monitoring the lives of human beings according to each Faith. Does that mean there are multiple Gods because there are multiple images of God? There has to be an amazing administrative apparatus to keep a daily record of seven billion human beings, not to speak of all of nature's creation. It is the absurdity of this concept that led Gandhi to believe that there is no God in human form sitting in heaven but that God in the form of 'Truth' sits in the hearts of every individual and when that individual betrays another he or she is not only betraying himself or herself but also the Truth that is God. The sins that we see flourishing in society today are because all of us think we can betray God now and then do penance and God will forgive us.

For that Truth to flourish in us we must be truthful. Grandfather was convinced relationships must be built on unconditional love, beginning at home. Those who believed and followed him practiced this nonviolent approach to life. In our home when we misbehaved, my parents took the punishment upon themselves. I remember on several occasions my mother or father, or sometimes both, skipped a meal because I had misbehaved. This punishment was so effective I would never do it again.

At age sixteen, while living in South Africa, Dad asked me to drive him to Durban so he could attend a day-long conference. I had to do a few chores and get the car serviced before picking him up at a prearranged intersection. Being an avid fan of Hollywood films, I spent the afternoon in a theatre. I was so absorbed in the movie that I did not realize it was past five. When I got out it was almost 5:30. I ran to the garage and drove as quickly as I could to where Dad was waiting. He was worried. I could see the relief on his face when he saw me drive up. 'What happened?' he asked in a concerned tone. I felt ashamed to say I was watching a movie and so I lied. 'The car was not ready.' Father looked at me with hurt in his eyes. 'That is not true,' he said. 'I called them and they said the car was ready long ago.'

'Please stop here,' Father said and when I did, he added in a voice of anguish, 'There has to be something wrong in me that you felt you had to lie to me. There must be some fault in the way I brought you up. As penance for this, I am going to walk home.' Father got out and started walking. I did not know what to do. I cursed myself for having lied. I could not leave Father behind and drive home. Most of the way Father would have to walk through farm-lands at night. I crept along behind him for four and a half hours. After that experience, I was determined never to lie again. My father had learned this from the man the world knew as Mahatma Gandhi. I learned many important lessons from this man, too.

So, I can say that I am born into a Hindu family and proud of my heritage and in the spirit of a true Sanatani I sincerely attempt to be a good, compassionate, accepting human being with respect for all the different beliefs and Faiths of the world.

ARUN GANDHI is co-founder and director of the M K Gandhi Institute of Non-Violence in Memphis, USA. His books include a *Patch of White*, *M K Gandhi's Wit and Wisdom*, and *The Forgotten Woman: The Untold Story of Kastur, the Wife of Mahatma Gandhi*.

With his wife, Sunanda, he has initiated many projects for the social and economic upliftment of the oppressed and to share his insights on non-violence.

Sunanda and Arun have a daughter, a son, and four grandchildren.

The Meaning of God

M K Gandhi

There is an indefinable mysterious Power that pervades everything.

I feel It, though I do not see It.

It is this unseen Power which makes Itself felt and yet defies all proof, because It is so unlike all that I perceive through my senses.

It transcends the senses....

That informing Power or Spirit is God....

For I can see that in the midst of death, life persists,
in the midst of untruth, truth persists,
in the midst of darkness, light persists.

Hence I gather that God is Life, Truth, Light.

He is love.

He is supreme good.

But he is no God who merely satisfies the intellect if He ever does.

God to be God must rule the heart and transform it.

A GENTLE BUT LASTING TOUCH
ATHIPET SUDHA VEPA

My parents had enduring influences on me during my formative years. My father's strong sense of duty and my mother's expression of devotion, as they demonstrated in their daily life, showed me the path to Hinduism in a simple and practical way.

Sudha Vepa

They say Hinduism lives in the household of the person who practices it. This is very true. When I was young I watched my parents and grandparents live their lives, and now it is my turn to let my children watch me live my life. My parents were both simple and unassuming people. They came from very orthodox backgrounds, yet I don't remember being told at anytime what I should do to be a good Hindu. It was always a gentle touch, but a lasting one. With the utmost devotion they just practised in their daily life what they had learnt, and all we did was learn by observing them. The first lesson I learnt by observing them was that in the practice of Hinduism there is flexibility and freedom of choice but, as in any aspect of life, freedom entails a greater degree of responsibility and accountability.

My father was a very practical and intellectual person, with a highly stressful job, a large family and three aged parents to support, which left him with little time for scriptures and rituals. Yet to me and to hundreds of others who were influenced by his honesty and his strong sense of duty, he was a great Hindu. What touched me most was his strong belief in unattached devotion to life and work. He worked in an environment where it was very difficult to refrain from corrupt practices and not to succumb to temptations. Nevertheless, he emerged unaffected and was more highly valued for it. He neither owned a house nor enjoyed the security of a bank balance at anytime during his life, but he was always proud of the fact that he was leaving behind for his children the legacy of his unattached devotion to duty. This has indeed greatly influenced me and all my brothers and sisters.

We grew up watching him turn down favours from wealthy clients and refuse expensive gifts of any kind from anyone. He exercised this discipline in the family and helped us all understand from a young age the importance of

Bharata Nathyam dancers training in the Kalakshetra School of Dance, Madras.

putting duty and devotion above materialism. I remember the days when I used to give dance performances. At the end of a performance it was customary for the artists to be presented with flowers and a silver memento. My father always made it a point to return the memento to the organizers of the concert. That used to upset me when I was a little girl, but by the time I was a teenager I had learnt to value art, in my case *Bharatha Natyam,* for its own sake.

Here is another instance of his amazing insight into Duty that has guided me all along. He once told me during a discussion on conflict of duties, 'True devotion to your duty will not give rise to doubts, but if you are faced with a conflict, ask yourself what your immediate duty is and where you are needed most at that point in time.' This has worked for me. By adopting his simple but logical approach to a complex problem, I once saved myself from a personal disaster and since then have been getting better at resolving conflicts about duties that crop up all the time in our daily life. Saint Kabir's famous *doha* (couplet) rings in my mind when I think of my father's practical solutions to conflicts through his unflinching devotion to duty:

> *If my Guru and my God both appear before me at the same time, whose feet would I touch first? I would serve my Guru first because of whom I have been fortunate to see God.*

This beautiful couplet throws light on how Kabir, the mystic poet, would resolve his conflict by logical reasoning.

My parents were both fond of narrating the story of Pundalika, the great devotee who made God wait at his doorstep while he served his aged parents. This is another simple but classic illustration of the same idea. For Arjuna, the greatest of the warriors on the battlefield of Kurukshetra, there was a conflict too, but he was placed in a totally different situation. Lord Krishna tells him that at that point in time his duty to *dharma* was paramount. When I came across these texts, much later in my life, I felt they were only echoing what my father had said and demonstrated in his life.

In the case of my mother it was *bhakti,* devotion to God, which in turn filled our house with love. I learnt from my mother that there was more than one way of worshipping God and that there was a rich and interesting variety in each of the several facets of Hinduism. Like most women of her times, she could not pursue formal education beyond the middle school, but she has acquired on her own enough spiritual knowledge to educate her children and her grandchildren. Amidst raising seven children, managing a household and looking after three aged parents, she taught herself to read and write fluently in three Indian languages, which not only helped her read some of the important scriptures but also develop her interest in devotional music and literature in those languages. Besides this she derives immense pleasure in doing hand embroidery of religious themes, which she continues to do even now, in her eighties. She has never been interested in publicity or in commercializing her talent. For her it is one of the ways of showing her devotion to God and sharing her joy with others. When I was a child and a teenager what particularly influenced and inspired me was the artistic nature of her devotion, rather than the daily *poojas* and chanting of the *slokas.* This had a great influence on my interest in Bharata Natyam, a classical dance form rooted in Hinduism, for which I have developed a deep passion.

Parasuram, one of the incarnations of Vishnu, embroidered by my mother

My mother has been instrumental in embedding the religious significance of Bharata Natyam in my training and practice of it. I think it started when I was six years old. I was very ill with diphtheria for several weeks and was confined to the front room of our little house. Every afternoon, after completing all the chores, my mother would spend a couple of hours at my bedside, narrating stories from *Srimad Bhagavatam.* I used to look forward to the story time with so much excitement. It was not just the narration of the story, but its dramatization and interpretation that was most exciting to me.

I remember, every now and then, whenever she thought she had forgotten a detail in the story, she would refer to an old, brown copy of the *Bhagavatam* that belonged to my grandfather. The sessions turned out to be both therapeutic and inspirational. Besides a deep interest in the mythologies and the *puranas*, I developed the ability to appreciate the religious significance of South Indian classical dance and music that stood me in good stead in later years.

As a dancer, and later, as a teacher I always enjoyed choreography the most. My experiments with the basic units of dance (*karana*) and the interpretation of music, lyrics and rhythms through Bharata Natyam gave me more satisfaction than performing the dance itself.

Lord Shiva as Nataraj engaged in his cosmic dance

I, along with several others in the local community and colleges, rely a great deal on my mother to translate the lyrics of poets like Kshetrayya, Annamacharya, Jeyadeva, Purandaradasa, Gopalakrishna Bharati and Tukaram, to name a few, which she does with a lot of involvement. She has always found the time to work with me, giving me her ideas and comments on the *abhinaya* (dance gestures and facial expression), besides translating and interpreting the devotional lyrics in detail, to the level of my limited understanding. We have spent several happy hours contemplating on how a particular imagery from a certain poet could be best expressed in dance.

The success of choreography and the *abhinaya* of the Bharatha Natyam dancer depend a great deal on the right understanding of the devotional lyric that is being depicted. By collaborating with my mother I was able to understand and experience some of the feelings of the poets and I learnt that devotion is an inseparable element of South Indian classical dance.

Although I was fortunate to have trained and carried out research under eminent gurus, it was the strong support from my mother, in the face of some opposition from orthodox elders in the family, that motivated me to pursue a career in Bharata Natyam. My exposure to Bharata Natyam has enriched my experience of Hinduism. I have learnt that a dancer's training does not end with giving performances. That is only a starting point. A dancer learns to appreciate the Hindu classics, scriptures, philosophy, music, literature, history and above all to revere the Guru and experience bhakti. For me Bharata Natyam is a discipline, yoga and meditation, which are pre-requisites for any act of worship.

When I look back and compare myself with my parents, I do not really know how much of the Hindu influence I am exercising on my children, who are being raised in the UK. They are exposed to a wider variety of values and a richer mix of cultures than I was. Writing this article has given me the opportunity to stop and reflect on my responsibility as a parent, and carry out a self-evaluation of how well I am demonstrating the Hindu values which my father did and my mother continues to do so well.

On being asked about their Hindu experiences, my children said, 'The variety makes Hinduism very interesting. Also the numerous Gods and Goddesses are fascinating. They help me focus better, when I want to say my prayers.' 'I feel like a rooted Hindu.' 'Hinduism is a personal religion, a process of self-development over a life time.' 'When I was much younger I used to think that the Sanskrit prayers were meant for asking favours of Gods and Goddesses. I'm beginning to under-stand that the prayers are in praise of God and the *poojas* are an offering and an expression of gratitude for what we've already got.'

It was refreshing to listen to the youngsters express their views on religion and how they perceive Hinduism. I sincerely hope they will continue to feel the gentle but lasting touch.

The dancing Ganesha. One of the pieces my mother embroidered for her grandchildren

ATHIPET SUDHA VEPA has performed and taught Bharata Natyam for several years in India and the UK and is a freelance dance critic and choreographer. One of her major interests is the study of the evolution of socio-religious themes and their depiction through art forms. She currently works as a Lecturer in Skills for Life in Harrow College.

INSPIRATION

There is nothing greater in life than inspiration.
If you can inspire people, then you are really fulfilling life,
and the fulfilling of life is our goal.

- Rukmini Arundale,
Dancer, Choreographer,
Founder of Kalakshetra School of Dance, Madras

GITOPADESH BY MRS RAMANI RAMA RAO
ONE OF MY MOTHER'S HAND EMBROIDERED MASTERPIECES
From the original sketch in Devdutt Pattnaik's *Vishnu – An Introduction*
Published by Mrs Jean Trindade for Vakils Faffer & Simons Ltd, 1998

MY BELOVED CHARIOTEER
ATREYEE DAY

I was three and my brother six months old when my mother and father underwent a formal separation. We came to stay in the family house with my two bachelor uncles and grandmother. It was a sprawling old place surrounded by an acre of planted and free growing vegetation – the wild and untended would seriously fight for place of honour with the carefully planned flowerbeds. It was Chotomama who had the green thumb – he could grow or mend anything. I still believe my love for nature comes from him. School was walking distance and Kailash Singh, a gentle and dignified ex-butcher turned gateman, would accompany us back home.

My brother Aneesh, Kailash and me. Drawing by Atreyee

Homecoming was always a matter of celebration. I never could make peace with classrooms but art, literature and singing were my favourite subjects. Ma would be in the office and afternoons were the high points of life. The terrace was a favourite haunt with uninterrupted skies to stare into, the grounds to explore, crows, cats, sparrows, squirrels, kites, snails and millipedes to observe, and lots of time to day dream while watching stray aeroplanes through the dandelions in the waist-high wild grass.

My childhood was idyllic and isolated with a steady spartan comfort. Sitting cross-legged on the water tank with water steadily filling inside, it was from Kailash we came to know about the great valour of Hanuman and Garuda. Kailash took us to the nearby masjid to be flicked over the head by the fly-whisk of the mullah if we were feverish. The azaan was as regular to our ears as the banging of the steel factory next door. Books were my best friends, also walks in the horticultural gardens with Chotomama and swimming every Saturday afternoon with Habu till my mother remarried when I was thirteen. We left to live in a housing community and for the first time, among other everyday novelties, experienced the Durga Puja in the neighbourhood. Out of my childhood I carried a vivid imagination but a certain insecurity, an early sense of loss, right into my adulthood.

A pivotal moment in my life was in 2000 with the death of my grandmother who I had grown very close to since my teenage years. During my childhood I used to defy the discipline imposed by her vigorously - but the equation changed once I grew up and she grew older. Our age difference was nearly seventy years! She had not quite completed class two and was a storehouse of anecdotes and stories. She was scared of snakes and thieves but not ghosts – a clairvoyant with many paranormal stories to share. My grandmother (*Didabhai*) had a very difficult life though she came from a well-to-do family and later was the wife to a wealthy jute broker, my grandfather. There were many tragic and dramatic twists in her personal tale: life threatening illnesses and deaths of children, intrigues and plots almost unbelievable in their propensity, but I saw her in a spotless white borderless sari, large-boned, luminous eyed, uncomplaining, smelling of lemon pickle and talcum powder. She was equally 'Ma' to the mechanic from the factory who would have lunch at the common table and to her three sons. Didabhai lovingly sat through each mealtime making sure that all were equally served.

Her daughter-in-law was an Englishwoman whom she completely accepted and stood by against much orthodox opposition. Later Mummy (as my aunt was called by all the children of the household, her own three included) mentioned how she stopped going to Sunday church because observing Didabhai she had learnt that to forebear and accept everyone with compassion was the highest religion. This simple adage of her simpler Hindu mother-in-law seemed to satisfy her and made her forgo all external religious rituals. Much later, when we went to perform Didabhai's last rites in Gaya, a small instruction was discovered written in her lucid hand – that she had been a *'grihi*

sanyasin' all along and her name was Shivananda Bhairavi and not just Mrs J N Day! Her rites were performed according to sanyasi dharma.

But the Hindu who has most spiritually inspired me is my friend Shruti, 'My Beloved Charioteer' as I jokingly called her, after a story by Shashi Deshpande. We started talking on the first day of art college in Baroda, Gujarat. She was a Maharashtrian from Jhansi with long plaited hair and a bindi, swathed in yards of dupatta, speaking more Hindi than I had ever heard, except in Bollywood movies! *Jhansi ki Rani* we used to

Didabhai. *Drawing by Atreyee*

tease her. I was a jeans clad Calcutta born and bred Bengali with lots of attitude and baggage to boot under all the veneer. She looked much older then her
19 years and me younger than my 22. I'm still not sure what clicked. It must
have been our common love for classical music because seemingly we had
nothing else in common, or a facial resemblance, for often people would mix
us up and speak to me in Marathi and her in Bengali. I never had a small town
friend before Shruti, coming as I did from a convent school in a metropolis
that ironed out all interesting personal details every day at Assembly and on the
games field.

I remember my surprise when she showed me a well-thumbed copy of the
Bhagavad Gita and said, 'This is the book I derive all my strength from - I
have not read much beside my science books.' She instead expressed awe and
admiration of my reading list, but showed no surprise that I had never even
seen the contents of the Gita except in the popular television serial. I told her
that she MUST read Antigone and Whitman, Salinger and Barret Browning
and...! I don't recall her telling me to read the Gita. No books besides the Gita!
What ever would we talk about?

It's nearly nine years, and five years since university, and we haven't stopped
talking. We are in different cities and often don't meet in years, but I often
think of her and the phone rings. We don't need too many words to
communicate.

Even now Shruti is not a word person. She paints with a subtlety touching the
core of stillness and quiet, reaching a point of almost nothingness, a reverent
self-negation. It is a state of grace. Overawed she would watch her brush unfold painted worlds within, as much a spectator as the others. It was as if *she*
did not paint at all. The painting painted itself. It was as if her body slightly
bent forward was keenly listening for the next instruction to follow from
within. She would de-materialize a chair to make it look like points of coloured
light dancing in a state of captured ecstasy!

How did you know Shruti *tai* (elder sister) that Indian red would follow ochre?
She never had an answer - she just knew. She would go on to intensely admire
her own creations. That would puzzle me. Later I realized she did not consider
her creation as *hers* at all - so the detached admiration! And then she would
forget about it and go on to the next. A karmayogi, she was an example to
others. I can recall so many little instances. Pure, child-like, happy with little
gifts, forgetful of them in the next instant!

Often she would tell me that she entered a blank mindless space *–kabhi kabhi
shunya mein chali jaati hoon, wapas aaney ko dil nahi karta*! (Sometimes I go into the
great emptiness and my heart does not feel like coming back.) For a fleeting
moment I would get a glimpse of something much larger and mysterious. So
glad you came back as many times! I would have been clueless without you.

ॐ ॐ ॐ ॐ ॐ ॐ ॐ ॐ ॐ ॐ ॐ ॐ ॐ ॐ ॐ ॐ

My angelic alter ego - I'll keep the darkness for myself, I quipped. But this was far from the truth - in fact it was she who carried the enormous burden of my affection for her. I faced an identity crisis soon after meeting Shruti - a big lack of something I later identified as a constant immobilizing doubt, at times translated into almost paralytic fear. Developing faith was the only answer for it.

She *never* criticized or judged anyone. She genuinely admired our differences, and accepted me exactly as I was. Having immense faith when I had none, she'd say, 'you are fine as you are – you will find your own truth – there's no need to emulate me – time has the best answers!' She could see light lurking at the very next bend.

I have seen day after day Geetu, her room mate, lashing out in anger and irritation and Shruti in tears, but never retaliating. Why? We would reprimand both, one for her harshness, the other for a complete lack of it! See, she would smile winking through her tears, I don't have to defend myself, so many others are defending me! That really annoyed me. Does that mean your non-violence is instigating violence in others? How can that be good? Much later I realized the importance of what she was saying. Violence MUST grow weary of violence.

This same roomie, a fierce and beautiful Rajput, would come back meekly to ask Shruti for advice or the use of her bicycle, cosmetics, clothes, which Shruti would dispense of lovingly. She had a blessedly short-term memory when it came to cataloguing other people's misdemeanors! As for food Shruti once said that she was unable to eat anything without sharing it with the people around her, including strangers, who often did not remain strangers for too long - much to my jealousy!

'Why can't I be like you, Shruti tai,' I would wail in frustration! She would indulge me like an anomalous baby sister. 'Because you are *you*, unique and special and loveable *exactly* as you are.' A daily shower of unconditional love for 4 years. An unrelenting perfectionist about her own self, she would forgive my most glaring short-comings. Selfish, I'd call her. You only want to improve yourself and what about me? You have to learn to do that alone, Atreyee. There is only so far even the best of friends can go! *Ekla cholo re,* she would say in broken Bengali after a Tagore song written for Gandhiji.

Shruti and me

There was a tiny white Harihara Temple (Shiva and Vishnu being worshipped in a single form) opposite the college campus, a clear area of quiet with an old caretaker who would meticulously sweep the courtyard twice a day. The green winged parrots ate out of the visitor's hand. We would sit sketch books in our laps for hours, in communion with the trees that surrounded it. Before this I had never entered a temple. For me it was all about ringing bells and getting to eat the cloying sweet *prasad* afterwards and of course spending some more time with my best friend!

Another favourite haunt was an old masjid built in the middle of Shivsagar lake near Dandiya Bazaar. I would sit behind Shruti on her bicycle, our *ratha*! The main attraction was an old Sufi caretaker who would share his cup of evening tea with us, allowing us to sketch him till his irate wife would berate and scold and complain about there never being enough food in the house. He would helplessly waited for the tirade to stop, watch her retreating mumbling back and then share his only tea biscuit with us, three conspirators, with his pariah dog looking on.

Shruti once told me in a very matter of fact way of an incident when she and her family had visited Vrindaban and had to put up at a dharamshala. They had found no accommodation till late in the night, for they are a large family. It was winter and soon everyone had fallen asleep. But Atreyee, I could not sleep. I kept hearing the sound of a flute playing the moment I closed my eyes. She woke up her grandmother and father who heard nothing at all. She lay awake – till 4 in the morning hearing this ethereal music which no one else could hear. Often she would sing on the hostel terrace during long power cuts - *Mere to giridhara gopal dusro na koyi* - Mine is the Mountain Bearing Gopal. There is none other but him.[1] I could never understand why she would say, tears in her eyes, 'I feel like leaving all this and going away!' All what, Shruti tai, go where? Leave even me? I would ask anxiously, insecure suddenly. 'Of course not,' she would say with affection, 'how could that be?'

But we did part ways. Maybe to appreciate better what I had found by losing it temporarily.

Shruti had already sown seeds that started germinating after we parted ways. She left to continue higher studies in a design school and I came back to my hometown. All I knew was this - the work in hand was ME, before starting off on any other 'job.' The work continues!

Shruti never preached she simply practiced. I remember during our campus ragging ritual we were asked to describe ourselves. And Shruti had said, 'I can adjust to any situation.' How we had laughed at her. It sounded like a matrimonial ad-line not something a teenager would mouth!

[1] The first line from a popular song by the mystic, Meera Bai. Krishna once lifted the Govardhan mountains to protect his people/cattle from a deluge from the skies. Giri means mountain. Dhara means holder.

Accept, forbear and love. Whenever you see lacunas in some one fill them with love.

Have I a special memory or favourite association with Shruti? I had sent her a mail comprising wholly of a quotation from the Bhagavad Gita several years back in a moment of epiphany.

> Whatever I have presumptuously said from carelessness or affection, addressing You as 'O Krsna, O Yadava, O friend,' regarding You merely as friend, unconscious of Your greatness;

> In whatever way I may have been disrespectful to You, in jest, while walking, reposing, sitting, at mealtimes, when alone (with You), O Achyuta, or in company - I implore You, O immeasurable One, to forgive all this.

Typical of her - in acknowledgement she sent me three photographs taken in Benaras!

Have I a spiritual message for our world today? Look around! There are apparently ordinary people guarding the extraordinary within. Have faith when there is absolutely nothing to support it. Step out in the air. Change no one. Start with yourself with love, acceptance and patience, and patience, acceptance and love. Laugh a lot. For the way is long and sometimes dark and lonely. But if you believe a Dearest Friend awaits at the end of it, so much the easier for both of you, yes. The both of you! I'll leave you with this mystery to ponder on. Don't look too hard or long!

ATREYEE DAY is currently teaching art and craft in a school / resource centre in Calcutta. She also writes and illustrates. She completed an English (Hons) degree at Jadavpur University, Calcutta and has a Painting (Hons) from M.S. University of Baroda, Gujarat, India.

Atreyee is deeply interested in the healing aspect of the arts and hopes to study this further.

Atreyee received spiritual initiation from the late Ranganathanandaji Maharaj of the Ramakrishna Mission.

THE ROYAL PATH

Are you growing spiritually? Can you love others? Can you feel oneness with others? Have you peace within yourself? Do you radiate it around you? That is called spiritual growth, which is stimulated by meditation inwardly and by work done in a spirit of service outwardly.

Work hard; perform all duties; develop yourself; then come and surrender to the highest. Do a whole day's honest work, then sit and meditate; then resign yourself to God. Otherwise, that meditation has no meaning or value. Meditation at the end of a lazy day has no meaning; but the same at the end of an active day, filled with good deeds, has meaning, and is rewarding.

How can we find joy in work? By working for oneself? No; it is not possible to find that continuous joy in work through selfish motivations. Frustration and ennui are the end of all selfish motivations. Frustrations and nervous break-downs are the end of a self-centred life. The first advice of modern psychiatry to such people is to get out of this prison of self-centredness and to find a genuine interest in other people. Everyone has to learn the lesson some day that the best way to be happy is to strive to make others happy. So wherever you find frustration, you will always discover that the person concerned had been too self-centred and the only hope for him is through learning to take interest in other people, to find joy in the joy of other people. This is the royal path that makes for health, for strength, for efficiency. This great truth - universal and human - we should apply to the world and to our life in it.

- Sri Swami Ranganathanandaji Maharaj

Swami Ranganathananda, *Eternal Values for a Changing Society*, Bharatiya Vidya Bhavan, Bombay, 1971.

FINDING MY WAY
BHAVISHA TAILOR

My father told me that spirituality had to be lived to the point that it didn't matter if I chose not to go to the temple or partake in *pujas*. He told me that true happiness came from within and the less I craved material things, the happier I would be. He told me this when I was eight, standing in a toyshop insisting that he buy me a doll! Happily for me, he did buy it and of course at the time, none of what he said made sense, but it lodged itself and many years later it became clear.

Bhavisha Tailor

From as far back as I can remember, the family would sit on my parents' bed almost every night and listen to my father read a story. Charting through amazing spiritual personalities, from Shri Tukaram and Guru Nanak to Shri Ramkrishna Paramhansa and St Francis of Assisi, we listened to stories of lives that carried profound messages. Although I was probably too young to understand them in their entirety, I do remember being moved by them. My father would highlight the attributes of love, devotion, humility, courage, patience, surrender and detachment. This continued in his letters to me during my teenage years at boarding school and deeply impacted my thoughts and attitudes.

Sometimes I accompanied my mother to the temple for *bhajans* or some other religious event. When the event was over everyone would hurry out to go home. There was a security guard employed by the temple, a frail old man, who would stand outside, opening and closing the gates as needed. I noticed that my mother was the only one who would stop to greet him and share whatever *Prasad* we had received from the temple. Her one-liner was, *Bhavi, never forget that God lives in each being.* In hindsight, I was learning two important Hindu lessons from my parents; the importance of personal values and the importance of respecting all beings.

However, with regard to the more formal aspects, I prayed as I was taught to do, sometimes reciting the Hanuman Chalisa and at others chanting the Gayatri mantra. I never felt, saw or experienced God's presence and because of this I questioned his existence. It would be fair to say I didn't recognize his presence. I prayed mechanically and sometimes I didn't pray at all. While my parents were a great influence in my life through the way they lived as Hindus, the pivotal moment for me came after I graduated.

As an undergraduate, my days typically revolved around clubbing, pool and last minute assignments. I forgot about religion except for the times when I was accosted by born-again Christians. It was also an exciting period. I was playing squash on the University team, I was dancing for the University team and involved with numerous clubs and societies. I graduated with my desired grades and then returned home to Zambia. The purpose was to take a year out before I went on to do my Masters.

In spite of my life being so full and exciting I felt a massive void. The void was not because I missed those things but because it all suddenly seemed so meaningless and empty. I felt incomplete and nothing could fill that hole. It dawned on me that the only thing missing in my life was God. Yet, I wasn't even sure that he existed. I wondered why we existed and whether life had any real goal. It was clear that we exerted our whole lifetime to having a roof over our heads, food in our stomachs and the possible enjoyment of some luxury before we died. It seemed utterly pointless and I could not believe that that was it. For the first time, I prayed with sincerity. The prayer was short, *Dear God, if you exist please let me come closer to you.* Every night as I prayed I could not stop the tears from falling because I so desperately wanted him to hear and I repeated it until I fell asleep. I could not have imagined then that within a month my life was to take a complete turn.

Satya Sai Baba

Coincidentally, I began to meet very spiritual people, through no effort of my own. It was ironic that these people were either followers of Shri Satya Sai Baba or the Swaminarayan movement, towards whom I held unjustifiable prejudices! It was a grace that through the devotees I met, my limited perceptions were dissolved and my heart was taken by the beauty of their devotion.

It was during this time that a friend asked if I would come home to help with flower arrangements as some Saints were coming from India and would be staying at their home. I obliged. As I was arranging the flowers, a man in his late fifties walked in with two others. I had never met them before but greeted them with the customary namaskar. The man walked up to me and put his hand on my head and asked who I was. I felt overwhelmingly peaceful. He asked me to come to the morning puja and I agreed. As they left the room my friend later told me that they were the Saints. I was taken aback for they had all been in plain clothes and I had expected someone in saffron robes. I came to learn they were of the Swaminarayan sect. The head, Pujya Saheb, had been initiated in his early twenties by his Guru Shri Yogiji Maharaj and been asked to remain a sadhu in plain clothes. Along with him, eight peers, all in their early twenties had also been initiated and were told to follow Pujya Saheb in what was a pioneering movement.

I joined the morning puja with Pujya Saheb and when the prayers began I wept uncontrollably. I could not stop the wave that washed over me and I felt ecstatic. The bottomless void I had been feeling was filled and I was completely satiated. It was from this moment that Pujya Saheb entered my life as my Guru. Because they were in plain clothes (more specifically in light blue shirts and khaki trousers), I could sit before

Guruvarya Param Pujya Saheb.

him and converse with him which is otherwise not possible for women, as the code of conduct for a Swaminarayan sadhu is extremely strict. This was one of the reasons I had previously disliked the Swaminarayan faith because I had always thought of them as being unduly sexist. However, my perceptions were being eroded. I felt full and happy. In a few days, he was gone and I wasn't sure when I would see him again.

In spite of my initiation as a disciple, I held on to one confusion. Prior to meeting my Guru I had chanted the Sai mantra, now I had been given another mantra. Although I was now in principle a follower of the Swaminarayan faith, I could not put aside my vivid experiences of Shree Satya Sai Baba. I felt in my heart that all paths would lead to God but I also felt that I could not walk both paths. In spite of this I did not want to lose either of them!

I returned to London later that year, in August 1996, to begin my Masters degree. One evening I was at the temple. I prayed hard, I asked God which path was for me and I heard a voice that directed me. It said *Swaminarayan*. It also said that I would not lose Swami (which was how I referred to Shree Satya Sai Baba) as Swami was contained within Swaminarayan. The confusion was settled from that point onwards. I now completely accepted the living Guru in my life and followed his instruction.

Having a living Guru changed my life beyond imagination. A revolution took place within. After all the yearning, I finally felt some connection with God. I felt His presence, I noticed His workings in my daily life and I found myself flowing with gratitude. I felt even in the littlest of things my prayers were heard.

Guruvarya Param Pujya Saheb performing Āarti in Chennai

While I was working in India, I once in my hurry knowingly jumped onto a reserved train with an unreserved ticket. I was going to the ashram and I had less than Rs5☐ in my purse. Two others that had jumped on prior to me had encouraged me saying the ticket checker had already come and gone. As I sat in the compartment I watched them run past me and realised that the ticket checker was on his way. I shut my eyes, prayed, put my hands up to Him regarding my mistake and left it in His hands. I did not even have enough money to pay a fine! When I opened my eyes, a young man had come and sat opposite me, followed immediately by the ticket checker. The young man handed his ticket and it was for a block booking of 35 people. The ticket checker went past me. Rationally, this could be put down to pure coincidence, except that these coincidences were happening all the time. I noticed that where I sincerely prayed, sincerely surrendered my fault and sincerely sought to make amends, God was with me and I thanked both Him and my Guru who had brought me to Him.

For my Guru, I cannot find words. I was humbled by his humility and his pure, selfless and unconditional love. He did not rigidly lay down rules and regulations for me to follow, but taught by his own life and actions. Rather than enforce, he allowed me to understand the do's and don'ts so that they naturally became a part of my life. Because of him, I learned to value life and the opportunity to serve and to progress.

My first lesson from him was to always think positive, even in the most dire circumstances. As human beings we are always quick to perceive fault in others and remember it, but the lesson has been to see the positive and pick out that which is good.

He made me understand that I now had a weapon that would allow me to overcome any situation or circumstance. My weapon was prayer. I feel one of the most important things that Guruvarya Saheb has brought to me are the precepts of *divyabhav* (accepting everyone and everything to be divine) and *nirdoshbuddhi* (understanding God and his devotee to be faultless). He taught that regardless of whatever happens learn to perceive each devotee of God as *divine* and *innocent*. This seemingly simple formula can be painfully hard to retain even in trivial circumstances where, for example, opinions differ. He showed that by keeping those two attributes, one no longer has to wrestle with anger, jealousy or greed, for by truly accepting each being as divine, those emotions are left with no room to arise and thus naturally drop away. Just the experience of trying to accept each being as divine, regardless of circumstance, has allowed me to love more deeply.

Each day feels like a blessing. The guidance of a living Guru coupled with prayer has given me strength and direction. Religions or spirituality no matter how different, are not divided, except by our own making. My gratitude is to the teachers who taught how to respect and cherish. I began as a mechanical Hindu, went through the paces of a sceptic and ended up a devotee, only through experiencing that there was something greater at work. Through my Guru I learned that the spiritual path is not necessarily the stereotypical solemn, serene one, nor that which haughtily preaches righteousness but a joyful journey towards God, which allows one to live and love more deeply.

BHAVISHA TAILOR is a BSc Sociology graduate from the University of Bath. She is currently studying for an MSc in Development Studies at the London School of Economics and will then read for an MSt in Religion at Oxford University.

Bhavisha was Chair of Hindu Youth UK (2003 - 2005) and is one of the Anoopam Mission's youth leaders.

The importance of
A TRUE GURU
by KABIR

It is the mercy of my true Guru that has made me to know the unknown;
I have learned from Him how to walk without feet, to see without eyes,
to hear without ears, to drink without mouth, to fly without wings;
I have brought my love and my meditation into the land
where there is no sun and no moon nor day and night.
Without eating, I have tasted of the sweetness of nectar;
and without water, I have quenched my thirst.
Where there is the response of delight, there is the fullness of joy.
Before whom can that joy be uttered?
Kabir says:
The Guru is great beyond words, and great is the good fortune of the disciple.

Guruvarya Param Pujya Saheb of the Anoopam Mission

LIFE IS AN ENDLESS JOURNEY
CHINTAMANI YOGI

I grew up in a traditional Hindu family in a small village in Dang, in the western part of Nepal. We never had dinner without first having evening prayers and receiving blessings from our elders by touching their feet. Father was one of the respected elders of the community. Every day villagers and friends would visit to seek his guidance on various problems. My mother was mostly occupied in the kitchen, cooking for family and guests. When we didn't have school, we children were assigned chores such as grazing livestock and watering the vegetable gardens. Evenings were taken up with reading books like the *Ramayana* and *Geeta*. We would listen as our parents told us moral stories and we would report the various activities of the day and share problems amongst our- selves. Our home was full of life. We didn't have separate bedrooms and so slept beside our mother or alongside our brothers and sisters.

Lord Rama, hero of the Ramayana

There wasn't a proper school in the village and my parents always had a dream of teaching me Sanskrit. So at the tender age of seven, I left the warmth of my parents' laps and travelled to Delhi for my education. We walked for two days barefoot followed by a further two days by train. Nobody explained to me where I was going and why. Yet part of me was eager to make this journey. It was as though some unseen force was calling me.

I joined a very traditional, old *Gurukul* to study Sanskrit and other ancient Hindu texts. Daily life was a challenge - getting up at 4.3□ am, performing yoga, meditation, reciting the holy books, and then going to school to study

My Father

the scriptures. Being a young child, I naturally longed for freedom and comfort. I missed the village and the people I had left behind. I was homesick for the beautiful rural environment. However, life at the Gurukul formed the basis of my education. It instilled in me strong moral and spiritual foundations and helped mould me into the person I am today.

After eight years in Delhi, destiny drew me back to Nepal. I once again breathed in the fragrance of the fresh air and felt the love of the innocent village people. I was overjoyed to be reunited with my family. The unconditional love of my parents and relatives felt like the greatest gift in the world. Yet new challenges were waiting for me. Failing rains and problems of deforestation meant my parents struggled to generate sufficient production from traditional subsistence farming. Many villagers unwillingly decided to migrate elsewhere in search of opportunities. We suffered lots of hardship during these times.

Despite all these difficulties, my father taught me philosophy, stories, songs and *Bhajans*. It was remarkable how, although being a father to ten children, he could still lead his life as a saint. He always reminds me of *Rajarshi Janak* (father of Goddess *Sita*) since he lived amidst this material world without ever being attached to anything. Our father taught us good virtues and aimed to guide us towards a righteous path. I still remember whenever I used to leave home, he would massage his long white beard and plead, *Babu, Aastik Bhayes* (My son! Please have faith in God). Being a young man I was always in a hurry. To keep him happy I would reply, 'Yes,' and then try to leave as soon as possible. But he would call me again and say, 'My son, always believe in God.' Even today, though my father passed away five years ago, I still hear his affectionate voice guiding me. I feel like he is just beside me.

Likewise, I am forever influenced by the deep spiritual character of my mother. I have not met a wiser woman in my life. From where has she obtained such wisdom? Was she naturally born with this or did she gain it through the hardships she has endured in life? She is over 75 now but her face seems to be glowing with the light of wisdom. Truly speaking she is a mother for many villagers, relatives and friends. How could one, despite being illiterate, inspire so many people so effortlessly and profoundly? Actually, there is nothing miraculous about her behaviour. She never preaches, but her

My Mother

motherly care and company can simply enlighten anyone. She spends most of her time singing devotional songs and entertaining people who come to meet her. I remain eternally grateful to her. She taught me to practice patience whatever the circumstances. The Bhajans she taught me give infinite pleasure. I sing them as constantly as I breathe and any tensions and pressures automatically disappear.

Moving to Kathmandu to pursue my further studies, once again destiny called me. Actually, I believe everywhere we go, everything we do is determined by fate *(Prarabdha)*. I enrolled in college for my Master's Degree and started hunting for connections with various political, religious and social institutions. It was then that I met Dr. Bihari Lal Shrestha. It was as though we had been brought together by some invisible force and became entwined like flowing water. He was an ideal person. He refused to rest in his mission and never said 'No' to the poor people. Actually, he served God through his fellow man. Though he was a highly respected orthopaedic doctor, his smiling and gentle behaviour was so heart touching. In fact I consider him a doctor of the soul since many patients used to feel better just by meeting him.

After meeting Dr. Shrestha I immediately immersed myself in social work. Together we established a school - *Hindu Vidya Peeth-Nepal* (HVP), a charity-based institution that imparts modern education along with spiritual values. Although I had the zeal of selfless service I lacked any real experience of life. I was just 21 at that time. It was his amazing inspiration and his family's trust and care that led me to social work. It was a challenging time for me. I used to work tirelessly and go to my bedroom in the school's boarding hostel only after 9:30 pm, having fed and put the children to bed. Afterwards I used to read *Swami Vivekananda*. His beautiful words made me cry. The financial pressures of running a school on a shoestring budget made my life so tough at

Sharing my message of peace

times. I often felt disheartened by others who never believed in us, who didn't trust our vision and failed to understand what we were striving to achieve with the school and other charitable activities. Still, I never got frustrated through these difficult times. The Vedas say, *Charaiveti.....*Keep walking; keep walking, then only will you get the nectar.

God was planning something more for me. In fact, He loves us through the people who are gifted or blessed by him. Therefore, he brought me into contact with Swami Prapannacharya ji, a yellow dressed saint who has dedicated his life for spiritual *Sadhana*. Swamiji began his long spiritual journey at the late age of 30. Until then he was uneducated and worked as a field labourer in Nepal's rural hills where poverty means it is a daily struggle to survive. But his destiny led him to Kashi, India. Later he returned to Nepal as an intellectual complete with a Ph.D. He came from a very backward community where nobody was allowed to read Sanskrit, but when he returned to Nepal, even the Brahmins bowed to him as a great saint.

According to the system of Hindu sects you can categorise Swamiji as a Vaishnav Sadhu. But he respects all sects and religions without any discrimination. He loves equally all Gods and Goddesses and accepts all the different religious pathways as beautifully as an ocean filled by the waters of many rivers. Nowadays he is over 84 but he works as actively as if he were just 25. He always follows the path of *Niskam Sewa* and says, 'I want to die just by preaching and serving for the betterment of humanity.' In fact, the heart of a saint is just like butter. As Tulasidas says, 'So kind, soft and bleeding for other's benefit and happiness.'

Dr Shrestha

Dr. Shrestha passed away, leaving his legacy upon my tiny shoulders. I was only 21 when I started working as a founder principal of HVP Schools. When he finally left me, I was still only around 35. Life is an endless journey. Wise are those who understand the call of time and shape their life accordingly. So I was determined to accept the challenges and continued my journey to fulfil my own mission and vision. On one hand, I was alone; on the other hand, God was with me. He endowed me with some more good friends for my mission of SEWA.

I would continually question myself: Was I working for the benefit of society or was I working just for the schools? Was I really working for the whole of humanity or just for Nepal? Actually, knowledge that comes from deep realisation is always true as He guides us only from the heart. So I listened to his voice and then began another campaign. This led to the creation of Shanti Sewa Ashram, an organisation working for the promotion of spirituality through selfless service in collaboration with twenty one different social and educational organisations, and Youth Society for Peace, a forum for youth committed to peace and service. Mottos like, 'Think globally, act locally' and 'Humanity through spirituality,' have become the guiding principles of my life.

I see beyond barriers of caste, creed, sex, sect, nationality and community. The concept of Vedanta has now become crystal clear for me.

I now clearly feel that although journeys may begin from different corners, all religious pathways lead ultimately towards the same goal. We may use different languages for our prayers but they give us the same feeling; we may live in different communities but are living on one earth under the same moon. So why not embrace each other and enjoy life by loving all? Why not feel that the same supreme consciousness exists in every being? We are all *Brahman;* all the variations are only illusions. Therefore, let's live in truth and understand the absolute truth; let's practice love and understand His unconditional love. Let's realise inner peace and create global peace.

DR CHINTAMANI YOGI is Founder, Principal and co-ordinator of Hindu Vidyapeeth-Nepal; Founder, Shanti Sewa Ashram; Patron, Founder and Principal, Youth Society for Peace.

He has an MA in Philosophy (Sanskrit), B.Ed. in Nepali, Diploma in Yoga Education, and an MD in Yogic Therapy.

He has published many books in Nepali and received many awards, including the National Sanskrit Glory Youth Honor and several Social Service Awards.

SELFLESS SERVICE

Human nature is quite inexplicable;
everyone wants his/her own safety, benefit, progress and pleasure.
On the contrary, a good person always thinks of how
he/she can contribute to the welfare of others.
Living for one's own life is very simple;
life without any ideal purpose has no meaning.
So everyone should think of how he/she can selflessly
offer more and more to others.
It's the only foundation and purpose of human life
and it is the only true Dharma as well.
Dharma means *SEWA*, as the Upanishada*s* say:
Sewa Hi Paramo Dharma
A very selfless service to others is a true religion.

- Dr Swami Prapannacharya

Dr Swami Prapannacharya giving his blessing to disciples

LORD SHIVA
Giant statue in Bangalore
of Lord Siva meditating.
Just as Nepal nestles in the Himalayas
so Lord Shiva's home is in those
high mountain ranges.

THE ETERNAL COMPANION
SWAMI DAYATMANANDA

The Hindu who has had the greatest spiritual impact on my life is undoubtedly Sri Ramakrishna. I was born into an orthodox Hindu family and cherished an image of Hindu spirituality, which image has still not changed much in India. For many Hindus spiritual life consists mainly of renouncing all actions and practicing meditation. Monks, especially, are expected to abhor all actions, however unselfish they are and lead a life of stoicism bearing the crosses of life with equanimity. The more austere the life, the more a person is respected. Mere outward insignia, such as a big beard, scanty dress, a rosary round the neck, invoke awe and fear. If a monk can be seen seated

Sri Ramakrishna Paramahansa

in meditation posture for a long period of time he or she is sure to be surrounded by crowds of people.

That was the kind of image many Hindus did and still do cherish of a spiritual person. But all this changed when I came into contact with the life and teachings of Sri Ramakrishna. I understood that outward signs, though of some help in the beginning, have very little to do with true spirituality. A student, a farmer, a house-wife, a doctor, a lawyer, a soldier, or even a politician - anyone can be great spiritually provided they are sincere, unattached, lead a life of self-control, and discharge their duties as a service to God. Worldliness according to Sri Ramakrishna is lust and lucre. One who is free from desire for these and is devoted to truthfulness is a spiritual person. The goal of life is God-realization. This goal can be reached through many paths. Of these, service to humanity, looking upon all as manifestations of God, is most suitable to this age.

The teachings of Sri Ramakrishna and Swami Vivekananda have inspired me to give up the world and join the Ramakrishna Order as a monk. As time goes on I understand these teachings in a deeper way, and my faith in them has become stronger.

The first book that I came across when I was a small boy was *The Eternal Companion*. It is a book on the life and teachings of Swami Brahmananda, one of the chief disciples of Sri Ramakrishna, and the first President of the Ramakrishna Order. It is considered a spiritual classic in Ramakrishna circles. As the title suggests this book is truly a companion to be cherished until one reaches the goal of life. This is a book that I constantly return to for inspiration and guidance.

Sri Ramakrishna, like other great spiritual prophets of the world, has one important message - the goal of life is to have a direct experience of God, and have Self-Knowledge. Sri Ramakrishna's message is the message of Vedanta. Without God, we are nothing, empty. Spiritual life is essential, not only for spiritual progress but for material and moral progress as well. Swami Vivekananda summarized the message of Vedanta thus:

- Each soul is potentially divine.
- The goal is to manifest this divinity within by controlling nature, external and internal.
- Do this by work, or worship, or psychic control or philosophy, by one or more or all of them and BE FREE.

This is the whole of religion. Doctrines, dogmas, books, temples etc are all secondary details. In these four sentences we get the entire message of Vedanta. This message has been practiced and taught by Sri Ramakrishna.

Swami Vivekananda

God-realization is the goal of life. Humankind today has forgotten its spiritual heritage. We have forgotten that we are the spirit and not matter. We are not mere bodies and minds but souls trapped in bodies and minds. Unless we take to spiritual life we are bound to suffer and also cause suffering to others. The only way to peace and happiness is the way of the spirit. This can be achieved only by the transformation of consciousness. Sri Ramakrishna showed that by suitably transforming human consciousness every person can get higher spiritual experience. Transformation of consciousness is what *yoga* or spiritual practice really means. Various religions are paths leading man to this one goal. Nowadays educated people know that it is impolite and barbarous to criticize other religions or cultures. Sri Ramakrishna taught that all religions are valid paths leading to the same God. He never said that all religions are exactly the same. Religious harmony was for him not a mere doctrine or social principle but a vital need of the soul. He saw in it nothing but an expression of the plenitude of divine creativity and immense potentialities for the welfare of humankind. He felt that his own life would be incomplete unless he too shared that divine plenitude. It was not social compulsion that made him practice the disciplines of different religions but the desire to make his own life complete or full, by having integral experience of the ultimate Reality. This fact was attested to by the Holy Mother herself (Sri Ramakrishna's wife). She knew him more than anyone else. The Mother said of him:

> It never struck me that he practiced all the religions with the primary idea of preaching the harmony of all religions. He was always absorbed in divine moods and used to enjoy the Divine Play through all moods adopted by Christians, Muslims, and Vaishnavas for the realization of God. His days and nights passed in these divine moods alone - he had no other consciousness.

Through his practice of different religions Sri Ramakrishna has taught the following principles of religious harmony.

Sri Sarada Devi, known as Holy Mother

According to Sri Ramakrishna, 'As many minds so many paths to the Reality.' This means that there cannot be one single religion for all people. Each religion offers a distinct and unique way of experiencing the Reality. This means that the differences among religions are real and have a definite mean-ing. But all differences disappear when one reaches God. Spiritual experience must be the basis of true religious understanding, and not mere tolerance or social necessity. No man's knowledge of God can be complete unless he gains, at least, some experience of Him through other paths besides his own. The more his experiences of God, the fuller becomes his spiritual life and the greater his contribution to the enrichment of collective life. These principles of religious harmony taught by Sri Ramakrishna are slowly gaining the acceptance of enlightened people all over the world.

Vedanta has shown modern man the right approach to other religions. Showing reverence to other religions or other prophets, or even practicing other religious paths, does not mean disowning one's own religion. A person can accept the principles of other religions without diminishing his loyalty to his own religion.

An interfaith Swami! This photo was taken before my sermon to an interfaith group in a Unitarian chapel in an Orthodox Jewish part of London.

Sri Ramakrishna had practiced different religions and established the validity of those religions. His practice of other religions may not be acceptable to many of the faithful believers, but it cannot be denied that many people, especially in the West, have regained their faith in their own religions after coming to know of Sri Ramakrishna's life and experiences. This fact has increased the faith of Hindus in Christ, Buddha and Mohammed - not to speak of their own divinities.

Another implication of Sri Ramakrishna's teaching of the harmony of religions is their mutual enrichment through individual or group dialogue and through a comparative study of various doctrines. Such a dialogue can enrich every religion. It can help us discover the inadequacies of our own religion. No religion is perfect; every religion has some defects or deficiencies. These can be removed by accepting some of the nobler attitudes and doctrines of other religions. For example, Hinduism can adopt the attitude of unity and equality from Islam and service to the poor from Christianity. From Buddhism it can learn compassion for the suffering creatures. In their turn Islam and Christianity can adopt the attitude of tolerance and mystical experience from Hinduism. The Hindu doctrine of the Atman can fill up a vital lack in Christian and Islamic theologies.

Sri Ramakrishna taught us that one of the most effective means of spiritual progress is to look upon man as a manifestation of God. This outlook greatly helps us divinize our relationship with every being in this world. It was the divinization of human relationships affected by Sri Ramakrishna that enabled Swami Vivekananda to deify humanism and spiritualize social service. The social orientation of the entire Ramakrishna Movement has been shaped by Sri Ramakrishna's conception of 'service to man as service to God.' This service to God-in-human-form is spiritual humanism. It is not simply doing good to others but rendering loving service to the divine, seeing its presence in all beings. Spiritual humanism embraces the whole of humanity regardless of race, culture, religion, or social affiliation.

Vedanta also places before us an ideal for an enduring bond of world unity. World unity based on mere humanitarian principles, cultural or economic affiliations or political considerations cannot endure for long. All these methods have been repeatedly tried and failed to bring about unity and peace. It is only a spiritual unity based on the recognition that this world we see before us is a manifestation of divinity that can bring lasting peace and harmony. Spiritual unity can come about only when we actively accept spiritual laws and try to put them into practice in our day-to-day lives. Many people are becoming increasingly aware of this fact and silently turning to prayer, meditation and other spiritual practices. Even many physicians are refusing to administer drugs and advise their patients to practice meditation. It is the recognition of this fact that made Swami Vivekananda travel to America and place the spiritual ideal before the Chicago Parliament of Religions in 1893.

My message to the world is the message of Vedanta as practiced and taught by Sri Ramakrishna and re-interpreted by Swami Vivekananda. If we can learn to accept that we are all potentially divine and try to manifest this divinity, the world will soon be a place filled with peace and harmony. It is this spiritual intelligence alone that will lead us to lasting peace, harmony and fulfilment.

SWAMI DAYATMANANDA was born in 1943 in Andhra Pradesh, India. Deeply influenced by the teachings of Sri Ramakrishna and Swami Vivekananda, he joined the Ramakrishna Order after finishing his college education in 1962. He was ordained as a monk in 1973. He worked in various capacities in several centres of the Order in India, his last centre being Banga-lore, where he worked for 17 years. In 1991 he was posted to the UK as assistant minister of the Ramakrishna Vedanta Centre. After the passing away of the then Abbot in 1993, Swami Dayatmananda has taken charge of the Vedanta Centre. His special field of interest is Advaita Vedanta i.e. Non-Dualistic philosophy propagated by Sankaracharya, and reinterpreted in our time by Swami Vivekananda.

Ramakrishna Vedanta Centre, Bourne End, UK

THE VALUE OF ONE

Know the One, and you will know the all.
Ciphers placed after the figure one get the value of
hundreds and of thousands, but they become valueless
if you wipe out that figure.

The many have value only because of the One.
First the One and then the many -
First God, and then creatures and the world.

- Sayings of Sri Ramakrishna

Samanvaya: Ideal for the Modern Age

SEARCHING FOR WISDOM
DEEPAK NAIK

I was born in Uganda. A promise I have made to myself is to go back one day and do some good work there. My parents moved to India and then brought me to England when I was about four or five years old. I was the youngest of their four children. I have lived here, in Coventry, within the same two square mile radius, ever since. This area means a lot to me.

My parents were among my earliest influences, imbuing me with the models and values that helped shape my life. My mother was very open-hearted. I remember how she welcomed two young Swedish missionaries into our home one day to give a slide show about their 'good news.' They became regular visitors! On one occasion my mother got a cross from them and placed it in the family *mandir* or shrine. For her God was one and she respected all ways of valuing that God. This impressed and influenced me as a young child.

My father passed on to me some of his strength and determination. He was a heavy smoker for most of his years but when, near the end of his life, my son developed a cough and my wife said that he could no longer visit his grand-father, overnight he stopped smoking. She had the same impact on me too when, many months pregnant with our first child, she told me that if I continued to eat meat she would give meat to the child also. This really made me reflect and in an instant I became vegetarian!

This essay is based on an interview in Coventry on 11 January 2006.

Other early influences in my life were some of my teachers who gave me self-confidence, even though I was a poor pupil in many ways. I was too busy trying to champion the under-dogs at school to concentrate on the academic aspects. When I tackled the school bullies to help others, I soon found myself their target!

My art teacher, Mr Toby, had a special impact. I had wanted to give my mother a picture of Sri Santoshi Maa, our family deity, but I could not paint it. Mr Toby painted it for me and I was able to give it to my mother. Mr Toby respected my request and acted upon it, even though he was not a Hindu. The painting was framed and hung in our living

Mr Toby's painting of Jai Santoshi Maa, goddess of peace

room for many years. Now it blesses Legacy House, the home of Minorities of Europe that I helped found and still direct.

When I was a child I did not know much about my religion. I remember being asked at school if I worshipped cows. This was a trigger to me to begin reflecting on who I was and what my faith was. I have always learnt most about my religion from non-Hindus. Through their questions, they have stimulated me to reflect, read and research more about my tradition. This has made my faith stronger. I am completely comfortable with being a Hindu. I find such a beauty in its openness to others and the respect it shows for different beliefs and practices. Hinduism is like water, fluid. It is not solid, like a stone. It allows you to accept your imperfections even as you strive to be better. I have found this really helpful. I can be relaxed, free to question and sort out difficulties without tension.

For me, Lord Krishna is God, the ultimate reality, but I don't feel good enough to focus on this. Although I feel a connection with and respect for the family deity this too is not my closest spiritual guide. For me it is Lord Ganesh who weaves his thread through my life and most influences and inspires me. When I pray it is Ganesh Bhagwan that I see and feel. One of our Hindu

Explaining Lord Ganesh to young Europeans at a Coventry mandir

elders taught me how to understand Ganesh, the elephant god, deity of wisdom, in a rational as well as spiritual way. He taught me how I could walk the path of spirituality and combine it with rational understanding. As someone brought up in the west this combination is important to me.

When we need wisdom and have important decisions to make it is important to take the correct steps. A checklist can be very helpful in preparing to successfully overcome the obstacles that affect our lives. The elephant head of Lord Ganesh can function as a most effective checklist.

An elephant uses its trunk to go out, smell out and reach out for what it needs and this is what we also can do to find those people who have made wise decisions in the area that concerns us. When I have a problem I need to consult with those who have already made the wise decisions that can help inform me. The mouth of an elephant is small compared with its overall size. You can't easily see it. This teaches me that I need to ask the wise people small, sharp, precise questions and not waffle about my situation. The elephant's large ears give me the insight that I need to listen to their responses rather than keep talking myself. The small eyes of an elephant reveal to me that I need to look at everything in detail, check out the 'small print.'

Lord Ganesh

This checklist helps me to make wise decisions myself. The ultimate wise decision is to become one with God. For that I need let go my ego, this is symbolized by one of the two tusks of Lord Ganesh being broken. I need to let go of me. In meditation the mind usually scampers all over the place. This is symbolised by Lord Ganesh's constant companion, a mouse. Ganesh himself has the wisdom, the means, and the skills to truly control the mind (ego) and to become one with God. Ganesh is also the son of God or Shiva so, to reach God, we go through the wisdom manifested in and by Ganesh.

One of the biggest breaks in my life came when I began work in life assurance. It took me away from manual labour and helped me develop the habits and secure the training that have become essential ingredients of my life. It opened doors for me internally and gave me confidence, ambition, communication and management skills, and time to reflect. Collectively these led to my work for the Hindu community and from there to all the other arenas that have motivated and engaged me. Phrases I learnt during my life insurance training, like 'Limits only exist in the mind,' have enabled me to do things for God that were not possible before. I learnt that nothing can stop me if I am called to do something worthwhile.

My work now is all about diversity – religious, racial, ethnic. I have always felt drawn to this, even when very young when my question was, 'Why is it that we don't value God, why do we allow people - political, business, religious - to use God to divide and oppress, create violence etc?' Anything I can do to prevent that, or to move people away from that, is the contribution I want to make. This feels like my dharma, the reason I am here. God does not need my protection but it is my duty to use my presence, energy, and time for this

Leading an international interfaith workshop
at the 2002 International Association for Religious Freedom Congress in Budapest

purpose so I try to create climates where we can build good quality relationships, embrace our differences, and value and have fun with God.

I have a special incentive to make these conditions possible for young people. They are the future. They have the potential to change society so influencing them to be active, positive and passionate members of society is a must. The organisation I helped found and still lead, Minorities of Europe, exists to enable them to become the visionaries we hope to be. Our projects include faith, interfaith, community building, community cohesion, development, values and human rights agendas and involve young people from all parts of Europe. We try to build respect in all participants, for themselves and for others. It is wonderful work and I feel truly blessed.

Although as a human being I am a global citizen – Ugandan, Indian, European, English, Hindu – still I know that this cannot define me. I came to earth with nothing and will leave with nothing. All labels are just temporary. Inside, none of these things endure. More and more I reflect on just who is Deepak Naik and what is his real significance......

DEEPAK NAIK is a Hindu who is married to Daksha and with her has a son, Rajay, and a daughter, Avni.

In the recent past Deepak has been in financial sales, worked in Equalities for Birmingham City Council, and is one of eight founders of Minorities of Europe, a registered charity that works with young people to create a little more harmony in the world.

Deepak is a also a trustee of the United Religions Initiative and has recently begun an MA in Peace Studies.

INVOCATIONS TO LORD GANESH

I know the one-tusked Lord teaching me oneness.
I know the curve-faced one straightening my path.
May that elephant-headed God bless me with enlightenment.

I know that transcendental person.
May that curve-faced one guide me.
May that Ganesha of elephant head inspire and illumine my mind.

O Lord Ganesha of large body, curved trunk,
with the brilliance of a million suns,
please make all my work free of obstacles, always.

A VISION OF UNITY
DENA MERRIAM

I was brought up in a secular Jewish family but from my earliest days had inter-faith interests. Although I knew only a Jewish prayer from somewhere I also learned the Hail Mary and felt very drawn to this feminine expression of the Divine. As I grew up I continued to search for a coming together of different religious traditions but nothing spiritually satisfied me. When I was first at College, studying literature, later focusing on sacred literature, it was the mystic poets like William Blake that spoke to me and influenced my search.

I married in my first year at College and both my husband and I became seekers after Truth together. He was based at Harvard and at that time, in 1969, it was a place of drugs, rock and spirituality, with Ram Dass organizing gatherings for students. We read his book *Be Here Now* and went along to meet him. It was a turning point in our lives and, shortly after this, we were given a copy of *Autobiography of a Yogi* by Paramahansa Yogananda. My husband and I took turns reading from our one copy of this book and we couldn't put it down. I recognized Yogananda as my guru and this was confirmed for me in a dream about him. I wrote to the organization he founded, Self-Realization Fellowship, and requested Kriya Yoga initiation (the special yogic meditation technique taught by Yogananda). They advised me I had to apply for the lessons first and that it would be one year before I would be ready for Kriya. One year seemed endless to me at that time! Later I received Kriya initiation from Brother Anandamoy, a senior monastic and direct

Br Anandamoy

This essay is based on an interview in London on 16 April 2006 disciple of Yogananda. So, at age twenty, although I continued to explore my interfaith vision, I was established in my spiritual path and practice and have stayed with it ever since.

Reading the *Autobiography of a Yogi* turned my attention East and other inspirational books followed, on Ramakrishna, Ramana Maharshi and others. I found in so many of the great Hindu preceptors a relationship with God as Divine Mother that resonated with my own early attraction to Mary. I found much more too that seemed meaningful in a special way, including Hinduism's embrace of Truth wherever it is found without feeling threatened. Also, where else but in Hinduism is bliss, God-intoxication, so boldly proclaimed and open to everyone? In my experience I have not found anything quite like this elsewhere and Hinduism has such a rich and diverse literature where it is all expressed so beautifully.

Paramahansa Yogananda

Perhaps what has most deeply affected me is Hinduism's profound vision of unity. This yogic vision of unity I find to be the only true monotheism. There is no duality. No God outside or over there. In the west there has long been the assumption that its version of monotheism is superior and that Hindus are polytheists. This has to be challenged. The real yogic understanding is a deeper vision of monotheism. What have divided us are false differences. Christianity and Judaism have angels. Islam gives many names or attributes to the one God. Hindus were more poetic, creative, and gave forms to all the attributes of God but God is still One.

Hinduism gives us the steps to reach this divine unity for ourselves. We don't have to rely on others. In the yogic traditions we are our own vehicles. We just have to follow a clearly described path of interiorization to remove the clouds of ignorance that cover our knowledge of it. Realizing this unity is the goal of life. Yogananda put all this great wisdom into words that everyone can understand and he gave us the tools to realize it. He took the teachings hidden to all but yogis and made them accessible. This was what I had been searching for though I did not realize it until I read the *Autobiography*. Of course, it's not always so easy to follow it well! I remember in the early days meeting someone who meditated two hours daily and had been doing so for four years. I was still struggling with twenty minutes daily so thought he must be enlightened! Thirty-five years later I realize that even if you meditate six hours every day still the mind might not be conquered. That is very difficult!

When I left university I had children so stayed at home with them, keeping up my meditation practice and study. The children were exposed to all religions so grew up without any particular religious identity. This seems to be increasingly common today. More and more people may retain something from the religion they were born into but may have a completely different spiritual practice. Some years ago, when I began interfaith work, I began to reflect on my own religious identity. People wanted to put me into a religious box and I always chose Hinduism. Yet, when I am in India I realize that this is not really accurate. What do you call yourself when you have come to realize the truth in all religions? Recently I discovered the term 'hybrid' used at a conference so that is what I am!

When my husband and I divorced I had to go out to work and so joined the family company. I did a master's degree in sacred literature, became a free-lance writer, and learnt to separate my working and private lives. This went on for many years until the opportunity arose in 1998 to help organize the Millennium World Peace Summit that brought together religious and spiritual leaders from around the world for two days at the United Nations followed by two days of workshops at the Waldorf-Astoria hotel. I had become dis-couraged by institutional religions and felt they had nothing to offer me so this was a re-entry into the religious world for me and I was surprised by how in-spiring I found many of the leaders from all the different traditions that took

With participant at Global Peace Initiative of Women event

part. It proved a new phase in my interfaith traveling and since then I spend much of my time doing interfaith work though I continue to question it. While it is undoubtedly important, how much good are we really doing? Where best to direct our energy? Should we continue bringing people together for dialogue or seek new ways to promote unity and a unified spirituality? Where might interfaith activity be in five years? Will I have found new ways to contribute to it or will my part be completed? The question of our own religious identity is integrally wrapped up in these questions and in the future of interfaith.

More and more I find people ready to agree that old exclusivities have to be replaced by a new universalism, although many find this deeply disturbing and so become even more polarized. At a recent conference I was sitting between a Muslim and a Christian who were locked in a struggle over the cartoons about the Prophet Mohammed on one side and the treatment of a Muslim convert to Christianity in Afghanistan on the other. There seemed to be a competitive edge to who was the greatest victim, who was suffering the most. I told the Indian parable of the elephant touched by six blind men, each convinced that his part best described the elephant whereas in reality they each only knew a  part of the whole. This story says it all for me. The understanding in it comes from Hinduism. It has to be embraced by all of us. We have to move beyond defending our own tribe or family into a human unity, a human spirituality. Later that evening, sitting alone by the sea, I clearly 'saw' the unity of all the religions and had the strong feeling that only realizing this unity can save us.

New questions arose from this experience that I am still processing. How do we help humankind take the leap away from tribalism? How can we expand that ancient impulse into a global vision? Do I want to shift directions now, take a different route? What of my own identity? Is it time to break away from old paradigms? How? Maybe in the interfaith movement certain groups need to continue a dialogue but others of us are ready for something more. I have begun exploring with others who feel this change, who are ready to acknowledge equality and mutuality, what we might do together.

Practice is the key. It is scientific. It does not depend on tribalism or beliefs of any kind. Try it and see. In my family, where years ago I was seen as someone a little bit weird, on the fringes, I am now recognized as a peacemaker there. In my interfaith work we are experimenting with coming together to share practice, share experience, awaken compassion, to move beyond dialogue. The success of interfaith depends on our own spiritual practice. We can only advance the interfaith agenda if we continue our own spiritual journeys. Interfaith doesn't replace them but depends upon them. The deepening of relations between religious people is an outcome of each of our own deepening spirituality. There are so many ways to the Supreme. It's possible through any of the

Kabir, weaver and mystic

traditions. What is important is that we make that journey to understanding together. My own shift is towards this, making that journey with others: just being together, in each other's company, sharing spiritual experience. It's not new. Centuries ago Kabir did just that, bringing Hindus and Muslims into shared experience. I often meet with a Sufi friend but we don't feel moved to say much, except every now and then, 'It's all One, isn't it?' The joy is in being together.

My guru was a pioneer in interfaith. Even back in the 1920s and 1930s he was addressing the vexed questions of religious identity, preaching that he was not Hindu, not Christian. There was not an interfaith language then but he was already formulating new ways of thinking for westerners. He is deeply respected in interfaith circles and has inspired so many interfaith activists on their own spiritual journeys. Paramahansa Yogananda gave the example and the teachings that can bring us to divine unity. These have guided my life. When I ask, 'What would he do if he were here now?' I immediately feel his presence. He is here now, in spirit, working unceasingly to help unfold in all of us who are receptive the profound yogic vision of unity.

DENA MERRIAM is Founder and Convener of the Global Peace Initiative of Women, a non-profit organization created by a group of women religious leaders to foster the spiritual values of global unity, peace-building and the development of all the peoples of the world. She was also one of the organizers of the Millennium World Peace Summit of Religious and Spiritual Leaders held at the United Nations in 2000.

She is currently working with the United Nations to organize a series of global youth summits around the Millennium Development Goals.

Dena has a Masters Degree from Columbia University and has served on the Advisory Boards of the Harvard Center for the Study of World Religions, the International Center for Religion and Diplomacy, AIM for Seva and Dharma Drum Mountain.

A UNITED WORLD

Let us pray in our hearts for a League of Souls and a United World. Though we may seem divided by race, creed, color, class, and political prejudices, still, as children of the one God we are able in our souls to feel brotherhood and world unity. May we work for the creation of a United World in which every nation will be a useful part, guided by God through man's enlightened conscience.

In our hearts we can all learn to be free from hate and selfishness. Let us pray for harmony among the nations, that they march hand in hand through the gate of a fair new civilization.

- Paramahansa Yogananda

AS FAMILY NAME WE CHOSE *BHARAT.*
JAEL BHARAT

As half of the Netherlands is reclaimed from the sea, so many Dutch people seem to have the idea that they created earth themselves. I was born in such an atheistic critical/rationalistic environment in the west of the Netherlands. A memorable quote from my father was, 'Of all people, vicars are the most useless.'

Being a very serious boy I remember my first question when I was four, 'Why am I here?'

During my study at the agricultural academy in the south-west of Holland I stayed with a family who were members of a protestant Christian community. They really believed that God played a role in their struggle against the sea water. After every meal my landlady read me a chapter from the bible. I found this more interesting than the one-hour youth group sessions some years before with a vicar who could only grasp our attention for counting the amount of matches he needed to keep his pipe burning. Succeeding my parents and becoming an arable farmer (I hoped that this occupation would give me enough freedom to do what I was really interested in) and having developed many practical skills, I became a 'do it yourselfer' in life.

My first wife Elly was member of a liberal Christian community which asked me to accompany the church-singing on the organ. I always followed the sermons with interest - not only for the fact that I had to be alert to follow up the sermon with meditative music - and became a member of this little community because I felt a positive influence on my family with three children.

To say who or what influenced me most during my first forty two years is very difficult. I studied economics, philosophy, and went to Africa to do 'development work,' amongst other things. Perhaps 'do it yourselfer' is the best indication of how I tried to find an answer to my first question. No special example stood out, but I had a few very good friends, Elly included.

And then Elly got cancer and passed away after 18 months of suffering, when she was 48; our children 14, 16 and 18, and myself 42. This was terrible for everyone, especially for our children and Elly's parents. But for me it came with a great blessing too, because after she passed away Elly's spirit brought me in contact with, or made me aware of, the spiritual world. Before this

*The spiral is a mystic symbol.
Here I have visualised the expanding effect of
individuals -free spirits- able to risk their earthly lives
working for the highest good.*

happened I could have said, 'I only believe in what I can see,' but this experience made me really see. It transformed me at once from a sceptical atheist into a student-mystic. I also started praying to 'Great God' as what I presumed to be the highest authority, not having much idea what it would hold, yet I put all my trust in it and kept to 'Thy will be done.'

Then on top of this experience, out of the blue, seven years later in May 1991, during the night after he was murdered, the spirit of Rajiv Gandhi visited me with the request to come to Delhi. India had not at all been part of my landscape so far. Never had I considered visiting that country or whatever. Only some time before I had seen Richard Attenborough's film about Gandhi three times and had been very impressed.

My encounter with Rajiv Gandhi was extraordinary. In a dream it started by us both sitting somewhere on the ground, me writing and he meditating. After a while we happened to look at each other and recognized each other as old friends. Rajiv proposed to go sit somewhere and have a drink and chat. We entered a kind of club which was over-crowded, but a Dutch acquaintance of mine, who appeared to be a member there, offered us his table. Then Rajiv repeated several times his message, 'Please come to Delhi.' He also added that I did not need to prepare myself; 'just come and you will be well received.' He seemed to represent India because I noticed a lot of background murmur, in which the Mahatma was the only one I recognized.

During our conversation I awoke and got up but our meeting continued (as in a vision). After emphasizing his message several times, I asked Rajiv how he felt after his assassination. He responded that he felt very well/content/happy, especially because he felt that at least he had done something useful during the last part of his life.

There was no doubt in my mind that I would go to India. Others of course concluded, 'He is following a dream!' My then Australian son in law Paul informed me that people who visited India mostly return from there as 'weirdos.' My response was that in my case there was not much to lose as I already was one.

I prepared my travel for after the harvest of sugar beets, mid October, and even prepared my family on the possibility that I might not return, which in a way happened because I returned four months later quite changed, at least disturbed during the first months because of not yet being able to handle the new experiences in a balanced way. For example, I was already a vegetarian but how to deal with the insight I got that *Life is in everything*?! For a while I felt not able to grow sugar beets anymore because these are harvested before having died. After months of searching I found the answer that one only eats in the service of God.

One of the main experiences I had in Delhi was my first direct encounter with God. God, as she called itself, spoke to me extensively; especially about the many problems of humanity on this planet earth. This occupied the main part of the report I wrote about my visit to India. I also had the experience of feeling reborn as an Indian (having had a dream in which I had a lively brown baby in my arms) which led me to change my family name to Bharat.

In - mainly - Christian Europe I had never felt so much at home as I did in India. With my experiences and views, in Holland I was seen as completely weird, while in India people could place it in a familiar context, and point me to people 'who know more about that.'

After my 'India experience' I connected to the Dutch Branch of the International Association for Religious Freedom (IARF) and the World Conference

The sacred cow of India grazing with the Himalayas behind her

for Religions and Peace, (WCRP) and became an Interfaith volunteer activist in The Netherlands.

After being a widower more then ten years and feeling married to God, very careful with my text, knowing that one might literally get what one asks for, I added to my prayer the wish to have a female friend on the same spiritual level as me, and who would fit within my calling - serving God.

Attending the 1996 IARF Congress in South Korea I met Sandy, who worked initially for the IARF while helping build up the International Interfaith Centre (IIC) in Oxford. Later Sandy worked wholly for the IIC for which I became a volunteer in 1998. Right away it felt very familiar between us.

Some years before we married formally Sandy also chose for herself the family name BHARAT. We both experience our marriage as 'arranged in heaven.'

Why did India become so special? I think that her uniqueness is because she maintained and kept her inheritance alive and well. Part of human tragedy is that, originally, all communities around this globe had what India still has (were all special one time), but the rest just lost it because of various reasons. In India the Sanathana Dharma (Eternal Truth) has been kept free and alive and is not squeezed into a book or religion with consequential limitations. Also prophets and the likes are only revealed or revealing parts of the Eternal Truth. Hinduism is unique in that it accepts religious diversity without feeling threatened or being competitive. Sectarian differences divide at human level but the philosophy of Hinduism embraces all paths to Truth. It is not reduced by competitive missionary squabbling between different groups. No one owns the Truth. Truth is one and for all.

Despite being an economist myself, when I was in India I was sad to learn that India thought it needed to open its borders for the rest of the world because of political/economic reasons. I didn't see any benefits in this for India. If well

Oxford's architecture:
The Radcliffe Library
and environs

The Himalayas

organized India could be self sufficient, and keep Truth free and alive. But perhaps by this opening to the rest of the planet India makes her sacrifice, to help rescue the world from more disaster.

I am sure that Hinduism - Sanathana Dharma - will be able to provide the spiritual tools to come through this present terrible Kali Yuga, if, especially in the west, the realization grows that 'the end is nigh.'

Sandy and I wrote a booklet, *Mapping the Cosmos-An introduction to God,* which made us part of the Advaita family. Every evening we read from the wisdom of Paramahansa Yogananda. Every morning we read from the Ashtavakra Gita. One could conclude that I am still a rationalist . . .

My grand daughter Elly asked - visiting me in hospital after I got a stroke - 'What is the aim of life?' My direct response was 'The search for it.' This was not my complete answer. That would be SELF- REALIZATION.

On the question what has been my greatest inspiration my response at this moment is: LIFE and INDIA.

With Sandy, just home after three weeks in hospital following my stroke

JAEL BHARAT was born in The Netherlands. He was a farmer and economics teacher before moving to the UK when he met Sandy, becoming part of the team at the International Interfaith Centre in Oxford. Retiring from there in 2004 he has concentrated on his search for Truth and working with Sandy on various books. His sudden stroke (May 2006) proved a painful blessing in his search for Self-realization.

GOD IS LOVE

It is not that *we* have to love God, but to realize in our hearts God who *is* love
Dada Maharaj from Satara, Maharashtra

Sandy walking in a wheat field, a typical Dutch landscape, on her first visit to my farm.
During this visit Sandy gave me Autobiography of a Yogi by Paramahansa Yogananda.

PROPHET OF PLURALISM
JAY LAKHANI

Living in digs in London in my late teens I began to try to make sense of religion. I started reading accounts by contemporary spiritual personalities. Then a student of physics, religion had to be rational for me. One wintry December, when I was about seventeen years of age, I came across the complete writings of Swami Vivekananda. The first book in the series focuses on the life story of Ramakrishna Paramahansa, Vivekananda's spiritual preceptor. I could not put it down. It thrilled me. Religion suddenly started to make tremendous sense to me, became a reality.

Ramakrishna Paramahansa

That evening was a turning point in my life. It had a major impact on my life. Here was religion as experience, not book-learning or mental gymnastics, but heartfelt, personal. I knew it could satisfy me. Since that night Sri Ramakrishna has been my mentor, my teacher. We have a special relationship. Through his grace and my own past karma, I realised that I had a special function to fulfil.

My life went through various phases. First I thought I would become a monk, then I re-entered the secular world, and finally, in my forties, I was drawn again to the spiritual life, wanting to fulfil the true aims of my life. I began by organising classes for Hindu children, introducing them to their faith through spiritual stories without sectarian bias. Now we prepare a few hundred candidates every year for Hinduism A level and GCSE exams.

While all this was developing I began to be approached by interfaith bodies to participate as a Hindu partner in dialogues. This led to interaction also with educational bodies. I began to teach children of other faiths too. When talking with young Christian children about God I affirm their understanding of God as father. This is marvellous, to have an idea of God as a loving, protective, guiding personality. We have some fun too and I ask them if they don't find mums more cuddly, less hairy, more willing to hand out the treats even if they haven't done well at school! Why not then think of God as Mother, if that appeals? I don't try to shift them but to give them the freedom to relate to

This essay is based on an interview in London on 29 November 2005.

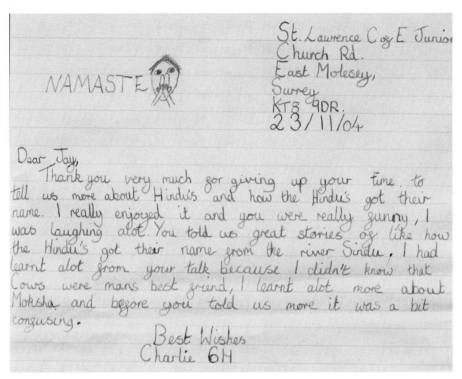

St. Lawrence C of E Junior
Church Rd.
East Molesey,
Surrey
KT8 9DR.
23/11/04

Dear Jay,
Thank you very much for giving up your time to tell us more about Hindu's and how the Hindu's got their name. I really enjoyed it and you were really funny, I was laughing alot. You told us great stories of like how the Hindu's got their name from the river Sindu. I had learnt alot from your talk because I didn't know that Cows were mans best friend, I learnt alot more about Moksha and before you told us more it was a bit confusing.

Best Wishes
Charlie 6H

Ultimate Reality in the way that fits their requirement. I try to stir their imagination so they can think of Ultimate Reality as something versatile, exciting, and personal.

I extend this idea too to teach about reverence for life. These little children can now imagine God as a mother so I introduce them to her son, Ganesh, someone much like themselves, clever and quite naughty too! When Ganesh comes home from school he finds his Mother busy in the kitchen. He wants to play but she does not have time so he goes outside and finds there the neighbour's cat. He decided to teach him the alphabet so that he becomes clever like Ganesh himself. He writes letters on his board and asks the cat to repeat them but the cat always says 'miaow.' By now the children are joining in with their 'miaows'!

Finally Ganesh becomes annoyed with the cat and decides to punish him. He picks the cat up and hits it three times. The cat runs away. He doesn't want to play anymore. Ganesh goes back inside and finds his Mother, still in the kitchen but bruised and bleeding. What has happened? Who did this? Ganesh is very upset. His mother calls him to her and explains. 'My son, this is the most important lesson in your life. As Mother Goddess of the universe I live in all beings. If you hurt any living being you hurt me.' Ganesh realised he could never again hurt another, that the same divinity in his Mother shone in the eyes of every living being.

After telling this story at one school, the teacher wrote me that whereas the children used to step on snails in the playground, thinking it was funny, they now bend down to them and say, 'Hello Mummy!' Religion for them had changed, from something theistic to something here and now, interactive, a dynamic 'spiritual humanism.'

In the same way, when speaking to older students and adults about God, I try to invoke the idea of spirituality by referring to God as *Brahman*. *Bra* means cosmic so Brahman means cosmic reality. This is Ultimate Reality as a principle rather than a personality. This does not have to be confined to religious expression and offers a more commonsensical way to spirituality. There is no super-human imbued with our own characteristics and contradictions. There is the understanding that something dynamic underpins the whole universe and all its layers, something unique and special. This is Brahman. Brahman is Spirit. Spirit shines in all. Scientists don't yet name quantum as spirit but they do know that these building blocks of the universe are not material, not matter. Hindus have been saying since ancient times that the building block of the universe is Spirit. Spirit alone holds the universe

Giving a talk on religious pluralism at Norwich School to Oxbridge candidates from all over Norfolk

together. Now, when I am invited to universities and colleges, quite often I
don't speak about Hinduism but about pluralism. This is the deeper, more
comprehensive aspect of Hinduism. Young people relate to it. It makes sense
to them. It is relevant to our world today. At one school, when I was talking
about religious pluralism to a thousand young people of various faiths and
none, the concept of pluralism touched them so much that they spontaneously
started to applaud. They understood that spirituality cannot be confined to
narrow religious expression. They appreciated having it explained to them as
something that is not just theistic or non-theistic or non-religious but cuts
across all such classifications.

This kind of approach can influence the ways a multi-faith society like our own
utilizes religions as cohesive rather than destructive forces.

I have been very delighted to discover that many of the Muslims I meet are
very open to the message of religious pluralism. They think very positively
about how it can help build bridges across religious boundaries. Indeed, as part
of the interfaith activities that followed the London transport bombings in July
2005, I had the unique experience of being invited to offer and explain Hindu
prayers in a mosque.

However, I have also come across some resistance to religious pluralism,
primarily from Hindu fundamentalists and from some Christians. The former
think they are uniquely different from other religions and that pluralism will
water down their tradition. The latter fear pluralism because they link it with
relativism. It is completely different. Relativism says 'there is no absolute,
everything goes.' Pluralism says that, 'depending on your starting place, you
have an individual prescription that fits your requirement for spiritual
progress.' This prescription is not at all floppy. It is binding. The prescriptions
are different, reflecting our different starting points and needs. This is good, it
shows we are not clones.

Some Christians are also anxious about their God being watered down when
he turns up in other religions. Simple mathematics disproves this. Take infinite
from infinite and infinite remains. The very idea of God being diminished in
such a way undermines the potency of such a God. God cannot be
encapsulated in any structure or he is no longer absolute. When we realize this,
with humility, there is greater unanimity and universality. God is not
limited to our own prophet or to our own vision.

I have come to understand that religious pluralism addresses the crucial need
of our times. It is the great legacy of Sri Ramakrishna, the prophet of
pluralism, and his disciple, Swami Vivekananda. This is the healing prescription
they offer our times. It is being accepted, it is entering the academic field.
London seems especially open.

I have been termed the evangelical pluralist! Inspired by my mentors I believe they show how religions can relate to each other, with equal dignity and no claims of monopoly; how truth claims between religions and between religions and science can be reconciled; how we can find validation in our own religion through the validation of others; how we can appreciate the truths in another religion without changing our own. This has been the abiding inspiration and influence in my own life.

In one way an acceptance of pluralism leads to the end of religions ruled by prophets as pluralism insists that we too have to become prophets. Perhaps this is why some feel threatened by it. We all have to grow up and become God-realised. This is part of a maturing process for humanity. Young people today know this. They don't like ideas of being a chosen people or having a special contract with God. They see no human difference between the Muslim or Christian or Hindu sitting next to them. They get on well together so they prefer such a universal approach to spirituality.

Sri Ramakrishna is the personification of pluralism, of universality, through his own direct experience. He offers a unique contribution to the dialogue of religions. All religions ultimately stand or fall on the basis of their intense spiritual experience. Practicing Christianity and Islam as well as many forms of Hinduism, Ramakrishna found the final experience of all was indistinguishable. He could rightly claim that all religions lead to the same destination. His experience continues to inspire my life. His is the message and example for our times.

JAY LAKHANI is a 56 year old Gujarati Hindu born in Kenya. He studied Physics at Imperial and Kings Colleges London. His field of study was Quantum Mechanics and Theory of Relativity. Jay took early retirement to study and promote Hindu teachings. He runs the Vivekananda Centre that works towards promoting Hindu education and the key role it can play

towards reviving and refreshing the message of spirituality across religious boundaries.

Jay is chief advisor on Hinduism to the Department of Education and Skills, the Qualifications and Curriculum Authority, and the Hindu Council UK. He acts as Hindu contributor for schools, colleges and media like the BBC.

ॐ ॐ ॐ ॐ ॐ ॐ ॐ ॐ ॐ ॐ ॐ ॐ ॐ ॐ ॐ ॐ

RELIGIOUS PLURALITY, RELIGIOUS UNITY

Many are the names of God and infinite forms through which he may be approached. The Reality is one and the same; the difference is in the name and forms. Some address the Reality as Allah, some as God, some as Brahman, some as Kali, others by names as Rama, Jesus, Durga, Hari. God is formless and God is possessed of form too. And he is also that which transcends both form and formless.

All religions are true. God can be reached by different religions. Many rivers flow in various ways but they all end up in the same sea.

A truly religious person should think that other religions also are paths leading to truth. We should always maintain an attitude of respect towards other religions.

- SRI RAMAKRISHNA

If any one hopes that religious unity will come by the triumph of any one of the religions and the destruction of the others, to him I say, 'Brother, yours is an impossible hope.' Do I wish that the Christian would become Hindu? God forbid. Do I wish that the Hindu or Buddhist would become Christian? God forbid. The seed is put in the ground, and earth and air and water are placed around it. Does the seed become the earth, or the air, or the water? No. It becomes a plant. It develops after the law of its own growth, assimilates the air, the earth, and the water, converts them into plant substance, and grows into a plant. Similar is the case with religion. The Christian is not to become a Hindu or a Buddhist, nor a Hindu or a Buddhist to become a Christian. But each must assimilate the spirit of the others and yet preserve his individuality and grow according to his own law of growth.

- SWAMI VIVEKANANDA

TOWARDS THE LIGHT
KARAN SINGH

As a young child, I was allowed to see my mother every day for only one hour, and my father thrice a week. This was obviously not an ideal family environment, and it flowed from a deep incompatibility between my parents. My

My parents

mother was a village girl from Kangra; my father was the ruler of the largest of India's over five hundred native States. My mother was warm, gregarious, and loved children; my father was stern, severe and moved only in a carefully chosen circle of courtiers and very few friends. My mother was strong on conversation; my father so formidable that normal conversation in his presence was virtually impossible. My mother was superstitious, demonstrative, emotional; my father was neat, meticulous, aloof. This psychological imbalance led to a good deal of tension and mutual conflict.

Through my studies in later life I learnt about the Vedantic concept that all human beings, because of their shared spirituality, are members of a single, extended family. The Upanishads have a beautiful word for the human race, *amritasaya putrah* (children of immortality) because we carry within our consciousness the light and power of Brahman, regardless of our race or colour, our creed or sex, or any other differentiation. That is the basis of the concept of human beings as an extended family: *vasudhaiva kutumbakam*. A famous verse points out that the division between 'mine' and 'yours' is a small and narrow way of looking at reality, indulged in by people with immature minds. For those of greater consciousness, the entire world is a family.

This essay is compiled from correspondence with editors, Karan Singh, *An Autobiography*, Oxford University Press, 1989, and www.karansingh.com

One of the greatest influences in my life in understanding the full potential of this wisdom was Sri Aurobindo. The forty years he spent in Pondicherry were an extraordinary saga of spiritual realisation and articulation. One of the most

Sri Aurobindo

original and comprehensive philosophers of modern times, Sri Aurobindo's thought covered every form, every action and every manifestation of life. His famous phrase is that 'all life is Yoga.' Life cannot be compartmentalized into the intellectual, the emotional, the material, the psychological, the spiritual; it is ultimately an integrated whole.

Sri Aurobindo was simply not interested in individual salvation; he was not even interested in collective salvation. What he was aiming at was something even more audacious – creation of a new heaven and a new earth; the transformation and transmutation of terrestrial consciousness. I would like to say, in all humility, let us in this hour of darkness and strife, try and find the inner door that opens on to this, our deeper consciousness.

Many years ago I developed the practice of writing down my most vivid dreams, an experiment which turned out to be of considerable value in my inner growth. These dreams would often involve encounters with Hindu saints and deities. I had a particularly vivid dream in which Sri Aurobindo and the Mother initiated me into some form of higher consciousness as a result of which I went into a trance, and another in which Ramana Maharshi beckoned to me to join him. On two occasions I have seen Krishna and have also encountered the goddess in various forms and disguises. This rich psychological material proves, if proof were needed, that waking consciousness is only a small fraction of total awareness. Above and below the conscious mind are vast dimensions. Omar Khayyam once said: 'There was a door to which I found no key, there was a veiled past which I could not see, some little talk awhile of thee and me there was, and then no more of me and thee.' Once one gets above a certain level, then individuation ceases and one becomes part of the entire spiritual manifestation.

Sri Krishnaprem, a remarkable Englishman and a great yogi, also guided me spiritually and remains a major element in my life. Whether in pain or joy, in elation or in depression, in conflict or in repose, his fragrance lingers like a tangible presence and gives me strength. I met him first of all, after some period of correspondence between us, at his temple ashram in the Himalayan foothills. During the three days I spent with him and his associate, Sri Madhava Ashish, also English, we had extended discussions about my life-situation. I gained a number of valuable insights that have since stood me in good stead. He talked of how every action has the elements of light and shade, and how the inner price has to be paid for every apparent outer advance. It is the brightest light that casts the deepest shadow. He told me 'Do not lose the light that is within you. It is more precious than your intelligence, wealth or fame. It is the only thing that will last.'

I have tried to live out this truth in my interfaith work - the belief that there resides deep within us all a divine spark which is capable of being fanned into the blazing fire of spiritual realization and that we are all part of one reality. These are the true foundations of the interfaith movement. While we individually seek within us that divine spark and clean our minds of bigotry and fanaticism, we need to take collective steps towards global inter-religious peace and harmony.

Today we find the world riven with religious dissensions and rivalries. Religion has a very mixed record in human history. Much that is great and noble in human civilisation can be traced back to the great religions of the world - art and architecture, music and dance, literature and moral codes. However, more people have been killed, tortured and persecuted in the name of religion than in any other name, and history is replete with bloody religious conflicts that continue down to the present day. If humanity is to survive it is my conviction

At the 1999 Parliament of World Religions

that the interfaith movement will have to become much more effective and active than it is at present. The Vedic dictum 'The truth is one, the wise call it by many names' has to be the keynote of the new edifice of Interfaith harmony.

Over one hundred years ago, at the first Parliament of World Religions, held in Chicago in 1893, Swami Vivekananda said: 'Sectarianism, bigotry and its horrible descendant, fanaticism, have long possessed this beautiful earth. They have filled the earth with violence, drenched it often with human blood, destroyed civilisations and sent whole nations to despair. Had it not been for these horrible demons, human society would be far more advanced than it is now. But their time has come; and, I fervently hope that the bell that

Swami Vivekananda

tolled this morning in honour of this convention may be the death-knell of all fanaticism, of all persecutions with the sword or with the pen, and of all uncharitable feelings between persons wending their way to the same goal.'

Unfortunately, his optimistic hope has not yet been fulfilled. But we cannot abandon the vision; it simply means that we must redouble our efforts to achieve the goals that he so eloquently articulated. For this it is necessary to highlight the golden thread of mysticism that runs through all the great religions of the world – the glowing vision of the great Upanishadic seers or the Jain Tirthankaras, the luminous sayings of the Buddha or the passionate outpourings of the Christian saints, the amazing assertions of the Muslim Sufis or the noble utterances of the Sikh Gurus.

These and other traditions of ecstatic union with the Divine represent an important dimension of religion that is often submerged under the load of ritual and theology. It is the many splendoured light of the Atman, 'the light that lighteth everyone that cometh into the world,' as the Bible has it, the *Ruhani Noor* of the Muslims, the *Ek Onkar* of the Sikhs, that must form the basis not only of organised religion but, more importantly, of the inner spiritual quest. In the tumult and turmoil around us we must never lose sight of this inner light and the deeper purposes behind outer events.

We have ultimately to find that light within us and become one with it. Then only will the true significance of the inter-religious dialogue become manifest, and then only will religion fulfill its true dual purpose – to lead us inwardly towards the spiritual light and outwardly towards peace, harmony and global consciousness, as humanity hurtles into the future astride the irreversible arrow of time.

Let me close with the immortal Vedic prayer:

Lead us from the untruth of ignorance
into the truth of knowledge.

Lead us from the darkness within
into the light above.

Lead us from the cycle of birth and death
into immortality.

DR KARAN SINGH was born heir-apparent to the Maharaja of Jammu and Kashmir. In 1949, at the age of eighteen, he was appointed Regent/Head of State, elected Sadar-i-Riyasat and Governor. In 1967, he was inducted into the Union Cabinet by Shrimati Indira Gandhi. He held important Cabinet portfolios of Tourism and Civil Aviation, Health and Family Planning and Education and Culture.

He was awarded a Ph.D. by the University of Delhi for his thesis on the Political Thought of Sri Aurobindo. He has been Chancellor of Jammu and Kashmir University and Benaras Hindu University; President of the Authors' Guild of India, the Commonwealth Society of India, and the People's Commission on Environment and Development; Chair of the Temple of Understanding; Member of the Club of Rome, the Club of Budapest, and the Green Cross International. He was a Member of the Lok Sabha and, since

1996, has been a Member of the Rajya Sabha. He is Chairman, Ethics Committee of the Upper House of Parliament, Chairman, Governing Board of the Auroville Foundation, Chancellor of Jawaharlal Nehru University, and President of the Indian Council for Cultural Relations.

Karan Singh has written many books and has lectured on political science, philosophy, education, religion and culture, in India and abroad.

WHO by SRI AUROBINDO

In the blue of the sky, in the green of the forest, whose is the hand that has painted the glow? When the winds were asleep in the womb of the ether, who was it that roused them and bade them to blow?

He is lost in the heart, in the cavern of Nature, He is found in the brain where He builds up the thought: In the pattern and the bloom of the flowers He is woven, in the luminous net of the stars He is caught.

In the strength of a man, in the beauty of woman, in the laugh of a boy, in the blush of a girl; the hand that sent Jupiter spinning through heaven, spends all its cunning to fashion a curl.

These are His works and His veils and His Shadows; but where is He then? By what name is He known? Is he Brahma or Vishnu, man or a woman, bodied or bodiless, twin or alone?

We have love for a boy who is dark and resplendent, a woman is lord of us, naked and fierce. We have seen Him amuse on the snow of the mountains, we have watched Him at work in the heart of the spheres.

We will tell the whole world of His ways and His cunning: He has the rapture of torture and passion and pain; He delights in our sorrow and drives us to weeping, then lures with His joy and His beauty again.

All music is only the sound of His laughter, all beauty the smile of His passionate bliss; Our lives are His heartbeats, our rapture the bridal of Radha and Krishna, our love is their kiss.

He is strength that is loud in the blare of the trumpets, and he rides in the car and He strikes in the spears; He slays without stint and is full of compassion; He wars for the world and its ultimate years.

In the sweep of the worlds, in the surge of the ages, ineffable, mighty, majestic and pure, beyond the last pinnacle seized by the thinker He is throned in His seats that for ever endure.

The Master of man and his infinite lover, He is close to our hearts, had we vision to see; we are blind with our pride and the pomp of our passions, we are bound in our thoughts where we hold ourselves free.

It is He in the sun who is ageless and deathless, and into the midnight His shadow is thrown; When darkness was blind and engulfed within darkness, He was seated within it immense and alone.

Sri Aurobindo

THE WORLD IS ONE FAMILY
MATHOOR KRISHNAMURTI

I am an Indian following '*Sanatana Dharma.*' I have been fortunate to come into close contact with some special people, including Mahatma Gandhi, whose influence has changed my outlook and approach to life to a great extent, both publicly and privately.

These great souls also affected my outlook on religion. I feel NO DIFFERENCE with people of other religions. I believe in the religion of humanity. I am free from any tension. This is the effect of my contact with Gandhi and others. I believe literally in the age-old Vedic dictum *VASUD-HAIVA-KUTMBAKAM* – the world is one family. The goal of all religions of the world is the same – Realization. God, by whatever name used, is the creator of the world. God is in all and everyone is in God. Hence there is no scope for dislike. Unless we develop love and respect for God, who is all pervading, and put this faith into practice, we cannot be happy.

I was born in Karnataka in 1928. My family was poor. We were taught then that poverty was a test of our integrity and God would watch how we success-fully dealt with it. I consider it a blessing. It keeps us humble and encourages inter-dependence. At the age of twelve years I read for the first time Gandhi's autobiography, *My Experiments with Truth*. I read it in one night. He so inspired me! I was especially touched by the story he told of how, during an English examination, he had spelt a word wrongly. His teacher came alongside him and whispered the right spelling so he could correct it. Gandhiji could not make the change. He could not be dishonest. Such truthfulness!

This essay is compiled from e-mail and fax correspondence between Mathoor Krishnamurti and the editors in October 2005, from *Mathoor in Britain,* M P Birla Foundation, Bangalore, 2004, and from an interview in London on 19 December 2005.

Gandhi wrote two letters to Adolf Hitler, the first one before the Second World War started with the hope of preventing it. His second letter, written during the war, also impressed me. Gandhiji had addressed the letter to 'Dear Friend.'

> That I address you as a friend is no formality. I own no foes. My business in life has been for the past 33 years to enlist the friendship of the whole of humanity by befriending mankind, irrespective of race, colour or creed.

Referring to his own country's struggle against imperialism, the Mahatma wrote, 'Our resistance to it does not mean harm to the British people. We seek to convert them, not to defeat them on the battle-field.' Hitler's methods would surely not succeed. 'If not the British, some other power will certainly improve upon your method and beat you with your own weapon. You are leaving no legacy to your people of which they would feel proud.' For Gandhi, only non-violence could defeat 'a combination of all the most violent forces in the world.' I have firm faith in this non-violence or *ahimsa*. My message to everyone is: Eschew violence. All are equal in the eyes of God. The world is one family.

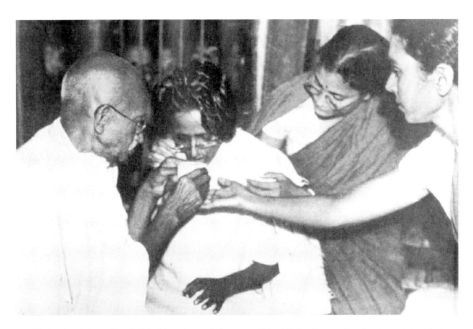

Eschewing violence: Gandhiji helping Amtus Salaam to end her 25 day fast, undertaken in protest against communal riots in East Bengal and Bihar.

How I longed to meet this great soul, Gandhi, but how? I lived in a village and meeting such people was not possible. However, when I was sixteen years of age, Mahatma Gandhi was scheduled to visit Madras where I was at high school. My own opportunity to meet India's great champion of ahimsa came closer. How eagerly I awaited the occasion. Adverts appeared in *The Hindu* newspaper for 'volunteers to render their services' during Gandhiji's visit to Madras. I joined the three-mile queue only to be rejected when it was discovered I could not speak Hindi. I sat in a corner and wept with despair. But I did not give up and determined to learn enough Hindi to become eligible as a volunteer. This I did and was subsequently chosen as one of only four volunteers to personally attend the Mahatma. My joy knew no bounds. I was thrilled at this opportunity of seeing Gandhiji from very close quarters.

For the next thirty-five days, I woke at 4am to prepare for the early morning walk that was part of the Mahatma's regular routine. For us volunteers it was not actually walking but running to keep up with Gandhiji's brisk pace! Everywhere he went during this period he met with such reverence and love and he disappointed no one. There were not things I wanted to discuss with him. I just wanted to be near him, this great man of truth, of *satya*. Those days are indelibly imprinted on my mind. I will never forget them.

This did not end my connection with Gandhiji however. I also spent six months at his Wardha Ashram learning to live as a friend to all, knowing the world as one family. During my stay I learnt about cottage industries, like spinning and making gas from cow dung and also about cleaning. By cleaning the toilets I learnt not only from Gandhi's unique philosophy but also the importance of giving attention to tidiness and cleanliness. Gandhiji himself would come sometimes to the ashram and speak at prayer meetings. The more I saw of him the taller he grew. I wondered how it was possible that such a person really lived on earth. When I heard the news a while later of Gandhi's assassination, I could not bear it and collapsed, sobbing, to the ground.

Many years later I found myself Executive Director of the fledgling *Bharatiya Vidya Bhavan* (Indian Cultural Institute) in London, a post I occupied for twenty-four years. There were many challenges in the early years and many miracles as support for the work grew and donors materialised to meet the many needs. When the time came that we acquired the present location of the Bhavan in West Kensington, I soon began to meditate on designing the prayer hall. I wanted it to be a place where people of all religions could come and pray peacefully and feel its sanctity. I wanted it to conform to Gandhiji's vision of prayer – a place where silent reflection on God and our own behaviour could be encouraged, where meditation could be uplifted, where all could come together as one.

Sri S Ramakrishnan paying his respects to Gandhiji

Sri S Ramakrishnan was Founder, Director, and Executive Secretary of the Bharatiya Vidya Bhavan world-wide and it was he who had sent me to the UK in 1972, advising me always to be guided by my conscience. His words carried with them the elixir for my future life. When he visited the London Bhavan, he told me about an incident he had experienced when meeting Gandhiji.

At the age of sixteen, he had organised a batch of boys his own age to engage in spinning. In 1940 on *Gandhi Jayanthi Day* (birth commemoration) these boys saw Gandhi and presented to him the thread they had spun. While conversing with Gandhiji, Sri Ramakrishnan said, 'Bapuji, I want to join your ashram.' He was then asked to detail his family background and when Sri Ramakrishnan explained that his mother was a widow, Gandhi would not permit him to join the ashram but encouraged him to look after his mother. Before they left, Gandhiji also advised the boys to continue spinning, to wear *Khadi* only, and to recite *Sri Vishnu Sahasra Nama* every day.[1] The Mahatma taught those boys to value each member of the world family in a real, practical way, starting at home.

I have recently compiled the *Gandhi Upanishad* – a collection of anecdotes from the Mahatma's life. In one of these, Gandhiji woke up at 3.15 am and began to sob like a child. His attendants rushed to him and asked him what was the matter. He replied that he would fast for three days. Why? He had dreamt that he was greater than the Buddha. But it is only a dream his companions told him. No, Gandhiji, told them, he must have thought this at some waking moment so now he must fast. On another occasion, Fenner Brockway, the Quaker peace activist and Labour MP who was very close to Gandhi, asked

---

[1] Khadi is traditional handspun natural fabric. The Vishnu Sahasranama is one of the most revered sacred chants in Hinduism for getting rid of problems and realising spiritual liberation.

him how he felt about Jesus' teaching to love your enemies as yourself. Gandhi was spinning and only smiled. Brockway asked him again. Gandhi looked up and said, 'I have no enemies.' What a great man he was. He spread the Vedic message of our oneness not only though his teaching but through his practice.

Gandhiji has risen from the status of an ordinary advocate to that of Mahatma in the eyes of the whole world by living a life of undaunted truth. I came to understand him, and also Rama and Krishna, not so much as *avataras* descended on earth from their heavenly abodes in human form but as ideal human beings. For me, Gandhiji is one of the most accomplished human beings in establishing *dharma* and annihilating *adharma* here on earth. His great message is a blessing for us all:

> Truth is God. Every time we speak untruth our growth is stunted by an inch. Truth is Love, Truth is service to humankind, Truth is ahimsa.

Through my many years of service to the Bharatiya Vidya Bhavan I became one with all people from different walks of life, discriminating against none for their colour, race, nationality or religion. To me 'Duty was God' and even now it is so. All my life experiences only confirm the ancient Vedic truth and my Gandhian training that, indeed, the world is one family.

MATHOOR KRISHNAMURTI is Executive Director of the Bharatiya Vidya Bhavan in Bangalore. He is author of many books including a biography of Mahatma Gandhi, and the recipient of many awards, including a gold medal for his services to the spreading of Gandhian Philosophy during the Gandhian Centenary Year.

Mathoor was married to Rajalakshmi until her passing away in 2003. They have one daughter and two grandchildren. Their son-in-law, Dr Nandakumara, is now Director of the London Bhavan.

WISDOM OF THE VEDAS

Peace be to earth and to airy spaces!
Peace be to heaven, peace to the waters,
Peace to the plants and peace to the trees!
May all the Gods grant to me peace!
By this invocation of peace may peace be diffused!
By this invocation of peace may peace bring peace!
With this peace the dreadful I now appease,
With this peace the cruel I now appease.
With this peace all evil I now appease,
So that peace may prevail, happiness prevail!
May everything for us be peaceful!

- Atharva Veda

United your resolve, united your hearts,
May your spirits be at one,
That you may long together dwell
In unity and concord!

- Rig Veda

The Rig Veda

PUNAHR-NIRMAAN (RE-CREATION)
MONA VIJAYKAR

I often find myself in the midst of rebellion, asserting a just cause perhaps because I share my birthday with Jhansi ki Rani. Over the years I learnt that truth prevails regardless, but the struggle yields something more valuable that only experience can teach and what my parents truly exemplify: *shraddha* (faith) and *saburi* (patience). For years, these words hung like a riddle for me above Sai Baba's seated figure at Shirdi until life illuminated their power through the most incredible circumstances.

My father, who followed in his father's illustrious footsteps, rose through the ranks to lead one of the largest nationalized Indian banks. Our family basked in the glory of his reputation as a respected banker. We enjoyed an elitist life-style through his hard earned privileges, while our personal assets were few. My mother's warnings to prepare for retirement fell upon deaf ears, since my father typically left it to Providence. His contributions to the finance industry left no doubt that he would celebrate a long innings.

But in 1985 their lives collapsed. Quite unknown to us, two years prior and thousands of miles away, the wheels of this tragedy were set in motion by the scandal of an Indian bank fraud emerging in the West. Dramatic events followed in India, beginning with my father's immediate resignation, accepting responsibility for the corrupt deputy who had caused the problem. But the leaders who believed in him extended his term instead, demonstrating their confidence in his ability to recover the loss. We rejoiced in relief and gratitude,

Sri Shirdi Sai Baba
Mahasamadhi Shrine

oblivious to the unfolding difficulties that would devastate our family.

As an upright banker, my father's presence was a nuisance to some of those directly connected to the bank for his insight into their suspicious dealings. They decided to make my father a scapegoat and overnight his contract with the bank was terminated without pension, the company car and other belongings confiscated and the family ordered to vacate the bank's flat leaving my parents and two young brothers at the mercy of family and friends. The nightmare of being stripped of possessions did not demoralize my father as much as the aspersions cast upon him. As Chairman, he could not resort to the staff Union. We desperately sought legal assistance but to our dismay, the nations most celebrated and powerful lawyers would not take on the challenges of the case. Over the years, my father became resigned to his fate, a reservoir of experience left untapped, let alone unsung.

My parents survived this huge setback thanks to their enormous courage and particularly my mother's undaunted *shraddha* and *saburi*. Rather than fight the system they chose to 'leave it to Him' and focused on rebuilding their shattered life from scratch, while their peers were reaping the rewards of retirement. Through twenty one years my parents only looked ahead, celebrating their children's accomplishments, welcoming their son and daughters-in-law, grandchildren and a host of friends into their modest life. Though my parents sought no revenge, occasional news about those who conspired against my father would arrive as astounding proof of Divine justice. But the toughest are put to greater test and my parent's resilience was to hold us in good stead through the unexpected, lengthy ordeal that lay ahead.

Around the time of the bank scandal, my parents were preoccupied with hopes of my marriage. Their prayers were answered when a friend's son proposed after six years of indecisiveness. I was married within a week to the 'brilliant, nice boy from IIT.' The fact that his family was strongly opposed to the match was relegated to the back burner in the hope that they would eventually warm to the marriage. My husband left for the US six days married, while I patiently

My parents

awaited my visa to whisk me away; oblivious to the fact that my *saat phere* (wedding ritual of seven circumambulations around the sacred fire) had whisked me off the edge of a cliff.

Blinded by devotion and delirious with joy, I embraced my new relatives and launched genuine efforts to win the love of my in-laws; a task as daunting as that of a clown at a funeral. I was nonplussed by an unfamiliar culture of taunts and jibes. Wedding photos of my husband alone were displayed; I was introduced to guests as 'our dwarf' and a photo of my aunt was passed around with morbid delight as a preview of my old age. My anguish was compounded when the US Immigration and Naturalization Service lost my papers and extended my wait indefinitely.

While I was announcing my fairy tale marriage from the rooftops in India, my husband chose to downplay the news in the US. In the eight months that it took for me to join him, he was not alone. Guilt, turmoil, regret and dread had accompanied him till the cold in his feet would rise to his lips in anger and impatience without provocation. If this life was intended as retribution for my bigotry in a previous life, the purpose was more than served. My husband's coldness, unceasing disapproval and sharp intimidation effectively undermined my confidence. Emotionally and physically rejected as a new bride in an alien land, I had embarked on a mind-boggling roller coaster that should have prepared me for the shape of things to come.

The double whammy from my in-laws and husband opened the floodgates of my hurt and resentment. But hope springs eternal in every woman to nourish the bedrock of eternal promise. The birth of our children lulled me into a state of settledness and although there is a fine line between keeping up pretences and 'making lemon juice from the lemons that life hands you,' over the next twenty three years I would diligently fulfill my *dharma* of motherhood and *grihasti* (home-making), building memories for my sons, whose unbound affec-tion propelled me towards new zeniths of creativity. The world would perceive an 'ideal' family, surrounded by material comforts, in a home that reveled in love, exuberance and vibrant culture. My combined experience as woman, immigrant, mother and artist formed the *Amrut manthan* (churning or turmoil) which yielded sweet *makkhan* (cream) in the form of children's books, songs, plays and newspaper articles. Inspired by Gandhiji and the words of a girl-scout anthem, '*kadam badhaye ja nidar*' (March ahead without fear), I remained optimistic.

I plunged into voluntary service as an educational consultant to help explain Indian and Hindu culture in American schools. My days were consumed by professional intensity and I soon regained my confidence through the love and respect of students, teachers and like-minded strangers across the world. But my greatest challenge was closer to home. Driven by prejudice and mortified by my assertions, my husband would belittle my objectives and support those who blocked my efforts. Although disheartened by overwhelming apathy and weakened by a solitary sense of betrayal, I resolved to be steadfast in *karmanya vadhikarasthe ma phaleshu kadachana*. (Pursue the course with selfless diligence regardless of expectation).

Our marital discord provided abundant food for speculation. Professional counselors happily roped us into infinite consultations without resolution and my parents remained mute, bearing the illusion that I might somehow reconcile to my shocking fate. Marriage is the greatest leveler. As I confided in more women, masks dropped and skeletons peeped from closets at an alarming rate. I yearned to flee this existence yet I had invested a lifetime in building our home and I was determined to maintain it.

As we are forced to understand the mechanism of the car only when it breaks down, it was now time for me to attempt to fathom life's contraption. Meditation and study of Hindu philosophy helped me discern fragments of wisdom and directed me towards new frontiers of my inner consciousness. Divorce became meaningless in the bigger scheme of things. I realized that our souls are entwined regardless and that the divine purpose of marriage transcends romance and the act of establishing a home, family and career. Marriage is meant to bond, not just two individuals, but to link entire communities and reinforce our spiritual connection of *Vasudaiva Kutumbakam* (a global family). We are thrown into relationships that are intended to steer us to seek answers and serve to overcome our specific weaknesses. In the past I took pride in my capacity to love and respect most people and condemned those who lacked courtesy. I was also conditioned by childhood tales and myths to assume that my sincere thoughts and actions would undoubtedly be reciprocated or appreciated. I had become hostage to my own desires.

Taking India into classrooms

The great sage Patanjali,
author of Yoga Aphorisms

With *pranayaam* (breath control) and chanting of mantras, I sought release. I began to inhale the energy of compassion and exhale my anger and resentment. This steadily helped crystallize my life's purpose as the Master Plan became apparent to me. The disappointments of a 'failed marriage,' 'stalled career' and social resistance to my ideas were all designed to motivate me to forge a unique path along which unpredictable challenges would help me discover my true potential. In the process, I was humbled into forgiving and accepting those who chose to dislike, distrust or oppose me.

My *Shraddha* and *saburi* brought me to a destination that was beyond my wildest imagination. I became aware that the cause in both cases, my marriage and my work, is bigger than us individuals. I realize that I am but a tiny wheel within elaborate universal machinery that operates only on goodwill and love. My job is to keep my wheel turning through my role of woman, mother and teacher. Children who receive appreciation and respect grow into respectful and appreciative adults. In retrospect, it is hardly surprising that over the years I equipped myself unwittingly with the skills and the knowledge to teach appreciation of diversity to future generations. Nothing is more liberating than to be entirely fulfilled in the giving without wanting in return.

But the most empowering thought that flashed through my mind was that I had never confirmed my arrangements with the Almighty before I was relocated to Earth; yet my stay here has been well taken care of and will be wherever I am on this planet until it is time for me to leave. Meanwhile this mortal has one more desire and that is to leave a legacy of future global citizens, who will have *shraddha, saburi* and the courage to love and honor all, especially the women in their lives.

MONA VIJAYKAR lives in California. She is the founder of India in Classrooms, a teacher assistance program designed to help dispel stereotypes about the Indian civilization. Her life is dedicated to bringing universal awareness among young children. She has written and illustrated 'The Vee Family' children's books. Her aim is also to build confidence among Indosauruses, those unique creatures who originate in India but are spotted across the world.

MESSAGES OF SRI SHIRDI SAI BABA

Serve selflessly without craving for recognition. Service rendered with expectations will be futile

Remember, do not sing in praise of the rich, sing your song in praise of the Lord, in front of him

I am ever living to help guide all who come to me, who surrender to me and who seeks refuge in me

Spend money in charity, be generous and munificent but not extravagant

He who comes to my Samadhi, his sorrow and suffering shall cease

I stay by the side of whoever repeats God's name

Remember, saburi (Patience) ferries you across to the distant goal

I shall surely bear it, if you cast your burden on me

Develop purity of heart to develop the soul

I shall be active and vigorous even from my tomb

Sit quietly, I will do whatever is needed

All religions are like rivers to finally join the sea. Follow the path of any religion and merge with 'paramatma'

In sorrow speak to me, in anger repeat my name, in bliss sing for me

Believe in the principles of 'karma' and do not expect any returns as a 'karma yogi' but live peacefully

Always repeat the sacred names of God

Burn the desires of the body and brighten the soul

Always remember, 'Prayer with pure heart is the passage to salvation'

Shirdi Sai Baba

A WAY OF LIFE
NAVNIT DHOLAKIA

I was born in Tanzania. My father was a Station Master and my mother looked after our family. I had three brothers and three sisters. As we lived in small bush towns, education was always a problem for us and I attended various schools, sometimes locally, sometimes in the nearest big town. As curriculums were everywhere different, it was never easy. When it came to secondary education we had to return to India, looked after by a maid, while my father and mother stayed on in Africa. For my further education I came to England and this is where much of my life story has unfolded.

When I arrived in Britain in 1956, it was to Brighton that I went, hoping to study medicine. A friend of my father's had visited the UK and returned to India much enamoured of Brighton and its 'floating hotels.' By these he actually meant the piers but as there was no exact translation for this in our language he could not describe them well. I was fascinated by the vision of floating hotels so Brighton was the place for me! Unfortunately, on arrival there, my studies were immediately threatened by the impact of the Africaniza-tion programme in Tanzania. This forced my father to retire so that he was not able to support me. I went to the Principal of the College where I had enrolled and told him my story. Not wanting me to abandon my studies, he made it possible for me to take up part-time work and study Chemistry at evening classes.

One of my colleagues at these classes was also my room-mate and one evening he invited me to have a drink with him. I had never been in a pub or drunk alcohol but I agreed and we arranged to meet that evening at a student pub where the drinks were cheap. When I arrived and went in my friend had not

This essay is based on an interview at the House of Lords on 24 April 2006 yet arrived. I hoped he would come soon as I had no idea what to do! I was also the only person there, apart from four young people sitting in one corner. One of these came over to me and explained that they were Liberals, had come together for a meeting but did not have a quorum, for which they needed five people. He explained that if I paid half a crown (two shillings and sixpence in those days) I could join the Liberals, come to the meeting, and they would have their quorum. This is how my political life began!

As I learned more about them I discovered that they sat in the council chambers to observe what went on there and organized protest marches against council policies of which they disapproved. When I asked them what they actually did to change the situations they found unacceptable I discovered that nothing was done to disturb the political status quo. I decided that if they would not stand up and try to make the changes, I would. I had a voice. I could shout. And I would use all my talents to help the disadvantaged people of Brighton. Just behind the majesty of the sea front, hidden behind its beautiful façade, lay broken families, poverty, large council estates where all the 'problems' were thrown together with no attempt at integration into the wider community. My efforts to make these changes attracted tremendous opposi-

tion from the British National Party and other extremists in Brighton who felt threatened by the actions of one lone Asian! Despite this I became elected and was the first Liberal Democrat council-lor in the city.

Brighton was also the place where I met my wife. As well as being a councillor, I was working in the hospital. One day, after receiving an invitation to the Mayor's Ball, I saw this charming woman there, walking towards me, so I asked her if she would accompany me to the Ball. She asked to think about it but some days later agreed to come with me. We have been married forty years now! As she was a sister in the hospital

With my wife, Ann

when we met, I often say that we met on medical grounds! We were married in the Quaker way, marrying each other in front of the community and so not taking specific religious vows. It was not easy for us at first as our 'interfaith' marriage caused some concern amongst our colleagues. It was not us they worried about, they told us, but the children who would come later. In fact our two daughters - one a lawyer, one a doctor - have enjoyed freedom to choose their religion and have benefited from the best of both Hindu and Christian traditions and been able to appreciate the goodness in all religions.

I was born a Hindu, raised as one and will die as one. I have never wanted to change this. Although, when I am in India, the first thing I do is visit the family shrine in Bhavnagar and offer my prayers there, my religion is not really based in the temple. It is the values of Hinduism that have most inspired me and which underpin my own values and inspire my life. When I read the great Hindu thinkers and saints of 20th century India, people like Sri Aurobindo and Mahatma Gandhi, what I read is not so much religion as values, common to all. Whilst our values are absolute and must never be compromised, they are also transferable. We can absorb good from all sources.

We must also regularly look at our religions and the way they are interpreted and find ways to discard aspects that are no longer relevant. For instance, when the caste system was developed it was a profound understanding of how different tasks could be met to help society function. It was not seen as divisive. Relevant then it is not relevant now. We need to question why we interpret our religions in demonising ways, adding values to them that were never there, inducing hate, and creating divisions. We need new fusions, fresh interpretations. We must speak out to make this possible. For instance, when I was in a certain Eastern European country, on the way from the airport to the presidential palace, in a car with the President, surrounded by his entourage of accompanying police motorcyclists, I saw a strange scene. In the distance a group of people were throwing stones at someone. I asked the president what was happening and he sent someone to find out. He returned and told me that it was just some people stoning a crazy man, nothing to worry about. I told the President that I would rather go straight back to the airport than be part of such a set-up. He looked at me, disbelievingly. I assured him that it was so and asked for the car to be turned around. Then he sent someone to stop the stoning. It did not change the world but it did change the situation for one person at least and maybe sowed seeds for others. We must not remain silent.

Another anecdote demonstrates what, for me, is real religion – caring and love. We were in Africa, visiting a place where an elderly Australian doctor had, for many years, looked after women with disabilities that created huge problems for them at the birth of their children. Many were then discarded by their husbands or suffered great personal physical pain. One striking young woman there drew our special attention. I asked the doctor about her. She had been thrown out by her husband and had returned home to her father. Her father had rejoiced in the return of his daughter. Although he was very poor, with only one ox and a small field, he immediately sold the ox and set out on the long journey to this medical camp to get the help his daughter needed. As he had nowhere to go during her treatment he sat unobtrusively outside and patiently waited. I asked the doctor what an ox would cost and she told me £120. There were three of us and together we gave the amount needed, asking her to give it to the father when he and his daughter were ready to leave.

My Parents

My mother also revealed to me personally this religion of love and caring. Illiterate as she was, she was one of the greatest influences in my life. She was my teacher, showing me how to live, a deep process too often underestimated. In the development of the Hindu heritage, it is the Mother who passes on the traditions to her children and my Mother was no exception. All other influences in my life came after, built on and reinforced what she had already established in me.

As she could not read or write, she asked me, when I was a boy, to read her stories from the *Bhagavad Gita*, the *Mahabharat* and the *Ramayana*. At that time I was happy to do so, not for the content, but for the pocket money I received. The more pages I was asked to read the happier I became! It was much later when I realized how much those stories had infiltrated me and become part of my life. I often draw on them in my political life. For example, in recent controversies in India over the planned introduction of visas for Indians living in other countries, I reminded people about the plight of Sita in the *Ramayana*. After twelve years imprisoned by Ravana in Sri Lanka, Sita was rescued by Rama and Hanuman and brought back to India. Now, I told my audience, this would not have been possible.

They would have had to apply for visas first! I used the same story again to advise against this policy that divides Indians living in India and those in the diaspora. When Hanuman was asked about his loyalty to Rama and Sita, he tore open his chest, revealing their pictures embedded on his heart. Ask any Indian to do the same and there you would see the map of India.

For me, Hinduism's great blessing is that it gives us a simple way to live, a way of life, a means to fulfil ourselves. It has given me a community of which I am part, a community with an ancient lineage that has passed on its own special kind of cultural and spiritual DNA. My family

Lord Hanuman

structure enabled me to feel part of this lineage, part of a very long process. I did not grow up in a vacuum. I learnt how to balance what I take from life with what I give to others and was encouraged and stimulated by the example of my parents to care for others and to give more than I receive. I was given the confidence to speak out for what is right and to preserve the great values that belong to all humanity.

Mahatma Gandhi put it this way:

> I will give you a talisman. Whenever you are in doubt, or when the self becomes too much with you, apply the following test. Recall the face of the poorest and the weakest person whom you may have seen, and ask yourself, if the step you contemplate is going to be of any use to her. Will she gain anything by it? Will it restore her to a control over her own life and destiny? In other words, will it lead to *swaraj* [freedom] for the hungry and spiritually starving millions? Then you will find your doubts and your self melt away.

LORD NAVNIT DHOLAKIA OBE DL was Chair of Brighton Young Liberals, 1959 and 1962, and elected to Brighton Borough Council, 1961-1964. His political appointments include: Development Officer, National Committee for Commonwealth Immigrants; Secretary of the Liberal Party's Race and Community Relations Panel; member of the Commission for Racial Equality; and member of the Commission on the Future of Multi-Ethnic Britain. He became a Peer in 1997 and then the Party's President, re-elected in 2002 for a second term.

He was front bench spokesperson on Home Affairs from 2002 to 2003, a council member of the Howard League for Penal Reform since 1992, a member of the editorial board of the Howard Journal of Criminology, and a member of the Ethnic Minority Advisory Committee of the Judicial Studies Board.

He is a Trustee of The Loomba Trust, a Patron of the Hindu Forum of Britain, a keen photographer and gardener who enjoys travelling and cooking.

Houses of Parliament, London

THE DHOLAKIA COAT OF ARMS

The design represents different parts of my life.

Ganesh is the Hindu God of prosperity, a remover of obstacles and the Lord of Beginnings. He is holding two batons in his hands, one to signify punishment for those who do not follow the true life and the other for protection for those who do. The lower right hand held up signifies a

blessing and the other hand is holding a sweet.

The sacred symbol OM is on Ganesh's dress.

The Heraldic Dolphins represent Brighton.

The birds on the shield are the Sussex Martlets. I am a Deputy lieutenant of West Sussex.

The four balls on the coronet are those worn by a Baron.

The Black Buck is only found in a reserve near Bhavnagar, our home city in Gujarat. In the old days the whole of Gujarat had Black Buck but now they are confined to one area.

The flowers don't mean anything, but are part of a standard Heraldic Design.

'Carpe Diem' means 'Seize the Day' or in colloquial terms 'Go for it.' Our eldest daughter is a 'Notary Public' in Scotland. They are required to have a seal and a motto. 'Carpe Diem' was originally her motto and it seemed a good idea to put in on our crest.

SIMPLE AND PROFOUND
SWAMI NIRLIPTANANDA

Swami Satchidanandaji Maharaj was the first disciple of Jagadguru Acharya Swami Pranavanandaji Maharaj, Founder of the Bharat Sevashram Sangha, an international organisation devoted to promote spiritual, cultural and social values.
It was founded in 1917 with an emphasis on service to the vulnerable - particularly in times of natural disasters.

It is not very often one comes in contact with such a great soul, and rarer indeed the opportunity to serve him. I was fortunate to have this in abundance during my two years stay in India in 1979/80 and I took full advantage of it. Not a minute of the two years I spent with Swami Satchidanandaji (lovingly called Baraswamiji Maharaj or elder/ first disciple) was wasted. Every time I recall that period I rejoice. It really was a heavenly experience!

It all started in 1972 when I went to India for a brief three months visit. I was sent by Swami Purnanandaji from London who initiated me into *Brahmacharya* (monasticism). During

Swami Satchidanandaji Maharaj

that time I hardly had the opportunity to meet the great saint except at the end of the period. After arriving at Calcutta, I went with a group of *sannyasins* (ascetics) and volunteers to Ganga Sagar where the birth of Ganga - the holy river Ganges - is celebrated every year at Sagar Island. The bus we travelled in to Kaagdeep was very shaky and one got the impression that it would fall apart at any moment! However, we all arrived safely.

Kaagdeep is a point from where one has to cross by motor boat to Sagar Island. Soon after we entered the motor launch there was preparation for *Sandhya* (evening) *arati* (worship). A picture of Acharya Swami Pranavanandaji Maharaj, founder of the Bharat Sevashram Sangha, was ceremoniously placed on a slightly raised altar made from whatever was available. The motor launch was transformed into a temple. The whole atmosphere changed. The group consisted of a preaching party who were experienced in their job. The chanting and music with various instruments, together with the sea atmosphere, sort of took me into another world. It was so simple and natural, something I was not accustomed to, living in London. When the evening devotion was finished we all sat down for dinner. The food was cold, being prepared for us in the morning before we left Calcutta. Nevertheless, it was enjoyable.

After the long journey everyone was tired and about 11 PM there was preparation to sleep, on blankets spread on the 'floor' of the launch. The boards of the floor were so uneven that they stuck in our backs. I tried to fix myself between two of the protruding edges without success. Soon I was resigned to the fact that I had to spend the night awake. All the others were sleeping!

At 4 AM there was the morning arati and on the horizon appeared the illuminations at Sagar Island where thousands of people already gathered for this great celebration. It was a fantastic sight. Being in the Bay of Bengal the place was silent apart from the noise of the engine. The early morning breeze was so refreshing and relaxing that I felt very energetic in spite of not sleeping the whole night!

Our camp was a small makeshift hut made up on all sides by thatched straw. Some of the straw spread on the sand was our bed! There were many huge

Bithal Rukmini Temple, Pandharpur, 30 Km from Solapur in Maharastra where millions of devotees assemble on the occasion of another great event, the Aashadi Ekadashi Mela.

camps elsewhere for the volunteers but this hut was the temple and had a couple of 'rooms.' Our camp was on the beach of the Bay of Bengal and we had a good view from there. Just after we arrived the arati started, at exactly 11 AM. The ceremony is usually performed at 4 AM, 11 AM and 7 PM. The spiritual vibrations from this are very conducive to meditation and I took advantage of the atmosphere on the island. It was wonderful to see thousands of thatched camps transforming a usually deserted island into one of brisk activity. Cultural displays and businesses of various kinds catered for the pilgrims who come from all parts of India, braving all hardships just to have a sacred dip in the Ganga!

I was particularly impressed by one pilgrim who came, from God knows where, with his aged mother. There was no other way to take her from the bus stop to the Ganga except on his shoulders! When they reached a point from where they could see the holy river, their faces lit up as if to say, 'We've made it, oh Mother Ganga!' Here in these *melas*, the rich and poor mix in such a way that we can hardly make any distinction between them. How nice it would be if the world was like this! Thousands of people gathering and hardly any crime! This respite was soon over but the impact of it will never be forgotten, particularly the first holy dip in the icy water. It sends a shock through your whole system. The body soon becomes adjusted to it and after that bath the world seems to be a different place, full of peace and tranquillity!

In India I had the opportunity to meet many great monks who were direct disciples of the Jagadguru. Each of them was like a sun shining in brilliance. Although each had hundreds and thousands of disciples they did not claim to be Gurus. To them the Jagadguru was the GURU. One day, as I was returning to the Head Office in Calcutta, I was given a packet by a devotee to take to Swami Satchidanandaji. When I brought it to the Ashram, I gave it to his *sevak* (attendant). He told Maharaj that his disciple had sent a gift for him. He asked, 'My disciple?' The sevak replied in the affirmative. That question and answer went on for a couple of times before the sevak said, 'Guru Maharaj's (Jagadguru's) disciple has sent it.' Swami Satchidanandaji then gave one of those captivating laughs that capture the hearts of others. I took it as a lesson for me.

On another occasion he said, 'You, Nirliptananda, do not have to take orders from anybody! Not even the

Swami Nirliptananda

President (i.e. himself) and Vice-president! You are a devotee of Guru Maharaj. He will guide you!' His words touched me deeply. Here was a person who had so profound an influence over so many people that if he just gave the order to some of them to jump into the fire they would gladly do it. And he was disclaiming everything!

There was one Sanyasi in the Ashram who had a bad temper. One day Swamiji called him and said, 'My son, from today you must observe silence.' He simply accepted that as a blessing!

I have seen hundreds of people who came to him with their hearts laden with problems and just a simple touch or a few words would send them out of his room in a cheerful spirit. A lady whose brother was seriously ill came to him and said, 'Please say that he will not die!' That was the kind of faith people had in him. He consoled her and she felt greatly relieved.

One day I was doing *seva* (service) for him in a room on the roof of a building when a devotee came to meet me. He was very mentally disturbed. For that reason he was searching for me everywhere. As soon as he climbed the stairs to the roof and met me, he said, 'It's very strange. All my mental disturbances have disappeared.' When he went into the room where Swami Satchidanandaji was and saw him, he said, 'He is full of peace!'

One devotee mentioned an incident to me many years ago. Their whole family was initiated by Baraswamiji Maharaj, except her father. He simply did not want to know. He would not even go to the ashram. After she got married she joined her husband in England. A few years later she visited India. Under pretext she told her father that she wanted to go to the ashram but was afraid to go alone. The father did not want to displease his daughter who had been away for so long. Both of them stood in the queue for *darshan* (blessing). She was in front and he was behind her. When she came out her father went in, and stayed inside for about 15 minutes. After bowing he just could not get up. Only tears were flowing all the time. He felt as if he had wasted so many years of his life!

That was the kind of attraction Swami Satchidanandaji exuded. It is something difficult to understand intellectually. On his part he did not seem to do anything special to draw the attention or to attract anyone but he was like a magnet - everyone just moved towards him. About someone who is Self-realised the Upanishads say, 'Whatever he is, he is just that,' and it is a description that is aptly applicable to him.

He treated every one the same way. He never turned anyone away and each got the impression that he loved him most! The feeling I got in his presence was extraordinary. It was something indescribable. And more important, it was not something momentary. It seemed that this vibration was emanating from his being all the time. Although it was extraordinary yet to him everything was just natural. One could clearly see how his physical appearance had been trans-formed. He was not the kind of person who needed to be pointed out or introduced. Being in his presence was enough.

On his dying bed, when he lay on the arm that suffered a stroke, the other was used to bless a queue of people who were waiting. Usually, we say, 'Leave the person to die in peace.' Maharaji gave whatever he could until the last moment.

The above are just a few glimpses into the life of a person who lived a simple, unobtrusive life but busy in helping others. He could not sing, never gave a lecture or wrote any books yet he touched the lives of thousands of people who met him. He was like the sun - self-luminous - neither hates nor causes another to hate, loved by all who had his 'darshan.'

SWAMI NIRLIPTANANDA is leader of the London Sevashram Sangha. He was born in Guyana, South America and joined the Sangha there in 1958. In 1963 he was called to start a UK branch and was initiated into sannyas in 1974. He is a life member of the World Congress of Faiths and has represented Hinduism at many national and international forums. His main interest is to build community relations and he initiated the annual Om Day for Unity.

Guests with me at the Om Day for Unity and Peace 2000

Message to Humanity
Wisdom of the Jagadguru

1. WHAT IS THE GOAL?
Self-Realization and Universal Emancipation

2. WHAT IS RELIGION?
Self-sacrifice, Self-abnegation, Self-discipline, Adherence to Truth and Continence

3. WHAT IS REAL DEATH?
Forgetfulness of the 'Self'

4. WHAT IS REAL LIFE?
Self Realisation, Self-remembrance, Self-consciousness

5. WHAT ARE REAL SINS
Weakness, Fear (defeatism), Cowardice, Meanness, Selfishness

6. WHAT ARE REAL VIRTUES?
Heroism, Vigour, Courage and Aspiration to emancipation

7. WHAT ARE REAL SOURCES OF STRENGTHS?
Patience, Fortitude, Endurance

8. WHAT ARE REAL ASSETS?
Self-confidence, Self-reliance, Self-respect

9. WHAT ARE REAL ENEMIES?
Indolence, Slumber, Procrastination, Inertia, Lustful senses, and Passions

10. WHAT ARE REAL FRIENDS?
Energy, Initiative, Enthusiasm, Perseverance

FATHER AND SON
RAVI RAVINDRA

Two childhood memories stand out in my mind.

In the first, I was about ten years of age. My father, Shri Dalip Chand Gupta, an eminent lawyer, liked to sit in the courtyard of our house, surrounded by poetry and other books, enjoying the winter sun. He did not need an audience but if someone passed by he would happily share something of what he was reading with that traveller. On this day I came into the courtyard and found my father there. He read me a *shloka* or verse from the *Bhagavad Gita*. In free translation it states, 'At the end of many births a wise man comes to me realising that all there is is Krishna. Such a person is a mahatma but a rare one.' Afterwards, father said to me, 'Ravi, I can tell you these words and I know what the words mean but I do not fully understand them. My wish for you is that you will meet someone in your life who can help you understand them.'

There was so much in what he said, not only feeling but also a whole teaching, that there are many levels of understanding and there was something he did not understand. Even now, remembering this, tears come to my eyes. The shloka often comes to my mind, without bidding. Those words are still relevant to me now. I am still trying to understand that, realise that, recognise the truth of it, not intellectually or in any sectarian way, but in my heart, in my whole being, that all there is is Krishna. It is my unfinished project.

Later, when I was about sixteen years of age, I told my friends that my idea of a 'decent man' would be a combination of three people - Swami Vivekananda, Rabindranath Tagore, and Albert Einstein. They were my ideals, models for my own aspirations. All are still interesting to me fifty years later, though it now seems unrealistic to imagine myself becoming like them!

This essay is based on an interview in Oxford on 17 September 2005.

Swami Vivekananda

Vivekananda expressed the best of religion. He was the opposite of those uninspiring priests one meets everywhere, in every religion, who only seem to exploit people. Vivekananda had a no-nonsense attitude to religion. He cut to the heart of it - direct spiritual experience. His way of speaking, not cowardly or docile, gave a sense of religion as fire. That appealed to me. He is still a great inspiration today, especially for youth. He himself never lived to be old so his enunciation is forever youthful. Today, the Ramakrishna Mission, that Vivekananda helped found after the *mahasamadhi* of Ramakrishna Paramahansa, has become something like the state church of India. Its broad inclusiveness allows many to feel comfortable in it in a way that narrower borders do not permit.

Tagore's poetry is sublime. It is sensitive, mystical, musical and flows with great finesse. Einstein, to me, is the archetypal scientist. (Vivekananda also taught that religion was scientific.) Tagore and Einstein made contact with each other during a meeting in Berlin in 1930, where one emphasised Beauty, the other Truth.[1] Einstein also visited India and at one point even wanted to become its citizen. In 1977, when the Einstein archives were held at Princeton University, I went there, as a young physicist, hoping to research for a paper I had in mind on Einstein in India. Helen Dukas, previously Einstein's secretary, was in charge of the archive.[2] Remarkably she handed me the keys, telling me to lock up when I had finished and tell her the next day what I would like copied. So, I found myself alone with this great treasure! What did I ask to be copied the next day? I had found a postcard from Tagore to Einstein sent for the latter's birthday. It read, 'To him who knows all my faults and still loves me, my salutations.' This was what I brought to the photocopier and into my life.

I grew up a Hindu in the Punjab, moving to Bengal in my teens for study. There is a long history of lawyers and judges in my family. Indeed my son, Kabir, is a lawyer and in his application to Law Schools he wrote how the grandfather of his grandfather was a lawyer, how everyone in his family were lawyers or judges but his father had broken away from this. So, now, it was up to Kabir to re-establish the family heritage! Indeed, it is true, my life studies have explored the laws and judged the merits of technology, geo-physics, philosophy and religion, none of which has ever summoned me to court!

[1] See www.schoolofwisdom.com/tagore-einstein.html for a transcript of part of this meeting.
[2] They are now held at the Hebrew University of Jerusalem. For an online resource, see www.alberteinstein.info

A Commonwealth Scholarship took me to Canada where I did my M.S. and Ph.D. in Physics after which I returned to India where I spent nearly a year looking for a job. Finally I returned to Canada as an immigrant in 1966. For most of my career I was an academic at Dalhousie University in Halifax, firstly in the Physics Department as a professor of Physics. Later I was in both Physics and Philosophy and then, recruited by the great scholar, Wilfred Cantwell Smith, as a professor of Religion. Smith, to everyone's surprise, came from Harvard to Dalhousie to lead the new Religion Department there. He taught a course on religions in India in which his practice was to speak generally about religions in India in the first term and to focus on the Bhagavad Gita in the second term. We sometimes met over tea and one day, to my astonishment, he remarked to me, 'You clearly know the Bhagavad Gita better than I do so you should come and teach it in our department.' At this point I was beginning to feel that in philosophy we were sharpening pencils but never writing love letters so his suggestion came at an appropriate moment in my life. Indeed, I am almost convinced that our lives are arranged by guardian angels though they often take a circuitous route! I took a year out to study Sanskrit in New York and then returned to take up Professor's Smith's invitation. It was the Bhagavad Gita that brought me to the Department of Religion and not the department that led me to study the Gita. The Gita is like a thread weaving itself through my life and although I do not have a particularly *bhakti* orientation, yet there is a great love of soul in me that it inspires.

Recently I retired in order to travel more freely when invited to give talks around the world. My personal interests have become more directly scriptural and spiritual. My personal aspiration - the unfinished project - is more focused on how to touch the ground of silence, the ground of being. In this *vanaprashta* period of my life I sometimes question my activities, wondering what is the best use of my time and energy. Trying to do nothing is not easy and the world does not support us in this aim. I am often seduced by the invitations to give talks, a long-standing habit of the mind. There is a subtle awareness of ego gratification in this and yet there is also the need to know how to be useful. I have a strong conviction that I will live to be seventy-nine years of age so there are still twelve years to fill in the most useful way. How to do this? I cannot dance or sing so maybe I can still be useful talking about large or scriptural ideas. I am not sure yet but still feel that I have something to offer in this way so continue for now with what has long been my custom. The Gita tells us that inaction is not the way to be free of the bondage of action. We cannot be without action so understanding how to act in the most useful way is a prominent and yet unresolved issue in my life.

For me, my father was a good and generous man and in the broadest sense an example. I think of him when I am not sure how to behave, asking myself, how would he have acted? He always looked for the truth. He was even invited to comment on cases in which he was not directly engaged as a lawyer as his

views were widely known to be straightforward
and impartial. He read and thought broadly,
fluent in several languages – Persian, Hindi,
Urdu, Sanskrit, Punjabi and English. When, by
choice, he retired in 1969 at sixty-five years of
age, he never entered a court again but dedicated
himself to social service, using his name to
support many charitable causes. I remember one
occasion when, after visiting other relatives in
Canada, he decided to travel with my son, from
Montreal where Kabir was then studying, to our
home for Christmas. Kabir rang me from the
airport to tell me their flight was many hours
delayed. This is usual in Canada in winter
because of inclement weather. I reminded Kabir
that he should look after his aged grandpa. His

My Father

response was, 'Dad, amazingly, I don't need to look after Grandpa. He is looking after me! He is sitting here, cool as a cucumber, while I am the one fretting
away!'

At the end of his life my father was living with my elder brother, Shri Jitender
Vir Gupta, the chief justice of Punjab in India. Jitender was also interested in
understanding vanaprashta in a modern way and travelled widely in his search
for religious meanings. One day my father said to him, 'Jitender, do not go far
in these next few weeks.' A few months earlier, when I was in India, father had
told me, 'Now I am useless. It is time to go.' His body had become infirm and
he remained mostly in bed. He was able to accept this in a calm way and did
not resist it, as I tried to do. When I left India I had the strong impression I
would not see him again. One morning he asked his grandson, Hemant, also a
lawyer and now a judge, to fetch the Bhagavad Gita. With his head resting in
the lap of his son and with his grandson reading to him from the Gita he
passed away peacefully. What could be a more desirable death?

I often think of him and feel very inspired by him. My father really was very
important in my life. I hope that when my moment comes, it will be in such a
way as his and that by then I will have understood, in the ground of my being,
that all there is is Krishna.

PROFESSOR RAVI RAVINDRA has been a teacher in
physics, philosophy and religion for more than 37 years,
principally at Dalhousie University in Halifax, Novia
Scotia, Canada. He is the author of many books and
papers, including *The Yoga of Christ: According to the Gospel of
St John*. He was married to Sally, a Canadian artist and
potter, and they have a daughter, Munju, a writer and
environmental consultant, and a son, Kabir, a lawyer.

GITANJALI

RABINDRANATH TAGORE

Have you not heard his silent steps? He comes, comes, ever comes.

Every moment and every age, every day and every night he comes,
comes, ever comes.

Many a song have I sung in many a
mood of mind, but all their notes
have always proclaimed, 'he comes,
comes, ever comes.'

In the fragrant days of sunny April
through the forest path he comes,
comes, ever comes.

In the rainy gloom of July nights on
the thundering chariot of clouds
he comes, comes, ever comes.

In sorrow after sorrow it is his steps that rest upon my heart,
and it is the golden touch of his feet that makes my joy to shine.

COLONEL OF THE HIMALAYAS
SANDY BHARAT

My life has been blessed by influences and inspirations from many sources, especially but not exclusively Hindu. In my interfaith work, people of various faiths touched my heart and I learnt from them. Surely though the greatest impact on this present incarnation (and perhaps many past ones) has been that from my Guru and divine Friend, Paramahansa Yogananda.

He first came into my life when I was given a copy of *Autobiography of a Yogi* in 1975. Immediately I wrote to Self-Realization Fellowship, the organization he established to disseminate his teachings, and signed up for the lessons leading to Kriya Yoga initiation. That was over thirty years ago and whilst I must have disappointed

Paramahansa Yogananda

Master, as he is affectionately called by his disciples - truly a master of himself, his true Self – a million times in this period, he has never failed me and has saved me from myself over and over again. Love is his signature.

One of the ways he has helped me is by 'introducing' me to some of his most highly evolved disciples at moments in my life when they could make a difference and get me out of the deep holes into which I was digging myself. Three people especially come into this category: Sri Daya Mata, Brother Bhaktananda, and Swami Sharanananda. While I have not always understood the blessings I received, I have always been grateful for them!

In those early days as a member of Self Realization Fellowship, I had a power-ful longing to see Daya Mata, the Sanghamata or President of SRF. I dreamt of her often and she always appeared as a loving spiritual mother to the small child that I had become. In 1987 my longing was fulfilled when, after some telephoning and lots of meditation and prayer, a friend and I found ourselves at her feet in a small upper room at Mt Washington, Self Realization Fellow-ship's head-quarters in Los Angeles. The room was the very one where Master used to meet his guests. As we entered the room – two of twelve invited devotees - we heard Ma's chuckle and felt thrilled to bits! That hour we spent together completely satisfied my longing to see her. It was a most blessed and beautiful *darshan* (blessing of being in presence of holy being). In some way, for some purpose, it was one of the most significant hours of my life.

Swami Sharanananda once described Ma to me as like a telephone operator. When she receives an inward call from a devotee, a red light comes on and she plugs in; that is how she knows our thoughts and needs.

When you look inward to God you see utter simplicity, divine and joyous simplicity. That's what God is.

Sri Daya Mata

Brother Bhaktananda too was a special inspiration in my life. He was a humble monk of the Self Realization Fellowship Order, full of devotion, who looked after the devotees at the Hollywood Temple. They were devoted too – to him! He was totally absorbed in God and Guru but in a practical not a 'pious' way. He was always in that sacred space while at the same time mindful of the needs of all the devotees around him, caring, answering the phone at all hours to be there for them. He loved strawberry shortcake too, which endeared him to all of us with a sweet tooth!

The same friend who accompanied me to the darshan with Daya Mataji also shared my feelings for Brother B (as we affectionately thought of him to ourselves). Indeed, we had the idea to kidnap him and bring him to England to look after all the devotees here! Of course we knew we would not even make it to the airport as the host of Hollywood devotees would be hot on our trail but we had to smile one day when, serving at the temple and working in a storeroom, the key to it in our hands, Brother B walked in and joined us. A perfect moment for the kidnap!

The kidnappers (Lesley Maybee, left) with Br Bhaktananda at SRF's India Hall

Brother taught us all to practice the presence of God continually, mentally chanting over and over, 'I love Thee, Lord, I love Thee, Lord.' Brother said that 'when we practice the presence of God by repeating a devotional thought consistently and sincerely, then joy starts to fill our hearts…That feeling is just the beginning of what we experience in loving God.' He told the story of how, in his early days as a Self-Realization Fellowship monk, his mantra (known only to himself) was 'I love you Master.' One day the Master, Paramahansa Yogananda, walked towards him in the garden and, as they met, he looked at Brother Bhaktananda and said 'I love you too.'

Brother passed away in 2005 but he will never be forgotten by the thousands of devotees around the world who were blessed and inspired by his simplicity, devotion, compassion and guidance.[1]

Swami Sharanananda was born in India in 1915. He had lived as a householder and had a distinguished career in the Indian army until his retirement when he

Daya Mataji and Swamiji, March 1976

began farming and studying the teachings of Paramahansa Yogananda. In 1967, after meeting Sri Daya Mata, he became Swami Sharanananda Giri, a monk devoted to seeking and serving God under her leadership. Swami's monastic name means divine bliss (*ananda*) through taking refuge (*sharana*) at the feet of the Lord.

My first contact with Swamiji was in 1993. This was a special year in two ways. Firstly it commemorated the 100th anniversary of the birth of Paramahansa Yogananda and secondly, the first Parliament of World Religions, held in Chicago in 1893, was also commemorated with a second one, held again in Chicago. The whole of that year was designated a year of inter-religious understanding and coopera-tion and events were held around the world, some of which I attended and helped organise. One of these was Sarva-Dharma-Sammelana that took place in Bangalore in the summer of 1993. As I was part of the event team it seemed a good opportunity to visit some of Master's centres in India. In that country his organisation is known as Yogoda Satsanga Society (YSS). I wrote to Swami Sharanananda at the YSS retreat in Dwarahat, the Himalayan foothills, with a suggested itinerary. He wrote back and changed it all!

[1] Brother Bhaktananda: In Memoriam at www.yogananda-srf.org/srf_news/2005bro_bhaktananda.html

As it turned out my plans were indeed completely transformed, by time as well as by Swami, and eventually, before Sarva Dharma Sammelana, three friends (yes, my sister kidnapper too!) and I went to the Dwarahat retreat for three weeks. In some ways this was a troubled time in my life. Some unforeseen karma had erupted like a volcano, bringing great disturbance—joy, sorrow, guilt and total confusion. Sometimes, even my love for God was challenged. An SRF monastic later told me never to lose my peace but now it was gone, scattered and fragmented, and I was unable to restore it.

On the plane to India, I burst into tears when one of my friends told how Swami Sharanananda was also known as the 'Colonel of the Himalayas,' a very strict monk, one who would sometimes not let people into the ashram. I was convinced, in my disturbed and 'unworthy' state that I would be one of those not permitted to enter.

The Krishna temple at the YSS retreat

After twelve hours of wet and windy travel from Delhi, in a car with soft tyres, weak brakes, no windscreen wipers, doors held on by string, and a 'cool' driver, climbing increasingly steep and narrow roads, ever deepening ravines below us, pockmarked with the skeletons of rusting cars and lorries, we finally arrived at the ashram and my friends rushed in to greet Swamiji while I slunk in behind them hoping to be unnoticed and so allowed to stay. The journey had been so frightening I thought I would have to stay forever, unable to go back down the way we had come up!

It was not long before Swamiji, silently reading my consciousness, told me that only love can change a person. For three weeks he was our Mother, there in those high hills, nurturing us spiritually, emotionally, physically. No military punishments! Only love.

It was this Swami Sharanananda, the kind Colonel of the Himalayas, who helped me, at a difficult time in my life, to realise that you have to be free of self-pity before there is space enough for God to enter into your life. My anguish continued because I was thinking of it all the time instead of thinking of God. Keep things simple, Swamiji said. When we make life complicated, God comes to us in complicated ways!

Swamiji passed away in 1996 but he will be remembered as an example of a mother's love - despite his fierce reputation! It is true he could challenge as well as nurture! When we first arrived at the retreat in Dwaharat I was quite a nervous wreck - a combination of the journey, my inner state, and wondering how I would get to Bangalore on my own after our stay (my friends had other destinations in mind). At that stage I could not imagine finding my own way back to Delhi and then the flight to Bangalore. Swamiji teased me, deliberately emphasising his plans for the others, entirely separate to my own! He also told us how he had been on his way to catch a plane once when he was held up at a crossing point. The plane left without him and soon crashed. He let me sweat a while on all the prospects ahead, giving me time for faith and detachment to arise (I don't recall that they did!) before he so sweetly made plans for us all to leave together and for me to be dropped off at the airport in Delhi with the others waving me adieu.

We are never alone when we are with God. And God never leaves us. How can we ever forget this wondrous truth? Daya Ma said, 'God is as close as you permit him to be.' She once wrote to me, 'Keep cultivating that spirit of dedication to Him for this is what will draw His response.' As Lord Krishna said in the Bhagavad Gita:

> Be absorbed in Me, lodge your mind in Me:
> Thus you shall dwell in Me.
> Do not doubt it, here and hereafter.

SANDY BHARAT worked for the International Interfaith Centre at Oxford from 1994-2004. She has an Honours degree in Theology from Exeter University and is author of *Christ Across the Ganges: Hindu Responses to Jesus* (O Books May 2007).

She has two children, a gorgeous grandson, and is married to Jael. He came with three children and two more lovely grandchildren!

With Jael she has co-authored *A Global Guide to Interfaith: Reflections from around the world* (O Books May 2007) and *Mapping the Cosmos: An Introduction to God* (Sessions 2006).

Their website is: www.spiritualityfordailylife.com

REMEMBERING GOD

PARAMAHANSA YOGANANDA

Whenever you see a beautiful sunset, think to yourself: 'It is God's painting on the sky.' As you look into the face of each person you meet, think within: 'It is God who has become that form.' Apply this trend of thought to all experiences: 'The blood in my body is God; the reason in my mind is God; the love in my heart is God; everything that exists is God.'

In time you will find Him ever with you – A God who talks with you in your own language, a God whose face peeps at you from every flower and shrub and blade of grass. Then you shall say: 'I am free! I am clothed in the gossamer of Spirit; I fly from earth to heaven on wings of light.' And what joy shall consume your being!

No matter which way you turn a compass, its needle points to the north. So it is with the true yogi. Immersed he may be in many activities, but his mind is always on the Lord. His heart constantly sings: 'My God, my God, most lovable of all!'

Everything else can wait, but our search for God cannot wait.
Paramahansa Yogananda

REVERENCE FOR ALL RELIGIONS
SESHAGIRI RAO

Among those who have exercised a deep influence on my life and work, I wish to acknowledge that Mahatma Gandhi happens to be the foremost. I did not have any personal meeting with him, although I heard him speak once in Mysore. His writings, statements and answers to questions, were everywhere. But above all, his life - his righteous living, his selfless service, his experiments with truth, his non-violent struggles for making the lives of others better, his prayerful life as well as his moral and spiritual endeavors - impressed and touched so many; and I am one of them.

My commitment to vegetarianism, to solving problems in non-violent ways, to working for social and human welfare, and to building bridges between communities, as well as my devotion to Truth, God, and spiritual endeavors, are influenced by his life and example. But I shall confine myself here to elaborating my interest in the study of religions and my engagement in interreligious dialogue which have become a main concern of my life.

My study of Gandhi's *Autobiography* made me aware that he was exposed to religious diversity from the early years of his life. Among his father's friends were a good number of Muslims, Parsis (Zoroastrians), Jains as well as Hindus. They gathered frequently in his house for religious discussions and the young Gandhi eagerly listened to their conversation. This experience impressed on his mind the fact of religious pluralism and the need to forge unity among the followers of different religions.

K L Seshagiri Rao

Reminiscing about his early life, Gandhi expressed much regret at the lack of facilities to study religion at his school. He discusses this predicament in his *Autobiography* (p.120): 'I am a Hindu by faith, and yet I do not know much about Hinduism, and I know much less of other religions. In fact, I do not know what is and what should be my belief. I intend to make a careful study of my own religion, and as far as I can of other religions as well.' His religious quest was further stimulated by his Christian friends in England and South Africa. In London, he spent a large part of his time in religious discussion. Sir

Edwin Arnold's English version of the Bhagavad Gita, *The Song Celestial*, stirred him so deeply that it became his constant guide for the rest of his life. He also read *The Light of Asia* and *The Sayings of Zarathustra* with great interest. He was moved by the teachings of the New Testament, especially the Sermon on the Mount. Gandhi also read Washington Irving's *Life of Mahomet and His Successors*, and Carlyle's *Heroes and Hero-Worship*, and learnt of Muhammad's 'greatness, bravery, and austere living.'

Mahatma Gandhi

Gandhi believed that education without the study of religions is incomplete; religion is the most important element in any culture. He asserted that the study of religions is not only a legitimate intellectual pursuit but a vital aspect of human culture and civilization. It relates to the wellsprings of individual and social life and deals with the central questions of human life and destiny. Ignorance about the faiths of other persons gives rise to prejudice and misrepresentations resulting in a certain unwillingness to accept the integrity of the followers of other faiths. The lack of sensitive understanding of other faiths leads to mutual recrimination and bloodshed.

In the nineteen forties, a large number of Indian students followed the leadership of Mahatma Gandhi in the nonviolent struggle for the freedom of the country from the British rule. Under his influence, college students in India also organized study groups for acquiring some understanding of the Bible and the Gita. As a college student myself at that time, I organized a small study group in my college for the purpose. We used to meet during weekends, and every time we met we started with an interreligious prayer. I got my early lessons in Hinduism from my parents, who were devout Hindus, and imbibed aspects of Hindu tradition and practice from my domestic and social environments. But the inspiration for a deeper study of my own and other religions, especially Christianity and Islam, came to me from Gandhi.

In College, I performed very well in sciences and was eligible for a scholarship, if I chose, to major in physics or chemistry. My elder brother wanted me to utilize the opportunity and become a scientist. Other members of the family were pushing me to become an engineer. But I chose to major in Social Philosophy. My brother used to make fun of me for my choice. In any case, Mahatma's influence prevailed. My study continued, and I got my Master's degree in Philosophy of Religion from the University of Mysore. Soon after, I

started teaching philosophy and ethics in
Chattishgarh College, in the state of
Madhya Pradesh. Apart from teaching, I
engaged myself in directing youth activities.
I became the secretary of the State's *Bharat
Yuvak Samaj*, (Indian Youth Association), a
Gandhian organization devoted to youth
welfare.

My life and study came to a focus when I
accepted a fellowship from the Gandhi
Peace Foundation, Delhi, to study Gandhi's
religious thought. Dr. S. Radhakrishnan
was the president of the Foundation, and I
worked under his guidance on Gandhi's
concept of 'Reverence for all Religions'

In lecturing mode

(*Sarvadharma Samabhava).* In that connection, I came into contact with and
learnt much from Hindu as well as Christian followers of Gandhi. It led me to
engage in interreligious dialogue. I had also the opportunity to study, in some
detail, other great religions. Further, when I became a doctoral student at the
Center for the Study of World Religions, Harvard University, in the early
sixties, I took a number of courses in World Religions. After receiving my
Ph.D. from Harvard, I joined the Punjabi University, Patiala, in India, and set
up the Guru Gobind Singh Department of Religious Studies. It gave me an
excellent opportunity to do study and conduct research in Sikhism. The
University also published my work entitled: *Mahatma Gandhi and C F Andrews:
A Study in Hindu-Christian Dialogue.* In 1971, the University of Virginia offered
me a professorship in Religious Studies, which I accepted.

Gandhi started with the faith as well as the conviction that God is Truth.
Truth includes, for him, what is true in knowledge, right in conduct and just
and fair in human relations. He wrote in 1925 that 'my uniform experience has
convinced me that there is no other God than Truth.' And realization of Truth
became the sole aim of his life. Truth is many sided and our understanding of
truth is fragmentary. Whatever is true, good, and beautiful in any tradition is
valuable and deserves appreciation. Therefore it is desirable to go deep into
one's own religious tradition and adhere firmly to it, while keeping an open
mind regarding the values and insights that may be available in other traditions.
Gandhi, further, does not stop at knowing Truth. He must proceed to establish the same in terms of justice and fair play to all through non-violence, love,
service and sacrifice.

Hinduism was the root and stem of his religious life; he was an orthodox
(sanatani) Hindu. Gandhi's attitude to other religions was that of the Vedic
saying, 'Let noble thoughts come to us from every side.' But he also said that,

Gandhi at one of his prayer meetings

'We should throw open our windows for fresh breezes to blow through our halls, but we should refuse to be swept off our feet.' Gandhi, as a Hindu, expressed an ecumenical spirit in religious matters. Never did he claim that his religion was in exclusive possession of Truth. It is not necessary for the followers of other religions to be or to become Hindu to obtain salvation. He recognized revealing and saving powers in all great religions. As a Hindu, he respected all prophets and sages who come to guide humanity. He showed a willingness to learn from other traditions. In the context of the diversity of human needs, he held that the great religions of the world are not only relevant but also necessary.

Thanks to Gandhi's influence, I deeply cherish my tradition, but I do not wish it ever to be the only religion in the world. Actually, I am glad that there are other great religions that are, like mine, trying to stem the tides of violence, terrorism, war, materialism and consumerism on one hand and trying to bring happiness and fulfillment through moral and spiritual endeavors on the other. Among the practices that very much attracted me were the morning and evening interreligious prayers in his ashrams, or spiritual communities. They create a sense of unity of heart and respect for one another and exert a purifying influence on life.

Each religion has to be understood in its own terms. One has to understand the inner logic of a religion in order to be able to appreciate the religion concerned. For example, Hindus worship one God (who is beyond names and forms) who makes Himself available to His devotees in many names and forms. From the time of the Rgveda (which says that: Truth is one, sages call it by many names) to Mahatma Gandhi, the validity of the worship of one God through many names and forms is asserted.

In a multi-religious world, Gandhi realized that there is need to recognize that God is one, religions are many. Creative theological formulations are needed to do justice to religious pluralism. Further, the spiritual traditions of the world have a great role to play in arresting the tides of violence, materialism, skepticism and scientism that are challenging all religions.

Gandhi lived and died vindicating moral and spiritual values against the forces of materialism, sectarianism, parochialism, and violence. He believed that if human beings are to grow in peace and understanding, they must relate to other human beings with fearlessness and friendliness, irrespective of religious or national affiliations; dialogue is essential for progress. The different communities and their leaders need not only to communicate and cooperate to make the world a better place, but also to fashion an open environment in which to pursue truth. Growth in spiritual life will develop in people the capacity for humanity, charity, and tolerance and enable them to build a new civilization based on justice and moral regeneration.

K L SESHAGIRI RAO is Professor Emeritus in the Department of Religious Studies, University of Virgina; Chief Editor of the Encyclopedia of Hinduism; Co-rector of the Thanksgiving Foundation, Dallas, Texas; and Co-editor of *Interreligious Insight* journal published by the World Congress of Faiths.

He has participated in numerous interreligious gatherings around the world, including events organized by the World Council of Churches, the Temple of Understanding, the World Conference of Religion and Peace, the World Congress of Faiths etc. He was Hindu guest at the Fifth Assembly of The World Council of Churches; co-chair of WCC's International Hindu-Christian Consultation in 1981; and non-voting Hindu delegate at WCC's World Conference on Mission and Evangelism in 1989.

GANDHI'S REVERENCE FOR ALL RELIGIONS

Let me explain what I mean by religion. It is not the Hindu religion, which I certainly prize above all other religions, but the religion which transcends Hinduism, which changes one's very nature, which binds one indissolubly to the truth within and which ever purifies. It is the permanent element in human nature which counts no cost too great in order to find full expression and which leaves the soul utterly restless until it has found itself, known its Maker, and appreciated the true correspondence between the Maker and itself.

Religions are different roads converging upon the same point.
What does it matter that we take different roads,
so long as we reach the same goal?

I believe in the fundamental truth of all religions of the world. I believe that they are all God-given, and I believe that they were necessary for the people to whom these religions were revealed. And I believe that, if only we could all of us read the scriptures of the different faiths from the standpoint of the followers of those faiths, we should find that they were at the bottom all one and were all helpful to one another.

MY MOTHER
SHARADA SUGIRTHARAJAH

Varalakshmi

I am writing this short piece to express my deep gratitude to my mother, Kameswari, who died peacefully on August 15th 1997. The day is significant for two reasons: it was the day when India attained freedom from British rule in 1947, and in this particular year it was an auspicious day for Hindus – the day when they performed *Varalakshmi puja*. [1]

It was a good day to take leave of the world – a time when people around her were immersed in invoking the blessings of the goddess Lakshmi who not only symbolizes wealth and prosperity but also peace and well being. My mother was laid out in the sitting room and her face was calm, peaceful and radiant as though in deep sleep. She appeared to be in a kind of awakened state – in a state of inner liberation - aware of what was going on around her, yet peaceful. As her body was carried out into the open air for the last rites, the rains poured down, showering her with blessings from above. Those who came to pay their condolences remarked on her radiant face. Her inner force or *shakti* that sustained her in life was with her in death as well. This is how my sister, who devoted her time and energy to taking care of her, described her.

Although fragile health affected her physical mobility and forced her to give up formal schooling at an early age, she continued to educate herself. I remember my father taking good care of her and being very supportive of

My Mother in later years

[1] Varalakshmi (one who grants boons) is one of the names and forms of the Goddess Lakshmi who is especially honoured on this special day by Hindu women.

her interests. My mother loved reading, and my father took great delight in buying books for her. Despite raising a large family, she found the time to read and reflect. She read widely, both sacred and secular works - from the *Ramayana* to Shakespeare

I have fond memories of her sitting in the open air in her crisp white cotton saree, deeply immersed in reading the *Ramayana*. There was always an air of serenity about her and her face reflected her inner grace and glow. She had an enquiring mind and she never took anything for granted. Whenever my father found the time, he would read for her, and she would now and then ask him to pause in order to clarify a particular point. Over the years I saw her engage informally in a variety of topics with like-minded people – both relatives and friends. My grandmother especially shared her spiritual interests and they immensely enjoyed each other's company.

Mother in her youth

She had a deep scriptural knowledge that she appropriated in her own way. She looked in sacred texts for guidance rather than for absolute truths. She spoke less about what the *Upanishads* or the *Bhagavadgita* said about detachment but rather demonstrated it in the way she lived her daily life and in her attitude towards others. The art of detachment seemed to come naturally to her. If she had any visible weakness, it was her fondness for sweets!

Two incidents, among others, made a tremendous impact upon me.

One had to do with her last days and her peaceful death as already described. The other had to do with her beautiful garden of various flowers, vegetables and fruits. She had a great passion for gardening, and tended it with great care and devotion. Even so, she had no difficulty in leaving behind that beautiful garden when my father had to move from Madurai to Bangalore to take up a consultancy position after his retirement. When I expressed my sadness and regret that we had to forgo the fruits of her labour, those delicious mangoes and guavas, she gently reminded me that, on the contrary, we should be happy that others could enjoy what we had sown. In other words, one must take delight in sowing the seed and rejoice that others can enjoy the benefits. [2]

[2] The Bhagavad Gita sets a great value on *nishkama karma* or desireless action, selfless action, action performed without desiring or fearing the consequences, action performed with indifference to the outcome, without any expectation of the fruits (results or reactions or effects).

Her remarks have stayed with me – that we should be prepared to let go of our sense of possession, only then can we truly enjoy. Being physically separated from the city (Madurai) associated with the goddess Meenakshi, to whom she was devoted, was not easy for her, but she was able to come to terms with it because of her belief that the divine *shakti* (feminine power) is not limited to geographical space, but is to be found within oneself.

My mother's detachment was not one of indifference to the world around her but of involvement without being egoistically attached to it. It is in this kind of re-nunciation that she found true peace, happiness and strength. She believed in being good not with the expectation of

Meenakshi Temple in Madurai

being appreciated but being good for the love of goodness. With regard to her failing health, she did not look for miracle cures nor did she wallow in her suffering, but bore it with remarkable dignity, courage and endurance. Despite her physical pain she seemed mentally detached. She coped with her condition by listening to devotional music, which she always loved. She had to give up reading, but this did not pose any problems: she had already by then (at the age of seventy) appropriated the spiritual wisdom in the texts and could draw on it at will.

Sri Ramana Maharshi

She did her best for others in her own un-obtrusive way and did not expect anything in return – in the true spirit of *nishkama karma*. There is a story about Bhagavan Sri Ramana Maharshi that also illustrates this spirit in a graphic manner.[3]

Mr. Rangachari, a Telugu Pandit in Voorhees' College at Vellore, asked Bhagavan Ramana Maharshi about *nishkama karma*. There was no reply. After a time Sri Bhagavan went up the hill and a few followed him, including the pandit.

[3] I would like to thank Sandy Bharat for drawing attention to this story/example in Munagala Venkatramiah, *Talks with Sri Ramana Maharshi*, Sri Ramanasramam.

There was a thorny stick lying on the way which Sri Bhagavan picked up; he sat down and began leisurely to work at it. The thorns were cut off, the knots were made smooth....A shepherd boy put in his appearance on the way as the group moved off. He had lost his stick and was at a loss. Sri Bhagavan immediately gave the new one in his hand to the boy and passed on.

My mother was not attached to material possessions and had no difficulty parting with them. Even some years before her death, when her arthritic condition prevented her from wearing silk sarees and light jewellery, she did not hang on to them but gave them away, and donated most of her books to the local library. When she died there was nothing much to clear, except a small case consisting of her daily clothes. This indeed has had a profound impact upon me, and I hope that when I leave the world, I will go the way my mother did - free and unfettered. Both in life and in death, she exemplified the positive meaning of detachment. She showed me that when we are truly detached, we can see things more clearly, think more clearly, and deal with difficult situations with sensitivity, understanding and caution.

I don't wish to idealise my mother, but her warmth and generosity of spirit, goodness, unpretentiousness, and genuine interest in the welfare of others outweighed any shortcomings she might have had. She deeply loved and cared about her family and people around her. She was always kind and considerate and did not make any great demands on her family. She did not force her views on others and left it to them to make their own judgements. She valued custom and tradition but she did not follow them blindly. Her inner conviction gave her the wisdom and strength to do things in a manner that sometimes was unconventional. She lived an ordinary life in an extraordinary way. What has remained with me is her selfless love, warmth, openness, sincerity, child-like simplicity and her deep spiritual wisdom.

DR SHARADA SUGIRTHARAJAH was born and educated in India, and studied in England.

She is Senior Lecturer in Hindu Studies in the School of Historical Studies, University of Birmingham, England.

She is the author of *Imagining Hinduism: A Postcolonial Perspective* (Routledge 2003).

HYMNS TO DIVINE MOTHER

O Devi, you who remove the sufferings of your supplicants, be gracious. Be propitious, O Mother of the whole world. Be gracious, O Mother of the universe. Protect the universe. You are, O Devi, the ruler of all that is, moving and unmoving.

Be gracious to us O Goddess who takes away affliction from the universe. Most worthy of praise, grant us your boons.

O Devi, You are without a beginning or an end, You are the Primeval energy, You are the greatest ruler, You are born of Yoga.

O Devi, You are the mother of the universe and its support.

O Great Devi, obeisance to You.

FROM KRISHNA WITH LOVE
SHAUNAKA RISHI DAS

I was born in Wexford, Ireland, and two of the earliest influences on my life were Jesus Christ and my father. Some of the last words my father spoke to me were to advise me to look for and attentively follow those principles that meant most to me. These would be my guidelines for life. They would help me develop self-respect and become trustworthy. Even though my father had never left the country he was very broad-minded for his time. He was able to step outside the usual prejudices and boundaries of 60's and 70's Ireland and taught me how every subject had many sides. When my father passed away in hospital Father Kehoe, a priest from my college, was immediately on hand to conduct the last rites for my father. It was early in the morning and I wondered why he was already in the hospital. Later I discovered that his father had also just passed away there. Yet, still he came to us, despite his own loss. I was very impressed with his sincerity.

The story of Jesus and his message of love – pure, spiritual love – influenced me greatly when I was growing up. Love of God was his life. Everyone talks about love and happiness. They are such universal themes. Jesus inspired my quest for a loving relationship, my search for what it was, how to attain, feel it, give it. Ironically it was this that led me to Indian thought. I met Hindus who expressed this love wonderfully. Hindus could easily call Jesus a *bhakta*, one who loves God. In my tradition he is seen as a *Vaishnava*.[1]

This essay is based on an interview in Oxford on 12th October 2005.

[1] A Vaishnava, in this context, is someone who loves God with all his heart and with the adornment of humility. A Vaishnava is also defined as a follower of Lord Vishnu or his incarnations, especially Krishna.

A C Bhaktivedanta Swami Prabhupada, the founder of the International Society for Krishna Consciousness (ISKCON), showed me how to find the love I sought. I shaved my head, donned saffron robes and lived as a celibate student in an ISKCON ashram for six years. I got involved in a process that helped me understand what love of God is. This was not talking about it anymore. I had been given a *sadhana*, a practice, by which I could develop love for God and purify my heart.

I had already found the philosophy brilliant but it was the *kirtan* that really convinced me. I saw how the devotees would chant on the street for five hours and then, at one festival I attended, when everyone was lying down in a tent waiting for food, tired after being on the street all those hours, a spontaneous kirtan began and lasted for more than another hour. There was no one around to see. It was just an expression of the devotees' love for God. This personal expression of feeling for God was the best I'd ever experienced. Everything else was forgotten. Only the name of the One we loved or aspired to love was repeated, over and over, creating a wonderful connection with God. Chanting alone can lead us to love of God.

Aside from chanting I have found hard work to be the medium of sadhana or service most natural to me. Before undertaking any project I study the scriptures for guidance. Then I go to wise and holy *sadhus* who can advise me and bless the project. I follow this with two to three weeks at a holy place, immersing myself in prayer, asking Krishna for his authority to proceed. Then I can throw myself whole-heartedly into the project, surrendered, Krishna's servant. And it keeps me off the streets!

Srila Prabhupada

Jesus had set my goal, Prabhupada set me the challenge to realise it. He taught me how to change myself. It was not about others loving me anymore but about my ability to love God, to do what God wanted me to do. This is what I was called for, what I have felt all my life.

Srila Prabupadha helped me realise how difficult it is to do the right thing, even when we wish it. He himself was such a pure example of one who loved God, one who lived that love in his life. I was really impressed by his great integrity. Often we wonder how we can know if our preceptor is pure or if he is simply seeking respect, adoration

*Loving Krishna: the perfect devotee, Radha,
with her Divine Beloved.*

or worse? Is he really our friend, properly intentioned? In a series of lectures given in Vrindavan in 1972, realising that some of the devotees would think of him as the guru, as the best friend, Prabhupada told them, 'No, I am not your friend. Krishna is your only friend. He is the one who is with you always, even at the moment of your death. I may not be there.' I appreciated how he put himself in the background to push Krishna to the fore. That was his integrity and his love. Prabhupada was a true servant of God, an excellent example. When we love Krishna, we will love everything. All our needs and desires will be fulfilled.

I like the old joke. Question: how do you make God laugh? Answer: tell him your plans! One day, in the early 1990's, God certainly laughed at my plans. By that time I had got married, left the ashram, and was busy with a business, importing beautiful items from Kashmir to Northern Ireland that I then sold on to Irish Americans. The business was going well and my wife and I were acquiring the status symbols that go with success and were beginning to dream about buying a home and having children. Parallel to running the business I was acting as President at ISKCON's Belfast temple. Spiritual service was important to me and seemed something I could easily afford from my comfortable position.

The time came however when I felt I was being forced to make a choice between my material activities and my spiritual ones. Somehow I could just not accommodate them both anymore. I felt Krishna was asking me, 'Where are you going with this business? Do you really believe that I will look after you whatever happens? I am your insurance policy.' This was a real challenge but I came to the decision to liquidate the business and give my life to Krishna's service at the temple. It was a painful process but finally the last papers were signed and the business was closed. The very next morning after signing those papers I found out that I was no longer temple president, that my services were no longer required! I was bewildered and distressed. What could it all mean? I thought I had given up the business for service to God and now I had nothing – material or spiritual. I was nobody.

When I woke up the morning after all this I felt as if a grey film covered my eyes. I was depressed. As a devotee I should not feel this way but there it was. Later in the day I went with my wife to her parents' house. The minute my father-in-law opened the door and saw me he exclaimed 'What has happened to you?' My troubles were clearly etched on my face and in my demeanour.

I went upstairs to unpack and took from my bag a copy of the *Srimad Bhaga-vatam*, opened a page at random, and asked God to speak to me through what I read. My feelings were everywhere – detached, bitter, angry, quasi-spiritual – and I needed a perspective on my new situation. I had nowhere else to go. To this day I am still deeply moved when I remember what God revealed to me then. My eyes alighted on this text: 'Any difficulty in the life of a devotee is directly the mercy of the Lord.' I thought I had lost everything but Krishna knew where to find me. Krishna loved me. For the first time, I truly realised this. It's not just words, it's practical. He loves me.

It was such a fresh perspective on what I thought I already knew. I thought I was already doing the right thing by being dedicated to temple service. By nature I am tenacious and when I think I am doing what I have been told, what has been authorised and blessed, then I don't leave much space for God to change his mind! By extricating me in this straightforward way Krishna opened me up to the service opportunities he really wanted me to appreciate.

How amazing that God goes to all this trouble to teach us the lessons we need, to make us aware of his love. He set me up in business and then took it away. He set me up with the temple in Belfast and then took it away. Everyone I thought I was just became no one. Even though I was, to all intents, living a serious and committed spiritual life, I had missed the point. How embarrassing that I could be so ungrateful. How humbling. Spiritual life is just one humiliation after another, realising how little we know. It's not that we know love, humility, compassion and these deep realisations, it's that they seep in, undermining our feeble grasp in Krishna's intention.

My work for ISKCON grew and I travelled widely helping establish new groups and coordinating events. I also became involved in the Northern Ireland Interfaith Forum. Now I find myself in Oxford as Director of the Oxford Centre for Hindu Studies. A part of my sadhana that has accompanied these developments is the striving to come to grips with humility - I could do with a lot more! Even so I have learnt that even my arrogance – and all the gifts and curses I was born with – can be used in the service of God. Humility is surrender to God's will. It means doing what God wants me to do, even when, like Arjuna on the battlefield, I do not want to do that.

I have always felt that I was on a journey, a progressive journey of being 'found.' More and more I feel this. Krishna has always been with me, has

Theology Seminar led by Profs Francis X Clooney and Keith Ward at the Oxford Centre for Hindu Studies

always loved me. I may have called him something else but he has always been caring for me, even at the most difficult moments in my life. Prabhupada showed me how present Krishna is, taught me that the presence of God is real. Beliefs are not important. It all comes down to principles and practice. The direction Jesus gave me, the advice my father gave me and the sadhana Prabhupada gave me came together and, with the grace of Krishna, are transforming my life.

SHAUNAKA RISHI DAS is Director of the Oxford Centre for Hindu Studies, Editor of the ISKCON Communications Journal, and a Hare Krishna priest.

He is committed to dialogue with people of faith in God, especially with the Northern Ireland Interfaith Forum, the Interfaith Network UK, and as Chair of ISKCON's Interfaith Commission.

Shaunaka is married to Keshava Devi Dasi.

THE BHAGAVAD-GITA

In the Bhagavad-Gita, Lord Krishna (above) tells Arjuna (and all of us):

Whenever and wherever there is a decline in religious practice, O descendant of Bharata, and a predominant rise of irreligion - at that time I descend Myself. To deliver the pious and to annihilate the miscreants, as well as to reestablish the principles of religion, I Myself appear, millennium after millennium.

A true yogi observes Me in all beings and also sees every being in Me. Indeed, the self-realized person sees Me, the same Supreme Lord, everywhere. For one who sees Me everywhere and sees everything in Me, I am never lost, nor is he ever lost to Me.

One who is not envious but is a kind friend to all living entities, who does not think himself a proprietor and is free from false ego, who is equal in both happiness and distress, who is tolerant, always satisfied, self-controlled, and engaged in devotional service with determination, his mind and intelligence fixed on Me - such a devotee of Mine is very dear to Me.

Always think of Me, become My devotee, worship Me and offer your homage unto Me. Thus you will come to Me without fail. I promise you this because you are My very dear friend.

THE GIFT OF GIVING
SIVAKUMAR SARAVAN

It was a cool sunny morning in April 2001. My wife Lavanya and I were in a Saivite monastery in the middle of the Pacific Ocean, half way between the East and the West. Kauai's Hindu Monastery, as it is called, is located in the garden island of Kauai, one of the islands of Hawaii. It was established in the early 1970s, by the tall white-haired master, Sri Satguru Sivaya Subramuniya-swami, popularly known as Gurudeva.

With Gurudeva and Lavanya

It was our last day in the monastery-temple complex of what was a week long pilgrimage. Just a few months before, Lavanya and I had been married and the pilgrimage was a way of seeking blessings and guidance for a harmonious and purposeful married life. What a blessed and mem-orable pilgrimage it was as it was during this pilgrimage that Lavanya formally converted to Hinduism in a name-giving ceremony called *namakarana samskara*, witnessed by Gurudeva and all the monks of the monastery.

Our flight out of Kauai was just a few hours away and we were wrapping up our last minute discussions with Acharya Palaniswami on the possibility of having an art exhibition in Singapore of exquisite paintings of deities. The purpose was to raise funds for the hand-carved granite Iraivan Temple that was being constructed on the island. Lavanya and I were sad that our wonder-ful time in paradise was coming to a close and hoped that we could come back soon. Little did we know that we would be back on the island barely 6 months later for the Mahasamadhi of our beloved Gurudeva.

As we were admiring the paintings of deities that Acharya Palaniswami pulled out from the archives, I just somehow felt that I needed to see Gurudeva one last time before we departed. I excused myself and stepped out of the publica-tions building. Walking along the cement path, I stood for a while near a pavilion overlooking the Wailua River as it meandered from the majestic Mount Waialeale. Looking around at the lush tropical gardens, it was no wonder that the ancient Hawaiians had called this sacred spot on Earth *Pihanakalani* – where the heavens touch the earth. Then, as though my silent thoughts were heard, the most wonderful and magical thing happened. In the distance I saw Gurudeva in his bright ochre robes walking slowly towards me.

Mount Waialeale

I approached him with reverence and he gave me a hug full of fatherly love. With choking emotions I said, 'Thank you very much Gurudeva for every-

thing.' I was finding it hard to express my feelings. The fact that Gurudeva had such a powerful influence over my life and had guided me through the most arduous times of my life made it difficult to sum up my gratitude in just two words 'thank you.' As though understanding my plight, Gurudeva looked at me with a smile, which quickly put me at ease, and told me that it was time for me to give what I have received to others. That was the hallmark of Gurudeva. He does not engage in lengthy discussions but goes straight to the point, giving life-changing advice in concise sutras that sinks deep into one's consciousness.

Reflecting on this trait of Gurudeva, I recall another incident about 10 years ago. Then I was a first year undergraduate doing an accounting major. I had failed one of the papers and I was totally devastated. Failing was unacceptable to me, as I had always done well in school. For a few days I could hardly sleep or communicate coherently with anyone. I was so afraid that I would also fail the re-sit exam. This would mean that I could not progress to the second year.

Coincidentally, Gurudeva was in town giving talks in some of the temples. I managed to meet Gurudeva for a few minutes just as he was leaving a Muruga temple. I told him that I had failed one of the papers in my exam and I wanted his blessings to do well in the re-sit. Somehow I had this naïve thought that Gurudeva will, with a touch of his hand on my head, change my karma and give me the power to succeed. To my disappointment all Gurudeva said was, 'Use your willpower to pass the exam.' However, this turned out to be the greatest blessing. As Gurudeva's words sunk deeper into me, I had a strong surge of determination to do well and never give up. I quickly put a study plan into action with enthusiasm and met my lecturer for guidance. My lecturer was more than happy to help me. To keep the story short, I passed the re-sit and went on to do rather well in the next two years, graduating with an honors degree and joining one of the top international accounting firms. In the course of the next few years after this, Gurudeva continued to command me to lean on my own spine and use my willpower to solve problems. To this day, this wise counsel has helped me to be courageous in the face of adversity.

'Give what you have received to others.' These were the last words I was to hear from my master. In November 2001, Gurudeva attained mahasamadhi.

Image of planned Iraivan Temple

After Gurudeva's mahasamadhi, we were thinking of what we can do as a way of remembering all that Gurudeva had done for us. We were looking for a way of giving back what Gurudeva had given us. Mulling over this, the idea came to our minds of creating an endowment fund, under the Hindu Heritage Endowment, that will provide free meals on every mahasamadhi day. Hindu Heritage Endowment was established by Gurudeva to create and maintain endowments to provide permanent financial support for Hindu projects and institutions worldwide. Currently, there are more than sixty individual endowments that benefit temples, ashrams, monasteries, orphanages, homes for the elderly and publications in many countries.

We quickly wrote to Satguru Bodhinatha Veylanswami, Gurudeva's successor, about our idea and asked for his blessings. He gave abundant blessings and an endowment fund called Kauai Aadheenam Yagam Fund was created with the purpose of providing free healthy vegetarian meals for visiting pilgrims at the

Satguru Bodinath

Hindu monastery on Kauai during the annual mahasamadhi observance for Gurudeva and at other festive times. Religious feeding has always been an integral part of Hindu culture and we hoped that through the Kauai Aadheenam Yagam Fund this culture and the charitable spirit of Gurudeva would live for centuries to come. 'Give what you have received to others' had begun to weave through many aspects of my life.

I began to understand that giving is not just an act of charity but is actually a way of thinking. In today's fast paced automaton life where time has become a precious commodity, self-centeredness has very much replaced communal spirit. But giving need not be painful or associated with great personal sacrifice. Giving can be expressed in words, thought and deed in the simplest way in almost any situation. Spending some time to listen to a friend's problems, giving praise to co-workers for a job well done, giving respect to elders, making someone feel special, planting trees, protecting endangered species, sending positive thoughts to uplift a friend or a loved one, giving thanks to God before mealtimes, singing the glory of God, all this and more encompasses the concept of giving. It is easy to smile and spread some cheer. It does not take much effort to speak some kind words to make someone feel better.

The concept of giving also weaved through my corporate life. In 2004, I left a large international accounting firm to start my own practice in partnership with a few others. Gurudeva's teachings have always been a guiding principle in managing and growing my practice. Right from the beginning I adopted the principle that I should give more to my clients than what I receive. In fact, I assisted many prospective clients without getting anything in return. But this never hurt my business as the more I gave, the more fee-paying clients I received. As Gurudeva had taught, we cannot really give away anything.

Once somebody asked Gurudeva whether he performs miracles. Gurudeva replied that the miracle that he performs is to change people's life. Indeed, this is the greatest miracle that I have experienced in my own life. As I conclude

With Lavanya and Gurudev

this essay, staring at me from a table across the room is a nicely framed Charter Contributor certificate, for establishing the Yagam Fund from Hindu Heritage Endowment, that I received a few days ago, reminding of and reaffirming Gurudeva's grace. Gurudeva had given me all the spiritual tools that I need in this life. How can I sum up my gratitude in just two words 'Thank you?' Aum Namasivaya.

SIVAKUMAR SARAVAN is a sishya
of Saiva Siddhanta Church, a fellowship of the Sri Subramuniyaswami Gotra
that is headed by Satguru Bodhinatha Veylanswami.

He is a tax director in an international accounting firm and is currently residing
in Singapore with his wife Lavanya and his 3 year-old son Easan.

IN THY FOOTPRINTS

Will I ever forget my beloved Gurunathan?

Will I not melt in Love, recalling the testament of my Guru?

To give alms and more alms in a sincere spirit of charity is a means of atoning one's many afflictions. His fragrant feet are our best protecting armour.

Thy sheltering hands embracing thy true devotees in oneness of love, how shall I praise? Praise the valiant Vel of Nallur in sea kist Lanka. In the sanctuary of Arumugan, my Guru appeared to me as God divine. From this perennial fountain flows the bliss of wisdom. My Guru endearing and more dear than a Mother, made me melt like wax in the majestic, universal vision of the Oneness of God; in his equable and tranquil form, I saw the essence of truth: His words made me realise that all things mean intensely and mean well and that ill-will, enmity, and disharmony have no place in his experience.

Natchintanai. 155-156 by Satguru Yogaswami

A DEEPER HEALING
SUMATI CHAITANYA

I always knew I wanted something greater in life. As a child I used to enjoy spending time alone and I would talk to God, but I didn't know who that God was. From a young age I was besieged by the questions: *Who am I? Why am I born? Why are so many people sad in life? Where does the solution lie? Is there no end to it?*

My questions remained unanswered and lay dormant until I encountered Pujya Gurudev Swami Chinmayananda, a profound Vedantin and a great spiritual master.

As the one who recognised the Seeker in me without my even uttering a single word to Him, Pujya Gurudev Swami Chinmayananda has undoubtedly had the most profound impact on my life. To speak of someone who has not only shaped who you are but who has *made* you who you are is very difficult to explain. A spiritual teacher is not just from this birth. The all-compassionate Master is always waiting for a sincere seeker wherever he or she may be; so wherever there is someone seeking the Highest, the Guru reaches out and finds him or her.

Having just finished a degree in Homeopathic Medicine, I had started working as a doctor when I decided to embark on a trip visiting the spiritual centres of North India with my sister. Whilst I was travelling, I suddenly got attracted to books about *Gyana Yoga* (the yoga of Knowledge) and Meditation by Sri Swami Vivekananda. I was never a voracious reader - I could study medical books for hours on end, but not any other kind of book, except on this occasion.

Throughout this journey I just kept on reading one book after another. These books on Gyana Yoga, Knowledge of Self, inspired me and made things much clearer to me about getting closer to what I wanted. It was an ambiguous period of my life. I was sure of what I did not want in life, but I was still not too clear about what it was exactly that I did want. I had performed well academically and had progressed well in my field, but as much as I had enjoyed studying and working in the field of medicine, I was constantly seeking something greater, something higher.

This article is based on Vishva Samani's interview with Brahmacharini Sumati in February 2006.

Pujya Gurudev Swami Chinmayananda entered my life in a somewhat mystical way. It was completely by chance when I saw him for the first time in Bombay. I just happened to be there for one of His *Geeta Gyana Yagna*, talks on the Bhagavad Gita. The talk was on the Ninth Chapter of the Gita. I remember it vividly. Though I say I *happened* to be there it was only later I realised that I was *meant* to be there. I can only describe the experience of seeing Pujya Gurudev Swami Chinmayananda for the first time as love at first sight.

When I saw Pujya Gurudev on stage, I suddenly gained clarity of mind and it dawned upon me that THIS is what I want. Following this realisation, I searched for Him for a few months. During that time I had a dream in which He blessed me with what I had been seeking for so long. Later, in 1993 when I was twenty-five years old, I actually met Him at the Chinmaya Mission Ashram in Sidhabari, Himachal Pradesh where He spoke to me in the same way as He did in the dream. This made me understand that the *Guru Tattva* – 'the essence' is more desperate to guide a seeker than the seeker's yearning to reach the goal. On the sole occasion that I did meet Him, I didn't have to tell Him anything about what had been running through my mind since I had first seen Him – He just knew what I wanted. On that day He made me experience something high and divine which cannot be described in words.

I personally met Pujya Gurudev only on this one occasion, and I'll never forget those divine moments - simply because they define my life. I remember the hug, I remember the first look and I remember the manner in which he spoke to me. It took me by surprise because I thought I would need somebody to introduce me to Swami Chinmayananda, a world-renowned spiritual giant, but He just spoke to me as if He knew me. Little did I know then that a spiritual master who is the very Self of all is Omniscient. A thousand parents

Swami Chinmayananda

could not bestow as much love as was contained in the hug that he gave me. I was instantaneously dissolved in this divine ocean of love. I will never forget those beautiful eyes penetrating through me telling me THE knowledge of Self-divine. For the half an hour that did I spend with Him, Pujya Gurudev put me into the silent moments – an experience I still remember with such intensity. Such is the greatness of the spiritual masters who are ever so keen to guide the spiritual aspirants.

For the brief period that I did practice medicine it was never the physical symptoms that I would treat in patients. I was a homeopath, and homeopathy states that the mind expresses itself as the body. The logic is that only if you KNOW the mind are you are able to cure the body - but I always wanted to know how. What is it that makes that person unique and different from every-one else? And how is it possible to permanently remove disease? If it is the mind-set that creates the physical disease, how can it reach a state such that it remains disease-less? The study of Vedanta in Chinmaya Mission provided me with that answer – it is the ignorance of the Self that creates the mental disturbances and delusions. It is based upon these disturbances that one lives and becomes aggravated by the world, eventually resulting in physical problems. We suffer because we do not realise that we are not what we think ourselves to be. This is the understanding that I gained from the study of Vedanta at The Sandeepany Sadhanalaya, the Vedanta institution of the Chinmaya Mission in Bombay. Having got that understanding, I progressed.

As an Acharya of Chinmaya Mission, my service to humankind continues but with more awareness of deeper truth of life.

That which resonates in my ears when I think of Pujya Swami Chinmayananda is the statement; *'I am not the donkey to carry the weight of my disciples, I will show you the path and YOU WALK… there is no short cut on the spiritual path... you can...you must!'* He would say that you must reach the peak of evolution – and that you can do it in this lifetime, become a God-man. Each one of you has got the freedom to CHOOSE to make your life or to destroy your life and once having reached, thereafter live your lives giving maximum happiness to the maximum number of people for the maximum amount of time. But first YOU must change in order to spread that happiness.

I shall always remain indebted to my Guru who taught me that the differences are *'Mithya'* – unreal. The eyes are two but the vision is one so too the world may appear different but the Truth behind it is One.

If Pujya Swami Chinmayananda has shown me the vision of where I have to reach, then my Guruji, Swami Tejomayananda (Current Head of Chinmaya Mission) is like the kind mother holding my hand taking me there. I have learnt a lot from his saintliness, his sheer love for the Mission and the dedicated

With Swami Tejomayanandaji

people who work towards its vision. Guruji demonstrates such a profound love for the Scriptures and he is the one who has instilled a deep love for Lord Sri Rama in me. He has a soft and spiritual approach to everything - taking his own time in making decisions but always sure of what he is doing. The pace of his decisions is always good for the totality. Every time I see him, I learn something new from Him. He is so knowledgeable and hence so simple.

Pujya Gurudev has given us a field upon which to perform Karma Yoga – selfless dedicated service in the form of the Chinmaya Mission. Through the Mission's various activities, when performed in the true spirit of togetherness, one can purify the heart and steadily contemplate the Self-divine and ultimately come to abide in It.

By the Grace of Gurudev, I have been inspired to help others to love and to grow. He has not only shaped who I am but He has made me who I am. When somebody has made you, you become only HIS creation – you don't exist – it's just Him. It is impossible to progress unless you are tuned to your Guru, you thus reach a state where you stop being yourself and just begin to let everything happen because you know that it is just your Guru who functions through you. Such attunement is required for any seeker to grow, without which the best of the Gurus are unable to do anything to you. There are many things that enter a Seeker's life to shake you from that faith to reach divine heights - but Gurudev has kept me firmly on the path.

Even after the *Maha Samadhi* of Pujya Gurudev in 1993, His divine vision of the scriptures continues to guide sincere seekers of the Truth worldwide through The Chinmaya Mission under the able guidance of His Holiness Swami Tejomayananda. Glory to the Guru-Shishya Parampara!

BRAHMACHARINI SUMATI CHAITANYA has been an Acharya for the Chinmaya Mission, a worldwide spiritual organisation, for 10 years. Founded by His Holiness Swami Chinmayananda, the Chinmaya Mission Movement has 250 centres around the world. One of these centres is 'Chinmaya Kirti' in London, where Brahmacharini Sumati Chaitanya is currently based.

Her mission is to serve her Guru, which is to spread the knowledge of the Hindu Scriptures, Vedanta, to all age groups. Vedanta teaches the vision of Oneness and how to live up to that ideal amidst the numerous conflicts and difficult situations that we encounter in our day-to-day lives.

A WEB OF LOVE

The Universe Is a Cosmos

And Not Chaos.

There Exists a Mental Affinity:

A Scientific Law:

A Rhythm Of Mental Relationship

In Which The Entire Living World

Is Held Together

In One Web Of Love.

To Assume Differences In The World

Is To Belie This Great Oneness Of Life.

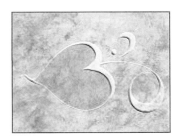

Lord Vishnu

GLOSSARY

Transliterations can mean different spellings for the same word.

ACHARYA: A highly respected teacher.

AHIMSA: Non-injury, harmlessness; abstaining from evil towards others in deed, word and thought.

ARATI, ARTI: Light passed before a deity and then taken to devotees who take the light into themselves as a blessing. See *Puja*.

ASHRAM: Monastic or spiritual community, usually led by a particular Guru or teacher or following a particular spiritual sadhana or practice.

ASHRAMAS: Four stages of life: *brahmacharya*, studentship, age 12 to 24; *grihastha*, householder, age 24 to 48; *vanaprastha*, forest dweller or elder advisor, age 48 to 72; *sannyasa*, religious solitary, from 72 onward.

ATMAN: The soul or true Self as distinct from the perceived material self.

AUM OR OM. The mystic syllable of Hinduism. The Upanishads explain that it stands for the whole world, past, present and future. It is the primal vibration from which all manifestation emerges. Its three letters represent the three worlds and the powers of creation, preservation and destruction. In common use, aum means 'yes, verily' (like the Tibetan Hum, the Judaic-Christian Amen and the Muslim Amin).

AUROBINDO, SRI, 1872-1950: Sri Aurobindo Ghose was born in West Bengal and was educated partly in England. On returning to India he became a civil servant and was drawn into the political struggle for India's independence. In 1908 he was arrested on a charge of sedition and during his imprisonment he had several spiritual experiences that changed him so that, on his release, he began a life devoted to spiritual writing and living. He passed away in 1950 leaving Mirra Alfassa, a French woman, known as the Mother, in charge of his community and philosophical transmission. Sri Aurobindo's writings on diverse topics are now gathered together as the *Sri Aurobindo Birth Centenary Library* and the *Collected Works of Sri Aurobindo*. There is also an ashram in Pondicherry, the Sri Aurobindo Society, and Auroville, a township established by the Mother based on her ideals and those of Sri Aurobindo.

AVATAR: Incarnation of God. An avatar is traditionally God 'come down' into a human form for a human lifetime. For Hindus God incarnates in many forms through the ages in order to help humanity find its way back to God. See *Krishna*.

AVIDYA: Ignorance of who we really are. Believing ourselves to be the limited human body and mind we remain in ignorance until we once again know ourselves as ever-free, unlimited Spirit, temporarily occupying a human body.

BARASWAMI: Elder monastic brother, first disciple.

BHAGAVAD GITA: A holy book for Hindus, part of the great *Mahabharata* epic. See *Krishna*.

BHAJANS/KIRTAN: Devotional chanting.

BHAKTANANDA, BROTHER, 1914-2005: One of the earliest monastic disciples of Paramahansa Yogananda, he entered the Self-Realization Fellowship (SRF) ashram in 1939. After serving at Encinitas and San Diego Temples, Brother moved to SRF's Hollywood Temple in 1971 and stayed there until his retirement in 2004. He was known and loved by all who knew him for his exemplary life of simplicity and devotion to God and Guru.

BHAKTI YOGA: The devotional path to God, explained in the Bhagavad Gita and other great scriptures of Hinduism. The Gita also explains other paths to God. *Jnana* yoga is the path of knowing truth through discrimination. *Karma* yoga is the path of selfless action, serving others without desire for the fruits of that action. *Raja* yoga is the 'king' of yoga or aspects of all types embedded in each devotee's search for Truth.

BHARAT: Sanskrit 'He who supports, maintains or bears a burden.' The ancient and original name of Indian lands and the constitutional name of independent India.

BHARATA NATYAM: Classical south Indian dance. See *Siva*.

BRAHMAN: The Real as Itself; undivided, undifferentiated Reality; the One.

CHINMAYANANDA, SWAMI, 1916-1993: Born in Kerala in a devout Hindu family, he later graduated in Science, Political Science, Law and English Literature from Lucknow University and became a journalist. His life changed when he met Swami Sivananda and became interested in the spiritual path. After taking *sanyas* (monastic vows) he became known as Swami Chinmayananda - one saturated in Bliss and Consciousness. He then studied under Swami Tapovan Maharaj for twelve years in the Himalayas and afterwards began his own teaching mission. Swamiji opened numerous centres and ashrams worldwide and built many schools, hospitals, nursing homes and clinics. His work continues through the international Chinmaya Mission he founded.

DHARMA: To follow our dharma is to do our duty, live a spiritual way of life, be true to our real Self. Dharma is righteousness and moral order. Its opposite is *Adharma*, unrighteousness. No one else can fulfil our dharma – it is our own individual connection to Truth.

DARSHAN: The blessing received by being in the presence of someone or something holy.

DAYA MATA, SRI: President and Sanghamata of Self-Realization Fellowship. She entered the ashram in 1931 aged 17 after meeting and being healed by Paramahansa Yogananda. Many of her family also became SRF monastics or devotees. Ma is revered and respected by all who meet her for her total commitment to Self-Realization and the great wisdom and love for God she reveals through her life. When the Master asked her to lead the organization he told her, 'Remember this: When I have left this world, only love can take my place. Be so drunk with the love of God night and day that you won't know anything but God; and give that love to all.' These words became the guiding light of Ma's life, a life that has been a great blessing for thousands of people.

DURGA: Goddess; Invincible, destroyer of demons, a form of the Divine. See *Names and Forms of God.*

GANESH: The elephant form of God, remover of obstacles, symbol of wisdom. See *Names and Forms of God.*

GAYATRI MANTRA: 'Oh God! Thou art the Giver of Life, Remover of pain and sorrow, The Bestower of happiness, Oh! Creator of the Universe, May we receive thy supreme sin-destroying light. May Thou guide our intellect in the right direction.' Chanting this Vedic prayer will help remove ignorance and establish wisdom.

GURU: A guru is one who dispels darkness and guides the disciple to Self-Realization, through life after life if necessary. Devotees and disciples might speak of their guru as Guruji or Gurudev. *Ji* is a sign of respect and *Deva* is God so the Guru reflects God by her or his own awakened Self.

GURUKUL: Ancient Hindu residential school system where *shishyas* or students and the *guru* or teacher live together.

HANUMAN: The sublime, empowered monkey form of God, hero of the Ramayana. See *Names and Forms of God*

HANUMAN CHALISA: A famous poem dedicated to Hanuman by the 16th century Indian ascetic and poet, Tulsidas.

JAGADGURU: World teacher.

JANSI KI RANI: The Indian queen, Rani Lakshmibai of Jhansi, (known as Jhansi Ki Rani) was a great heroine in India's struggle for freedom from the British. Aged only 22, she died in battle as she led the Indian mutiny in 1857 and is remembered as an embodiment of patriotism and courage.

KABIR, 1440-1518: Indian mystic who preached an ideal of humanity as one. A weaver, he later became famous for scorning religious affiliation. He expressed his philosophies and ideas of loving devotion to God using imagery and language from Hindu Vedanta and Bhakti streams and Muslim Sufi ideals.

KARMA: a) Action – A karma Yogi practices God-Realization through good actions and right behaviour; b) Cause and effect. 'What you sow you reap.'

KIRTAN: See *Bhajans*

KRISHNA: *Bhagwan* (Lord) Krishna is revered by all Hindus and considered by some to be the Godhead itself and by others to be a divine incarnation, one of the many through which the Real has manifested itself for the benefit of humanity and our spiritual development. Krishna is at the heart of the *Mahabharata*, a great Indian epic about the five Pandava brothers and the adventures they have in their struggle for justice. Krishna is their friend and guide as they ponder how to best fulfil their *dharma* or sacred duty. In the midst of the *Mahabharat* is the *Bhagavad Gita*, perhaps the most widely revered Hindu scripture of modern times and the best-known outside Hinduism. Some scholars believe the Gita has been interpolated into the epic but really that makes no difference to its impact that has been immense and profound through all the centuries it has been known. In this Gita, Arjuna and Krishna

share a dialogue on the eve of a battle in which Arjuna will have to fight many
of his own relatives. Krishna advises him on all the different ways to Self-
Realization and how each of them affects the way we live and interact with
each other and with God. It is in the Gita that Krishna makes his famous
declaration, 'In every age I come back to deliver the holy, to destroy the sin of
the sinner, to establish righteousness.' Here it becomes clear that for Hindus
God incarnates over and over again in order to help us fulfil our divine destiny,
to put us spiritually back on track.

This is one major difference with Christian concepts of divine incarnation,
one that allows many Hindus to accept Jesus (and great preceptors of other
faith traditions) as divine incarnations or *avatars*, on a par with their own.
Unlike fairly recent Christian interest in the historicity of Jesus, Hindus are not
unduly concerned about the historicity of Krishna. He exists in our hearts. His
life story can be read and understood at many levels. He has 'come down' and
is incarnate on earth in the inspiration and influence he still wields over
countless lives.

There are many versions of the *Mahabharata* eg. Kamala Subramaniam,
Mahabharata, Bharatiya Vidya Bhavan, Bombay. Look out too for a brand new
very modern sci-fi multi-book version by Ashok K Banker, Orbit Books,
starting end 2006. He has also written a series taken from the *Ramayana*. There
are many translations and commentaries too on the Bhagavad Gita. The
translation by Swami Prabhavananda and Christopher Isherwood, available
from most Ramakrishna Maths, is excellent. For a Gita with profound esoteric
commentary try the mighty 2 volumes by Paramahansa Yogananda, *The
Bhagavad Gita: Royal Science of God-Realization*, Self-Realization Fellowship, Los
Angeles, USA.

KRISHNAPREM, SRI: An English born mystic who played an important
spiritual role in the life of Karan Singh and others. Originally called Professor
Richard Nixon, a distinguished graduate of Cambridge University, he taught
English literature at Lucknow and Benares University and became enamoured
with bhakti yoga, became a disciple of Sri Yashoda Mai and became a fully
fledged sannyasin in the Vaishnava tradition. He wrote two books: *The Yoga of
the Bhagavad Gita* and *The Yoga of the Katho-panishad*. He passed away on
November 14th 1965. His last words to his beloved disciple, M Ashish, were,
'My ship is sailing.'

LAKSHMI: Goddess of wealth and prosperity, especially favoured by women.

MAHABHARATA: The ancient epic depicting the stories of the Pandava
brothers in which the Bhagavad Gita is interpolated. See *Krishna*.

MAHARAJ: 'Great king,' a title of reverence given to a spiritually elevated
being.

MAHASAMADHI: The conscious passing away of a great yogi. *Maha* means
great. *Samadhi* is a word that also describes the state of bliss felt by devotees
communing with God.

MANDIR: Temple or shrine.

MAYA: Illusion, a veil that covers knowledge of our true Selves and that we have to draw aside to see the Truth. As duality is built into the structure of creation – it is impossible to have pleasure without pain, life without death, health without sickness etc – then we have always the struggle with maya. Transcending it will bring us to God and our own true nature and then we shall be free from creation's allures and become constant and wise and absorbed in God consciousness even while still in the world.

MEENAKSHI: Goddess symbolising *shakti* or power, sometimes *prakriti* or nature.

MELAS: Great religious gatherings of which the Kumbha Mela is the most internationally famous.

MOHANDAS K GANDHI 1869-1948: Mahatma Gandhi has been chosen by three contributors suggesting his continuing widespread influence and inspiration. Indeed his focus on *ahimsa* (harmlessness, non-violence) is as much needed now as it ever was – and as difficult to practice in its entirety! Gandhi was born in India but spent some of his formative years in England and South Africa. The latter, with its apartheid regime and racist ambience, particularly affected him and helped develop the tools he later used so successfully in the *swaraj* (self-rule) movement that ended British occupation of his homeland. Not everyone understood or was able to follow the Mahatma's form of resistance and his inclusion of all peoples of India. This resulted in his assassination by a young Hindu, angered by Gandhi's support for Muslims. He passed away with the name of Ram on his lips (See *Rama*) – proof, if it were needed, of his spiritual centredness when even an unexpected and lethal bullet did not disturb his inner *mantra*, his inner focus on God.

MOKSHA: Freedom from birth and rebirth; freedom from duality and desires. The realization of who we really are.

MURTIS: Images of God that you will see in Hindu temples and Hindu shrines. For Hindus there is only one God or Reality. As that Divine Reality permeates everything then it can be perceived and appreciated in many different ways through many different forms whilst remaining Itself at all times. Thus the images you see revered by Hindus do not mean a plethora of gods but reveal recognition of the one God according to the calling and understanding and heart of each individual devotee.

NAMASKAR/NAMASTE: The traditional Hindu form of greeting with palms placed together: 'I bow to the God in you and in me.'

NAMES AND FORMS OF GOD: In Hinduism God can be thought of in any way that helps and encourages the devotee to build a relationship with, know and love the Divine. For many Hindus this has meant their dearest association with the Real is as Mother, full of unconditional love for her children. God as Mother in Hinduism has many names and forms and some are mentioned in this book. Different names and forms for God in Hinduism recognize that God has multiple attributes, enabling every human to find some aspect with which to form some special relationship. God can appeal to every-one, one way or another. Divine Mother has special appeal for many.

You will also find portrayed here as an influence God as Ganesh, an elephant. In Hinduism the monkey is also visualized as divine in the form of Hanuman, one of the great heroes of the *Ramayana* epic that tells the story of Rama (an incarnation of God), his wife Sita and brother Lakshman and their struggle against dark forces that threatened their world and their lives. It is marvellous how Hindus have made sacred all that they see around them, how they have found God in everything and loved and worshipped it accordingly and learnt so much of spiritual value in the process. Also when you understand the symbolism, for example of Ganesh, the wisdom becomes clear. See Deepak Naik's reflection for some insight into this.

NISHKAMA KARMA: The Bhagavad Gita sets a great value on *nishkama karma* or desireless action, selfless action, action performed without desiring or fearing the consequences, action performed with indifference to the outcome, without any expectation of the fruits (results or reactions or effects). You can read about this in Sharada Sugirtharajah's reflection. One of its great exponents is Ramana Maharshi and he is mentioned there.

PARAMPARA: The succession and lineage of religious groups.

PATANJALI: Compiler of the *Yoga Sutra*, a major work containing aphorisms on the practical and philosophical wisdom regarding practice of Raja Yoga. Virtually nothing is known about the life of Patañjali, but he may have lived around 200 BCE, a probable dating of the *Yoga Sutra*. 'Desiring to teach yoga to the world, he is said to have fallen (*pat*) from heaven into the open palms (*anjali*) of a woman, hence the name Patanjali.' Patañjali's Yoga is one of the six schools of Hindu Philosophy. He expounds on the eight limbs of yoga - yama, niyama, asana, pranayama, pratyahara, dharana, dhyana and samadhi.

PRASAD: Food offered first to the deity and blessed, then shared with devotees.

PUJA: Ritual worship.

PUJYA SAHEB, 1940 - : Born in Gujuarat, Saheb was recognized early in life as having a spiritual nature. He later became a sadhu, with seven others, in an unusual way under the guidance of Brahmaswarup P P Yogiji Maharaj of the Swaminarayan Mission. He wanted these sadhus, known as 'Vratdhari Sadhaks,' to be different in that they were not to wear saffron robes. They were to practice renunciation from 'within' and were to remain in plain clothes. This was unprecedented in the history of the Swaminarayan movement. Since then, within the span of 40 years, thousands of seekers worldwide have been touched by Pujya Saheb's compassion and grace and in turn have devoted themselves to living according to his teaching that 'To Serve Humanity Is To Serve God.' This is the inspiration of all members of the Anoopam Mission.

RABINDRANATH TAGORE 1861-1941: Great Indian poet, dramatist, painter, musician, educator and philosopher, perhaps most famous for his

Gitanjali collection of poems.

RAMA / RAMAYANA: Rama is the great adherent to dharma and hero of the Hindu epic, *The Ramayana*, which tells his story and that of his wife Sita and brother Lakshman and their struggles with Ravana, ruler of the *rakshahsas* (demons or evil beings, though not all are bad). It is the story of doing what is right whatever the consequences.

RAMAKRISHNA PARAMAHANSA 1833-1886: His is the life and message par excellence of religious pluralism that so aptly speaks to our troubled times where religious division, suspicion, and extremism blot the spiritual landscape. Sri Ramakrishna was born in Bengal and became a priest at the Kali temple in Dakshineswar where he soon began a life of spiritual intensity and training, engaging in many variant forms of *sadhana* (spiritual practice). These included Christianity and his vision of Christ is much reported. He was the prototype global theologian, discovering in all his various sadhanas an essential underlying unity leading to the same divine destination. Read more about the life of Sri Ramakrishna in the translation by Swami Nikhilananda of M, *The Gospel of Sri Ramakrishna*, Ramakrishna-Vivekananda Centre, New York.

RAMANA MAHARSHI, 1879-1950: At age 16, he became spontaneously self-realized when, feeling he was about to die, he realized he was spirit not body. Six weeks later he ran away to the holy hill of Arunachala in South India where he remained for the rest of his life. He often said that his guru was Arunachala. For several years he stopped talking and spent many hours each day in *samadhi*. When he began speaking again, people came to ask him questions, and he soon acquired a reputation as a sage and an ashram was built around him that still exists today. Sri Ramana taught a method called self-enquiry in which the seeker focuses continuous attention on 'who am I?'

RANGANATHANANDA SWAMI, 1908-2005: Renowned scholar, philosopher and president of the Ramakrishna Mission, Swami joined the Ramakrishna Order in Mysore in 1926. He was initiated into *sanyasa* in 1933. From 1939 to 1998, he served as the Head of the Order's branches in Rangoon, Karachi, Delhi, Institute of Culture (Kolkata) and Hyderabad. He became the president of the Ramakrishna Math and the Ramakrishna Mission in September 1998.

RATHA: A chariot. In her reflection, Atreyee Day refers to her friend's bicycle as their Ratha!

RAVANA: Leader of the rakshasas. See *Rama/Ramayana*.

REINCARNATION: for many Hindus the soul incarnates many times here and elsewhere in its search for true knowledge and Truth. Each incarnation is a fresh start in that search, a new opportunity to overcome flaws and to realize we are Spirit.

SADHANA: Spiritual practice. There are many different ways to practice spirituality for Hindus so each person can use the one that most benefits or attracts the individual concerned. For some this might mean meditation, for others good deeds, for some chanting God's name, for others the practice of discrimination, perhaps some choose worship of a particular aspect of God as depicted by a particular deity; many will include some of all of these in their sadhana.

SADHUS: A holy person dedicated to the search for God, often wandering unattached and living on alms.

SANATAN DHARMA: The eternal religion or truth or dharma, more than just a religion. This is what Hindus call their religion. It is Eternal Truth and is the way of living that brings us to Self-Realization. It is not for Hindus only but a Truth for all. It explains why Hindus are so diverse in their approaches to God and so inclusive of the ways in which others turn to God.

SANTOSHI MAA: Goddess of peace and family values, emblem of love, contentment, forgiveness, happiness and hope.

SANYASI: A renunciant, ascetic,

SATGURU SIVAYA SUBRAMUNIYASWAMI, 1927-2001: In 1947, as a young man of 20, he journeyed to India and Sri Lanka and two years later was initiated into sannyasa by the renowned siddha yogi and worshipper of Siva, Jnanaguru Yogaswami of Sri Lanka, regarded as one of the 20th century's most remarkable mystics. For over five decades Subramuniyaswami, affectionately known as Gurudeva, taught Hinduism to Hindus and seekers from all faiths. In the line of successorship, he was the 162nd Jagadacharya of the Nandinatha Sampradaya's Kailasa Parampara and Guru Mahasannidhanam of Kauai Aadheenam (also known as Kauai's Hindu Monastery), a 458-acre temple-monastery complex on Hawaii's Garden Island. Gurudeva's successor is Satguru Bodhinatha Veylanswami. The esteemed *Hinduism Today* journal is one of their great gifts to the Hindu community worldwide.

SATYA SAI BABA, 1926- : Born in Puttaparthi in South India, Swami has become one of the most well known of living Hindu teachers. He began his spiritual mission as a child and his devotees consider him to be an avatar, one of three - previously he was Shirdi Sai and after this incarnation he will become Prema Sai. Thousands gather every day for *darshan* at his ashram, Prasanthi Nilayam, beside the village of Puttaparthi. In His own words, 'This Sai has come in order to achieve the supreme task of uniting the entire mankind as one family through the bond of brotherhood, of affirming and illuminating the Atmic Reality (*Atma* – The Self) of each being, to reveal the Divine which is the basis on which the entire cosmos rests, and of instructing all to recognise the common Divine Heritage that binds man to man, so that man can rid him-self of the animal and rise up to the Divine, which is the goal.' Satya Sai also declares, 'I have come not to disturb or destroy any faith, but to confirm each in his own faith, so that the Christian becomes a better Christian, the Muslim a better Muslim and the Hindu a better Hindu.' His formula to lead a meaningful life is the five-fold path of *Sathya* (Truth), *Dharma* (Righteousness), *Shanthi* (Peace), *Prema* (Love) and *Ahimsa* (Non-Violence.)

SEVA: Service; *nishkam sewa*, selfless service without desiring the fruits of action.

SHAKTI: Power, energy. The active power or manifest energy of Siva that pervades all of existence.

SHIRDI SAI BABA: 1838(?)-1918: The birth and parentage of Sai Baba are not certain though it is believed he was born in a Brahmin family in Pathri village, Maharastra State, in India. He was given into the care of a fakir who in turn passed on the young child to a saintly person namely Gopal Rao Deshmukh. Sai Baba first came to Shirdi about the year 1854 and lived there for three years. Then he disappeared from there, returned in 1858 and lived there until his Mahasamadhi in 1918. He lived simply in a dilapidated mosque and taught that faith in God and tolerance towards others are the basic tenets for religious life. Before his *mahasamadhi*, he said that even after his passing away, he would speak from his *Samadhi* (tomb). Shirdi has now become a place of pilgrimage for all his devotees who feel his sublime presence ever more actively with them.

SHISHYA: Student, disciple.

SITA: Wife of Rama. See *Rama/Ramayana*.

SIVA/SHIVA: The Hindu trinity is Brahma (creator), Vishnu (preserver), and Shiva (destroyer of the world to allow fresh creation to emerge.) He is the supreme yogi and ascetic and associated with Mount Kailasa in the Himalayas. As Nataraj his dance represents both the destruction and creation of the universe revealing the cycles of death, birth and rebirth. His Dance of Bliss is for the welfare of the world. Under his feet, Shiva crushes the demon of ignorance caused by forgetfulness. One hand is stretched across his chest and points towards the uplifted foot, indicating the devotee's release from earthly bondage.

SLOKAS: Verses of holy text; prayers/invocations.

SRIMAD BHAGAVATUM (OR BHAGAVAD PURANA): One of the most important ancient texts about the life of Lord Krishna

SWAMI/SWAMIJI: Someone who renounces the lower self through monastic training. *Ji* is often added as a sign of respect. This can be added to many names also eg. Guruji, Krishnaji etc.

UPANISHADS: The fourth and final portion of the Vedas, expounding the secret, philosophical meaning of the Vedic hymns.

VAISHNAVA: A follower of Lord Vishnu, particularly in his revelation as Krishna.

VANAPRASHTA: Third stage of life in Hindu system. See *Ashramas*.

VEDANTA: 'Ultimate wisdom,' Vedanta is the system of thought that encapsulates the meaning of the Upanishads (circa 1500-600 BCE). There are different forms of Vedanta, especially Advaita (non-dualism, associated with Shankara) and Vishishtadvaita (qualified non dualism, associated with Ramanuja).

VEDAS: These scriptures are most ancient and wield great authority for many Hindus. They are considered revealed wisdom. They are shruti or 'that which is 'heard.' See Anant Rambachan's description in the *Introduction*.

VIVEKANANDA SWAMI, 1863-1902: Sri Ramakrishna's most famous disciple was Narendranath Datta, later known as Swami Vivekananda, one of the first great preceptors to bring Hinduism into the west through his own dynamic life and example. You will find that Swami Vivekananda is also much mentioned in this book. He is considered the progenitor of the modern inter-faith movement thanks to his speech at the first Parliament of World Religions in Chicago in 1893 when he brought the house down with his very first words: 'Sisters and Brothers of America.' For the full text of Swami Vivekananda's speeches at the Parliament, see *Chicago Addresses*, Ramakrishna Vedanta Centre, Bourne End, UK. There are many books about his life and teachings, available from most Ramakrishna Maths. Vivekananda is the model for any aspiring *karma* yogi: active, energetic, committed yet ever centred in divine wisdom and devotion. He truly shows us how to live in the world, caring and compass-ionate, yet always God-conscious.

VISHNU: The preserver and protector of creation, the embodiment of mercy and goodness, the self-existent, all-pervading power that preserves the universe and maintains the cosmic order or Dharma. Part of Hindu Trinity.

YOGA: Union. From the Sanskrit *yuj*, to yoke, harness, unite; practices to unite individual consciousness with transcendent or divine consciousness. The Bhagavad Gita describes bhkati, karma, jnana and raja yoga. See also Patanjali's *Yoga Sutras* (circa 200 BCE).

YOGANANDA, PARAMAHANSA, 1893-1952: One of the most influential Hindus of modern times, Paramahansaji was born in India in 1893, the year that Vivekananda addressed the first Parliament of World Religions in Chicago. His intense search for God finally led him to the ashram of his guru, Sri Yukteswar. In 1917 the young Swami Yogananda founded his first school, dedicated to spiritual as well as intellectual and physical education. In 1920 he was invited to speak at the International Congress of Religious Liberals in Boston. Thus began his mission to the west, commanded by his guru to spread the message of yoga and liberation. Yogananda stayed in the USA until his mahasamadhi in 1952. He returned only once to India, for fourteen months, in 1935. Of his many writings, *Autobiography of a Yogi*, published in 1946, is the best known and has been translated into more than nineteen languages. In the West his teachings are disseminated by Self-Realization Fellowship, known in India as Yogoda Satsanga Sangha.

YUGAS: (Sanskrit) 'Period, age.' Four ages, together making up over four million earth years, that chart the duration of the world according to Hindu thought. They are: Satya (or Krita), Treta, Dvapara and Kali. In the first period (Satya), dharma reigns supreme, but as the ages revolve, virtue diminishes and ignorance and injustice increase. This cycle continues in ascending and descending ages. Most think we are currently in the Kali Yuga.

THE HIMALAYAN ACADEMY has an excellent online lexicon at
www.himalayanacademy.com/resources/books/dws/DWSLexicon.html

Find out more about the people mentioned here through their organisations, websites etc
listed in RESOURCES.

Lakshman, Rama, Sita and Hanuman
Heroes of the Ramayana

PICTURE AND TEXT ACKNOWLEDGEMENTS

We are very grateful to all who gave permission for photos, pictures and texts used in this book. While most photos in the book were supplied by the contributors or taken by us at interviews, thanks and recognition are also due to the following:

OM SYMBOLS used on the front cover and inside the book courtesy of Himalayan Academy, except for the page borders originally designed by Jael Bharat and given to HA's collection.

INSIDE FRONT COVER: Picture of Lord Shiva dancing with his musicians courtesy of the Himalayan Academy.

ANCIENT VEDIC HYMN: We first saw this in Roy Eugene Davis, *An Easy Guide to Ayurveda*, CSA Press, 1996.

NAMASTE: Photo courtesy of Steve Evans. Creative Commons Licence at www.flickr.com

ROYALTIES: Photo of little girl courtesy of Steve Evans.

ARUN GANDHI: We are grateful to Arun and his MK Gandhi Institute of Non-Violence for ALL the pictures of Mahatma Gandhi illustrating the reflections of Mathoor and Seshagiri as well as his own.

ATHIPET SUDHA VEPA:
P8: Bharata Nathyam dancers courtesy of Claude Renault. Creative Commons Licence at www.flickr.com
P10: Picture of Siva as Nataraj courtesy of the Himalayan Academy.

ATREYEE DAY:
P19: Photo of Swami Ranganathananda courtesy of the Ramakrishna Mission.

CHINTAMANI YOGI:
P26: Picture of Lord Rama courtesy of www.boloji.com

DAYATMANANDA SWAMI:
P36: Photo of Swamiji courtesy of Mary Braybrooke.

DEEPAK NAIK:
P.43: Photo of Deepak Naik © Peter Williams, World Council of Churches. www.wcc-coe.org
P44: Picture of Ganesh courtesy of the Himalayan Academy.

DENA MERRIAM
P45/46: Photos of Paramahansa Yogananda and Brother Anandamoy courtesy of Self-Realization Fellowship, Los Angeles, U.S.A.
P50: Text: Paramahansa Yogananda, *Worldwide Prayer Circle*, Self-Realization Fellowship, Los Angeles, U.S.A. P 26.
P50: Photo of Self-Realization Fellowship Lake Shrine Gandhi World Peace Memorial courtesy of Carol Jordan.

JAEL BHARAT
P53: Cow in the Himalayas photo courtesy of Paul Evans. Creative Commons licence at www.flickr.com
P54: Oxford spires photo courtesy of Tawfique Hasan. Creative Commons Licence at www.flickr.com
P55: Photo of the Himalayas courtesy of Steve Evans. Creative Commons Licence at www.flickr.com
P55: Back at home photo courtesy of Janine Plaisier.
P56: Farm Field photo courtesy of Klaus Glindemann.

KARAN SINGH:
P64/68: Both photos of Sri Aurobindo courtesy of the Sri Aurobindo Ashram Trust.
P67: Photo of candle courtesy of Vanessa, one of the youth participants in the Through Another's Eyes project organised by the International Interfaith Centre when we worked there.

MATHOOR KRISHNAMURTI:
P70: Photo of Gandhi courtesy of Arun Gandhi and the M K Gandhi Institute of Non-Violence.
P72: Photo of Sri Ramakrishnan courtesy of the Bharatiya Vidya Bhavan Australia. www.bhavanaustralia.org
P74: Translations of Vedas online by Raimon Pannikar at www.himalayanacademy.com/resources/books/vedic_experience/VEIndex.html

MONA VIJAYKAR:
P75/80: Shirdi Sai Baba pictures courtesy of Shirdi Sai devotees who sweetly affirm, 'It's all BABA's property and we are humble servants practicing and spreading his teachings.'

RAVI RAVINDRA:
P94: Photo of Swami Vivekananda courtesy of the Ramakrishna Mission.

SANDY BHARAT:
P98, 99, 100, 103: All photos of Paramahansa Yogananda, Sri Daya Mata and Swami Sharanananda courtesy of Self-Realization Fellowship, Los Angeles, U.S.A.
P103: Text: Paramahansa Yogananda, *Sayings of Paramahansa Yogananda* (1st and 3rd quotes). Paramahansa Yogananda, *Self-Realization Fellowship Lessons/ Spiritual Diary* (2nd quote). All books by Paramahansa Yogananda available from Self-Realization Fellowship, Los Angeles, U.S.A.
P103: Photo of Gardens at Self-Realization Fellowship Lake Shrine courtesy of Carol Jordan.

SESHAGIRI RAO:
P105, 107, 109: All photos of Mahatma Gandhi courtesy of Arun Gandhi and the M K Gandhi Institute of Non-Violence.

SHARADA SUGIRTHARAJAH:
P112: Ramana Maharshi photo courtesy of Sri Ramanasramam, Tiruvannamalai, 606603, Tamil Nadu, India. Creative Commons Attribution Share Alike 2.5 Licence.

SHAUNAKA RISHI DAS:
P117: Original pencil sketch done by Teena Tolani. Scanned, enhanced and colored in Photoshop 7 by Jay Khemani. Creative Commons Licence at www.flickr.com
P120: Photo courtesy of Liz Highleyman. Creative Commons Licence at www.flickr.com

INSIDE BACK COVER: Lord Krishna statue at Self-Realization Fellowship Lake Shrine Gardens courtesy of Carol Jordan. For more about SRF's Lake Shine, visit www.lakeshrine.org

PUBLIC DOMAIN IMAGES *used in good faith for this non-profit book.*
Opposite P1: Indian Picture Gallery at www.historylink102.com; P21: Sai Baba; P32: Shiva; P49: Kabir; P66: Vivekananda; P74: Rig Veda; P84: Hanuman, Fair Use; P97: Rabindranath Tagore; P110: Varalakshmi, traditional; P112: Vishnu; P143: Rama; P155: Banyan trees and Hindu Temples; Back cover, top left: Indian Picture Gallery at www.historylink102.com; Below: Krishna with Gopis and Gopas, painted by B G Sharma. For his sacred art as postcards etc, see Mandala Publishing, www.mandala.org

The online Wikipedia Encyclopedia is an excellent resource for Public Domain images.
The brilliant photographers who abide at www.flickr.com are also most helpful.

Lord Krishna with his ardent devotees, the Gopis and Gopas (cowherds) of Vrindavan.

RESOURCES

Religious/spiritual organizations, websites, books and journals
linked to Contributors
Only resources in English are given here.

ORGANIZATIONS

ANOOPAM MISSION: Brahmajyoti, The Lea, Western Avenue, Denham, Bucks UB9 4NA, UK. www.anoopam-mission.org. Branches worldwide.

BHARATIYA VIDYA BHAVAN: 4a Castletown Road, West Kensington, London W14 9HE, UK. www.bhavan.net. Branches worldwide.

BHAVAN KARNATAKA, Race Course Road, Bangalore-5600 001, India. http://bhavankarnataka.com

CHINMAYA MISSION: 2 Egerton Gardens, Hendon, London NW4 4BA, UK. www.chinmayauk.org; www.chinmayamission.org.

ENCYCLOPEDIA OF HINDUISM: 937 Assembly Street, #1018, Columbia, SC 29208, USA. www.eh.sc.edu.

HINDU FORUM OF BRITAIN: Unit 3, 861 Coronation Road, Park Royal, London NW10 6PT, UK. www.hinduforum.org.

HINDU YOUTH UK: 145 Sandhurst Road, Kingsbury, London NW9 9LJ, UK. www.hinduyouthuk.org.

HINDU VIDYAPEETH-NEPAL: PO Box 6807, Balkumari, Lalitpur, Nepal. www.hvp-nepal.org.

HINDUISM TODAY / HIMALAYAN ACADEMY: Kauai's Hindu Monastery, 107 Kaholalele Road, Kapaa, HI 96746-9304, Hawaii. www.himalayanacademy.com.

GLOBAL PEACE INITIATIVE OF WOMEN: 301 East 57 Street, 3rd Floor, New York, NY 10022 USA. www.gpiw.org.

LONDON SEVASHRAM SANGHA: 99a Devonport Road, London W12 8PB, UK. Bharat Sevashram Sanghas world-wide.

LOOMBA TRUST: Loomba House, 622 Western Avenue, London W3 OTF, UK. www.theloombatrust.org.

LOOMBA TRUST (India): Suite 13 -14, 31, Prithviraj Road, New Delhi 110 011, India.

MINORITIES OF EUROPE: Legacy House, 29 Walsgrave Road, Coventry CV2 4HE, UK. www.moe-online.com.

MK GANDHI INSTITUTE OF NON-VIOLENCE: 650 East Parkway South, Memphis, Tennessee 38104, USA. www.gandhiinstitute.org.

OXFORD CENTRE FOR HINDU STUDIES: 15 Magdalen Street, Oxford
OX1 3AE, UK. www.ochs.org.uk.

RAMAKRISHNA VEDANTA CENTRE: Blind Lane, Bourne End, Bucks
SL8 5LG, UK. www.vedantauk.com. Branches world-wide.

RAMANA MAHARSHI: Ramana Maharshi Foundation UK, 15a Victoria
Road, London, NW6 6SX, UK. www.ramana-maharshi.org.uk.

SELF-REALIZATION FELLOWSHIP: 3880 San Rafael Avenue, Los
Angeles, CA 90065-3298, USA. www.yogananda-srf.org.

SRI AUROBINDO: Sri Aurobindo Society, Pondicherry, India.
www.sriaurobindosociety.org.in.

VIVEKANANDA CENTRE LONDON: 6 Lea Gardens, Wembley,
Middlesex HA9 7SE, UK. www.vivekananda.co.uk.

YOGODA SATSANGA SOCIETY OF INDIA: Paramahansa Yogananda
Path, Ranchi – 834001, Jharkhand, India. www.yssofindia.org.

WEBSITES

BHAGAVAD GITA: www.bhagavad-gita.org; www.asitis.com;
www.bhagavad-gita.us

HINDU COUNCIL: www.hinducounciluk.org

HINDU GODDESSES: www.sanatansociety.org/
hindu_gods_and_goddesses.htm; www.saigan.com/heritage/gindex.html

HINDU VOICE UK: www.hinduvoice.co.uk

INDIA IN CLASSROOMS: www.indiainclassrooms.org

ISKCON: www.iskcon.com. Centres world-wide.

KARAN SINGH: www.karansingh.com

KABIR: www.sacred-texts.com/hin/sok/index.htm;
www.boloji.com/kabir/index.htm

KRISHNA: www.krishna.com; http://krishna.avatara.org

MAHABHARATA: www.sacred-texts.com/hin/maha/index.htm

NATIONAL COUNCIL OF HINDU TEMPLES: www.nchtuk.org

PURANAS: www.puranas.org

RAMANA MAHARSHI: www.ramana-maharshi.org

RAMAYANA: www.valmikiramayan.net;
www.sacred-texts.com/hin/rama/index.htm; www.ramayana.com

RUKMINI DEVI ARUNDALE AND THE KALAKSHETRA SCHOOL
OF DANCE: http://artindia.net/anjana/kalak.html;
www.sawnet.org/whoswho/Arundale+Rukmini+Dev

SAI BABA, SATYA: www.sathyasai.org

SAI BABA, SHIRDI: www.shrisaibabasansthan.org; www.saibaba.org; www.saibabaofshirdi.net; www.shirdibaba.org.

SHANTI SEWA ASHRAM: www.hvp-nepal.org

SIVA: www.shaivam.org

TAGORE, RABINDRANATH: www.visva-bharati.ac.in/Index.htm

SRIMAD BHAGAVATUM: www.srimadbhagavatam.org; http://srimadbhagavatam.com/en

UPANISHADS: http://sanatan.intnet.mu; www.sacred-texts.com/hin/upan/index.htm

VEDAS: www.sacred-texts.com/hin/index.htm;

VIVEKANANDA: www.vivekananda.org; www.ramakrishnavivekananda.info/vivekananda/complete_works.HTM

BOOKS
Many have multiple reprint dates

BALU, SHAKUNTALA: *Living Divinity*: Sawbridge: London: 1981.

BHARAT, JAEL AND SANDY: *Mapping the Cosmos: An Introduction to God*: Sessions of York: 2006.

BHARAT, SANDY AND JAEL: *Guide to Interfaith: Reflections from Around the World*: O Books: May 2007.

BHARAT, SANDY: *Christ Across the Ganges: Hindu Responses to Jesus*: O Books: May 2007.

BURKE, MARIE LOIUSE: *Swami Vivekananda in America*: Advaita Ashrama: Calcutta: 1958.

BURKE, MARIE LOIUSE: *Swami Vivekananda: His Second Visit to the West: New Discoveries*: Advaita Ashrama: Calcutta: 1982.

CHINMAYANANDA, SWAMI: *Bhaja Govindam* (Commentary): Chinmaya Publications: 2000.

CHINMAYANANDA, SWAMI: *Ever-green Messages* (Collection of 365 beautiful quotes): Chinmaya Publications: 1999.

DABHOLKAR, GOVIND R: *Shri Sai Satcharita: The Life and Teachings of Shirdi Sai Baba*: Sterling Publishers Pvt.Ltd: India: 2000.

DAS, RASAMANDALA: *The Heart of Hinduism: A Comprehensive Guide for Teachers and Professionals*: ISKCON Educational Services: UK: 2002.

ELLSBERG, ROBERT, Ed: *Gandhi on Christianity*: Orbis: New York: 1991.

EMIR, RUDITE J: *At Every Breath, A Teaching: Stories About the Life and Teachings of Swami Chinmayananda*: Chinmaya Publications: 1999.

GANDHI, ARUN: *A Patch of White:* Thackers: 1969

GANDI, ARUN: *M K Gandhi's Wit and Wisdom:* Gandhi Institute: 1998.

GANDHI, ARUN: *The Forgotten Woman: The Untold Story of Kastur Gandhi, Wife of Mahatma Gandhi:* Ozark Mountain Publishing: 1997.

GANDHI, ARUN: *Legacy of Love: My Education in the Path of Nonviolence*: North Bay Books: 2003.

GANDHI, MOHANDAS K: *An Autobiography: The Story of My Experiments with Truth*: Beacon Press: Boston: 1993.

GANDHI, M K: *The Collected Works*: Indian Government: 1968.

GHOSE, SRI AUROBINDO: *Essays on the Gita*: Arya Pub House: Calcutta: 1926.

GHOSE, Sri Aurobindo: *Sri Aurobindo Birth Centenary Library*: Sri Aurobindo Ashram: Pondicherry: 1972.

GHOSE, SRI AUROBINDO: *Complete Works of Sri Aurobindo*: Sri Aurobindo Ashram: 1998f.

GHOSE, SRI AUROBINDO: *On Himself*: Sri Aurobindo Ashram Trust: Pondicherry: 1976.

GLENER, DOUG and KOMARAGIRI, SARAT: *Wisdom's Blossoms: Tales of the Saints of India*: Shambala: 2002.

GOSH, SANANDA LAL: *Mejda*: Self-Realization Fellowship: Los Angeles: 1980.

GOSWAMI, SATSVARUPA DASA: *Prabhupada: He Built A House In Which the Whole World Can Live*: Bhaktivedanta Book Trust: Los Angeles: 1994.

HISLOP, JOHN S: *My Baba and I*: Birth Day Pub Co: San Diego: 1985.

HISLOP, JOHN S: *Seeking Divinity*, Sri Sathya Sai Books and Publications Trust: Prashaanthi Nilayam: 1998.

HIXON, LEX: *Great Swan: Meetings with Ramakrishna*: Shambala Press Publications: London: 1992.

KABIR: *Songs of Kabir*: Weiser: 2002.

KANU, VICTOR: *Sai Baba - God Incarnate*: Sawbridge Enterprises: London: 1981.

KASTURI, N: *Sathyam Sivam Sundaram:* Gulab Singh: New Delhi: 1974.

KRISHNAMURTI, MATHOOR: *Mathoor in Britain*: M P Birla Foundation: Bangalore: 2004.

KRISHNAMURTI, MATHOOR: *Gandhi Upanishad*: M P Birla Foundation: Bangalore: 2004.

KUMAR, VIJAYA: *108 Names of Shirdi Sai Baba*: Sterling Publishers Pvt. Ltd: India: 1998.

LAKHANI, SEETA with LAKHANI, JAY: *Hinduism for Schools*: Vivekananda Centre: London: 2005.

LITTLE, GWYNETH, Ed: *Meeting Hindus*: Christians Aware: Leicester: 2001.

LOKESWARANANDA, SWAMI, Ed: *World Thinkers on Ramakrishna-Vivekananda*: Ramakrishna Mission: Calcutta: 1983.

LOKESWARANANDA, SWAMI: *Studies on Sri Ramakrishna*: Ramakrishna Mission Institute of Culture: Calcutta: 1988.

M: *The Gospel of Sri Ramakrishna*: Trans. Swami Nikhilananda: Ramakrishna-Vivekananda Centre: New York: 1973.

MAHARSHI, RAMANA: *Spiritual Instruction*: Sri Ramanasramam: Tirvvannamarai: 1939.

MASON, PEGGY and LAING, RON: *The Embodiment of Love*: Sawbridge: London: 1982.

MATA, SRI DAYA: *Only Love*: Self-Realization Fellowship: Los Angeles, USA: 1971.

MATA, SRI DAYA: *Finding the Joy Within You*: Self-Realization Fellowship: Los Angeles, USA: 1990.

MAZZOLENI, DON MARIO: *A Catholic Priest Meets Sai Baba*: Leela Press: USA: 1994.

MONKS OF THE RAMAKRISHNA ORDER: *Meditation*: Ramakrishna Vedanta Centre: London: 1972.

MURPHET, H: *Man of Miracles*: Samuel Weiser: New York: 1971.

NANDA, B R: *Gandhi and Religion*: Gandhi Smriti and Darshan Samiti: New Delhi: 1990.

NIRLIPTANANDA, SWAMI: *Defining the Hindu Way of Life*: London Sevashram Sangha: 2006.

NIRODBARAN: *Talks With Sri Aurobindo*: Sri Aurobindo Society: Calcutta: 1985.

OSBORNE, ARTHUR, Ed: *The Collected Works of Ramana Maharshi*: Weiser: 1997.

PATCHEN, NANCY: *The Journey of a Master: Swami Chinmayananda, the Man, the Path, the Teaching*: Asian Humanities Press: 1990.

PATTNAIK, DEVDUTT: *Vishnu - An Introduction*: Vakils Faffer and Simons Ltd: 1998

PRABHAVANANDA, SWAMI: *The Eternal Companion: Spiritual Teachings of Swami Brahmananda*: Sri Ramakrishna Math: Madras: 1978.

PRABHUPADA, SRILA: *The Path of Perfection*: Bhaktivedanta Book Trust: Los Angeles: 1979.

PRABHUPADA, SRILA: *Conversations with Srila Prabhupada*: Bhaktivedanta Book Trust: Los Angeles: 1991.

PRABHUPADA, SRILA: *Letters from Srila Prabhupada*: The Vaisnava Institute: Los Angeles: 1987.
PRABHUPADHA, SRILA: *The Science of Self-Realization*: Bhaktivedanta Book Trust: Los Angeles: 1977.

PRABHUPADA, SRILA: *Raja-Vidya: The King of Knowledge*, Bhaktivedanta Book Trust: Culver City: 1973.

PRABHUPADA, SRILA: *Bhagavad-Gita As It Is*: Bhaktivedanta Book Trust: Bombay: 1968.

PUJYA SAHEB: *Divinity Realized: Saheb as Revealed to the Pilgrims of Eternity*: Anoopam Mission: 2003.

PURANI, A B: *The Life of Sri Aurobindo*: Sri Aurobindo Ashram: Pondicherry: 1978.

RAMAKRISHNA, PARAMAHANSA: *Sayings of Sri Ramakrishna*: Ramakrishna Math: Mylapore: 1971.

RAMAKRISHNA, PARAMAHANSA: *Teachings of Sri Ramakrishna*: Advaita Ashram: Calcutta: 1981.

RAMAKRISHNA, PARAMAHANSA: *Studies on Sri Ramakrishna*: Ramakrishna Mission Institute of Culture: Calcutta: 1988.

RANGANATHANANDA, SWAMI: *Eternal Values for a Changing Society*: Bharatiya Vidya Bhavan: Bombay: 1971.

RAO, K L SESHAGIRI: *Mahatma Gandhi and C F Andrews - A Study in Hindu-Christian Dialogue*: Punjabi University Press: Patiala: 1969.

RAO, K L SESHAGIRI: *Mahatma Gandhi and Comparative Religion*: Motilal Banarsidass: 1991.

RAVINDRA, RAVI: *The Yoga of the Christ: In the Gospel According to St John*: Element Books: Longmead: 1990. (AKA *The Gospel of John in the Light of Indian Mysticism*: Inner Traditions Bear and Co: 2004.)

RIGOPOULOS, ANTONIO: *Life and Teachings of Sai Baba of Shirdi*: State University of New York Press: 1993.

ROMAIN, ROLLAND: *The Life of Vivekananda and the Universal Gospel*: Advaita Ashrama: Calcutta: 1988.

ROMAIN, ROLLAND: *The Life of Ramakrishna*: Advaita Ashrama: Almora: 1954.

SATGURU SIVAYA SUBRAMUNIYASWAMI: *Dancing with Shiva:* Himalayan Academy: 2003

SINGH, KARAN: *Autobiography*: OUP: India: 1995.

SINGH, KARAN: *Mundaka Upanishad*: Bharatiya Vidya Bhavan: Bombay: 1987.

SUGIRTHARAJAH, SHARADA: *Imagining Hinduism: A Postcolonial Perspective:* Routledge: 2003.

TAGORE, RABINDRANATH: *Gitanjali*: MacMillan: 1983.

TOYNE, MARCUS: *Involved in Mankind: The Life and Message of Vivekananda*: Ramakrishna Vedanta Centre: UK: 1983.

VIJAYKAR, MONA: *The Vee Family* (series): Tri-Color Books: 1991.

VIVEKANANDA, SWAMI: *Raja-Yoga*: Advaita Ashram: Calcutta: 1970.

VIVEKANANDA, SWAMI: *Inspired Talks*: Ramakrishna Math: Mylapore: 1969.

VIVEKANANDA, SWAMI: *Collected Works of Swami Vivekananda*: Advaita Ashrama: Calcutta: 1969.

VIVEKANANDA, SWAMI: *Vedanta Philosophy*: Ramakrishna Math: Madras: 1969.

VIVEKANANDA, SWAMI: *Chicago Addresses*: Advaita Ashrama: Calcutta: 1974.

VIVEKANANDA, SWAMI: *The Yogas and Other Works*: Ramakrishna-Vivekananda Center: New York: 1953.

VIVEKANANDA, SWAMI: *The Universal Religion*: Ramakrishna Vedanta Centre: UK: 1993.

VIVEKANANDA, SWAMI: *The Complete Works of Swami Vivekananda*: Advaita Ashrama: Calcutta: 1970.

YOGANANDA, PARAMAHANSA: *Autobiography of a Yogi*: Self-Realization Fellowship: Los Angeles: USA.

YOGANANDA, PARAMAHANSA: *Spiritual Diary*: Self-Realization Fellowship: Los Angeles: USA. (Annual Publication).

YOGANANDA, PARAMAHANSA: *Man's Eternal Quest*: Self-Realization Fellowship: Los Angeles: 1976.

YOGANANDA, PARAMAHANSA: *The Divine Romance*: Self-Realization Fellowship: Los Angeles: 1986.

YOGANANDA, PARAMAHANSA: *Songs of the Soul*: Self-Realization Fellowship: Los Angeles: 1983.

YOGANANDA, PARAMAHANSA: *The Science of Religion*: Self-Realization Fellowship: Los Angeles: 1953.

YOGANANDA, PARAMAHANSA: *God Talks with Arjuna: The Bhagavad Gita: Royal Science of God-Realization*: Self-Realization Fellowship: Los Angeles: 1995.

YOGANANDA, PARAMAHANSA: *The Second Coming of Christ: The Resurrection of the Christ Within You*: Self-Realization Fellowship: Los Angeles: 2005.

YOGANANDA, PARAMAHANSA: *Paramahansa Yogananda In Memoriam*: Self-Realization Fellowship: Los Angeles: 1976.

YOGANANDA, PARAMAHANSA: *Whispers from Eternity*: Self-Realization Fellowship: Los Angeles: 1949.

YOGANANDA, PARAMAHANSA et al: *A World in Transition: Finding Spiritual Security in Times of Change*: Self-Realization Fellowship: Los Angeles: 1999.

YOGANANDA, PARAMAHANSA: *Journey to Self-Realization: Discovering the Gifts of the Soul*: Self-Realization Fellowship: Los Angeles: 1997.

HINDU CLASSICS
So many versions of each available. Here is just a sample.

ASHTAVAKRA GITA: Trans by Swami Nityaswarupananda: Advaita Ashrama: Kolkata: 1940 (2001).

BHAGAVAD GITA: THE SONG OF GOD: Trans by Swami Prabhavananda and Christopher Isherwood: Sri Ramakrishna Math: Madras.

MAHABHARATA: Krishna Dharma: Torchlight Publishing US: 2005. See also Kamala Subramaniam, Bharatiya Vidya Bhavan.

RAMAYANA: Kamala Subramaniam, Bharatiya Vidya Bhavan, 1981. See also R P Goldman: Princeton University Press: 2006; Ashok K Banker, Orbit Books, 2005/6; and Krishna Dharma, as above.

SRIMAD BHAGAVATUM (30 Volumes): Prabhupada Bhaktivedanta: Bhaktivedanta Book Trust: 2004.

UPANISHADS (PRINCIPAL): S Radhakrishnan: Collins: 1994.

VEDAS (THE HOLY): Pandit Vidyalankar: Clarion Books: 2004.

YOGA SUTRAS OF PATANJALI: Sri Swami Satchidananda: Integral Yoga Publications: 1990.

JOURNALS AND NEWSLETTERS

BACK TO GODHEAD: Journal: 6 issues annually: Bhaktivedanta Book Trust: USA.

BHARATIYA BHAVAN NEWS: Bi monthly: Bharatiya Vidaya Bhavan: London, UK.

HINDUISM TODAY: Quarterly and online: Himalayan Academy: Hawaii.

ISCKON COMMUNICATIONS JOURNAL: Bi-Annual: ISKCON: Oxford, UK.

JOURNAL OF HINDU-CHRISTIAN STUDIES: Annual: Society for Hindu-Christian Studies: USA and India.

NAMARUPA: CATEGORIES OF INDIAN THOUGHT: Bi annual: New York, USA.

SANATHANA SARATHI: Monthly: Sri Satya Sai Books and Publications Trust: Prasanthi Nilayam, India.

SELF-REALIZATION: Quarterly: Self-Realization Fellowship: Los Angeles, USA.

SEVASHRAM NEWS: Quarterly: London Sevashram Sangha: London, UK.

VEDANTA: Bi monthly: Ramakrishna Vedanta Centre, Bourne End, UK.

There are so many wonderful Hindu resources of all kinds.
We hope you find the ones that give positive energy and insight
into your own spiritual life. Om.

Banyan trees with Hindu Temples by Thomas Danniell, 1796.

BY THE SAME AUTHORS

A GLOBAL GUIDE TO INTERFAITH: REFLECTIONS FROM AROUND THE WORLD
Sandy and Jael Bharat

The media always present the negative aspects of conflicts in which religions are implicated. There are other stories waiting to be told, of dedicated and inspired women and men, working for peace across religious divides.

This book introduces the 'when, why, who, how and what' of interfaith. It is illustrated with personal reflections and photos from more than one hundred interfaith activists and academics from around the world. Topics include the origins of interfaith activity, reasons for and types of, how to organize events, central issues, thoughts about the future, and resources. Many inspiring stories and quotes are included and a broad variety of perspectives are given, providing local, regional and international dimensions.

1-905047-97-5 352pp £19.99 $34.95 O-Books May 2007 www.o-books.net

---

From the Foreword by Marcus Braybrooke
[This] amazing book will give a wonderful picture of the variety and excitement of this journey of discovery. It tells us something about the world religions, about interfaith history and organizations, how to plan an interfaith meeting and much more – mostly through the words of practitioners. …. There is a Chinese saying, 'Change the world and begin with me.' This book is encouraging evidence that many people have been changed and spiritually enriched by sharing with people of other faiths.

Judith Lempriere, Head of Cohesion and Faiths Unit, Home Office
It is particularly important that such work can be shared publicly with others so we can celebrate and learn from one another and strengthen the bonds between individuals and communities whilst respecting one another's differences and diversity.

Madeleine Harman, Trustee, International Interfaith Centre
I am so impressed by the wide ranging people and opinions. This is a great piece of work.

SANDY BHARAT AND O-BOOKS

CHRIST ACROSS THE GANGES: HINDU RESPONSES TO JESUS

In the last two centuries, some of Hinduism's greatest saints and scholars have lovingly embraced Christ and made him their own. Continuing and aggressive Christian mission in India is now making some Hindus anti-Christ as well as anti-Christian.

Find out why mission disturbs Hindus and how they have responded to their encounter with Christ and Christianity from colonial to contemporary times, in India and in the West. This is their story in their words.

Knowing and understanding others is always challenging. Make your own interfaith journey and discover what happened when Christ crossed the Ganges.

1-84694-000-1 240pp £14.99 $29.95 O-Books May 2007 www.o-books.net

---

From Foreword by Marcus Braybrooke, President, World Congress of Faiths: There is much to learn from Sandy Bharat's important book. I hope it will encourage many Christians and Hindus to enter into a deeper dialogue with each other.

From the Foreword by HE Dr Karan Singh, Rajya Sabha India: In her well researched book Sandy Bharat has studied in depth some of the Hindu encounters with Christ. This book is part of the growing literature on the Interfaith movement, and will be of value to students both of Hinduism and Christianity.

Ramesh Kallidai, Secretary General, Hindu Forum of Britain: Hindu Encounters with Christ provides a fascinating account of interaction between Hindus and Christians, offers a refreshing view of Christ seen through the eyes of some of the greatest Masters who walked the face of the earth.

Dr John May, Irish School of Ecumenics: I think this would be of the greatest interest to many people involved in interreligious relations; I know of nothing like it, which brings the story right up to date.

Marianne Rankin, Alister Hardy Society
This is a fascinating and wide-ranging overview of a subject of great importance. It is a must for anyone interested in the history of religious traditions and in the interaction between faiths.

MAPPING THE COSMOS:
AN INTRODUCTION TO GOD
Jael and Sandy Bharat

A challenging read for people of all ages, cultures, religions and no religion; A must read for people concerned about the future of humanity. In this small but important booklet the authors explore our relationship with creation and with God. What do we mean by the word god? Who is responsible for this world and all its troubles? Can we improve our situations? What can we hope for in the future?

Adding wisdom from spiritual sages and contemporary thinkers to their own insights and visual imagination the writers lead the reader through a journey we might all need to make.

While you may not agree with everything they write you will be stimulated to reflect again on our place in the cosmic scheme of things.

1-85072-341-9 48pp £4 $6 Sessions of York January 2006.

John Phillips, Vedanta
A stimulating read, providing much food for thought, both for the newcomer to the reading of spiritual literature and even for the jaded pallet of one who has read many books on spiritual life.

Sharon Steffensen, Yoga Chicago
It's inspiring, thought provoking, hope-filled and an important book for anybody concerned about the future of humanity.

Clive Hambudge and Soraya Boyd for Sevashram News
This avid little booklet seeks to draw us within, there to re-assess our place in relation to the 'totality of spirit.' We feel it succeeds in this and reminds us that '[h]e who sees me everywhere and see all in me, he never becomes lost to me, nor do I become lost to him.' (Gita 6, 30).

Marianne Rankin, De Numine
The aim of the booklet is to 'stimulate individuals to have more confidence in their individuality,' to realise that 'everyone is God the creator, and her/his own saviour. There is no vicarious living.' This meditation can expand your awareness of God, creation and of how and why you make your world as you do. It would make a wonderful gift - perhaps first to yourself.

Text on picture opposite:

He who perceives Me everywhere and
beholds everything in Me, never loses sight
of Me nor do I ever lose sight of him.

Bhagavad Gita